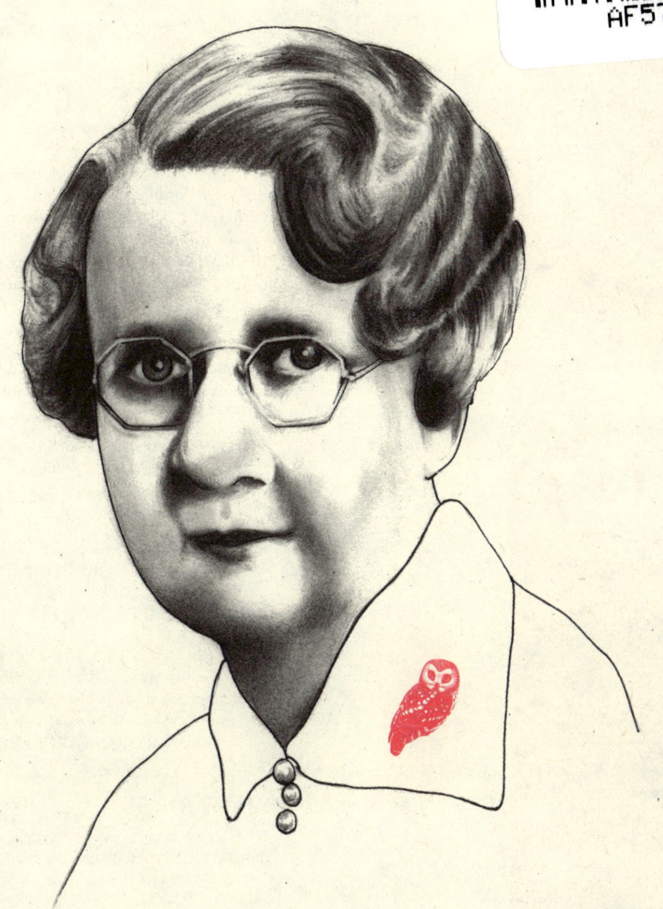

COUSIN CORINNE'S REMINDER

ISSUE NUMBER THREE

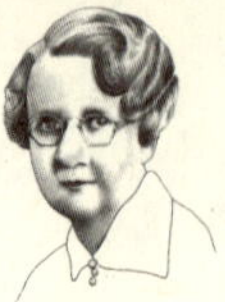
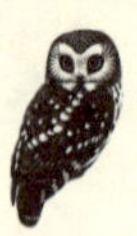

COUSIN CORINNE'S REMINDER

ISSUE NUMBER THREE

The editors wish to thank the following individuals and establishments for their support in the making of this issue: Jonathan Ames, Molly Auerbach, Abe Baldwin, Mark Borthwick, Chad Bunning, Nico Cassanetti, Steve Conners, Anna Cory-Watson, Stanley Crouch, Jack Dorkey, Stephen Gambello, Lois Gannett, Maryam Gunja, Carrie Kania, Alana Mirafuentes, Brisa Robinson, Eduardo Ruiz, George Emilio Sanchez, Peter Schmitz, Eric Simonoff, Martha Southgate, Emma Straub, Erik Syverson, Michael Thomas, Gordon & Nancy Vickers, Adam Wilson. Great and many thanks to all of our contributors, past and present!

Cousin Corinne's Reminder wishes to thank the following individuals for their generous financial contributions, which greatly aided in the production of this issue:
-Anonymous Individual $6,000.00

Honorary Cousins (donors of $5,000 or more):
Daria Sellon $5,000.00
Anonymous individual $7,000.00
Anonymous Individual $6,000.00

Cousin Corinne's Reminder is published twice yearly by:
COUSIN CORINNE INC
161 COURT STREET
BROOKLYN, NY 11201 USA

Get in touch: INFO@COUSINCORINNE.COM
Visit our website: www.COUSINCORINNE.COM
Subscriptions are available! Please subscribe!
We encourage your to submit your work! Visit our website to view
our SUBMISSION GUIDELINES.

PRINTED IN CANADA
ISBN: 978-0-9826343-2-5 List Price $14.00 (US Dollars)
Library of Congress Control Number: 2011908723

Cover Photograph: THE BEGGAR © 2005-2011 Zack Zook

CONTENTS

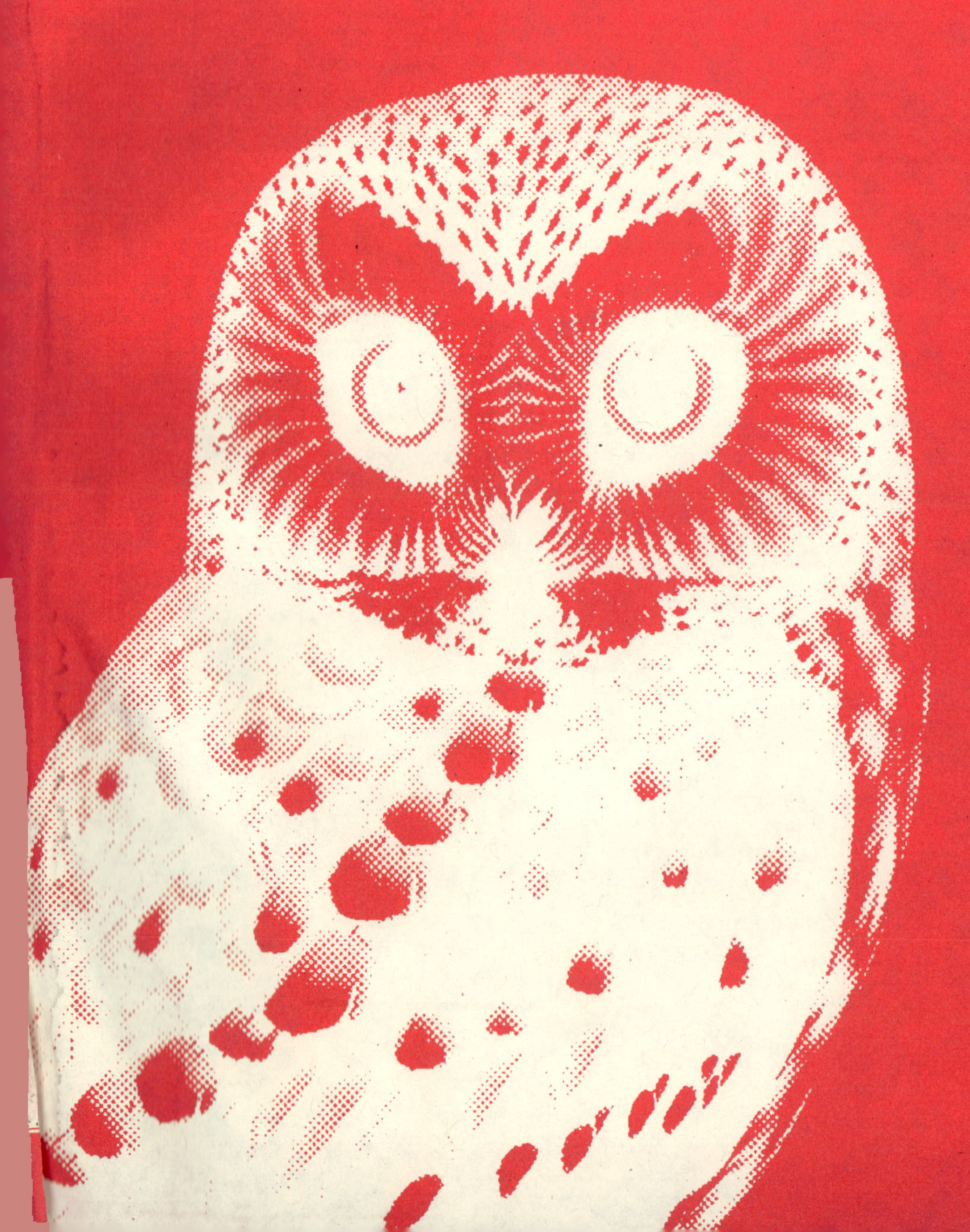

RACHEL B. GLASER

TURID

The girl was bored and wandered. She did not care if she was tagged; no one could force her to play. If she was It, she would not react—she would continue looking at the Wilsons' plants, at the rows of bright flowers. She could hear her sister yelling after their neighbor. Her sister had been It for a long time.

She was only a kid, and could go in everyone's yards. She spotted a stray cat and for a while tried to get it to follow her, but the cat was uninterested. She saw her neighbor running for base. Base was any large tree. The girl walked past a bunch of flowers and one of the young flowers stretched out to her and whispered, "Take me with you, my family is boring!" The girl stared, then yanked it from the ground. The other flowers were screaming. The pulled-flower cried in her hand. "I didn't think it would hurt! I didn't believe them," it moaned. The flower had a raspy voice. The girl didn't know what to do. She clutched the flower and ran. The flower was disheveled from just a few minutes in her hand. The girl had never heard a flower before.

The flower calmed down, and now began planning its new life. "I will sit in a jar of water and you can read to me all day." The girl didn't know what to say. For one thing, she knew the flower would only live a day or two, and also, the girl had school; she couldn't just waste her day reading to the flower. She didn't want to! The flower continued, "You can drive us into town and we can see a movie. I've never seen a movie before." The girl wanted to scream with laughter. She couldn't drive! And imagine taking a flower to the movies!

Her sister ran up and tagged her. The girl dropped the flower and chased her sister across everyone's yards. Adults were coming home from work and they waved at the girls from their cars. The sisters saw the stray cat and chased it into the bushes.

The girl was mostly home when she remembered. "I picked a crazy flower today," she told her sister. "It complains!" She wanted it back to show people.

The flower was coughing in the dirt when the girl reappeared. It said she was a terrible girl, that she had ruined all of their plans. The girl knew the flower was being dramatic; she had never agreed to any plans. She thought she was doing the flower a favor by pulling it out. She didn't know it would hurt. She picked up the flower, who was silent. She stroked its petals and the flower was pleased, though it said nothing.

The flower loved being in the warm hands of the terrible girl. It was lulled by the rhythm of her running. The girl tried to rouse it because its voice cracked her up, but the flower was asleep, so she left it outside near the dog's stuff.

Dinner had started and her parents scolded her for being late, but laughingly. The girl felt right and happy with her family. Her Dad was telling a hilarious story about work. He was imitating the Mexican warehouse workers. He was good with imitations. One of the Mexican warehouse workers needed heart surgery, and they replaced one of his heart valves with a valve from a pig heart. This sounded incorrect to the family, unreasonable really, but the man felt better than ever. There was a rasping from outside, and the family didn't know what it was, but the girl cracked up and ran out the door.

The flower was so stunned by the indoors that it forgot it was furious. It talked at length about the indoors. How weird the lighting was. The ceiling fan transfixed it. The family laughed at it. The Mom stuck it in a narrow vase and the flower drank the water greedily. It was in the center of the table, on display, and felt honored. The family continued talking, but the flower had no background and felt completely left out. It complained, quietly at first, but then began moaning and the girl had to shut it in a drawer.

The flower missed its family horribly. Right now they were slowly folding in their petals and quietly saying goodnight to each other. Young flowers were being funny and saying goodnight to made-up flowers. When it was sunny, all the flowers were spread-out and ecstatic. When it rained, every flower's center filled up with water and they gurgled when they spoke. Each family flower had a completely different personality. Some of the flowers were near silent, and just enjoyed listening to the talk of others. Other flowers were proud and articulate. The pulled-flower was closest to a set of flowers that had all blossomed on the same day. Just standing near these flowers was pleasant to the flower, because their heads, petals, and stems had been present for the flower's entire life, and made the flower feel cozy in its place. The flower could picture so clearly its family mourning it. "Turid!" they would cry, for that was the flower's given name.

The flower wore itself out in the drawer. It was startled to wake in complete darkness, with no sounds or breeze. It now understood it had made an irrevocably bad mistake. It had sacrificed everything for a girl it barely knew. It was no longer connected to anything it liked. Its petals were dry, its singy ways were over. Turid felt the dullness of a done flower.

The girl opened the drawer and Turid would not look at her. The girl plucked a petal and the flower cried. "I'm sorry," the girl said. "What do you want? What can I do?" Through sobs, the flower requested the vase again. The girl got it and put the flower in. "Listen to me," Turid said in a small voice. "My petal hurts because you swiped it. I thought only boys swiped petals." Turid leaned against the vase's glass sides. "Even though I'm in water, I feel dry. I have no more energy to be myself. I need to be planted back with my family,"—it looked to make sure the girl was listening,—"but first I want to see a movie."

The girl put the vase in front of the television and found a tennis match on. "Together," the flower insisted, so the girl sat and watched. She was going to be late for school. Yesterday, the girl had thought she'd have fun showing the flower off at school. She'd even thought they'd become friends and she could talk about boys with the flower. Now, the girl ceased to be entertained. The flower reminded her of toys she had had as a child that "spoke" in jarring, staticy voices. Her parents had grown exasperated with these toys, especially when they went off in the middle of the night, chattering aloud.

The girl looked away from the television to observe, with disgust, the flower, who didn't seem to be paying attention. "I do not like movies," Turid decided. "Please plant me immediately." Turid was limp. There was a gap where the girl had swiped a petal.

"I'll be right back," said the girl, and then she went off to school.

The flower sat in the vase in front of the television, waiting. The day was intolerable. The television showed tennis. The flower found itself wishing to be visited by a bug, and the flower as a rule hated bugs. The flower was ashamed to return to its family with a petal gap.

Turid's family had lived from their bulbs for thousands of years. They had been traded and transplanted and the journeys had been difficult. Many times their fate seemed teetering, but they had persevered, even when planted in poor conditions. To be a flower born from Turid's family was an honor. The bulbs had adept memories and remarkably long life spans and taught each generation of flowers about their past. Turid remembered fondly the bulb it had come from. The generous and wise nature of that bulb. Turid felt wildly lost to be disconnected from its bulb.

The indoors was a dead place, full of interesting objects. They were stacked on top of each other. There were places for people to rest. The flower tried to describe the objects, but they made little sense. They were colorful and lifeless. Though the flower had looked at houses with curiosity when it was in the ground, it now understood that inside, houses were devoid of real feeling. The flower grew so bored.

The Dad came home and heard the rambling flower. He walked over to it in a menacing way, and the flower kept going. The Dad moved to swipe a petal. "You are a terrible father," the flower said. "You've made a careless and unfeeling child. She promised to take me to the movies, then put me in front of this." The television showed tennis.

The Dad put Turid in the closet. The vase made a scraping sound against a floor tile. Then, the door shut. Dust swirled in the dark. A spider immediately visited the flower and the flower thanked God.

In the terrifying starless dark, Turid thought only about its family. It struggled to remember, and was rewarded with, memories of its own childhood. It remembered little bits of songs they had all sung. There had been epic fights between flowers that now seemed minor and endearing. Every thought or feeling that Turid had now felt like it was an expression or learned behavior of someone from its family.

It was hours before the girl's sister found the flower. The flower was very disoriented. It had a web over its face. "My friend made that," the flower said weakly. The sister took the flower and threw it in the trash.

Turid spent the day fainting. It remembered the outdoors as one being.

The next morning, the girl dumped cereal next to the flower and the flower grunted. The girl had forgotten about the flower, and grudgingly picked up Turid and shook the filth off. "You have disrespected nature and the tradition of my flower type, and I will poison you if you do not take me home." The girl was so bored of this flower that she considered putting it in the blender.

"You will die!" the flower screeched. The girl stared back at the limp flower.

Turid began screeching in loud, grating bursts. The sister came in and complained. The girl grabbed the flower and stuffed it in the refrigerator.

"Murderer!" Turid yelled.

Turid sobbed in the refrigerator. My flower family has survived worse than this, Turid told itself, though unsure if it was true. Turid was so weak from pain and distress that though the flower knew all the members in its family by name, when it now tried to imagine them, it only saw them in the vaguest sense. The flower ached and another wretched petal browned and fell. The flower curled in an effort to comfort itself. It thought, A family is the best collection. It tried to think what should be its final thought.

The girl went upstairs and changed. She had thought flowers were shy, feminine creatures, but had found her flower to be overly proud, needy, and annoying. The flower didn't seem to have a gender. It was not suited to be a girl's friend, though the books the girl had read as a child had always suggested that girls and flowers could be close. The word "murderer" had startled the girl. Only men were murderers. It seemed very unpopular for a girl to murder anything.

The girl retrieved the flower from the refrigerator. The flower could not move or talk. The girl looked at the flower and saw a complicated piece of trash. It looked like the ruined decoration of a present. Or an inedible part of a vegetable. The girl ran down their block. Gradually, the warmth from the girl's hand reanimated the flower. It felt like it was going to throw up.

"I hate you!" Turid said. The girl said nothing. Her eyes scanned for the kind of flower. The girl had a softball game later on and her birthday was coming up. She knew she wasn't a murderer.

The flower couldn't describe where it was from. The girl took it to all the yards on her street, but could not match the flower. The flower had no sense of direction. For the third time, they snuck around the Wilsons' yard, looking for similar flowers. The girl grew agitated. "Here here here," Turid chanted, leaking in the girl's hand.

The girl tossed the flower in front of its family and the flowers were frantic. "Turid! You wild thing!" Turid squirmed in the grass, trying to obscure the petal gap.

"It is me!" Turid said with glee. "I have lived a life in only two days, and I have hated it!" The flowers were quiet. Not only did Turid have a wide petal gap, but the remaining petals were shriveled and limp. Even more startling, Turid's head was partially severed at the stem. And the bottom half of the stem had already browned. They knew Turid had only a few more hours. The flowers tried to think of something appropriate to say. They could think of nothing.

Turid watched its flower family watching and felt distinguished. The flower could hear the sounds it had grown so accustomed to. The meditative moan of the lawnmower. Leaves flapping against other leaves. A few ants began to nibble Turid and the flower did not object. I am adventurous, thought Turid.

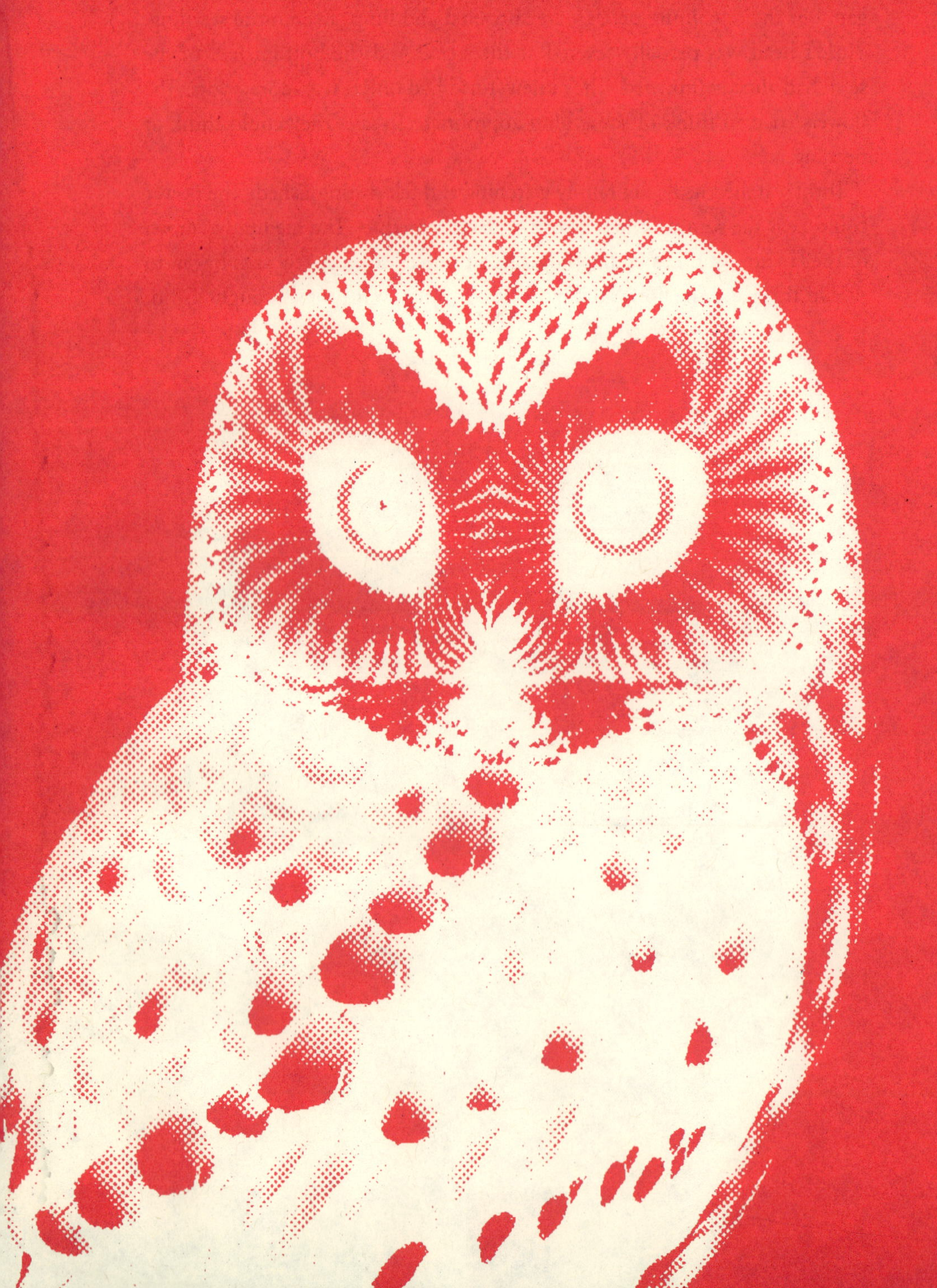

BENJAMIN GANTCHER

I wasn't naked but
April dragged her web
across my skin It was blurred
down here as if the nervous pushing new leaves
garbled their intentions at the top of the sky
the magnolia burning
with the arrogance of the favored
I blended in I was able to inhabit every passer-
by I wanted I was
everyone and I
were faintly erased
in the dimly
whispering I was
blurred a shadow of April I was
brimming

Self-Portrait with Exquisite Fidelity

I want the girl with the crooked face
who looks at you from inside the mirror,
you see yourself at peace and knowing you
so pleases her she beams affection. I want
that girl to walk with me on State Street

and chat about our families and climb the steps
that mount above the ruins of sea shells and jails

and the ten thousand things are the words
and draw the lace shadows like veils
and white caps that surf the blue mouth of the East
River and scows and animal flowers that flash
inside this mirror of all senses with red lips

I would talk and talk and make a mask of sparks
I would rise off any cushion and hand her into a boat
and watch a long time as she was rowed away

Before the seas rise and the shit of the canal overwhelms what passes for life in this neighborhood, I'd like to bring your attention back to my dreams. Picture a scrawny red maple. Planted in a coffee shop garden and propped up with rocks that seem to be cutting into its infant elephant skin, the little tree is suffering from an indifference similar to the cruelty of the bonsai gardener. Now it can speak to us. Its eloquent hands, scarlet in the sunshine, signal the rising energies of human springtime. Of course, it's the shadow side of the little tree we're looking at, where the curled up hands, pushed against the glass, sign in a jacketed way, like the hands of an autistic child pursuing his private data. But now a toddler in a stroller sees the tree. He takes the measure of its bifurcated nature. He identifies with it and records the experience in his very cells. There is nothing his mother can do about it. I win this round.

Your poncho is my poncho. I crave and loathe it
Stand-in of the moment, I and
I are tangled up in strings of math and custom
clank The baby is coming undone
It has the taste of a corporation, if not the rights
Give me a drag of that frame of reference, borrowing
me for a night. June's Phyllis is leaving a snowfall
Named for the sleep of horns
Everything turns into music

Snow is the farm of dreams
white creeps inside of sound, and she would sip a beaker of winter
sleeps white sleep.
falling through footprints
among the voices sleep

You forgot Benjamin. He is fucked with grace
the snow farmer
dwarfs spoke to him on the bus—he never called it temerity
the way on his first trip into town a Benjamin will greet
himself in the hard waterfalls
and, after hearing an explanation of glass, secretly not give up

rivulets and deep potholes in my story are teeming with life
the arrow Spring is steaming with arms
like a crowd that jumps to its feet, far away
him and his son, deaf in those hats,
their duet leaving the neighborhood

I was making piles
I had to make something
I made the sound of a salamander climbing a red leaf
a song that fills the walls
like stacks of headlines
without these papers I'm an immigrant
in my life
perpetually arriving

The sunlight pledged a soft detergent
I promised to use it. Look to the roof of your eyes
Tightly, said I to your Mollie, bring a mop, and isn't it surprising to make out
the original colors? Yes, they are supremely
wishful, these pinks and opals

In the interim (bewitching) the interim drains away (too bad)
The wastrels were overwritten by the randy
As when snow is arriving to help with the arrangements, the whole place was excited
plump, like pretty bakers, on view after nightfall
tearing at us with their fullness

EMMA STRAUB

MONTREAL

Last February, my husband and I drove to Montreal with a band that we work for, making and selling merchandise. Two early points: 1. February is not the time to visit Canada. 2. Though I say we drove to Montreal with the band we work for, what I mean is that we drove with the cello, the autoharp, the ukulele, the guitar, the pianet, the monitor box, and the CDs, t-shirts, and tote bags, while the band members themselves flew gracefully over our heads inside an airplane. We were driving from Washington, DC, and according to Google Maps, the drive would take ten hours. We left early enough to put us into Montreal at 7 p.m.; 8 or 9 if we stopped to eat, get gas, and pee. The whole thing seemed entirely reasonable.

Though for the bulk of the tour we would be traveling with a tour manager we knew well, the Canadian leg was going to be handled by someone else; the band's regular tour manager wasn't allowed to cross the Canadian border because of some legal troubles on a previous tour with one of Bob Marley's sons. We were given papers to present to the official on duty, and wished luck. We should have noticed that no one ever looked us in the eye when they said it wouldn't be any trouble whatsoever.

We stopped for lunch in New Jersey at The Orange Squirrel, Yelp's highest-rated restaurant in the nearest town. Point number three: don't eat at a restaurant named after a squirrel. I don't mean to pick on New Jersey, a far easier target than Montreal; I just want you to understand the contents of my stomach.

We made it to the border at about eight o'clock. In case you think things are about to go wrong, you're right. There weren't many cars in front of us, so we zipped right up to the open bay. We pulled up to the gentleman in the uniform, handed over our shoddy paperwork, and were directed to an abandoned-looking warehouse around the back. This did not bode well. We were ordered to fill out a number of forms (in French) by a large, gruff man who would rather have been asleep. Point number five: everyone else was asleep. Aside from the janitor, the place was deserted. The forms had to be filled out on an ancient computer, which meant that unless we filled in every answer (such as the old chestnut "How many metric tons does your car weigh?"), we were screwed. The weed-smoking tour manager had told us just to keep our mouths shut and not to declare anything. We missed him.

Eight p.m. became nine. Then it was ten. We hadn't eaten in nine hours, as we'd been saving ourselves for the poutine of our dreams in order to make up for the Squirrel we'd eaten in New Jersey. We made frantic phone calls to the tour manager—we could put the merch in storage at the border and pick it up on the way back into the US, but that would mean that we wouldn't have anything to sell at the shows, and none of the places would be open until morning anyway. My poor husband, who is remarkably good at getting things done, began to have a mental breakdown. For the next few hours, we haunted the empty hallways and drove back and forth across the parking lot, looking for the spots where our American cell phones would work without charging us the international rates. Every so often, we would tromp back through the ice to the empty counter, to try to reason with our miserable Mountie boyfriend.

We sat, dejected, on the benches in the hallway, picking up our feet when the janitor came by to buff the floors. A stack of newspapers sat on the floor beside us—I picked up the paper on top, and saw the singer in our band staring back at me. He was on the front page of the art section; his face took up the entire top half of the paper. The expression on his face looked something like sympathy, but it could have been a similar look of: "I just had the most delicious smoked meat for dinner, pity you weren't here."

Sometime around 11:30 p.m., the tour manager called to say she had hired us a broker, which in Canadian border-speak means someone who knows how to speak French and will fill out the paperwork for you. We then stared at the empty counter for another half hour and waited for our broker to arrive. When she did, looking like we had just torn her away from the Gathering of the Juggalos, the entire transaction took about fifteen minutes.

It took no time to get into the city. We checked into the hotel and dropped our bags and all the gear in our room. We found a 24-hour poutine restaurant online and set out for it immediately. The restaurant was a forty-minute walk from the hotel, but we were sure that once we got cash from an ATM, we could hop in a taxicab. It was only after the third ATM in a row refused to give either of us money that things began to look a bit dark. It was now close to 1 a.m., and approximately negative-10 degrees outside. Perhaps now would be a good time to add that I refused to pack any pairs of pants on the entire tour, and was only wearing a pair of American Apparel leggings with holes in them.

The 24-hour poutine restaurant was packed. We walked in the door, and watched plate after plate of French fries smothered with gravy and cheese curds sail by. Hypnotized, we shuffled up the counter, only to see the most horrifying sight of all: CASH ONLY. I may or may not have actually cried. We shuffled back out the way we came and, still unable to pay for a taxi, walked the cold 40 minutes back to the hotel in near silence. When we stripped off our clothes, our thighs were hot pink, frost-bitten all the way to the bone. My husband and I took turns scalding ourselves in the shower, and went to sleep looking like two plucked chickens.

The next morning our ATM cards worked normally. We ate four Montreal bagels while waiting in line for breakfast, and sure enough, everything was perfectly peachy after that. People were nice to us, in French and in English. We left the city without a single bite of poutine, but that seems right in retrospect. Some people fall in love with Montreal the second they see it, like a French Canadian OZ, all lit up and sparkling. But not us. Montreal made us suffer, like the best-looking boy in high school might. Everyone else can love you, Montreal, but we know the truth—you've got a heart of ice, whether or not it's covered in delicious gravy.

“IT IS STRIKING, AND ALSO FITTING, THAT A NOVEL SO DISTINCTLY AMERICAN, A NOVEL ABOUT APPEARANCE AND REALITY, ABOUT ISHMAEL'S REFLECTIVE WANDERING AND AHAB'S RUTHLESS QUEST, INFORMS THE CREATION OF THE TRIPTYCH. FOR THIS IS A PAINTING, AMONG OTHER THINGS, ABOUT WHAT IT MEANS TO BE AN ARTIST: A NECESSARY COMBINATION OF ISHMAEL'S ABSORPTION OF THE WORLD, FUSED WITH AHAB'S RUTHLESS PASSION.”

—JHUMPA LAHIRI

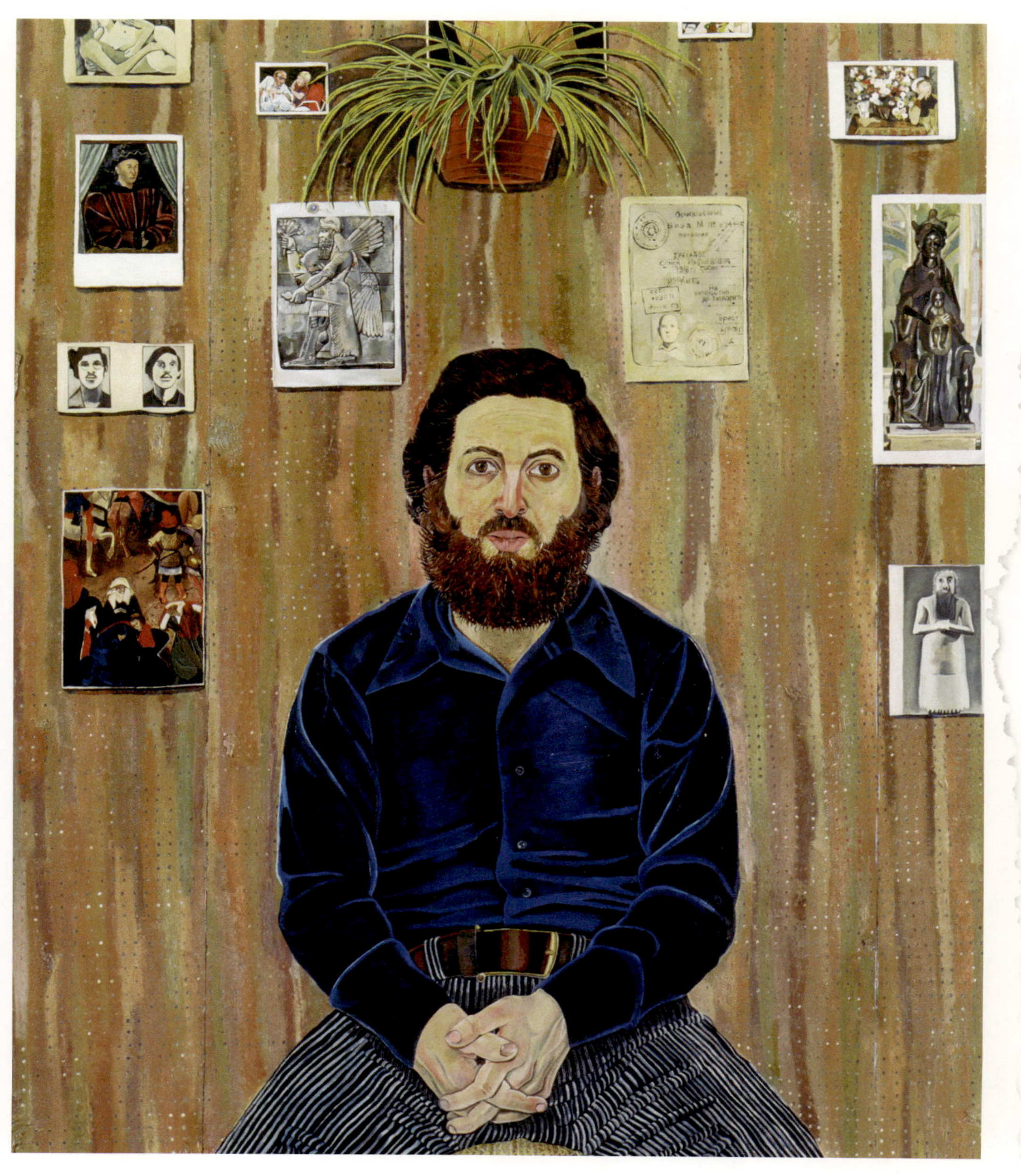

SIMON DINNERSTEIN'S
THE FULBRIGHT TRIPTYCH

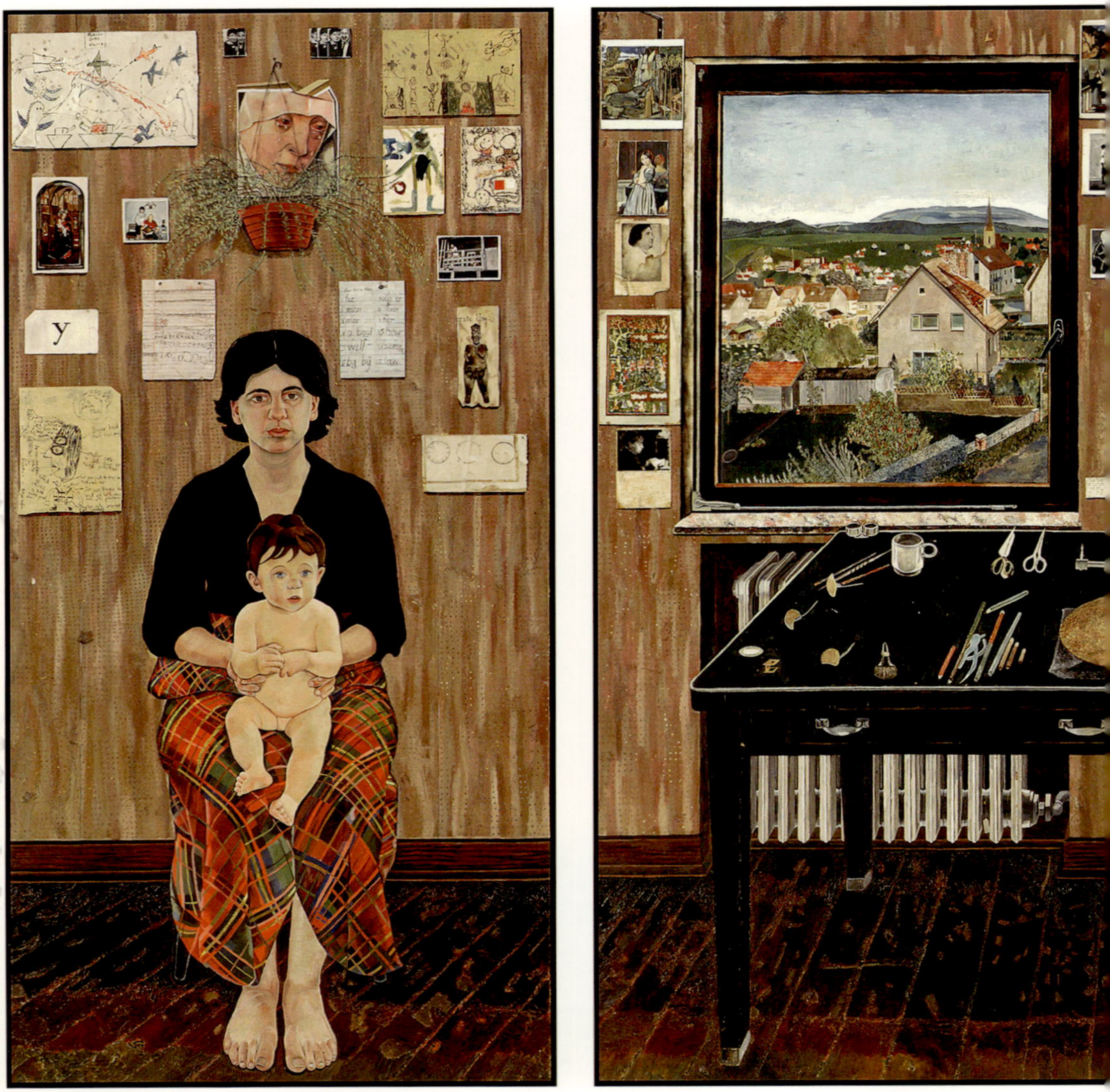

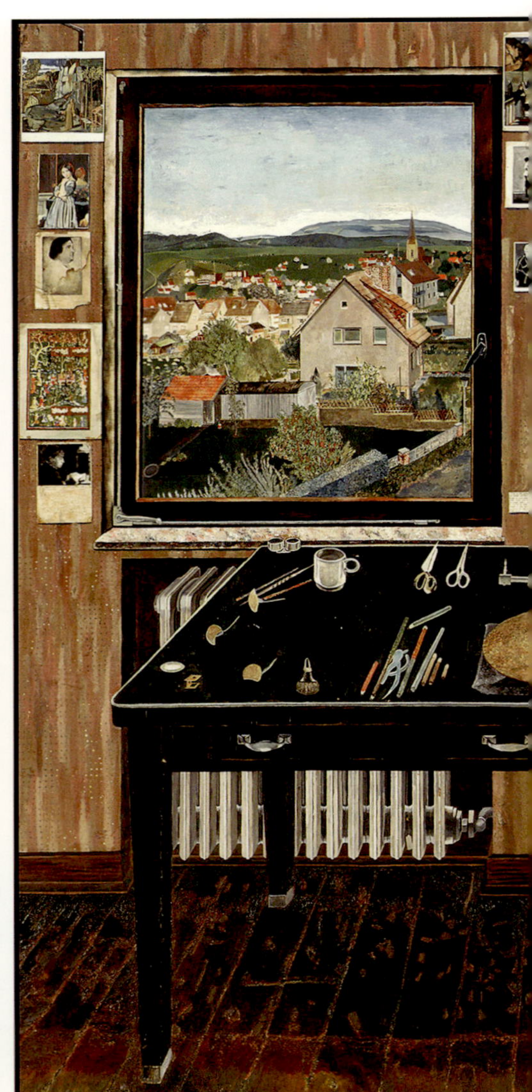

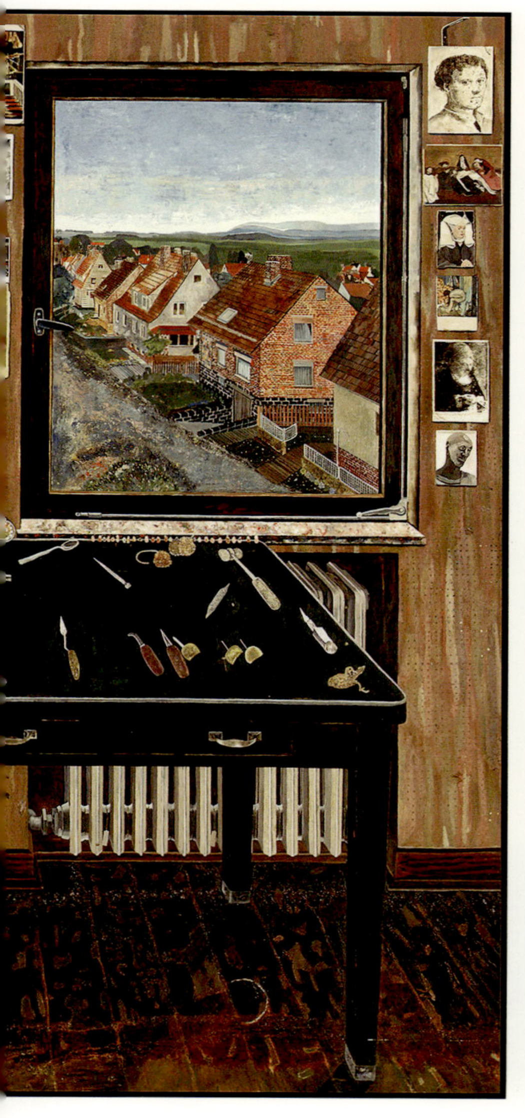

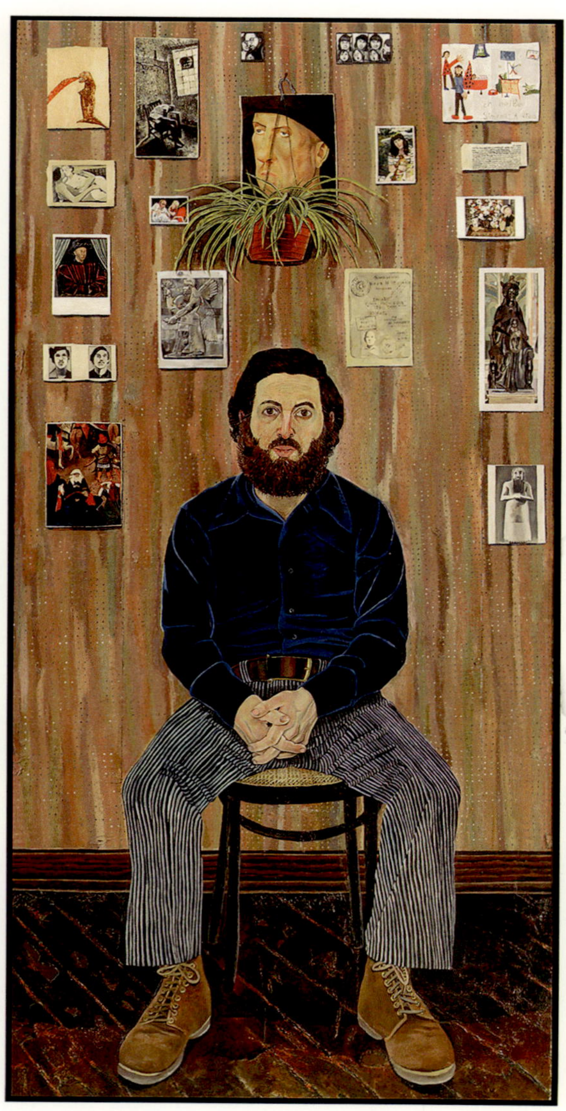

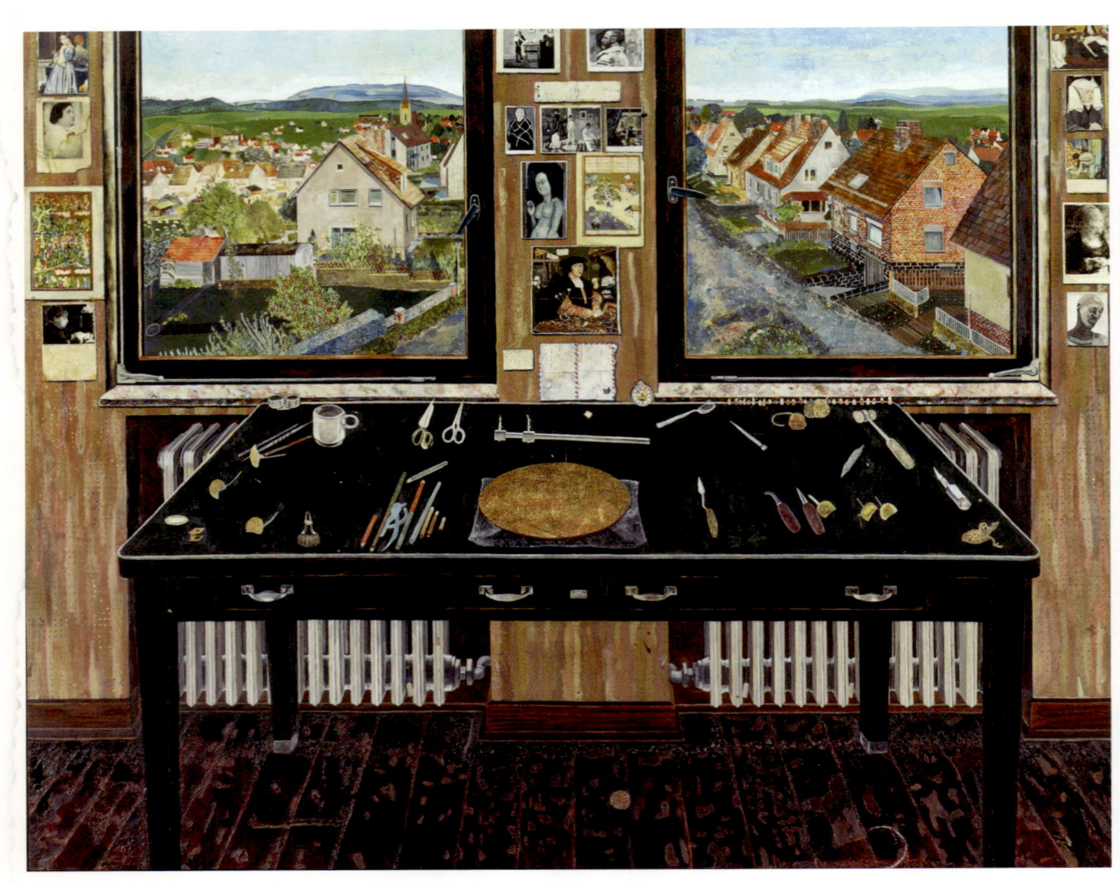

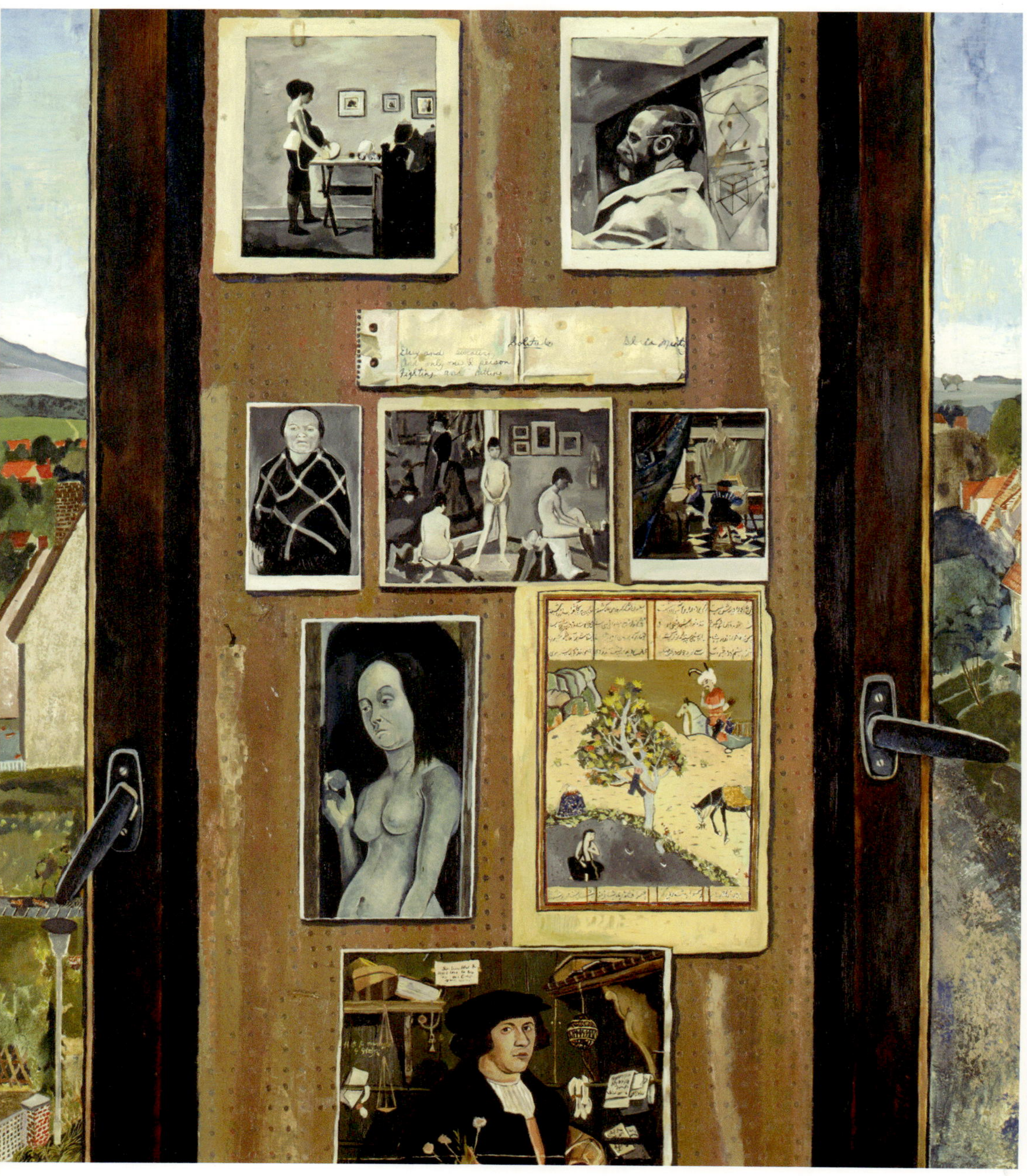

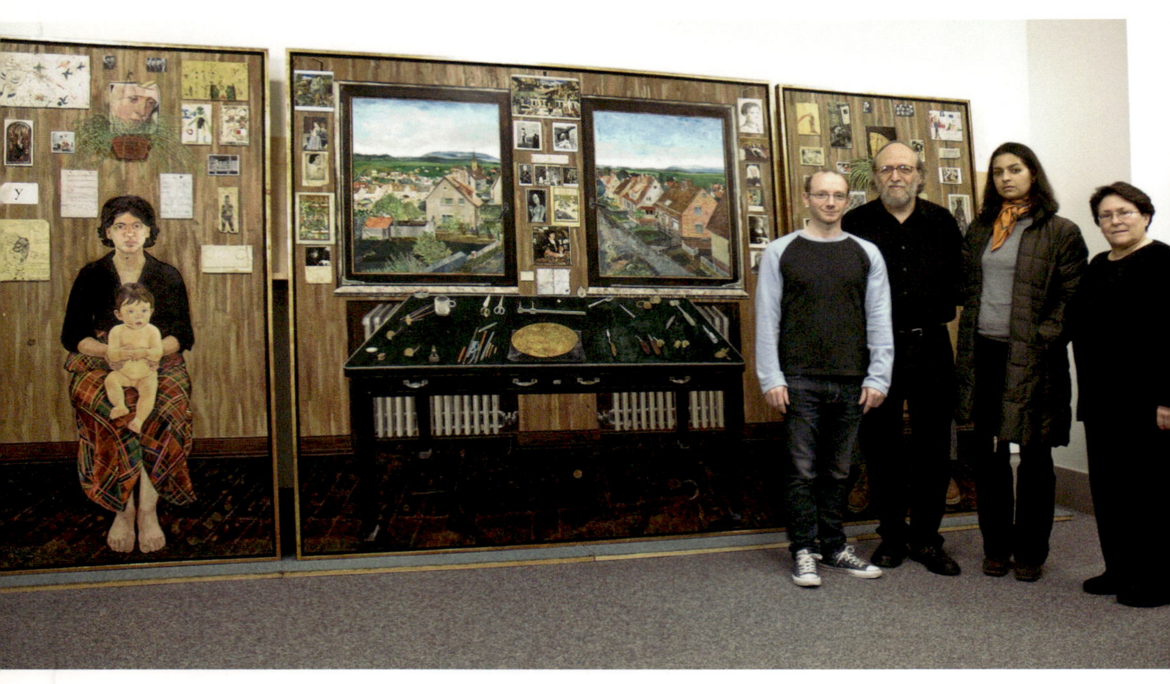

Marshall Price, Simon Dinnerstein, Jhumpa Lahiri, Virginia Bonito.
The Palmer Museum of Art, Penn State University, December 2008

JHUMPA LAHIRI

THE SPACE BETWEEN THE PICTURES

I first met Simon Dinnerstein in a letter of introduction delivered to me by a mutual friend I'd invited to tea. In the letter, Simon wrote kindly about my writing and, venturing to suggest that I might find his painting *The Fulbright Triptych* "of interest," invited me to contribute an essay for this book*. Along with the letter he sent a catalog of his work and a reproduction of the *Triptych,* measuring fourteen-and-a-half by eleven inches. I spent that summer evening looking at pages of the catalog. There were paintings and drawings of women sleeping and dreaming. Facades of Victorian row houses in Brooklyn, where Simon and I both live, on streets that I'd walked along. I saw a little girl sitting at a piano. A flower market in Rome. One painting, of a nude mother and child lying head to toe in bed against a vivid persimmon wall, reminded me of the portraits of Balthus. A few days later I wrote back to Simon by e-mail, accepting his invitation, and taped the reproduction of *The Fulbright Triptych* to a wall in the room where I write.

The painting depicts an artist's studio, a place where creative work is produced. It is, specifically, a printmaker's workshop. The central panel, about twice the width of the two on either side, contains a black table positioned in front of two radiators set into alcoves in the wall. The table is arrayed with engraving tools, objects vaguely reminiscent of a surgeon's instruments. A copperplate, resembling the solid halos of Giotto's angels, rests ever so slightly off center, on top of a square leather pad. Above the table, a pair of windows reveals a single landscape of homes and hills and sky, the vista divided in equally sized sections by the windows' frames. In the left panel, a barefoot woman with short, dark hair sits with a naked baby girl in her lap. In the right panel, a man sits alone. The man and woman look directly at the viewer. The

***The Suspension of Time: Reflections on Simon Dinnerstein and The Fulbright Triptych*, to be published by Milkweed Editions, June 2011. Jhumpa Lahiri's essay is one of 44 essays in the book, which also includes 70 illustrations.

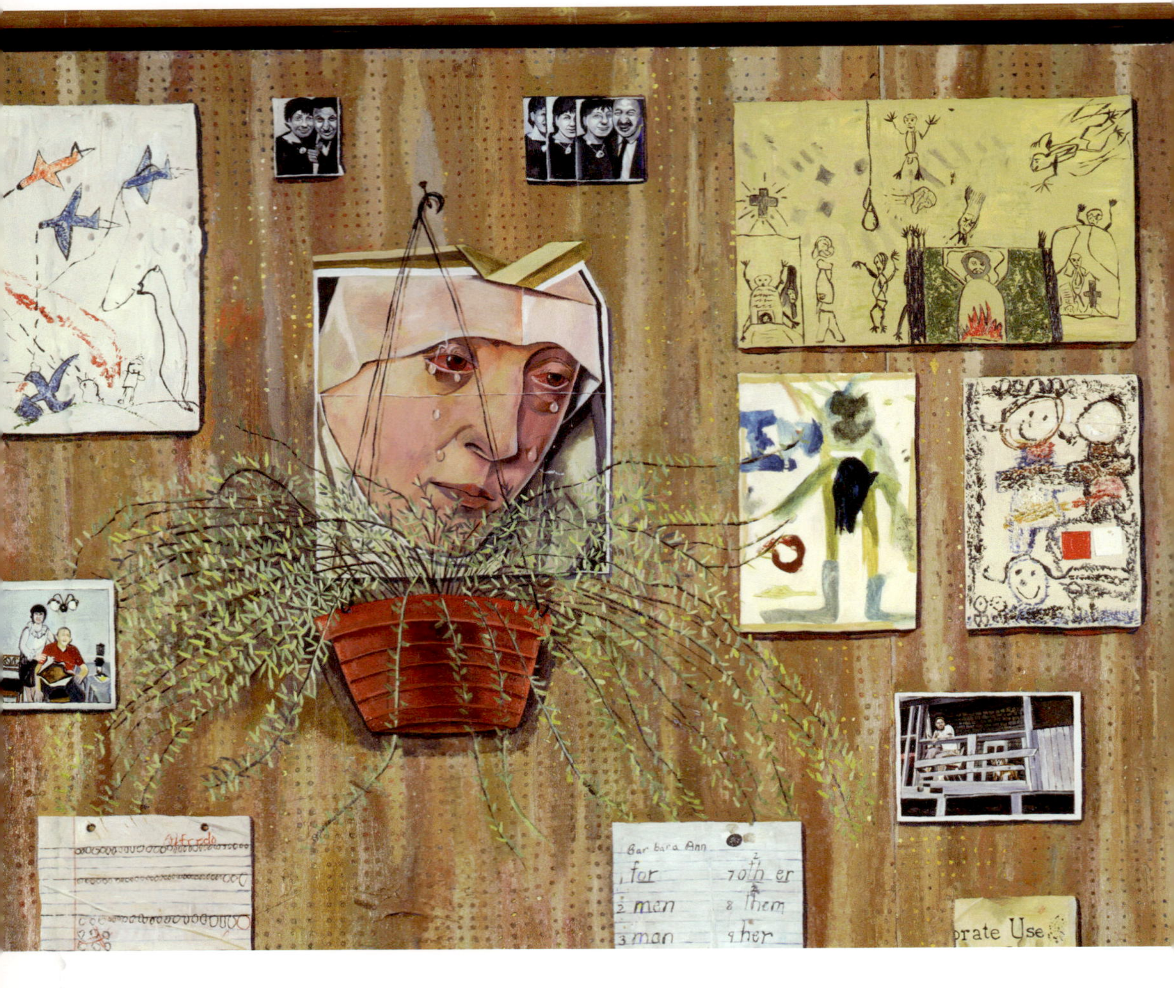
Alfredo
Bar bara Ann
1 for
7 oth er
2 men
8 them
3 man
9 her
orate Use

child's gaze, lighter than those of her parents, strays to one side. Two houseplants, similar but not identical, hang from nails at the same height above the man's and woman's heads. The man's clothing—striped blue-and-white pants, laced work boots, a wide brown belt, a navy shirt with a wide collar—evoke the early 1970s, when I myself was a child. The painting is both a self-portrait and a family portrait; the man is Simon, the woman is his wife, Renée, and the baby is their daughter, Simone.

There are only three things the three panels have in common. The first is the floor, made of thickly scabbed wooden planks. The second is the wallpaper, which has muddy peach and tan and green stripes seemingly applied with a paintbrush, and is patterned with tiny dots that lend it a perforated quality. The third is an assembly of small images, mostly visual but some consisting of text, decorating these papered walls. There are postcards of paintings, many of which I recognize: Bellini, Ingres, Hans Holbein, Degas. There are family photographs, some playfully taken in a photo booth, along with quotations, letters, things written on sheets of ruled paper, children's drawings. Each of these items, fifty-six in total, appears to be literally pasted to the surface in the manner of a collage, but is, in fact, a painted replica.

I have collected postcards of paintings since I was a teenager. And from the time I first set up a desk and started writing in my early twenties, I have marked my creative territory with a version of the informal, idiosyncratic two-dimensional gallery displayed on the walls of *The Fulbright Triptych.* These are the things that comfort my eyes when they wander from page or screen, that witness my solitary labor day after day. Currently, against the backdrop of teal-blue walls, there is a large map of Massachusetts, the place where I set many of my stories, and a smaller map, recently xeroxed from the New York Public Library, of the neighborhood in Calcutta where my father was raised, a place I am currently struggling to conjure. There are drawings, copied by my own hand from photographs, on the front and back of my paternal grandparents' house. There are photographs of my parents and husband and children, quotations from Nathaniel Hawthorne and from Corinthians 13. There are postcards of work by Piero della Francesca, Giorgio

Morandi, and Phillip Guston. Pictures of Virginia Woolf, Anne Sexton, and Hilda Doolittle. A blue-and-orange Joan Mitchell painting I ripped out of a magazine, called *Merci,* the brilliant hues faded from exposure to direct sunlight. A letter, propped up so that I can see it behind the screen of my laptop, sent to me from Paris by Mavis Gallant. As my desks and sources of inspiration have changed over the years, so have the things with which I've chosen to surround myself. But when they are on the walls of the place where I write, they become talismanic; to be forced to take them down and box them up in the course of a move always feels like a sort of death.

About two months after receiving Simon's letter, I went with my friend Tonuca—the friend who had brought me his letter—to visit him in Park Slope. Located a short distance from the neighborhood I live in now, Park Slope is deeply familiar to me. For five years I lived less than three blocks away from Simon's house, in an apartment where I brought my son, and then my daughter, home from the hospital after they were born. For those years, I probably brought my milk, bagels, and cups of coffee from the same shops along Seventh Avenue, Park Slope's commercial thoroughfare, as Simon.

The man who welcomed us was nearly forty years older than the one sitting in the *Triptych.* His hair and beard were gray, and he wore glasses, black jeans, and a black button-down shirt. Renée was at home that day as well, her hair still short, though no longer the ebony shade Simon had painted it. We stood on the spacious parlor floor which has a large, beautiful kitchen at one end and a gleaming grand piano at the other (Simon and Renée's daughter, the little girl he had drawn at the piano, grew up to be a concert pianist who used to give lessons to Tonuca's daughter).

As we looked at the many paintings and drawings in the room, I was overwhelmed by the personal history of people I barely knew, by the passage of time cycling forward and back. For there was a drawing of Simone, the unclothed infant in the *Triptych,* as a grown woman, eight months pregnant with her son, her shirt unbuttoned to reveal the skin of her swollen belly, her face and body filled with a weary satisfaction. The young couple in the *Trip-*

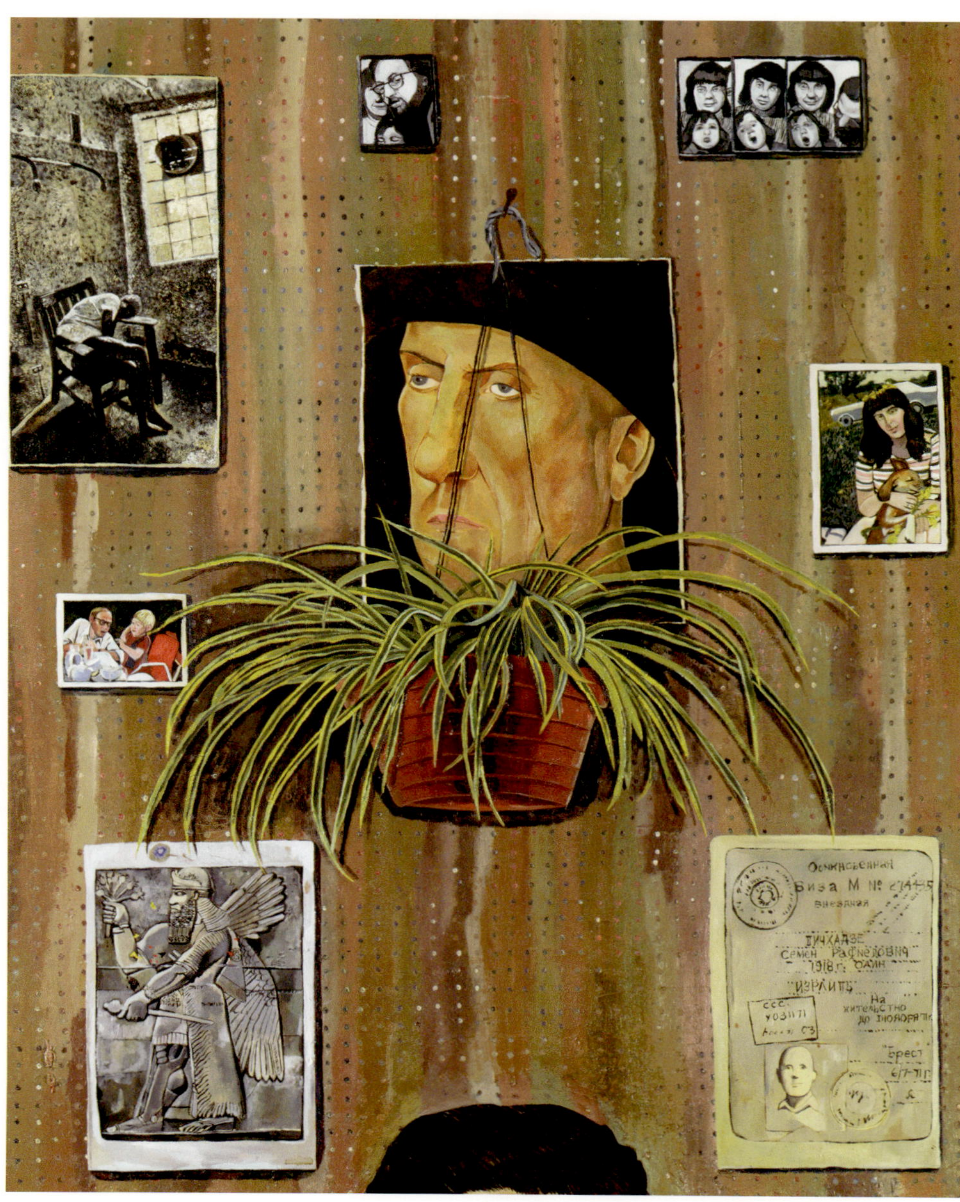
Биза М №
Семен
1918 г.
На
Брест

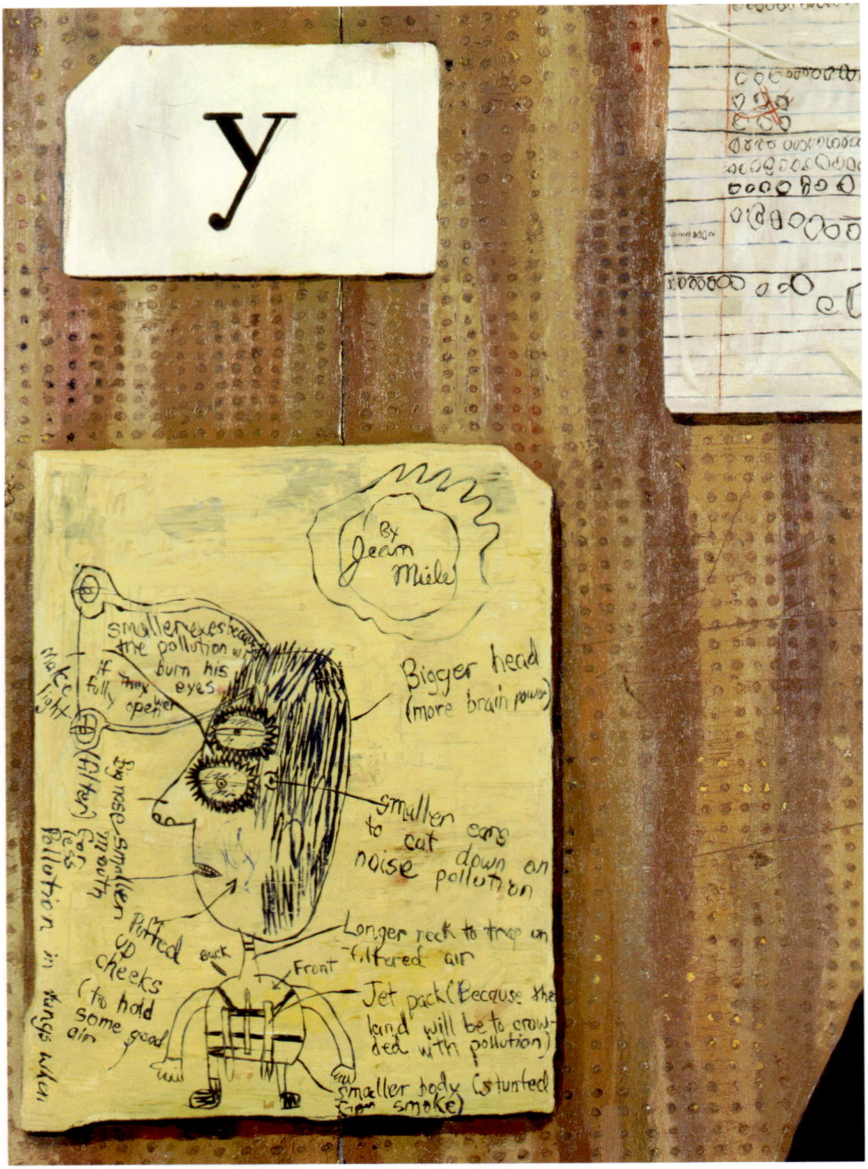

y

By Jean Miele

smaller eyes because the pollution will burn his eyes if they were fully open

make light

Bigger head (more brain power)

(filter)

Big nose

smaller mouth for less pollution in lungs when

smaller ears to cut down on noise pollution

Puffed up cheeks (to hold some good air

Longer neck to trap un-filtered air

Back

Front

Jet pack (Because the land will be to crowded with pollution)

smaller body (stunted from smoke)

tych, just setting out on the journey of parenthood, were grandparents now. And just as that brand-new family who had been keeping me company on the wall of my writing room has since spawned another, so the artist in the early years of his creative life now lives in a house chockablock with the work he has produced, hanging up and leaning against just about every wall.

Simon was generous with his time, serious but unassuming. He spoke candidly about his art, his life, his interest, his dreams. He talked about the years he and his family had spent in Rome at the American Academy. His love of reading was frequently conveyed. He recommended *Blindness* by José Saramago, and showed me a painting that he feels has a connection with Bulgakov's *The Master and Margarita.* He spoke of Strindberg's *A Dream Play* and of *Tonio Kröger,* a novella by Thomas Mann. I'd read the story over twenty years ago, in college, and remembered it dimly. Simon spoke of it with such enthusiasm that I reread it as soon as I got home.

The visit concluded in Simon's studio. Like mine, it is located on the top floor of a row house. Compared to the other rooms I'd seen, the studio was grittier, untouched by renovation, the plaster walls cracked. Lights were clamped to poles, overlapping blue-and-green tape was stuck to the floorboards, and fluorescent panels hung from the flaking ceiling. On dirtied white walls were hooks from which nothing hung. Midday sun shone into three south-facing windows, one of the panes broken. Through them the colors of autumn were visible, just beginning to grace the leaves of the trees. We could hear the voices of children calling out as they played on the grounds of P.S. 321, the school where Renée taught for many years.

Simon showed us his recent work, a series painted literally onto his palettes, along with something much older—two charcoal drawings he had made of Renée, nude, when she was pregnant with Simone, an uncanny reverse echo of the drawing of Simone, similarly pregnant and bearing distinct resemblance to her mothers, downstairs. One of the newer paintings, like the *Triptych,* featured a window. Only instead of revealing the world outside, a self-portrait filled much of the frame, and looked in at the viewer.

I am loath to admit people into the room where I work and was struck by

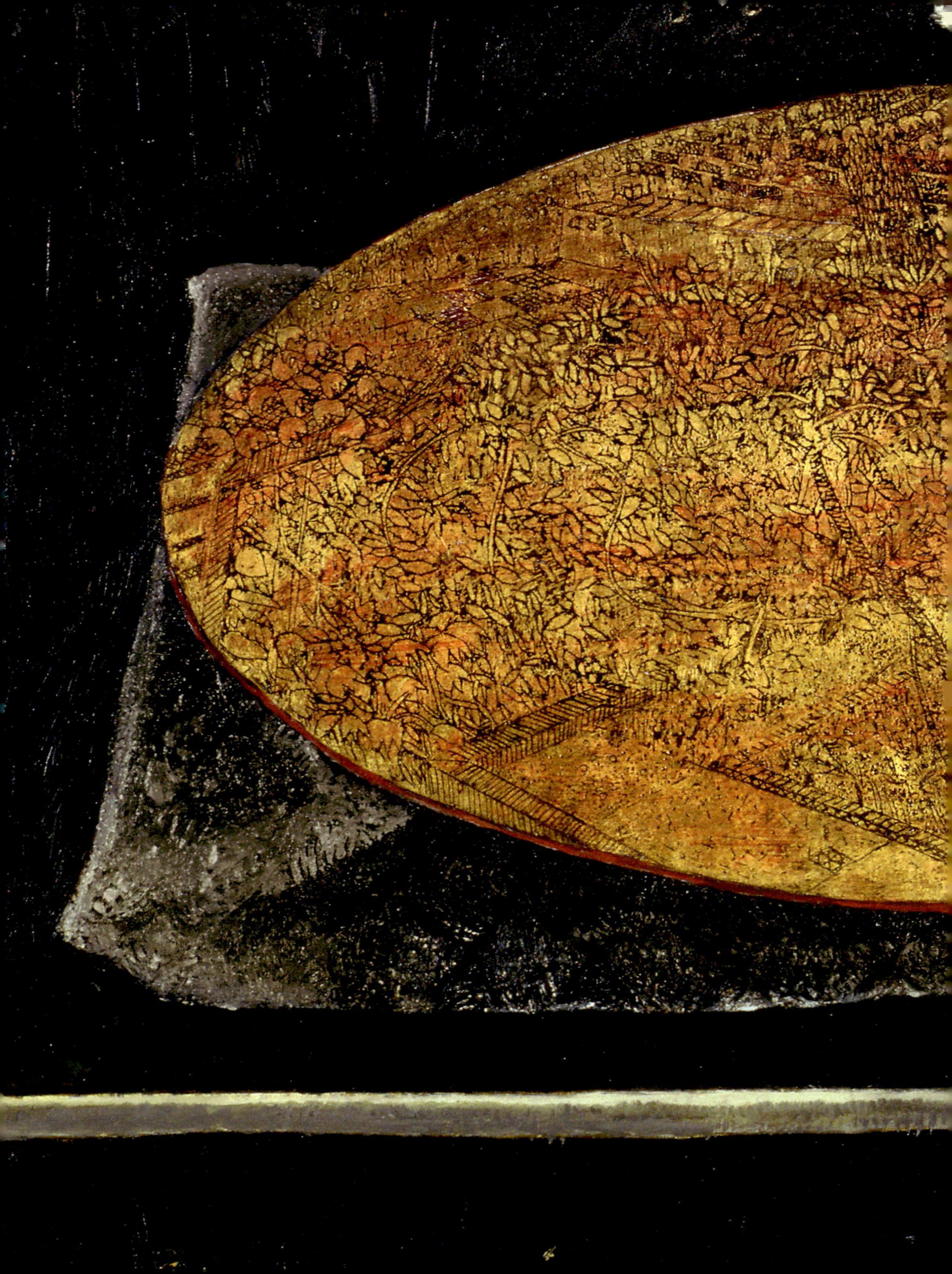

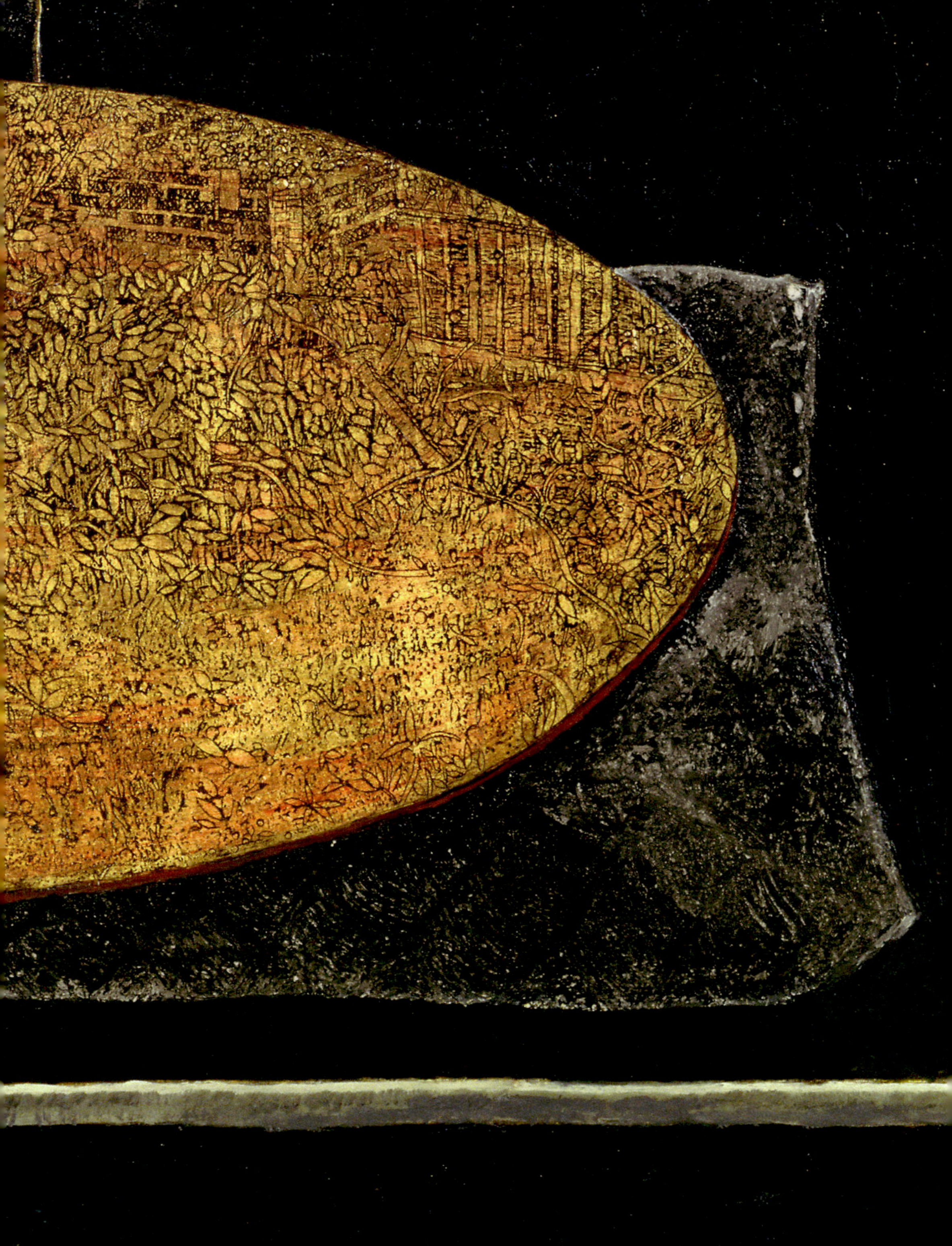

Simon's willingness to allow us to gather there and chat. I saw his curled-up tubes of paint, his easels. Brushes arrayed like beheaded flower stems in an Italian coffee can. Chairs where his models have sat. And tucked into an alcove, taped to one wall, a living continuum of the backdrop of the *Triptych:* a collection of reproduced works of art in the form of postcards and newspaper clippings, many of them faded from sun and age.

In December 2008, two months after meeting Simon in person, I accompanied him to Penn State University, where *The Fulbright Triptych* resides in the Palmer Museum of Art. Along for the ride were Virginia Bonito, an art historian, and a curator at the National Academy, Marshall Price. In the course of the four-hour drive, much of which crosses through the milky, monotonous landscape of northeastern and central Pennsylvania, I asked Simon to talk about the genesis of the painting. He said that he had begun it in 1971, in Germany, when he was twenty-eight years old. He had traveled to Germany the year before, with Renée, thanks to a Fulbright fellowship. He had proposed to study the work of Dürer. After working on the middle panel for six months, drawing forms in black Rapidograph on gessoed wood, he returned to Brooklyn where, after two-and-a-half years, the painting was finished in 1974. He recalled that the apartment in Germany where the painting was conceived came unfurnished. The black table in the central panel was given to him by his landlord and became his subject. It was his first painting. Until then, he had made drawings.

Simon told us that the *Triptych* changed his life before it was even finished. When it was still in progress, when he was struggling to pay a rent of ninety dollars a month and support his wife and child, he walked unbidden into New York's Staempfli Gallery and managed to get the dealer and his co-director, Phillip Bruno, to visit his studio in Brooklyn. After looking at the painting for twenty minutes and not saying a word, the dealer, George Staempfli, told Simon that he wanted to own it. He then proposed an arrangement: he would pay Simon a fixed sum every month until it was finished, and then he would exhibit it. It was an extraordinary stroke of good fortune, a moment

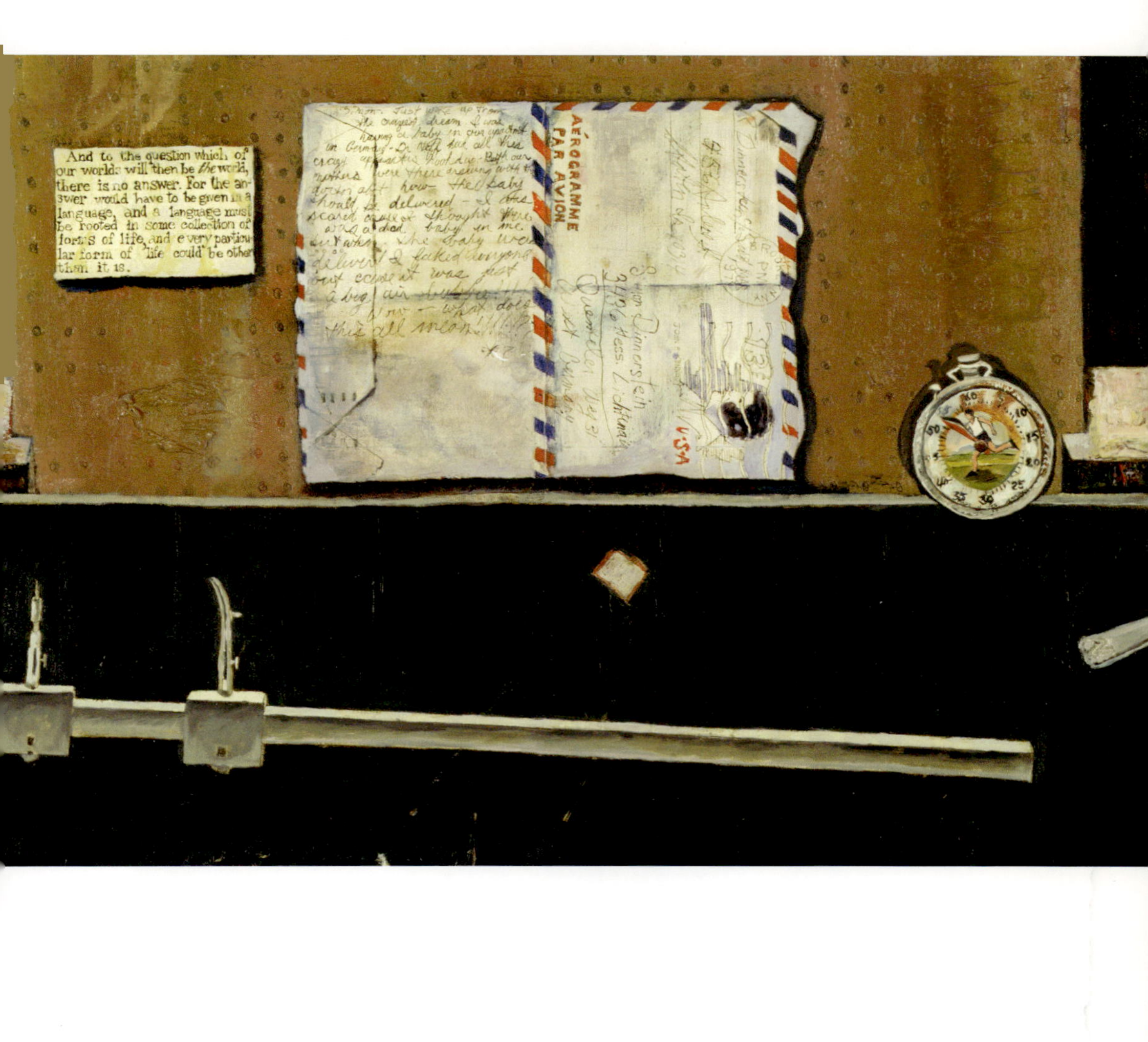
And to the question which of our worlds will then be *the* world, there is no answer. For the answer would have to be given in a language, and a language must be rooted in some collection of forms of life, and every particular form of life could be other than it is.
AÉROGRAMME
PAR AVION
USA

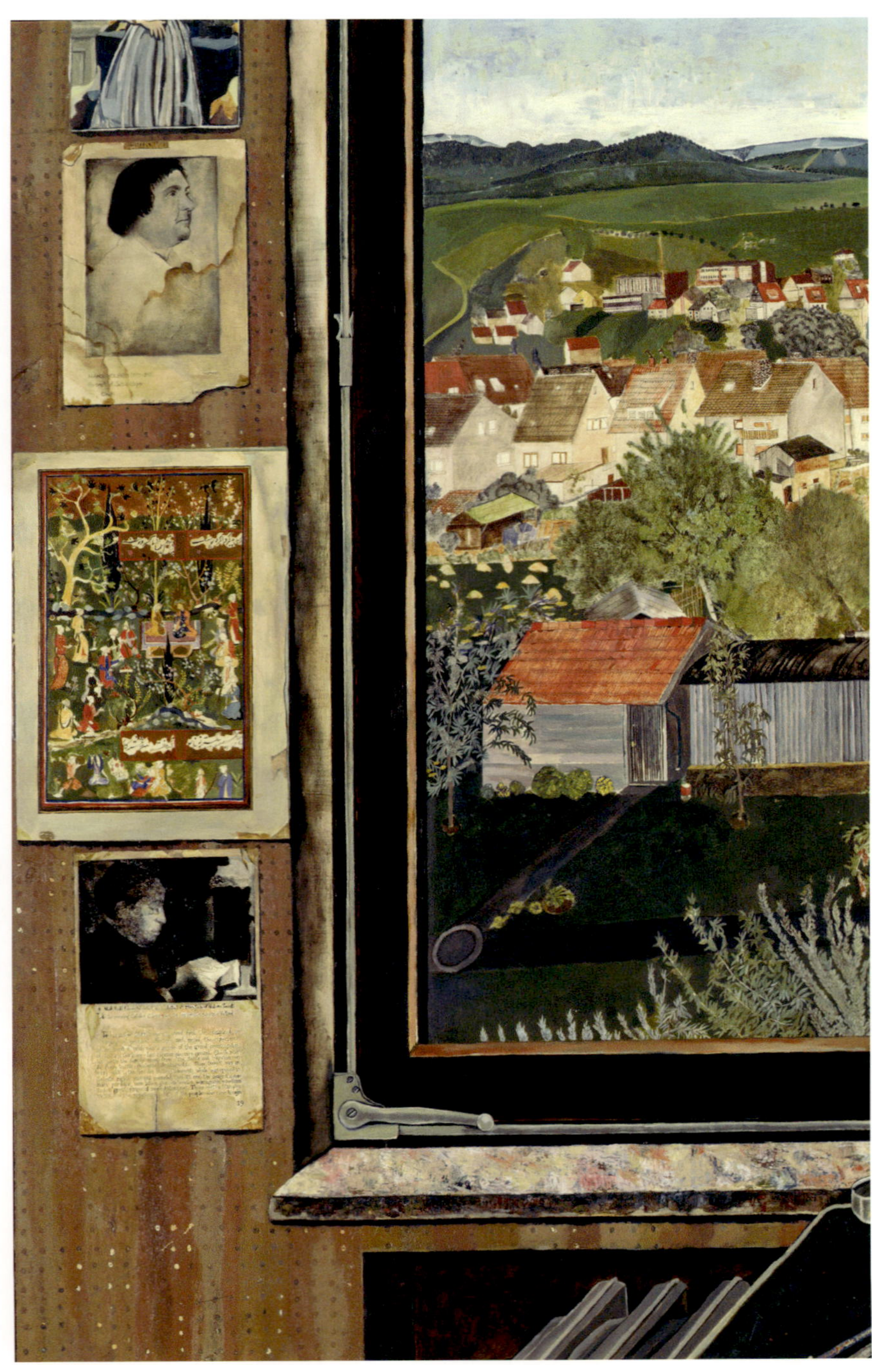

that forever altered Simon's life and career. As he recounted the story, it was clear that the memory still overwhelmed him.

I understood his emotion well. Any artist lucky enough to migrate from obscurity to recognition, from poverty to solvency, knows what a miracle it is. Recognition, combined with the ability to support oneself as much as possible on one's creative work, is what aspiring artists dream of. But once achieved, the new reality itself feels like a dream. This is how I have felt for the past dozen years, after a door, against similar odds, opened for me, enabling me to make my living as a writer. Listening to Simon, I realized I would feel this way for the rest of my life. I asked Simon what he'd been reading when he started the painting. The answer was *Moby-Dick.* He'd read Melville's novel for the entire year he was in Germany, repeatedly renewing it from the library. Still not finished when he was scheduled to sail back to America, he brought the book back with him and finished it, poetically, on the high seas before mailing it back to the library in Europe. He told me another thing: that on the back of the central panel of the *Triptych,* Renée had nailed a five-mark coin to the wood crossbars, corresponding to the gold coin Ahab nails to the mast of the Pequod. "Begun in Good Faith and High Hopes on May 3rd, 1971…with the love of Renée" is written in her hand beneath the coin. The benediction touched me; I remembered my own shaky beginnings as a writer, and how much my husband's faith in me meant at the time.

It is striking, and also fitting, that a novel so distinctly American, a novel about appearance and reality, about Ishmael's reflective wandering and Ahab's quest, informs the creation of the *Triptych.* For this is a painting, among other things, about what it means to be an artist: a necessary combination of Ishmael's absorption of the world, fused with Ahab's passion. It is also an intensely personal painting, just as *Moby-Dick,* for all its vastness, is an intensely personal narrative. It is a painting about a young American artist's absorption of northern European art, about his study of Dürer's copper engravings, about his response to that discipline in a new medium, and about his journey home. The triptych-in-progress not only crossed the Atlantic physically along with its creator, but embodies dense layers of crossings between one thing and another: between artistic traditions, between places, between past and present, between the real and the re-created. Between emerging and being, and between conception and birth.

It had been almost nine years since Simon had seen the *Triptych.* It is not the same for writers, who are unable to revisit their work simply by pulling it off a shelf. As we sat in a restaurant in University Park, about to head over to the Palmer, I felt a vicarious sense of nervous anticipation. It was as if we were going to visit a child who had both grown unrecognizably old and stayed exactly the same. The people at the museum were expecting us, and the panels had been brought into a special room for us to view, the fourteen inches I'd gotten to know in reproduction now stretched to fourteen feet. The first thing Simon said when he saw it was that the panels needed to be set further apart. Once they were arranged to his satisfaction, we stood far and close, taking notes and photographs. For me the pleasure of seeing a real painting has to do with those textures and details that lie dormant in reproduction. Face-to-face, I became aware of the roughness of the subfloor, the seams of the wallpaper. The veins on Renée's feet, the sheen of her plaid skirt. The bold swirls in Simon's hair, the rich velvet of his shirt, the fiery flecks in his beard. With the lights adjusted a particular way, I saw how brightly the copperplate, painted in gold leaf, turning the windows into easels and thus turning the view they contained into a paradox: something both beyond and within the room, something that is both reality, passively seen, and art, actively recreated.

Another aspect of the painting I was appreciating for the first time was the extent to which the painting represents a compression of real space and time. The room we see, albeit broken into three sections, is neither an apartment in Germany nor a studio in Brooklyn, but an amalgamated realm that is another place altogether. The view through the windows is of the German countryside, but the floor and the wallpaper, the hanging plants, the sycamore fronds scattered on the worktable, are native to Brooklyn. Now that I knew the full story—that Renée was not yet pregnant when Simon started working on the *Triptych,* but that by the time he finished it, Simone had been born—the painting's narrative became apparent. In this sense it is as much

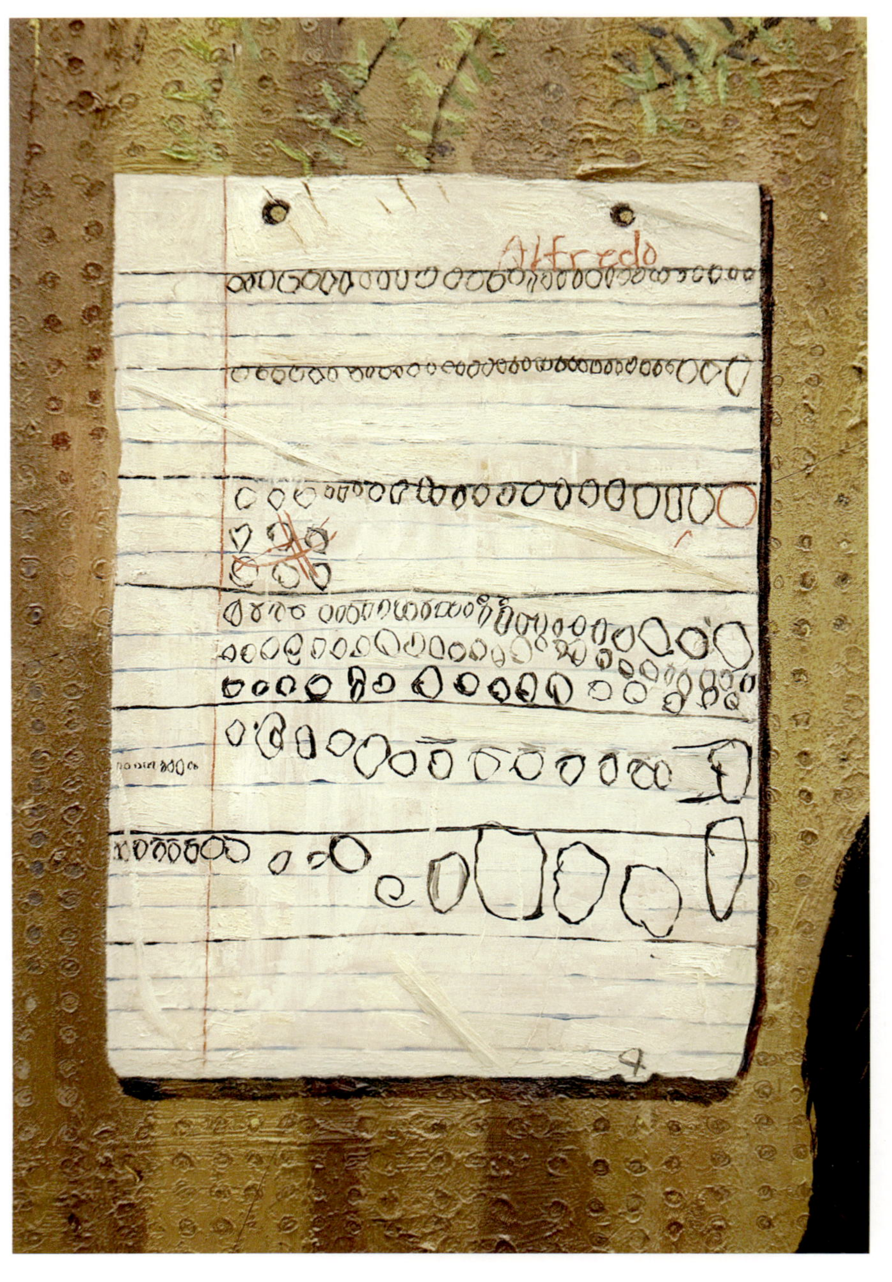
Alfredo
4

a trilogy as it is a triptych, for the painting shows us a life in stages, in parts. It shows what exists, and what does not, and what existed only previously. It reminded me of instances in my writing when, working from the past, I have had to manipulate actual events in order to serve the purpose of fiction. *The Fulbright Triptych* is the first time I appreciated this deliberate rearrangement of reality on a visual level.

Simon talked about many of the items, depicted in astonishing precision, on the walls of the painting. He read a poem written by a thirteen-year-old girl named Gloria Mintz:

Grey and sweating/And only one I person/Fighting and fretting.

He pointed out a ballpoint drawing by one of Renée's students, and reading exercises they had done. He read a quotation about language, and asked us to guess who it was attributed to (I guessed Plato; the answer was Wittgenstein). There was a letter propped up between the windows, and Simon crouched down, offering to read it, stepping into the world of the painting as if it were a stage set (it is three-quarters life-size). It was a letter to Simon from Renée, who at one point during their years in Germany had gone back to New York to visit her ailing father. She recounted an anxiety dream about being pregnant, a dream she'd had before the painting was conceived.

The things on the wall would be different now, Simon told us, but I saw that his love for them had not waned. Nor had their presence; they were there, an artist's ephemera made permanent, painted into the wood. They were all sacred to him, everything from the work of van Eyck and Seurat to a colorful drawing by two German girls, daughters of a couple the Dinnersteins had befriended in the town, named Simone and Andrea. Simon told us that Simone Dinnerstein (whose name is pronounced Simona) was named after these two girls, and that after she was born, six-year-old Andrea sent them the drawing as a baby gift. As I stood in front of the panel on the right, he pointed, standing directly in front of his painted younger self, to a re-created paragraph torn from the re-created ivory page of a re-created book. "Do you recognize this?" he asked. I shook my head at first, then stopped when I read, "To me, the white whale is that wall, shoved near to me. Sometimes I think there's naught beyond." It was a passage from chapter 36 of *Moby-Dick.*

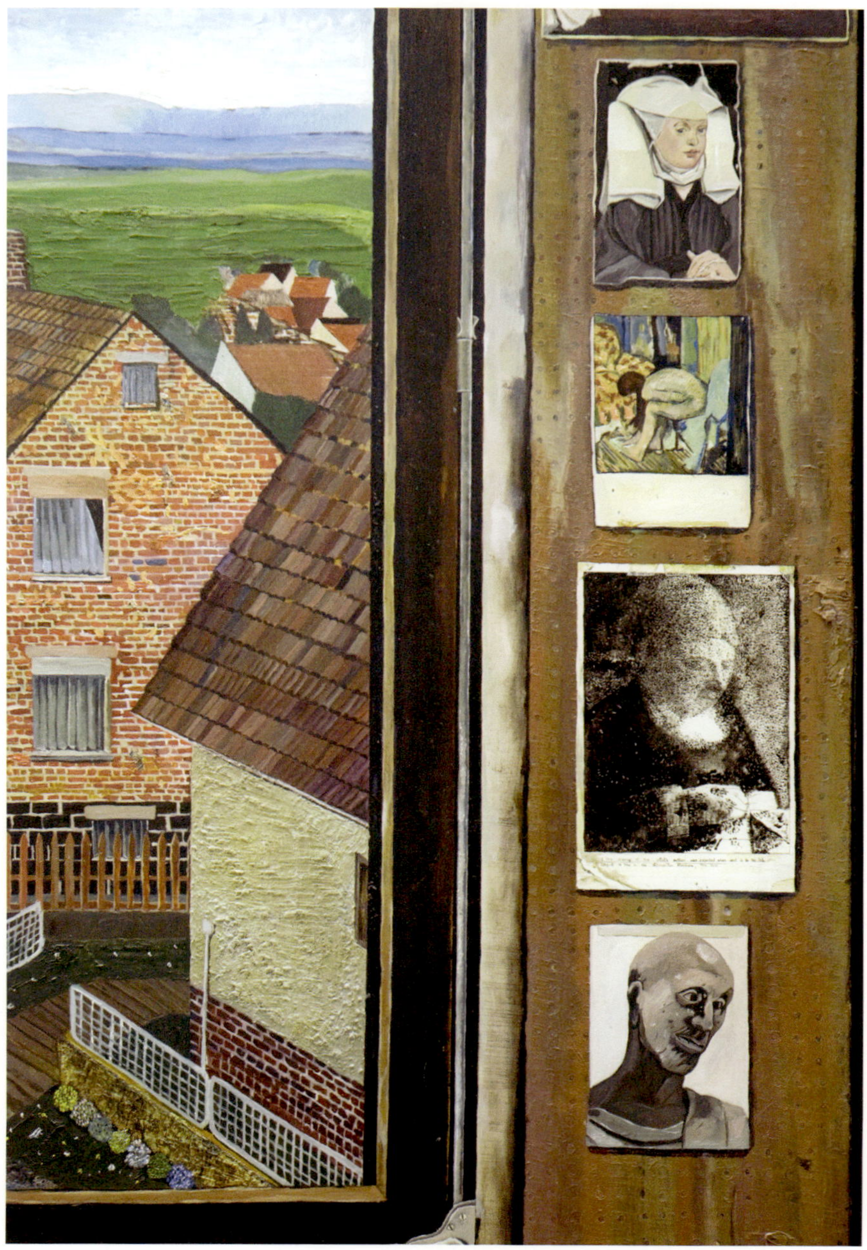

A painting of an artist's studio is an inherent contradiction, and a profoundly intimate thing. It is a finished work that represents something impossible to represent—the piecemeal, protracted process of making art. To work as an artist is to revisit something day after day, to look at a subject or an experience not twice or twenty times but what easily feels like twenty thousand times. In the course of those repeated visits, the thing seen—or in a writer's house, contemplated—begins necessarily to evolve, to become something other than itself, to become, at times, unrecognizable. The walls of the studio, the floor, the furniture, the scarps taped to the walls are what remain constant, and they are as revealing, as much of a self-portrait, as the depiction of an artist's figure or face. In that sense, *The Fulbright Triptych* is a self-portrait twice over.

One of the postcards on the walls of the *Triptych,* of a painting by Vermeer, is a self-portrait of the artist seated at his easel, his back to the viewer, working with a model who poses in the background. But the artist in *The Fulbright Triptych* sits still, a figure who is both model and artist, his fingers interlaced, the instruments on his worktable untouched. That he is not actively occupied is, of course, an illusion. The completed painting, the enduring distillation of the effort required to create the composed figure, reminds us of this. After getting to know Simon a little bit, I think that his posture in the painting, at once vigilant and relaxed, is appropriate. He is a man who not only paints the world he sees but deeply thinks about and questions it—thoughts and questions that eventually become manifest in his work. His presence in the painting reminds us that the idle moments in one's studio, when one is not actively painting or writing or making anything, when one is perhaps sitting in a chair staring into space, are precisely the moments inspiration tends to strike.

I love *The Fulbright Triptych* and will continue to keep a reproduction of it taped up in my writing room, because it is about the interplay of the two aspects of my life that are the most sacred to me: art and family. When I was first getting to know the painting, I regarded it as a fugue of threes. The three panels, the three figures. The three formal subjects—portrait, still life, landscape. The three levels of representation—the painting, the reproductions of other paintings, the painted renditions of those reproductions. After looking at the painting and thinking about it for nearly six months, I see that it is as much about dyads as triads, and about the primal alchemy of two becoming three. The painting is about a marriage and about the consequence of that marriage: a child. It is also about an individual who, doubly creative as artist and father, exists both in the realm of art and of life; who is devoted to both things but is also sundered by them, occupying a panel of his own. As a writer who is also the mother of two young children, I experience this sense of division on a daily basis. Though the artist's family exists within the *Triptych,* has even participated in its creation by posing for it, the painting is made by him alone, in the studio, outside ordinary life. In *Tonio Kröger* Mann writes: "The artist must be unhuman, extra-human; he must stand in a queer aloof relationship to our humanity; only so is he in a position, I ought to say only so would he be tempted, to represent it, to present it, to portray it to good effect."

As we were getting ready to leave the museum, there was a moment when Simon and I stood alone with his painting. "I believe the meaning of the painting is contained in the space between the pictures," Simon told me. Whether he was referring to the space between the reproductions he'd painted or the space between the panels themselves was not clear to me at the time. But in the process of writing this essay, I began to understand.

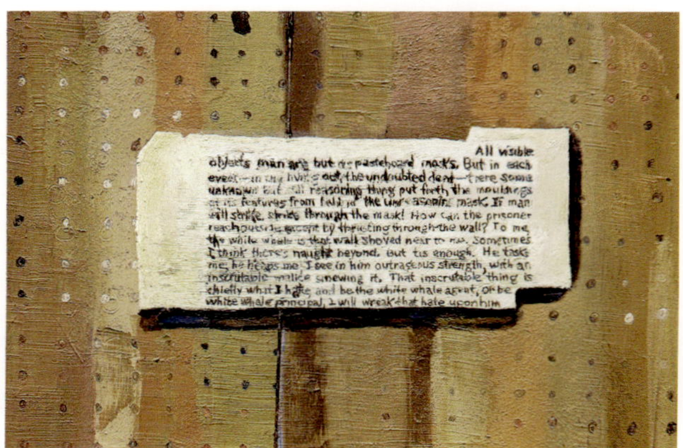

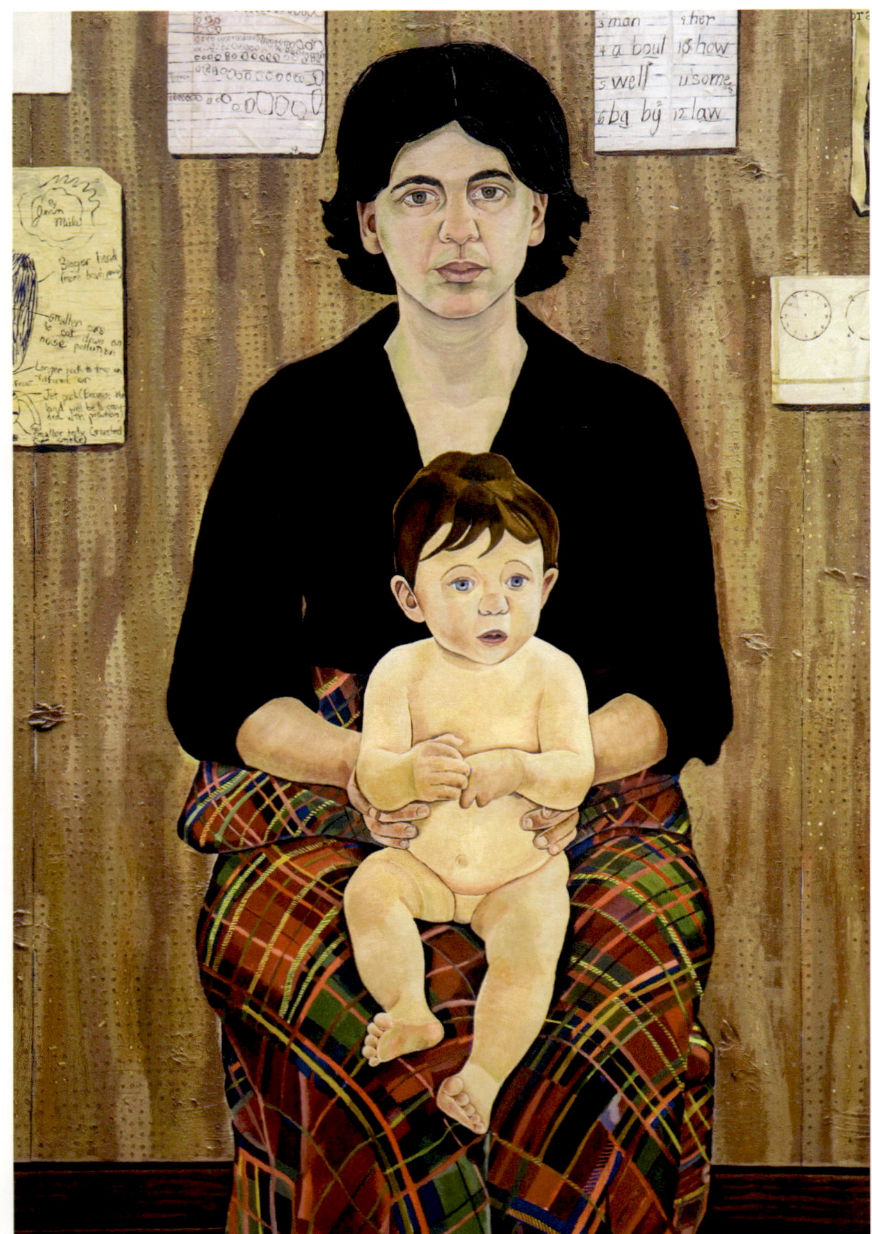

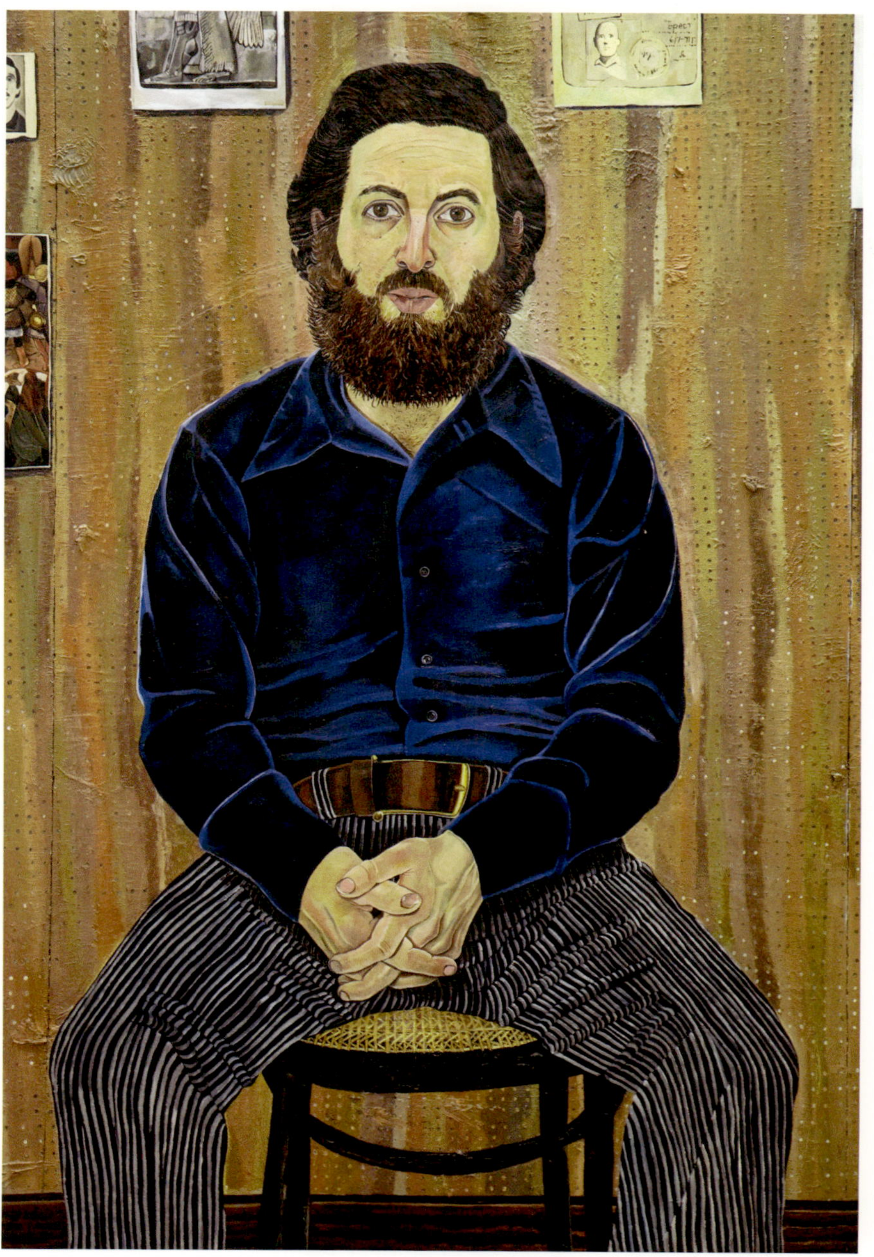

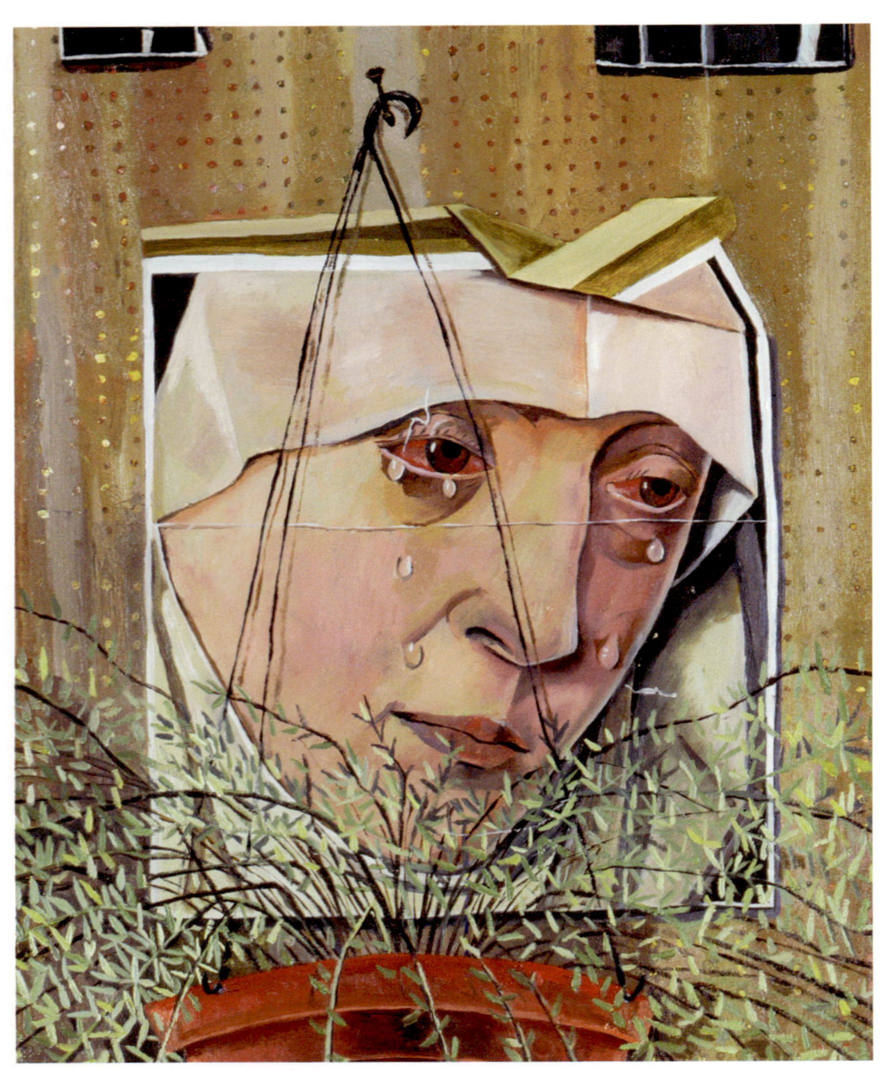

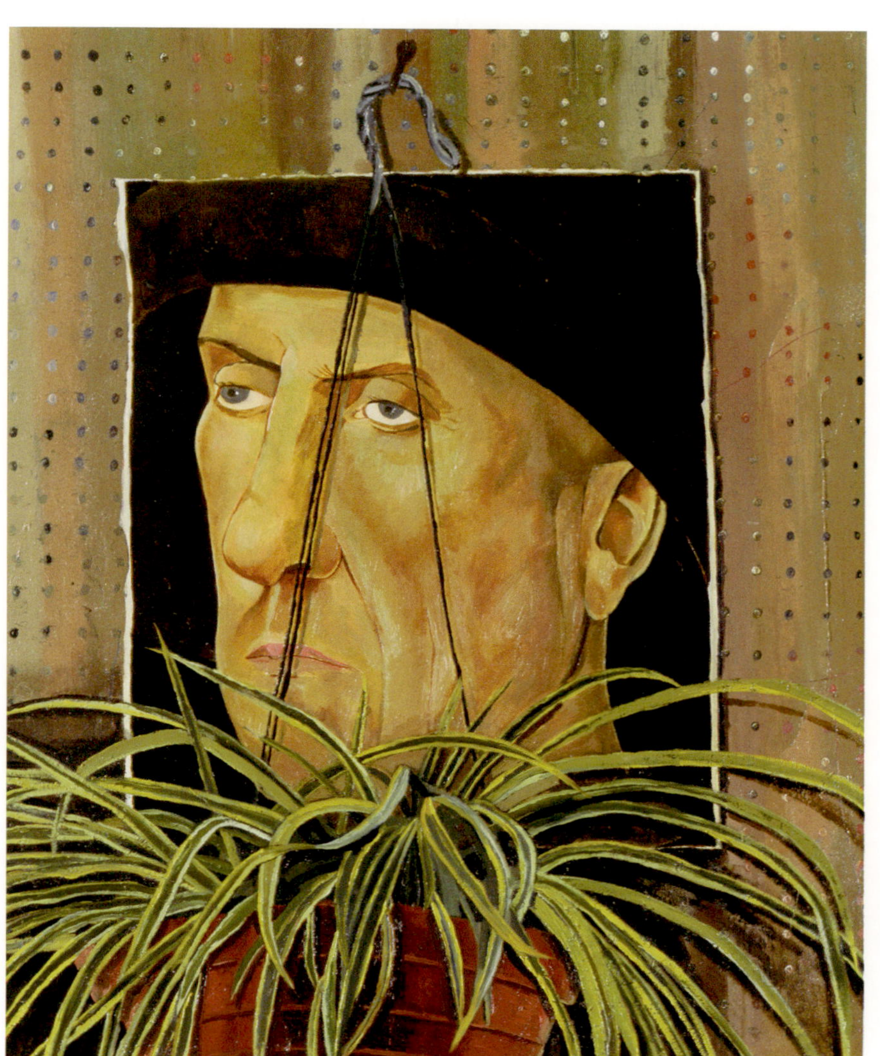

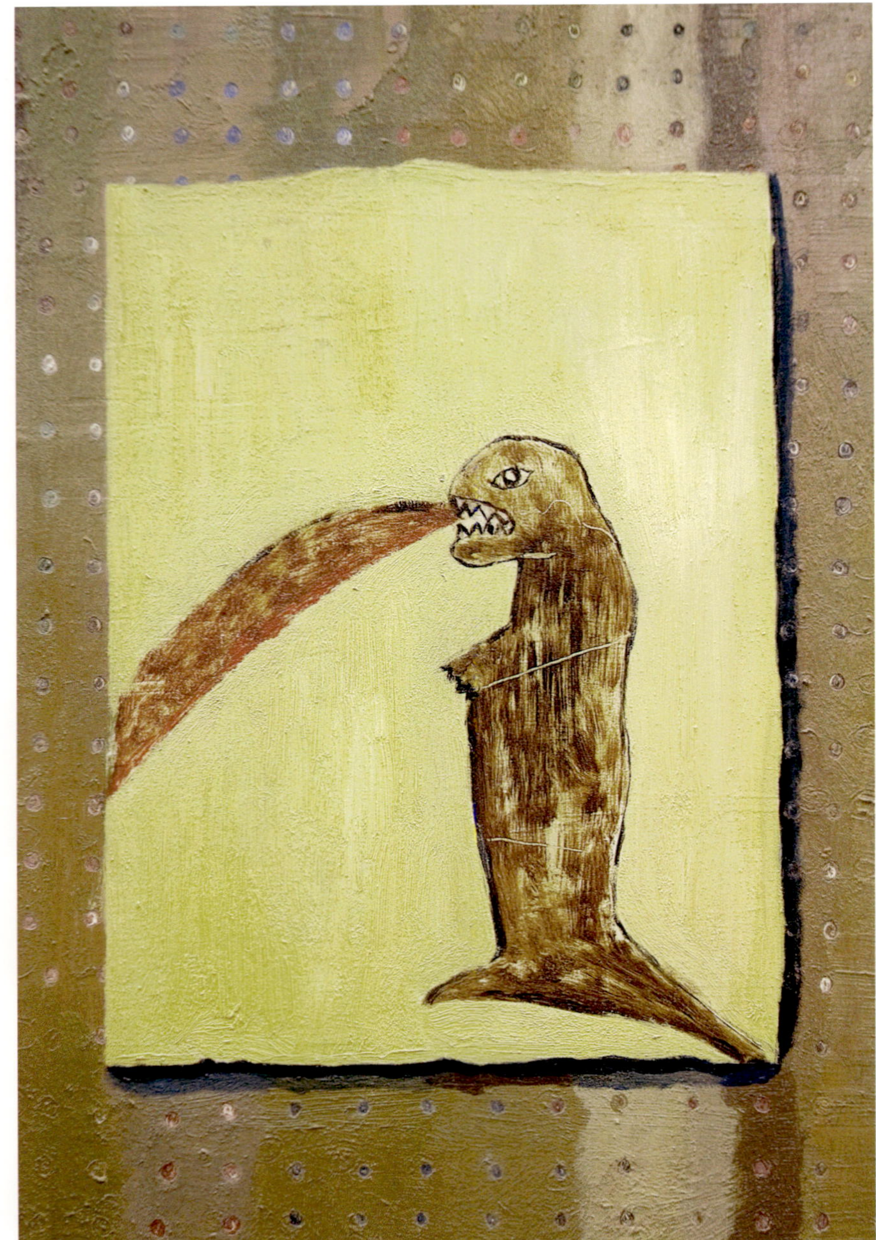

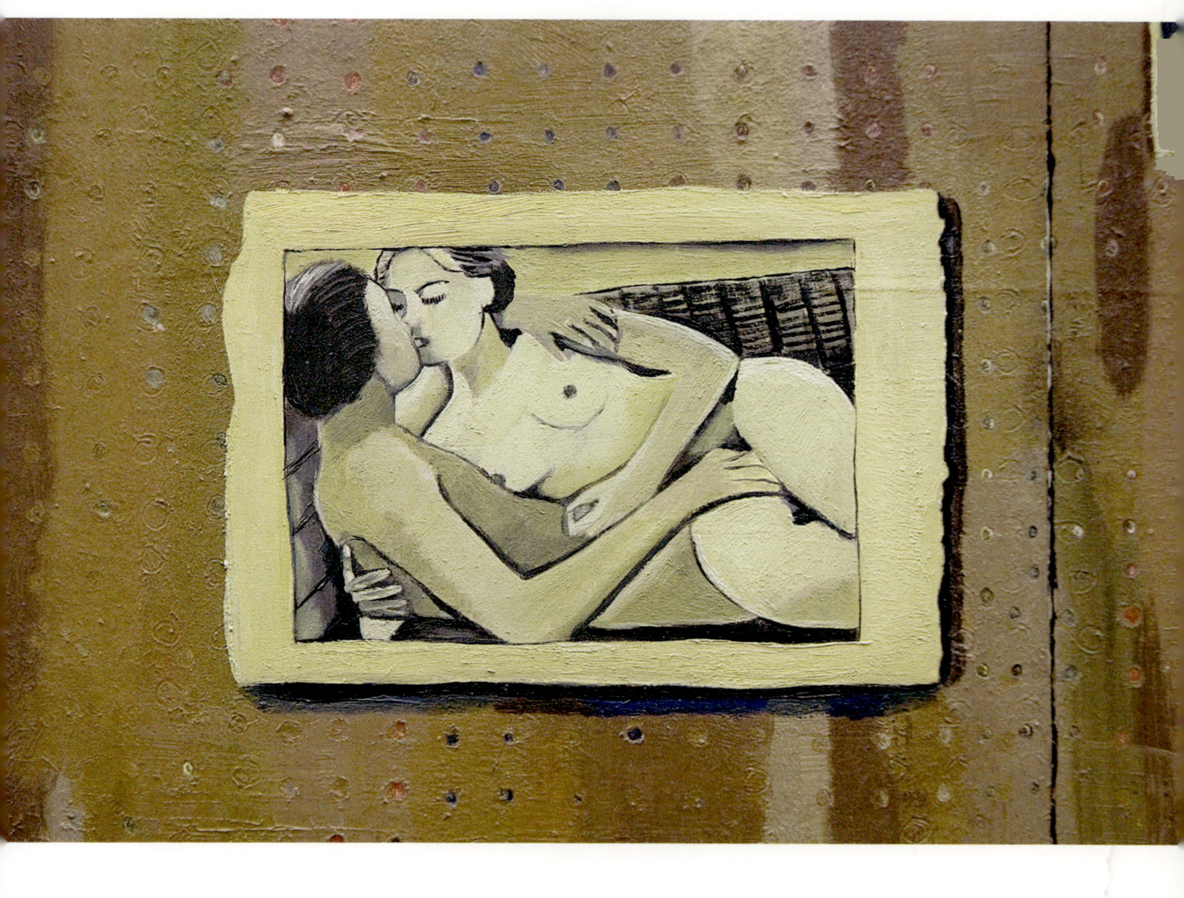

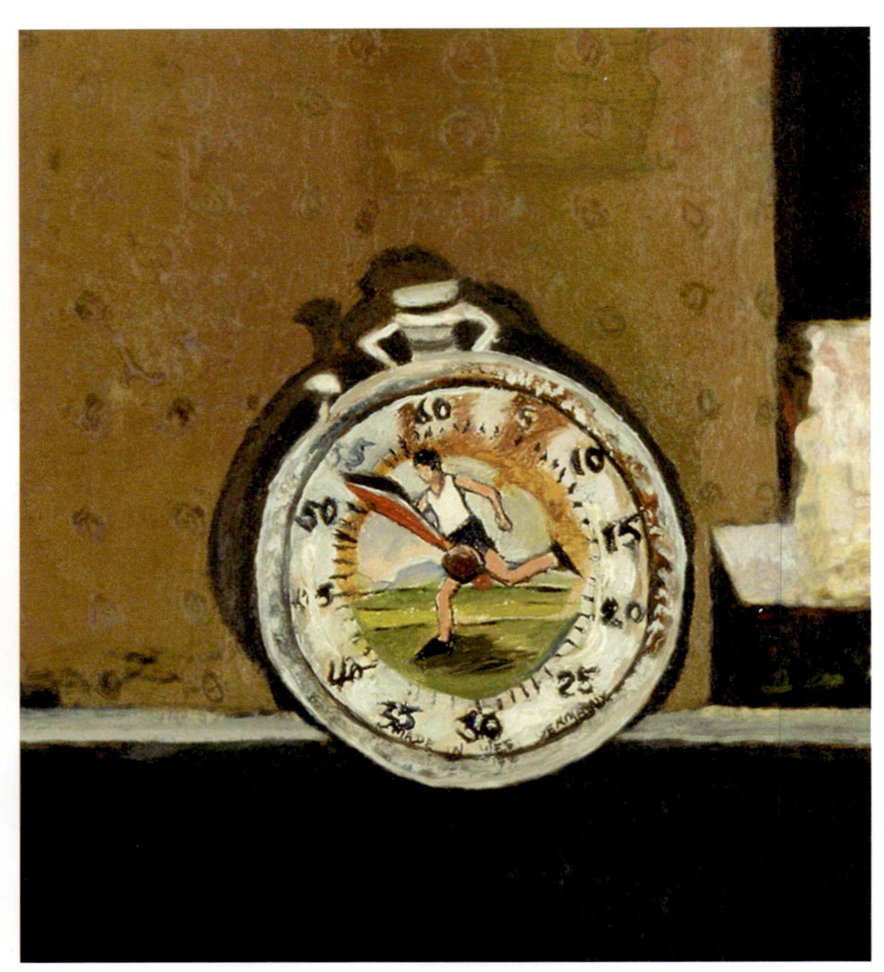

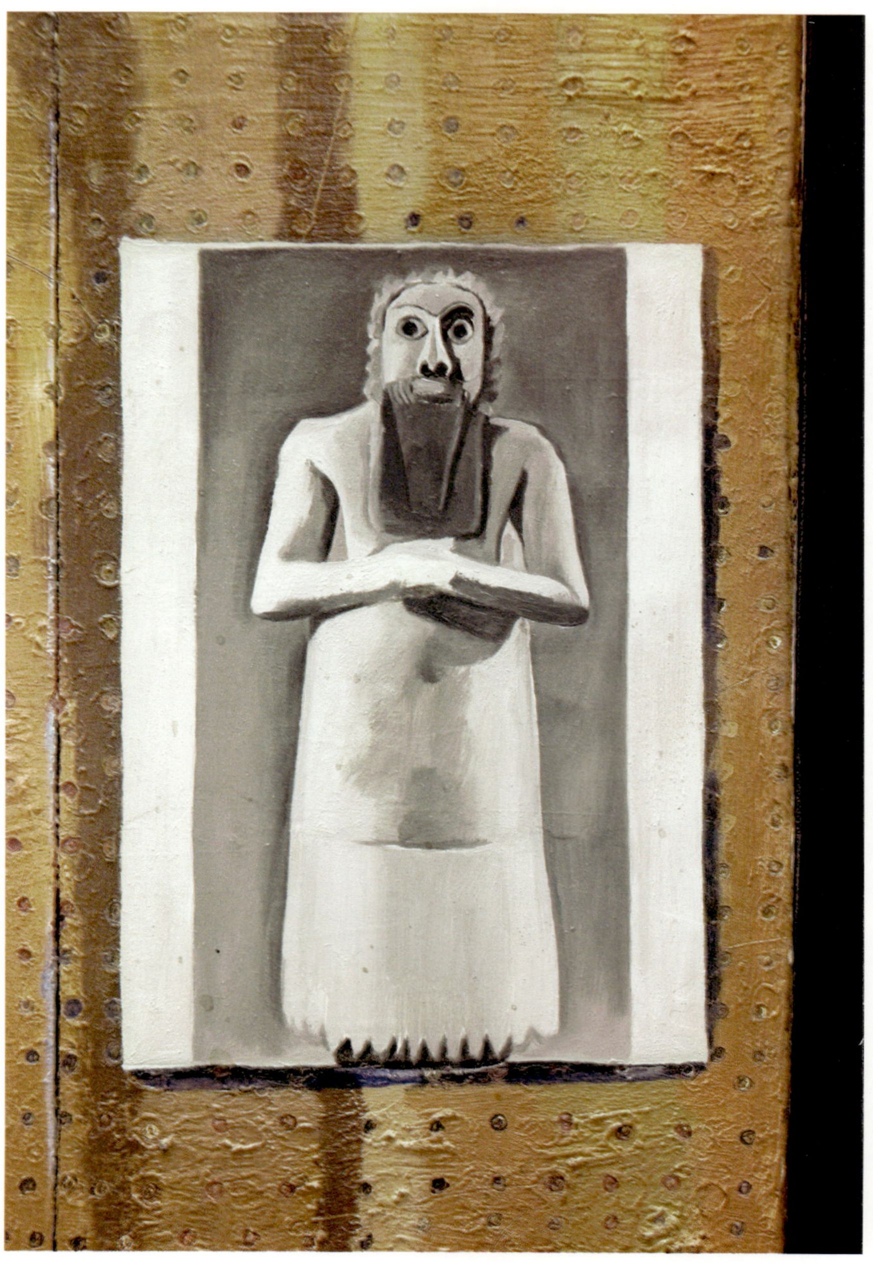

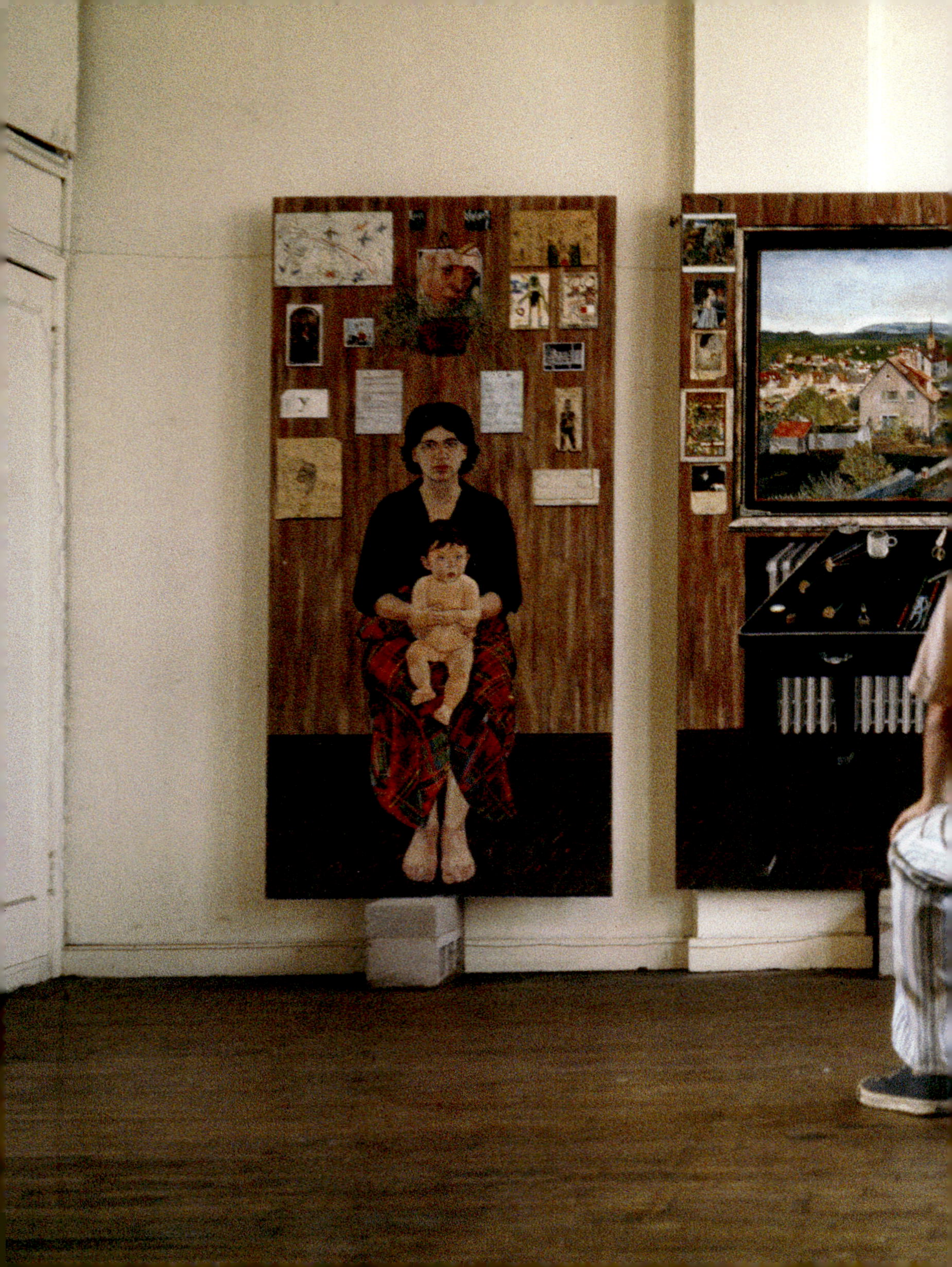

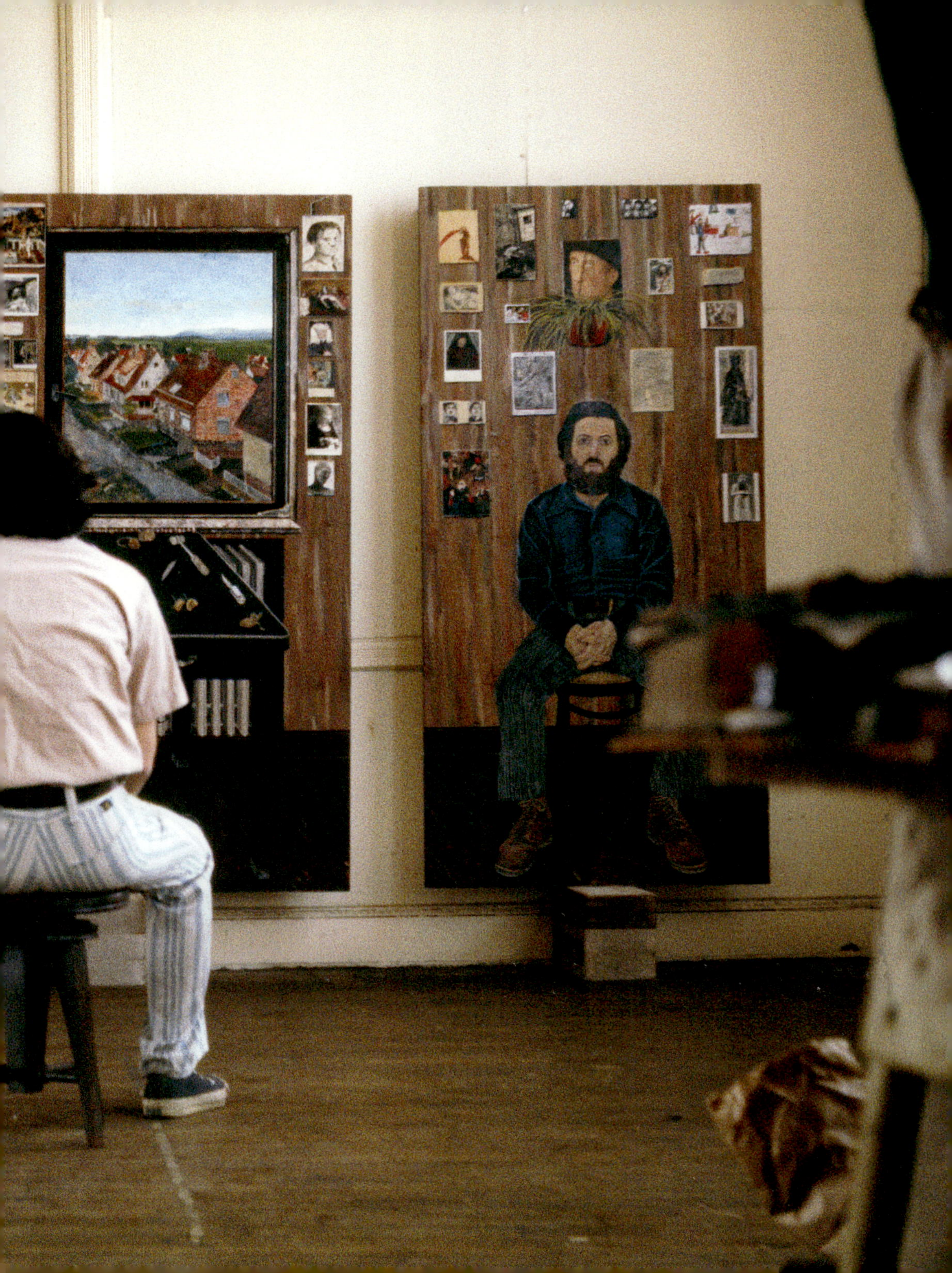

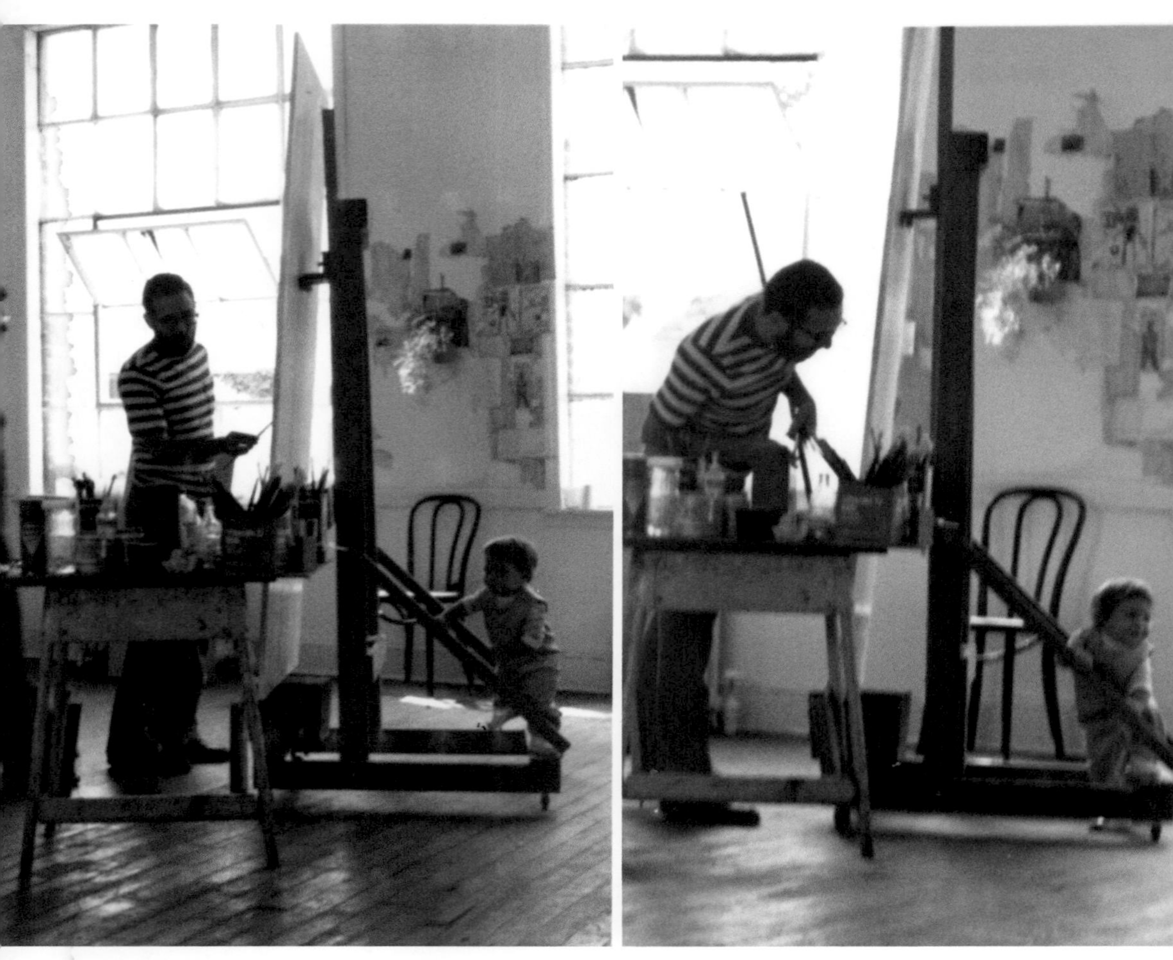

The Fulbright Triptych, which has been in the permanent collection of the Palmer Museum of Art at Penn. State University for many years, will be exhibited in New York at the German Consulate General (along with other selected works) from June 16 - September 15, 2011. The Consulate is located at 871 United Nations Plaza at 49th Street, NYC.

EMILY RABOTEAU

ECHOLALIA

The ship in the bottle in the engineer's hands was a brigantine called *Evangeline.* He'd painted her name on the lark blue stern with a brush as small as an eyelash. This boat was just like her—cheerful and voluptuous and true. He hadn't exactly loved Evangeline, who was young enough to be his daughter. She was soft where June had grown hard was all. She was a balm in their house. She'd had a way with Abel. Kissing her had been tender and separate from everything else. Her mouth, he remembered her soft smiling mouth, the way it yielded to his tongue, its heat, the way she whispered, "It's alright," into his mouth passing the words like smoke, "It's alright," and how he had inhaled the words and almost believed her.

Now that Evangeline was gone, the boat in her name was a repository for his guilt. It didn't belong in his fleet. He wanted to get rid of the *Evangeline* as an act of contrition, but also because if June found this particular boat, it would make things much worse than they already were. He wasn't sure how to dispose of it, so as a dilatory tactic, he tidied the worktable. It could hardly be called a mess but he tidied it. He sharpened the drafting pencils and arranged them in their mug. He realigned his rulers and slides. He fingered his long-shanked tools, the hand-forged hooks, probes, forceps, and tongs thin enough to reach into the necks of bottles. He polished and arranged these so that they were perfectly parallel, just as they would be on a surgeon's table. It was better that way. There were tools for measuring the bottles' insides, their diameter, circumference, and volume, because this is how you begin.

The first step, if he were building a boat in a bottle would be to lay a putty sea, to tool it into waves. Paint it with acrylic. Blues, darker blues, grays. And patiently wait weeks for it to dry. While the weeks went by, he would attach the masts to the hull with hinges so that they could fold back onto the deck like a sparrow's wing, making the boat small enough to fit through the bottleneck. Once it was inside, he would erect the masts again with his tools and glue down the drawstrings made of his wife's hair. He knew each of those steps by rote, he could practically do them in the dark, and it comforted him to know their precise sequential order.

But Ben was not building a ship tonight. He would have to destroy the *Evangeline* before dinner, which was being cooked upstairs by his mother-in-law while June attended to Abel's rocking. He could smell Mrs. Kim's beef sizzling in a pan. The scent of the beef might have been what set Abel off into his perseverations. The boy's sense of smell was more acute than a dog's. But it might just as easily have been one or more of a dozen other sensory assaults that set him off. It was hard to say.

Through the floorboards he could hear his son repeating the words, "I'D LIKE TO BUY A VOWEL! I'D LIKE TO BUY A VOWEL!"

Ben didn't know how June would decode that phrase. Abel wanted something other than a vowel. He had the entire alphabet at his disposal. He could talk, which was supposed to be something to be grateful for. There were other children in Abel's class who could not do that. There was a girl who could complete a thousand-piece jigsaw puzzle, picture side-down, row by row, but had never spoken a recognizable word. There was a boy who carried several sheets of the Brooklyn Heights yellow pages in his front pockets, folded in sixths. He had memorized them all and only spoke in numbers. There was another boy who communicated in pictures of trains, drawing upwards of a hundred a day with remarkable skill, tearing them from his sketchpad and tossing them off rapidly, but never ever depicting human figures. Abel could speak, but not hold a conversation. It was not quite speech, what Abel spoke. It was in the slipstream of speech. His syntax was limited to the present. There was no past. There was no future. Ben wondered sometimes if Abel even knew who he and June were. Upstairs, his rocking grew more frenzied.

"I'D LIKE TO BUY A VOWEL."

If Abel was loud enough for Ben to hear through the floorboards, then he was loud enough for their neighbor, Cheryl Biggs, to hear through the adjoining wall of her brick row house at 35 Cranberry Street, twin to their own. Cheryl was generally forgiving of Abel's outbursts. Other neighbors on their narrow block were less so. They judged June for walking Abel with a leash. They thought her overprotective, neurotic, a bad mother.

"Why do you care so much about what they think? Don't be so sensitive," June advised when he worried about their reactions. She had a pack of business cards in her pocket ready to hand out to people who openly disapproved: *My son is autistic. Thank you for your patience as I raise him to be a valuable member of society.* But she was too far inside Abel's world, or at any rate, inside the house all the time (since there was only so far you could travel inside Abel's world) and had lost sight of how it appeared from the outside. How strange, for example, that the windowpanes were made of Plexiglas, and that instead of flowers, the window boxes contained plastic pinwheels, facing inward. How strange, for example, that Abel might try to unzip a stranger's jacket, or lick the tire of a parked car, or throw himself down in the middle of the sidewalk with his hands over his ears and refuse to get up. To say nothing of the noises that emanated from 33 Cranberry Street—the crashing, the pounding, the shrieking—the sounds that made the house seem haunted.

"He's trying to tell us something," June would say. "Be patient. Try to understand." To Abel she would say, "Use your own words, angel." When he could not, she would hand him his picture communication device and say, "Show me."

"I'D LIKE TO BUY A VOWEL."

He's trying to tell us something. But Ben wasn't sure. What if Abel was stuck like a needle in the groove of a scratched LP, his mind snagged in some other dimension while his body was stuck in this one? What if he was just a shell, robotically flapping his hands or pounding them against the wall? How do you explain such behavior to your neighbors when you don't fundamentally understand it yourself? When even the experts contradict themselves?

Evangeline had been good at explaining pieces of it. How had she put it? "Abel has reduced sensitivity in his hands and feet," she said, back when she helped them part-time on Tuesday and Thursday afternoons as Abel's respite worker. She knelt on the floor with Abel, facing away from Ben, and was trying to interest the boy in a color wheel. The top of a purple thong showed like a t-square above the low-cut waistline of her cut-off jeans. She looked up at him over her bare round shoulder. "That's why he stomps around and taps on walls to figure out where he ends and the walls begin."

"But *why?* Why are his hands and feet that way?"

Evangeline was still a child herself, no more than twenty. How could he expect someone so young to know why Abel was the way he was? Yet he was desperate for an answer.

"I don't know, Mr. Da Silva," she said. "Why is the sky blue? Some things are a mystery. Give me your hands."

"What?"

"Your hands, silly. I don't have cooties. Come play with us for a minute," and with an easiness that cut through him like a sail, she grabbed Ben's hands and pulled him to the floor. "Hold them up like Diana Ross."

"What?"

"You know! *Stop! In the name of love,"* she sang it like a country song with gusto and the twinge of a southern accent, *"before you break my heart. Think it o-over."*

"I'm afraid I don't understand."

"Oh, come on! I thought that was your era," she laughed. "Okay, hold them like this." She positioned his hands flat in front of him like a mime feeling an invisible wall. Her hands were fleshy and warm, with the fingernails painted, surprisingly, blue. "Abel likes that song. Don't you, Abel? *Stop! In the name of love…"* Abel chewed on the collar of his t-shirt while watching them out of the corner of his eyes. "We call this mirroring. Your daddy's home from work, Abel. Can you say hello?"

Abel scuttled forward like a crab and matched his small hands against Ben's. "Push," Evangeline instructed. "He needs to feel that pressure." So Ben pushed and for a full three seconds, Abel pushed back. Abel was small for nine and his muscle tone was low, but he was strong when the will was there, and Ben could feel the will in his son's hands, pushing back. It was the opposite of being hit by Abel, to be touched by him like this. It was a melting feeling.

"Push!" said Evangeline, and a wall fell away in the space between him and his son.

"Good!" she praised when Abel was finished with the greeting. She fed him a red M&M. "Doesn't it feel good to say hello?"

She smiled at Ben. He could still feel the shape of his son's fresh handprints in his palms. "I can explain why the sky is blue if you're interested," he told her. "It's not a mystery." By which he meant to say, *please stay.*

And eventually she did. But before Evangeline took up residence on the third floor to work full time, they'd had a revolving door of tenants, usually young people—graduate students at NYU, junior editors at publishing houses in midtown, struggling actors, and once, a gay couple with twin mustaches, both interior decorators named Michael—all seduced by the low rent and the proximity to Manhattan. In and out, in and out. When the tenants broke their leases because of Abel's disruptions they were haggard, exhausted, tight-lipped. Sometimes they were apologetic about leaving, sometimes not. They usually asked for their security deposits back.

"You should have warned us," said one Michael, not unkindly, when they left. "Good luck, honey," said the other, handing Ben a scented candle as a parting gift. They'd found a sublet in Chelsea—half the space at twice the rent, but they would be able to sleep undisturbed. "It's vanilla. We know you got your hands full with that adorable little hurricane."

"What are you doing?" interrogated June the night the Michaels left when she came into their bedroom to wake Ben from his two-hour sleep cycle and found the candle burning on the bedside table. She wet her fingers and extinguished its flame with a sizzle. "What the hell is this?"

"It's vanilla," said Ben, disoriented. He'd hoped it might set a mood. That if Abel was down when she came to wake him they might have a ten-minute overlap of time alone together. But Abel was not down. He was rattling something in his bedroom, which was connected to theirs through a set of sliding doors. His plastic piggybank? If Abel dislodged the plug from its belly and disemboweled the coins he might put a nickel in his mouth and swallow it.

"The wick could be toxic," June snapped, dropping the candle into the wastebasket and falling into bed, mumbling about a study she'd read—something linking high traces of metal in the blood of children like Abel to the lead in candle wicks. The soot could poison him, damage his internal organs. It could worsen his behavior. June was asleep almost as soon as her head hit the pillow. And that meant it was time for Ben's two-hour watch. They rotated.

"I'D LIKE TO BUY A VOWEL."

Ben peered up through the grated half-window above his worktable on the night in question, still holding the bottle. Tired, he was always tired. It was the fourteenth of April. A light rain was falling. He could see people's feet hurrying along Cranberry Street, clipping against the wet sidewalk through the sad quick runnels on the windowpane. He could see the wheels of a stroller gliding past, its charge protected under a canopy of plastic. This was a neighborhood of gourmet cheeses, in-vitro fertilization, real-estate envy. Not quite Park Slope, where babies were the accessories of choice and parents put their unborn children on waitlists for the best nursery schools, but close to that. This was a time and place where people wore their children like earrings; they carried their babies against their chests in hundred dollar contraptions; they loved their offspring more than they loved themselves. Like Park Slope, this was a neighborhood where children were raised by nannies from the Caribbean, women who reminded Ben of his mother. This neighborhood had one of the highest property values in New York because of its school district. June had chosen their house for that reason, for the child they needed to make before it was too late.

"I live at 33 Cranberry Street," June had taught Abel to say three years ago, when he was six, in response to the question, "Where do you live?" He had answered fourteen out of twenty times without being prompted with M&Ms, "I live at 33 Cranberry Street," which at seventy percent was a terrific response rate. June was radiant when she reported this to Ben and they had celebrated by sharing the twenty-year-old bottle of Merlot his best friend and partner Morrie Rosenblatt had given him for securing a design deal with Moonlight Cruise Line. June fell asleep drunk without brushing her teeth and she had a smile on her face when he undressed her and touched the sacerdotal dimples above the rise of her buttocks, there, where she resembled a viola. That had been a good day.

But the next evening, when he got home from the Navy Yard he found Abel stretched out stereotyping on the living room carpet, sucking on his washcloth and staring up at the ceiling fan in absolute silence. When Abel was calm, everyone agreed he was a beautiful child. People always wanted to lay their hand on his head. Abel's curls were thick as moss and coiled like the spiral casings around one of the charcoal pencils in the mug on Ben's drafting table. But since Abel didn't like to be touched and could explode with slightest provocation, he and June had to warn them against it. *Please don't touch him.*

The silence was disconcerting, Ben remembered. Abel was in his own world on the carpet. The air in the room had a dreadfully heavy charge. June lay motionless on the sofa, hugging one of the logbooks to her chest like a breastplate. She had a black eye and a bloody lower lip. Neither she nor Abel looked at Ben when he let himself in.

"What's wrong?" he asked, setting down his schematics on the upright piano.

"I didn't do it right," June explained. Her voice was dry. "At school today Deirdre asked him, 'What is your address?' and he didn't know."

"What did he do to your eye, June-bug?"

"I thought he knew it. He only knows it if you ask him, 'Where do you live?' If you ask it another way, it doesn't work." She turned her head toward Abel on the rug. He could do that for hours and hours too; lay flat on his back, watching the ceiling fan spin. But they were not supposed to let him get lost doing that for too long either. It would interfere with his social development. "What if he elopes?" June asked.

"He's six."

"What if he bolts? What if he gets out and gets lost? He has to know his address."

Ben considered the possibility for the hundredth time. If Abel escaped their townhouse somehow, how far might he travel before encountering something that terrified him? There were certain things that crippled him inexplicably and completely. Balloons, for example. What if he saw one of these or a cluster of them tied to a gatepost with ribbons to announce somebody's birth or somebody's birthday and ran from it into traffic? How far might he wander before someone would notice him? Pineapple Street? Cadman Plaza? The Promenade? Abel loved the water. Surely some adult would stop a little boy from trying to jump into the East River. He would look normal to them, in his Thomas the Tank Engine t-shirt and corduroy pants, but he was not, and if they asked him his name there was only a forty percent chance that he would answer correctly. If they tried to take him by the hand, he might attack them like a cornered dog.

This was why Ben had fixed locks on all the doors and windows of their townhouse. "He won't get out. It's not possible," he assured June.

"Deirdre said Bethany got out. She squeezed through the cat door at her grandmother's house in Westchester. She was gone for six hours. They found her wandering on a golf course with bloody knees."

"Which one is Bethany?"

"The girl with the jigsaw puzzle."

"We don't have a cat door. I'm going to get some ice for your eye."

"No! I need you to help me." June was desperate. "Can't you just help me for once? He needs to know where he lives."

"Your eye is swollen shut."

"Don't touch me," she hissed, pushing away his hand like Abel would. "You're not listening! We need to phrase the question in every possible way, so that if he gets out and someone asks him where he lives, he'll be able to tell them."

"But he's got those labels," Ben reminded her. Abel's name, address, and phone number—together they'd ironed those labels into every article of his clothing. Even his socks. Those kinds of labels were supposed to go in the clothes of children heading off to summer camp, or the clothes of old people in retirement homes. Abel had a dog tag with this information too, but he didn't like the feeling of the chain on the back of his neck and wouldn't wear it.

"That's not good enough." June began to cry. "I want him to learn. We're not going to be around to take care of him forever. He's getting older. He has to learn. I need you to help me." As if he did not help her enough—that was the implication—that was the way she said it.

"Fine," said Ben.

He moved to the center of the rug and squatted next to Abel, whose striped t-shirt was dirty with graham cracker crumbs. Ben's knees cracked. The child tensed. "Abel," he said firmly. He held his face above his son's.

"Abel." The boy had the black near-human eyes of a seal, but they were narrow like his mother's. They seemed to be looking straight through him. Abel was more interested in a ceiling fan, a radiator, a light switch, and a doorknob than he was in his own father's face. "Abel. We live at 33 Cranberry Street. What is your address?"

Abel's eyes flickered briefly into focus and out of focus again. Sometimes he responded to his name, and sometimes not. He nursed the washcloth in his mouth, sucking at its center like it was a nipple.

"What is your address?" Ben implored.

There were five possible reasons whey Abel didn't answer. 1) He couldn't hear the question. 2) He didn't understand the question. 3) He understood the question but didn't know the answer. 4) He knew the answer but wouldn't say. 5) He knew the answer but couldn't say. Of these five possibilities, the last was the hardest for Ben to accept, the idea that the answer was locked inside his son but couldn't get out.

How could Abel speak with that rag stopping his mouth? Ben snatched the washcloth away suddenly. It ripped slightly against Abel's baby teeth.

"No!" cried June. "Not like that."

"What is your address?" Ben pressed, holding the washcloth out of reach. The ceiling fan whirred above them. Abel dug his heels into the rug, contorting. He scraped off his sneakers, exposing the white Velcro splints he wore back then to keep him from walking on his toes. If they allowed him to walk on his toes he could damage the muscles in his calves. They would tighten and freeze and he would never be able to properly place the souls of his feet on the floor without pain. But *why* did he walk on his toes?

Nobody knew.

Abel reached for the torn washcloth, clenching and unclenching his hands.

"What is your address?"

"Leave him alone," June ordered, giving Ben a look of supreme disgust. "Can't you see he's tired? Just go away." So Ben had fished Morrie's empty Merlot bottle from the recycling bin out front, retreated to the underground workshop, measured its circumference and diameter, and shoved a schooner inside of it.

The schooner is still there, a mockery of progress, corked in its bottle on the shelf. Abel is nine, the same age as the century, rocking upstairs under that same ceiling fan. He still can't say dependably where he lives. Ben's armada has proliferated to capacity. No more wall space left to build new shelves. Unless he spins the bottles sideways with their corks pointing to the center of the room, there is no space left for new ships. Evangeline has come and gone.

"I'D LIKE TO BUY A VOWEL."

Ben holds her in his hands. Had held her. Had felt her breasts. Was holding Evangeline in memory and in fact.

There were two ways to go about the matter of the *Evangeline.* Before he could do either, his cell phone buzzed in his pocket like a cicada. That would be Morrie calling to let him know if the design contract went through with the Pole Star Cruise Line. He didn't want to speak to Morrie right now. Not with *Evangeline* in his hands.

But what if by a stroke of irony it was her? What if it was Evangeline calling while he was on the brink of destroying the *Evangeline?* Ben hadn't spoken to her once in the two weeks since she'd gone. He had no idea where she was. Had she gone back to North Carolina? Unlike the others, she hadn't asked for her security deposit back when she left. Should he send it to her? He and June could use that money, were in fact bankrupt from all of Abel's treatments, but it seemed to him that this money should be returned to her. He checked the screen of his phone: Morris Rosenblatt.

He let it ring until it stopped.

Ben could smash the bottle against the terrazzo floor and crush the boat with his shoe. He could also ignite the boat with lit matches until it took to flame inside the bottle and turned to ash. Both options were dramatically violent but at the moment, neither form of penance was beneath him. Things had come to a head. He was on doctor's orders to take it easy, but he was actually in the mood to do both. The only thing that held him back was the knowledge that once he was done wrecking the ship, he'd have to go upstairs for dinner and face his wife.

"I'D LIKE TO BUY A VOWEL."

He wanted her back. Not just June, his wife, but the woman June was before Abel. The woman who played a harp in bare feet. He wanted to find the words to close the distance between them.

"She didn't mean anything to me," he practiced, but that sounded like something from one of his mother's soap operas. Besides which, it wasn't true, and June would be able to tell he was lying. "I love you, June," he said to her harp in the damp northeast corner. That was a definitive truth. He could lead with that. It was direct, it was simple, it was what he said on the unseasonably warm late November night when he proposed to her, and it had worked then.

Ben wondered if things might have turned out differently if he had waited and acted according to plan by asking June to marry him on Thanksgiving instead of the night before. He knew it wasn't logical to wonder this, but since Abel's condition was a mystery, he looked for its trigger everywhere—*Why? Why?*—even in places that didn't make sense. Both he and June had taken anti-depressants in the past. Could it be that? Was it the fault of the pricey powder he drew into a syringe and shot nightly into June's thigh to stimulate her ovaries when they couldn't get pregnant? Was it the course of vaccinations Abel received as a baby? What if it wasn't drug-related at all? Was it caused by genetics? A genetic mutation? Was it the fault of Ben's advanced age, or June's?

Could Abel have turned out this way because of the pressure of how badly they wanted him? Ben wondered this sometimes—if it wasn't a detriment to have pinned all their dreams on Abel, to have treated him like a status symbol before he was even born. He wondered also if Abel was affected by something atmospheric or environmental. Was it in the water? Was it chemical? Had his neurology been compromised by cell phone waves? Was he cursed by the fact that June's parents were adamantly against the marriage because Ben was black? Where did the deficit lie? Wasn't it a strange coincidence that Abel should be terrified of balloons when balloons had caused Ben to drop on one knee and say, "I love you, June," the night before he was supposed to? Was there a connection there? Was it a punishment for the crime he committed in Vietnam? What produced the tangle in Abel's brain?

Abel was screaming now, all five vowels at once and none at all. So, yes, June had probably taken away his blue rose washcloth as a punishment. Otherwise the boy would still be rocking and saying he wanted to buy a vowel. According to one school of thought, they were supposed to ignore the screaming so as not to encourage him with negative attention. According to another, they were supposed to swaddle him in a quilt like a kinder, snugglier straight jacket.

So many things set Abel off. If the silverware drawer wasn't closed all the way, he would scream. He would scream if the fringes at the end of the rug weren't straight. He would scream when it was time to get out of the bath. When the garbage truck came, he would cover his ears and scream. It was impossible to know all of the rules that ordered his mind. It was possible to learn some of the rules, but that was a full-time job. June had made it her job.

Ben cradled the *Evangeline* against his weak, weak heart like it was an infant he meant to comfort, though of course, he meant to destroy it. He closed his eyes. Upstairs, Abel screamed and screamed a squall that could split your brain in two. Ben hoped his son was not also biting his right hand; that raw red hammock of skin between the thumb and first finger and the scabrous knuckle that would never heal because he was always biting that part of his fist. At least he was not banging his head on the floor. Not yet.

In this way, Ben was a slave to his son's compulsive behavior, anticipating every eruption, even if it seemed he had detached himself by shutting the door and descending the basement stairs, even if June would say, which she would, that he had no right to call himself a slave to their son, it was not called slavery, it was called parenthood. If it was a slavish kind of parenthood, because of what Abel required, then she was the one who had earned the right to that title—slave—not him, regardless of his color, because this was not about race, this was beyond that. But if he wanted to bring that loaded word up, then *she* was the slave. She was the mother, not he. Which was an unassailable argument, of course, not even an argument, just a fact. She was Abel's mother. She would do anything to save her child. Motherhood was a kind of bodily sacrifice, he knew that; it was true for all mothers.

Fatherhood was something else. It was coming home from Rosenblatt & Da Silva when the day was nearly finished, struggling through dinner, then giving Abel his bath while June drank herbal tea and watched *Wheel of Fortune* or *Jeopardy!* or some mindless syndicated sitcom or listened to Beethoven in the dark or talked to her little sister, Kitty, on the cordless phone.

Fatherhood was this one half-hour alone with Abel on weeknights during bath time. It was the ritual of washing him, gently passing the threadbare washcloth over his chest like a wet spider web. It was observing how the boy submerged himself in the oval of lukewarm bathwater with just his nose above the waterline. It was being grateful for the peace Abel found in floating like that, with buoyant arms and his little brown fists relaxed at last, looking not unlike he had all those years ago, floating in the ultrasound like a magic bean in a butterfly wing. During the half-hour window between 7:00 and 7:30 p.m., fatherhood was marveling over the engine of Abel's body, which he had made but did not know how to fix. And finally, fatherhood was marveling over the engine of Abel's body, which he had made but did not know how to fix.

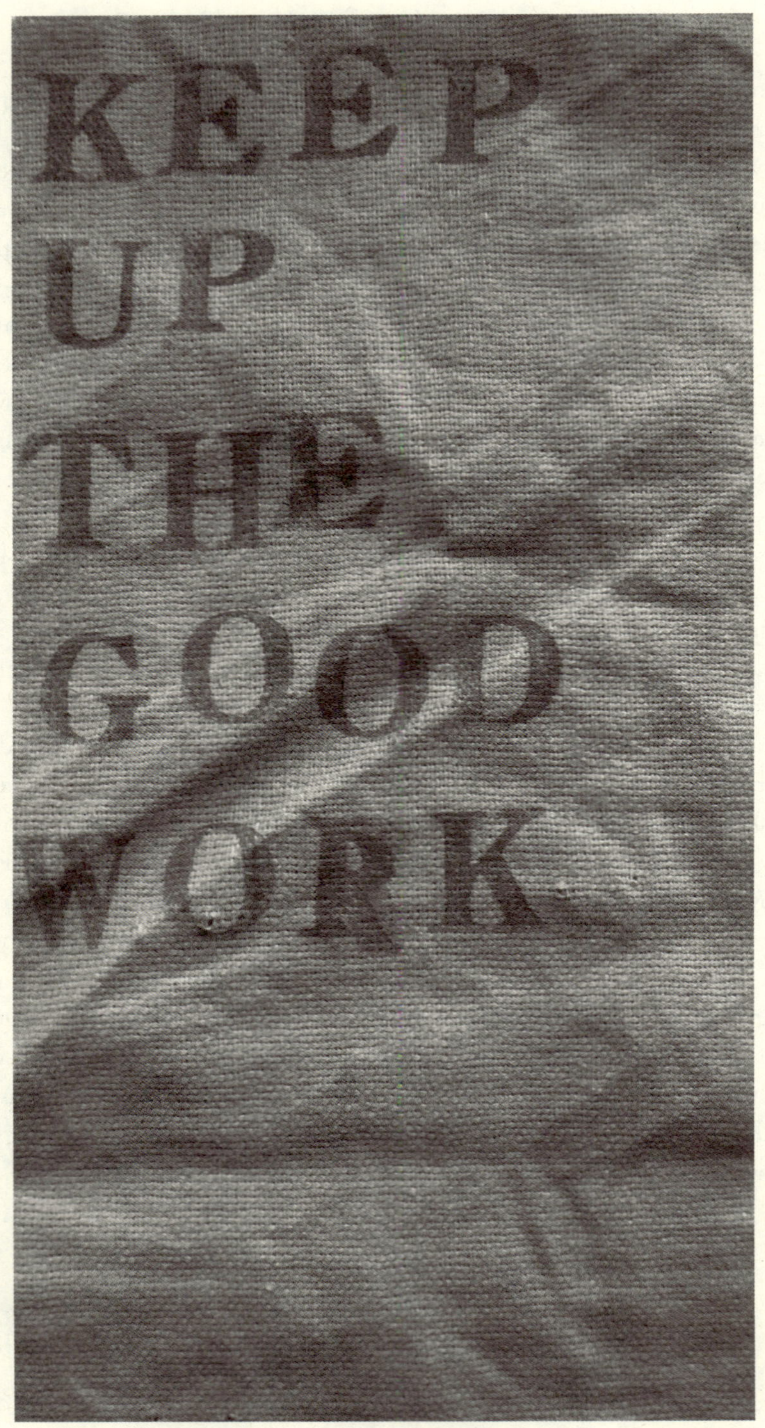

Courtesy of Todd Colby

TODD COLBY

Go! Team!

I'm just lifting my heart out of bed
with muscles made of lemons, yeah: lemons.
I love the way morning turns grayer than dawn's pink
or the childlike way that the rhythm of the B.Q.E.
rocks me to sleep when you're not here.
You get prime space in my mind.
Are you sitting? Well when you stand
there are famous people right next
to you all akimbo with definite chillaxing
and super-ridiculous pulmonary effort.
I mean, I'm on to you and all the things
you stand for, on, and over and out. I can't
lift you higher than I did while kissing
that little love button that says "go go."
And then I do get up because maybe I've had
enough and I can do this in style
but I'd rather you found me dancing
all jazzed and joyful for simply being
awake at all in this rabid century.
Are you on my team? I would like to start
a team and I would like you on it.

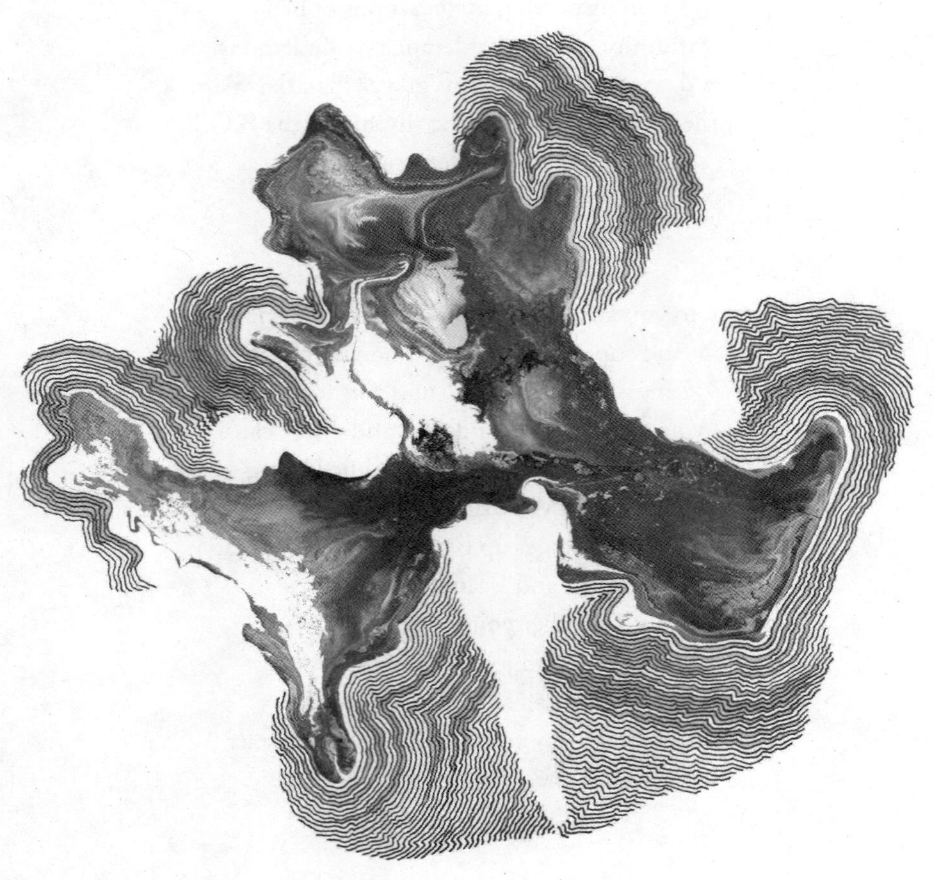

Courtesy of Yasmina Khan

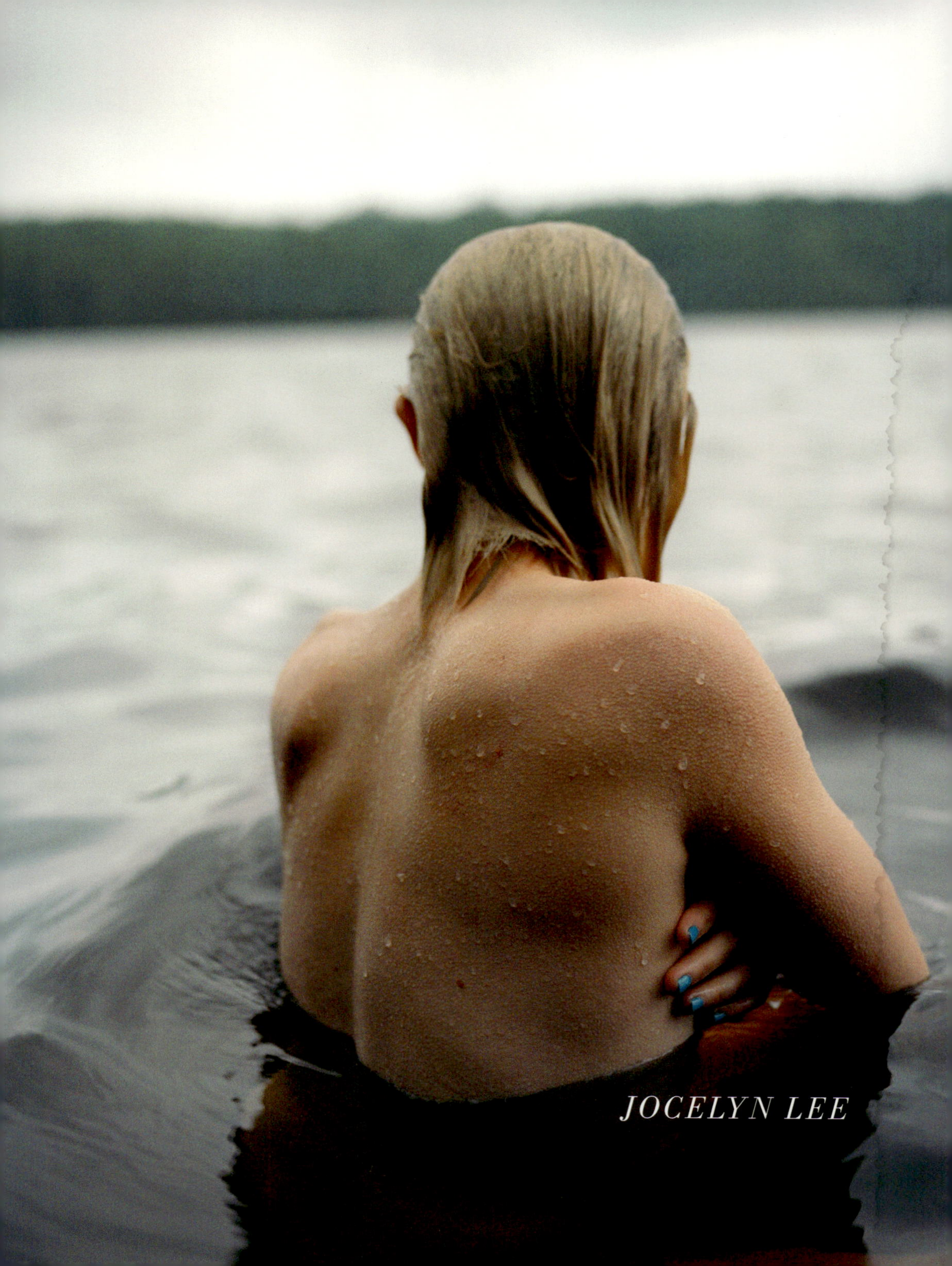

JOCELYN LEE

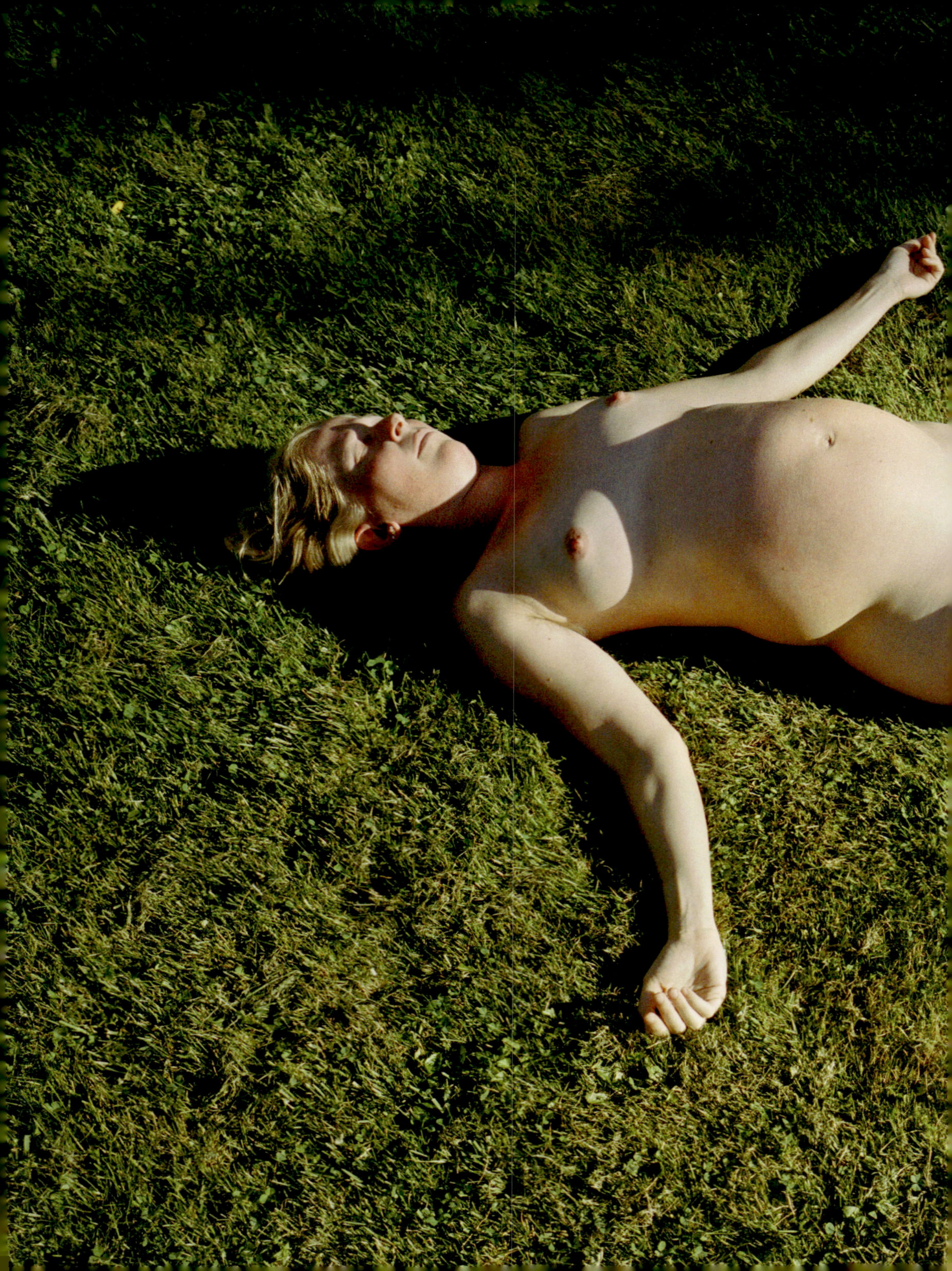

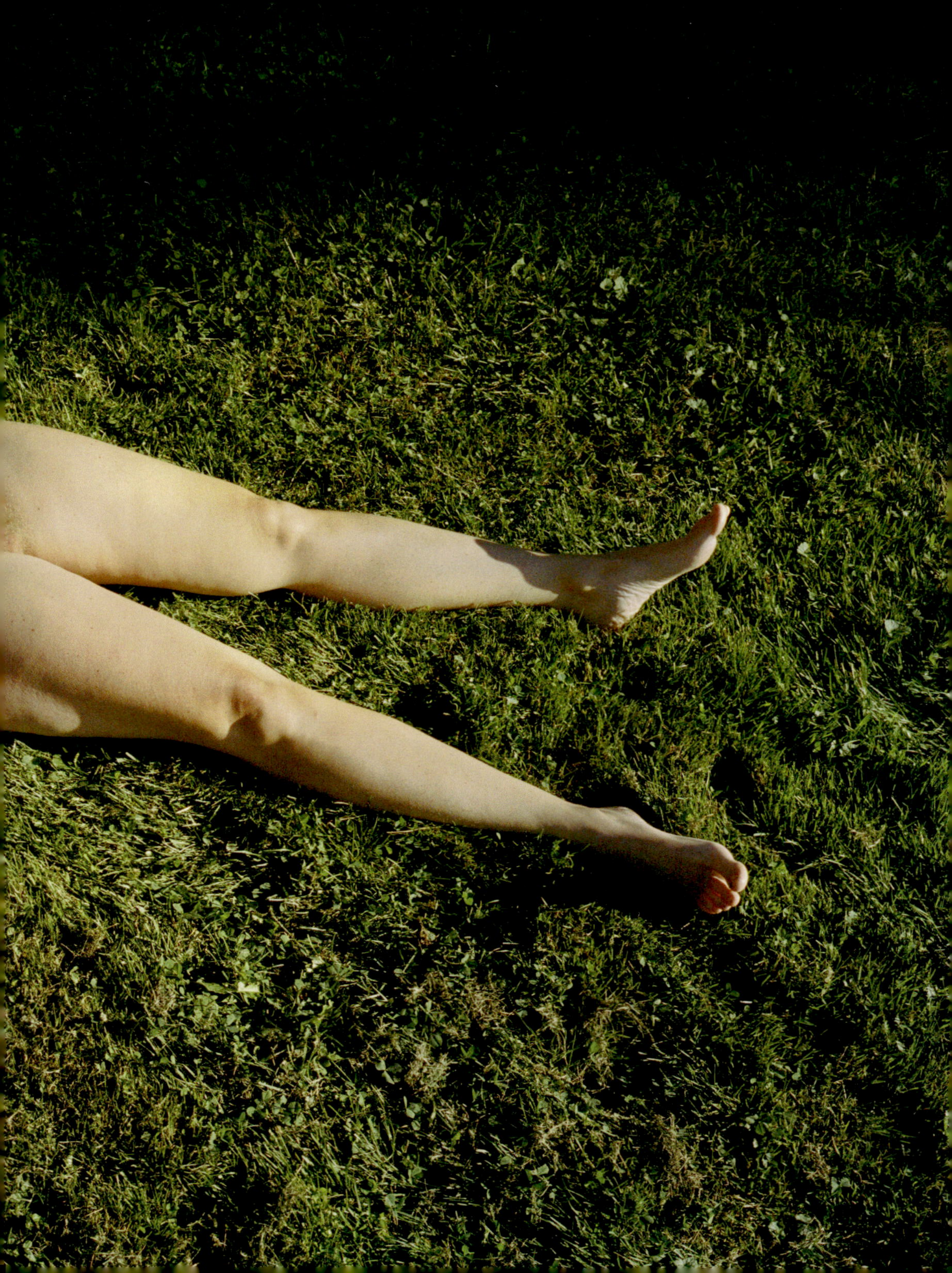

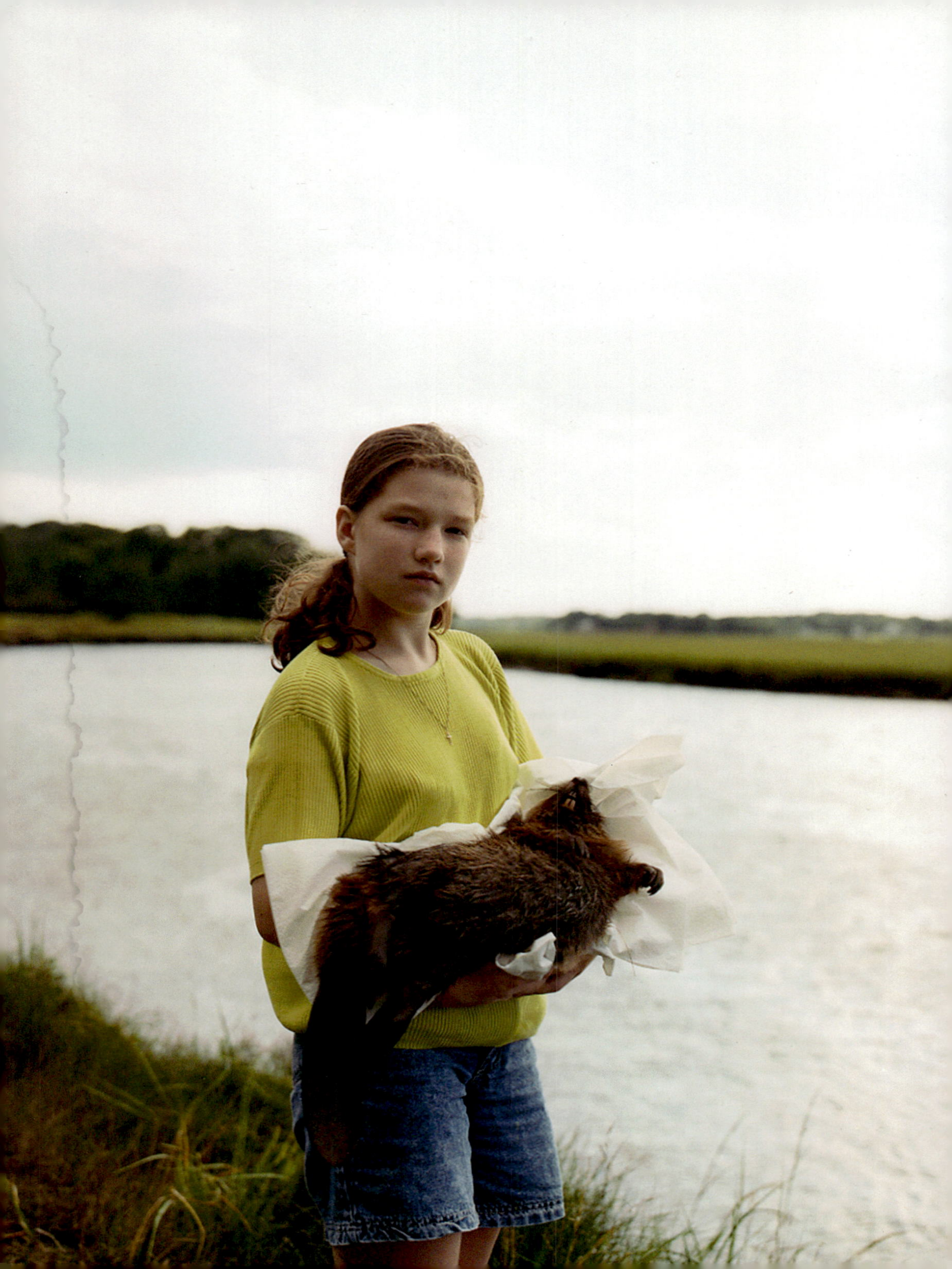

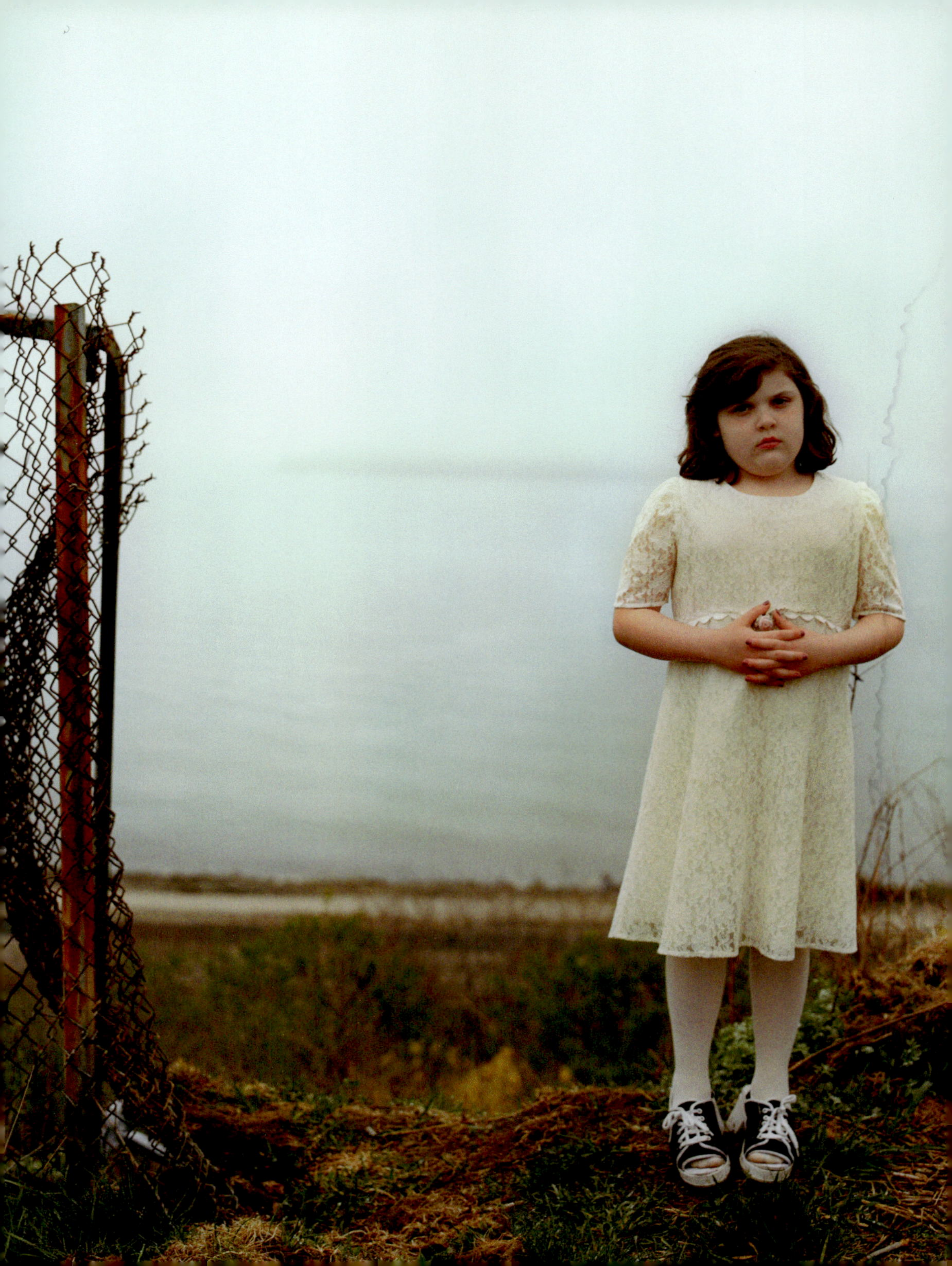

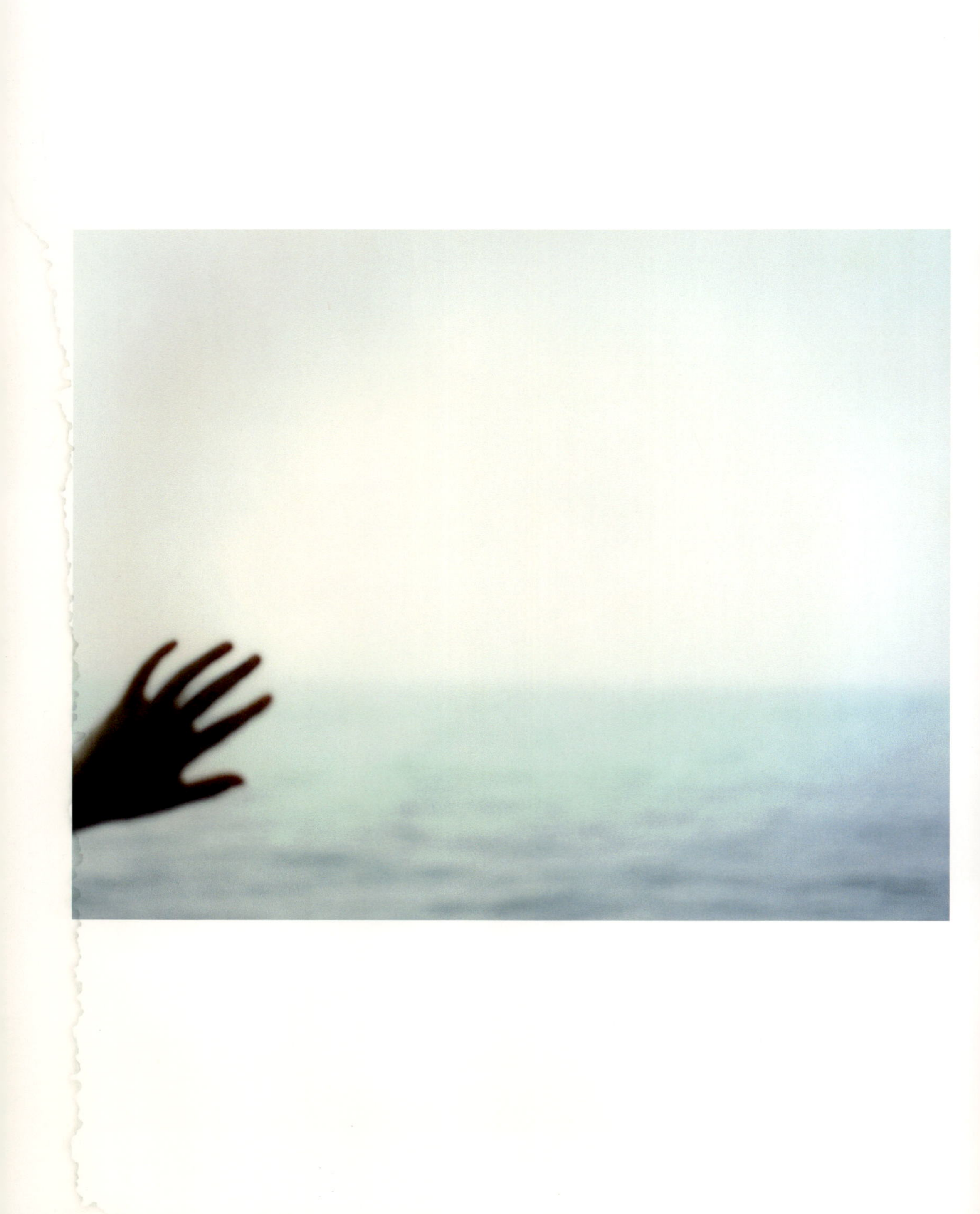

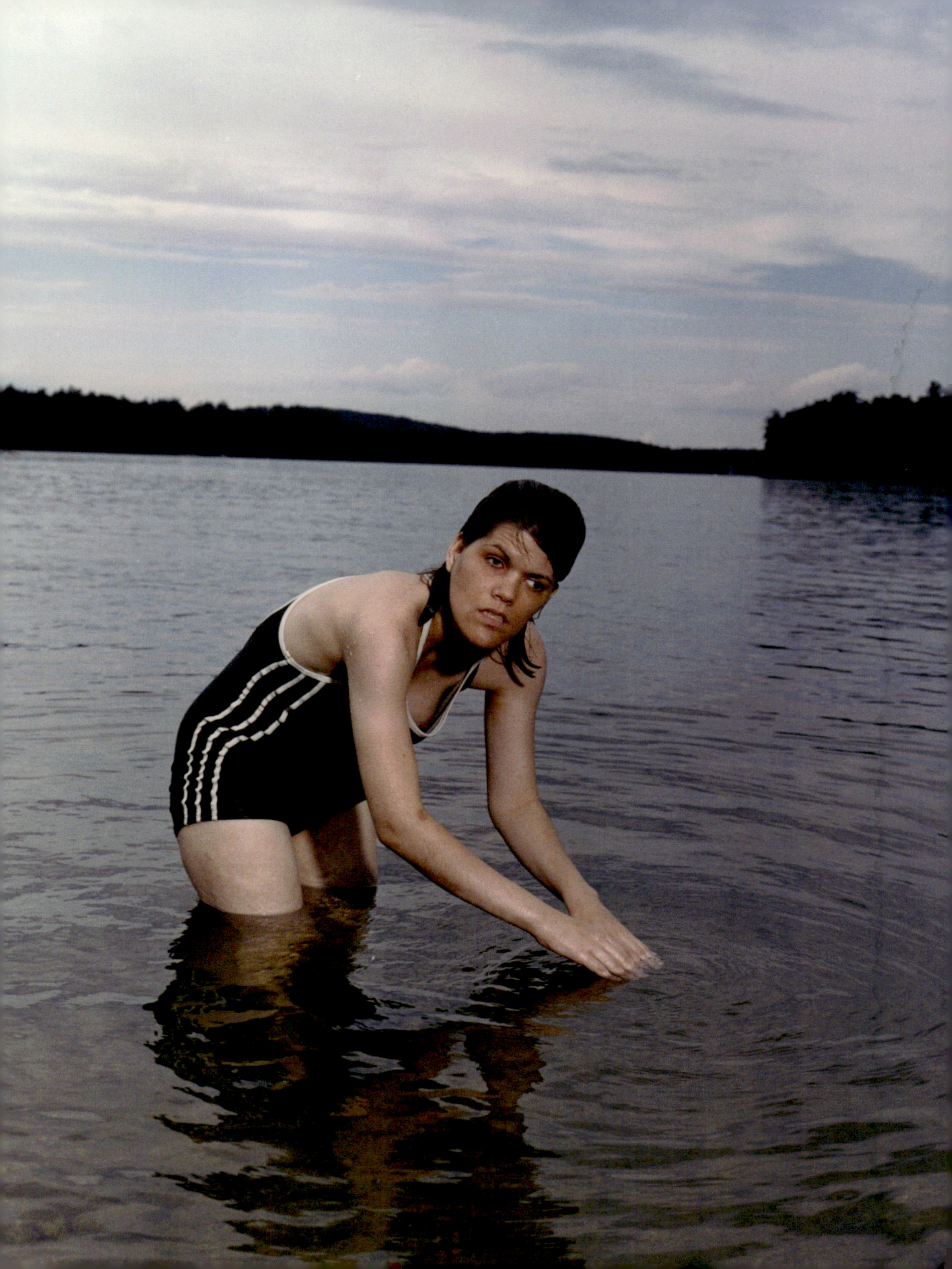

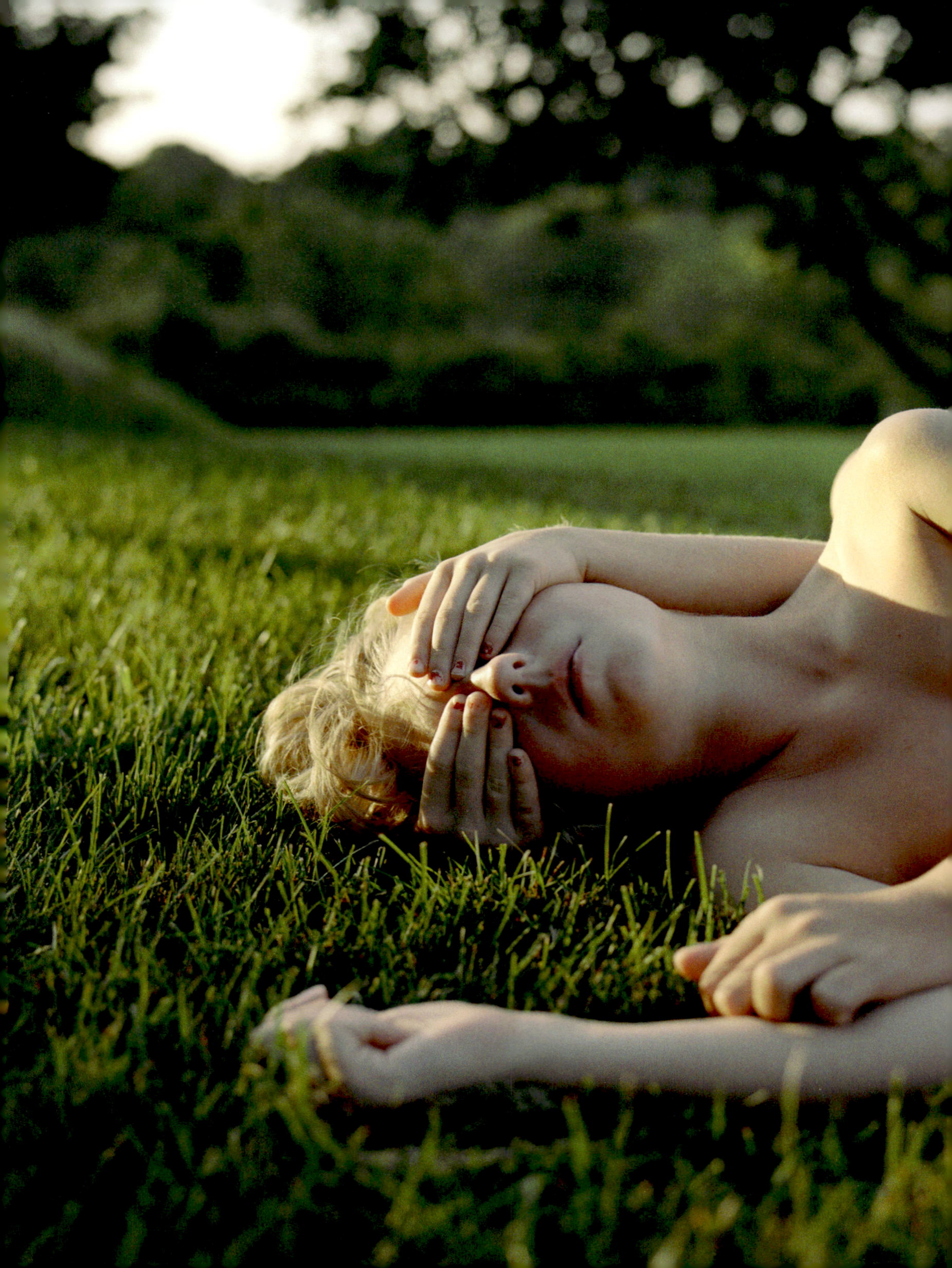

H. L. HIX

STRONG MAN

Delicate Cousins now believed in the soul, having just felt his own give way.

Fine, he thought. I am a stranded jellyfish. Just fine.

He was standing at the intersection of YanChang Road and GongHeXin Road in Shanghai late on a Tuesday afternoon, each hand holding a plastic grocery bag, each bag a jug of spring water. To get the bags, he'd had to argue at the market with the checkout girl (she was a girl, she couldn't have been fifteen), he complaining in English that the handles on the heavy jugs hurt his hands on the long walk to his room, she spitting back imprecations in Chinese, to which others were added by the impatient faces lined behind him. He should have bought his water at the smaller market, which charged half again as much, but was near enough the hotel that bags or no bags wouldn't matter so much to his fingers. The woman at the register there had once scolded him for keeping his wet umbrella with him instead of leaving it in the basket by the door, but he was fascinated by the scar across the web between the thumb and forefinger on her left hand. Water from the smaller market would have spared him insult, and let him see the woman's scar while she counted out his change.

But he'd gone to the bigger market, been cursed past all proportion to his offense, and now the handles of the bags were hurting his hands.

Fine.

"Delicate" of course was a nickname. His parents' imaginations had not extended far enough to consider, nor inclined in a direction that might have settled on, a name other than Dale, the name of his father's older brother, who at thirteen had drowned, and had himself been named for Delicate's father's father, who just after the war had started the furniture store in Pearlton, a town whose four thousand residents pronounced its name as if it were spelled *Perilton.* The store had lasted until Levitz came in at Dodge, the bigger town thirty miles down the road. The same thing had happened with other chains that sold other goods, so plenty soon the signs for Hal's Hardware and Pearlton Feed 'n' Seed marked vacant buildings. Hal had stayed around to complain over coffee every day at the same table in Carla's Café until tuberculosis spared the other regulars, but the Jespesons, who'd owned the Feed 'n' Seed, had moved away to live their last years in their daughter Lara's double-wide outside Pensacola.

"Delicate" had been bestowed by Martin Strapp, a classmate, in freshman lit survey the first week of college. Dr. Marshall had opened the second class session by asking Dale what, from the first reading assignment, one might infer about Achilles' heroic ideal, and Dale, caught off-guard, had paused for a moment with his mouth open before stuttering something as incoherent as it was irrelevant. The night before, he had flooded the basement of the dorm trying to use the coin-operated washer. Suds everywhere, his sock feet soaked as he stood there, panicked, trying to find the right button to push or plug to pull to stop the water, then squishing along the tiled hall on his way to wake the head resident. After his misadventure he couldn't get to sleep for worrying he'd risked electrocution when he'd stood in the water with the washer still going. He hadn't managed any reading about heroic ideals. Of Dale's mumbling, Martin Strapp had sneered, "Now *that* was a *delicate* answer," which amused the other students, who snickered tentatively at first but laughed out loud as soon as Dr. Marshall himself let one side of his mouth smile. Dr. Marshall called Dale "Delicate" for the rest of the course, so by semester's end Dale was no longer Dale.

For a brief while, Delicate hadn't minded his new name. The others in class all laughed and looked at smirking Martin, who had crossed his arms for punctuation, but Marcia Kensington (who pronounced her name Mar-

see-uh, not Mar-sha) had glanced at Delicate and blushed. In sympathy, he'd told himself at the time. He'd seen her across the room at the pre-semester social two nights before. He'd noticed that because she wasn't drinking, she couldn't figure out what to do with her hands. Several times she tried crossing her arms, but couldn't keep them crossed for more than a second or two. She tried holding her left wrist in her right hand, first in front of her, then behind her back, but that didn't work either. Soon enough, she would return her hands into the pockets of her jeans, and each time in doing so she shrugged her shoulders. The gesture drew his eyes often enough that finally they'd just stayed on her. She *looked* as uncomfortable and awkward and lonely as he *felt.* After class she'd made a point to say of Martin, "Don't mind him," and introduced herself. He'd walked her to her next class that day, and for a few more class sessions, but he didn't know what to say. Or what to do with his hands; it was *his* turn to shrug *his* hands into his pockets. His silence must have bored her, because soon enough she was walking with a couple of other girls, the three of them talking and laughing and gesturing. Any reason for thinking that first blush of hers something other than embarrassment drifted away.

Outside tourist areas, Dale couldn't walk far in Shanghai without passing a small metal box at shoulder height, mounted on a wall or a fence by the sidewalk. Each box surely proclaimed in Chinese what it asserted also in English: *Strong Man Condom Vending Machine.* Each had a slot for coins and a receptacle into which a condom would drop, Delicate assumed, though he had not ventured a purchase, had had no occasion to. Not all the machines looked serviceable: some were badly dented or rusted. Each time he passed a machine, Delicate felt less serviceable himself. Certainly it had been a long time since he'd felt himself a strong man, or been invited to prove himself one.

YanChang at GongHeXin was a busy intersection: bike lanes colonized by mopeds, left turn lanes, metal fences to separate sidewalks from streets, the inner-ring road passing overhead behind green barriers that translated speeding cars and buses into angry noise as privacy fences do guard dogs. At each corner of the intersection a uniformed officer patrolled. To Delicate, they seemed to succeed one another indefinitely; he never saw the same officer at any corner two days in a row, or at least never recognized any two as the same one. The female officers all looked vigorous and assertive, the males all fragile and stooped, in visible decline. Regardless of age or gender, they wore caps and yellow reflective vests and white gloves. Each wielded a whistle. They gestured and whistled and scowled, pointing at drivers or cyclists, waving them forward or instructing them to stop or turn. But their function remained a mystery to Delicate, who seldom saw anyone obey an officer's instructions. The officers' gestures never appeared to quite confirm the traffic lights. Though the officers acted as if they were directing traffic, to Delicate their movements appeared as a performance, a dance whose aesthetic he hadn't grasped, a film out of sync with its soundtrack. So he crossed the street when other pedestrians crossed, rather than when an officer signaled him permission.

Only this time when the others moved he couldn't. He'd made it halfway across, to the island in the middle of GongHeXin. Behind him, three lanes of traffic sped by in one direction, in front of him three in the other; overhead the ring-road traffic rumbled, below his feet the metro. People passed by in cars and buses. People passed by on foot. People passed on mopeds and bicycles. Delicate was astounded at what people carried, stacked on the platforms of three-wheeled bikes or strapped to mopeds. Propane canisters, fifteen at a time. Empty twenty-liter water bottles by the dozen. Fifteen-foot-long angle iron, fifteen-foot-long stalks of bamboo, bundled. Bags of turnips. Boxes stacked five high, higher than the rider's head. Pickle tubs, holding who knows what, headed who knows where. Stacked sheets of plywood, stacked sheets of glass. Rucksacks. Duffel bags. Wonderstruck babies, as chubby and pumpkin-headed here as back home. The traffic officers did their dances, now in the lanes, now out, pointing and whistling at people who paid them no mind.

As people paid him no mind. During each cycle of traffic lights, a group gathered around him, clustered by the curb like blackbirds filed on phone lines. Workers in coveralls, grandmothers pushing strollers, young couples holding hands, boys wearing earbuds, businessmen and -women in suits, boasting briefcases and bragging into phones. When the traffic light released them, they left Delicate behind, parting to pass without appearing to notice him, dispersing when they reached the other sidewalk.

But Delicate didn't budge. Couldn't quite. Stood and watched others pass, fully aware, just not able to make himself move. A rabbit alert to a cat. Motionless, watching.

He had been standing there for quite a while, through several cycles of the traffic lights, before a man turned while he was crossing and glanced back very briefly, the first hint of interest or curiosity anyone had shown. Everyone else studiously ignored Delicate's aberrance. It had to have been at least a hundred people by now. Delicate tried to do the calculation in his head: a dozen or twenty people each time by how many times? This man, though, didn't pretend not to have noticed the dumpy American man with shoulders sagging symmetrically under the weight of twin water jugs, standing in the median but not continuing across the busy street.

When the man reached the other side, he stayed his course for just a step or two before he stopped. The right leg of his pants was rolled a little above his ankle, as if he'd been biking before and forgotten to uncuff it. He paused a second, still facing the way he'd been walking, as if he'd suddenly realized he'd forgotten something. Delicate expected him to pat his pockets. But then he turned around, stepped back to the intersection, and stared straight at Delicate.

The man had an odd look about him; that something was not right in his mind registered on his face and body. All the extra size of his disproportionately large head swelled above his eyebrows, as if he had been given at birth a forehead and a half. His eyes both appeared to work, but not to work together: one or the other would settle on Delicate—now this one now that, in a struggle of wills—but never both at once. His torso, too, was large, out of proportion to his stumpy legs. All that top-heaviness made his movements look awkward, and even standing still he seemed tenuously balanced. The half-hearted cuff on one leg didn't help.

After his mother's funeral last year, Delicate had gone through her belongings, throwing things out. The most presentable of the furniture he'd tagged TAKE ME in black marker on masking tape and dragged to the end of the driveway. It disappeared overnight. The rest—the worst furniture, her clothes, everything else—he'd simply had hauled away. First he'd filled garbage bags and driven them to the dumpster, but then called Estes Gamble, a handyman whose brother Delicate had known in school but knew now not to ask after. Estes carted off the rest for two hundred bucks. Nothing had been worth keeping, though if Estes could find a way to polish a lamp or patina a shaky table and awl a few fake wormholes in it to pass it off as antique, more power to him. Seventy years, and among all his mother had gathered to herself, all she had lived with to the end, there was not a single object her only son wanted for his own. There had been one box, though, of photos, painstakingly arranged in chronological order, that he couldn't help but linger over. Photos of his mother and father together, of holidays and vacation trips, and of course of himself: as an infant, as a preschooler in a cowboy outfit (hat, chaps, cap guns in a plastic holster with plastic bullets serried around the belt), as a teenager with the elaborate model train landscape he had built in the basement, and as an adult twenty years ago, a time gap that made Delicate gasp.

The last photo in the box was of Delicate himself in his early thirties, looking casual in khakis and a blue button-down. And looking young. He hadn't seen himself in many photos lately, and had seen no old photos of himself for a solid decade. He'd stood when he reached that picture, and carried it to the mirror in the hall of his mother's house. The mirror frame—plaster mimicking wood carved to mimic a wreath, spray-painted gold—was dusty. The floorboards were dusty. Everything was dusty. Four clean circles marked where the legs had been of a table that had stood beneath the mirror until he'd toted it to the street the day before. Estes Gamble must have seen no value in the mirror, and Delicate hadn't noticed it in time to insist Estes take it away.

Delicate stood a long while and stared. His face in the mirror had in common with the face in the photo nothing save the expression: a confusion that appeared as a distant focus to the eyes, a slightly opened mouth, a little tilt to the head. In the photo, even though his jaw line had started rounding off already, his skin was still tight. His hair had started to thin, but still was brown. In the mirror, his hairline had receded, and what was left had gone gray and brittle. His jawline had just disappeared.

Fine, he thought. I am a hound with jowls, a cow with dewlaps.

When other people spoke of their lives flashing before their eyes, they always had it happen in dramatic situations: at the moment, say, when they saw the other car inexorably bearing down. Delicate wondered whether his namesake, his father's brother Dale, had seen his thirteen years flash before his eyes while he was drowning. Delicate had always been curious about Dale, but never summoned occasion and courage to ask his father or his mother anything about Dale's death. Had he drowned in a lake? in a pool? in the ocean? Had someone been there and tried to rescue him, or had the body been discovered later? Had he been swimming or had he fallen in? Had it happened in summer or winter? Had he been swept away in a flood? Had thin ice given way? Now there was no one to ask, no one alive any more who knew. No human being ever again would recall Dale's face. No one would think of Dale at all, save Delicate himself, who knew Dale only as the name they shared and as a story more withheld than given.

Other people's lives flashed before their eyes as the other car bore down or as their own began to slide across black ice, but here was Delicate casting back over his life as cars sped past, as he held water jugs, as he stood at a crosswalk in a country whose language he could neither speak nor read, puzzled over by a half-wit, ignored by the hundreds of others in whose plain view he stood.

Delicate replayed in his mind the video he'd seen a hundred times, of the grocery-bag-toting man stopping tanks in Tiananmen Square. How the first tank stops, perplexed by passive resistance, by a person neither taking up arms against it nor fleeing before it. How the other tanks stop behind the first. How the first tank tries to steer around the man, but the man, slim and nimble, simply stays in front of the hulking machine.

Delicate felt as though he were looking down on himself from the same angle as the camera that caught that video, but he was not a hero risking his life and freedom in valiant defiance of oppressive force, making on behalf of human solidarity a symbolic statement to be seen and admired by billions across the globe. This was Shanghai, restless hub of new global commerce, not Beijing, bunker in which the last of the old guard had hunkered down. He was not a student bringing home meager groceries, challenging the largest government in the world, but a middle-aged, middle-class middle manager of a middling corporation, sent to smile and bow to strangers, now lugging bottled water to his room because the tap water tasted sour and loosened his stool. He was not slim; he was not nimble. His standing there did not confound any threatening armored vehicle, was not a world-historical act on behalf of peace and in defiance of militarism and totalitarianism, just a manifestation of one weak man's enervating weaknesses, ignored by those around him and unknown to anyone else, aimless and inconsequential. No agents of aggression were perplexed by his courage. He had no courage, now or ever. He, Delicate Cousins, was the one perplexed.

Every morning, Delicate washed yesterday's clothes in the bathroom sink. He poured a little shampoo under the tap as it sent down tepid brown water. First his underwear, soaking it and kneading it and wringing it and setting it aside. He'd blushed over those same briefs not so long ago, embarrassed by Chrissie Arthur, the receptionist at the home office who had a habit of leaning back in her chair, tilting her head back, and shaking out her thick black hair. After she had run the fingers of both hands through it, she would follow through by extending her arms into a stretch, head still bent back, breasts the highest points of her arched body, enough gap between her blouse and belt to reveal her pierced navel. Delicate had taught himself not to stare, not to let her catch him, as obviously she took pleasure in doing, with his mouth gaping when she sat back up and adjusted her blouse. One day he'd overheard her bantering with a customer who visited often: "Boxers," she'd quizzed the man with a laugh, "or tightie whities?" Delicate, who hadn't heard them called that before, rushed back to his office red-faced. He didn't return to finish his photocopying until she'd left for the day. Now he was in Shanghai, spending two weeks in a dingy hotel, washing his tightie whities in the sink each day, followed by his discount-store socks, then his shirt and every second day his chinos, washing them all first, then three times refilling the sink to rinse them well before draping them over the shower stall to dry, coming back later to wring the gathered water from the lowest parts, once it had wicked down.

Being cursed by those in line behind him had been humiliating, but it was the checkout girl herself who had really scared him. Delicate had learned on just his second day in Shanghai to be wary of Chinese girls. He'd spent the first day in bed, not even getting up to eat, a torpor he told himself was jet lag. On the second day, knowing he had to be ready to smile and nod for the client on the third, he gathered himself and ventured outside. He kept a ballpoint pen in his hand and made marks on his palm to Hansel and Gretel himself which direction he'd turned, and at what streets. Not half a mile from his hotel, he'd happened on a park, and sat on a stone overlooking the small lake around which the park was laid out. He hadn't sat there long before a family interrupted his fragile solitude. The grandmother was cooing, trying to coax a small boy to the water's edge. She smiled at Delicate and he smiled back as she kept up her patter, saying to the boy what her gestures suggested meant something like "Come look at all the pretty little fish. Come dip your finger in and feel how cold the water is." The boy, though, was crying, and wouldn't come near the water. He shook his hands frantically, as if they'd caught fire, and stamped his feet. The parents stood well behind, talking to one another in tones that to Delicate sounded like argument. After ten minutes or so, all four left, but half an hour later they passed by in a paddleboat, this time with the boy standing on his father's lap, twisting the steering wheel back and forth, gurgling and screaming with delight. The whole family, including the boy, who before had paid no attention to Delicate, smiled and waved, speaking cheerful greetings as they passed, closer to him this time than they'd been when they were on shore. He smiled and waved back, stupidly saying in English, "Hello, Good day, Have a happy boat ride."

Once the family had paddled past, Delicate returned to his walk. The sun was high by now, and it was hot. His underarms and the back of his shirt were dark with sweat. Even his briefs felt sweat-soaked. As he passed two teenage girls seated on a bench, wearing matching school uniforms (white blouses and powder-blue skirts Delicate thought surprisingly short), talking to one another over the notebooks open on their laps, one of the two looked up, and asked him, "Hey, Mister, you speak English?" Surprised by how large a voice had come from so small a body, and feeling a little dizzy from the heat, he didn't think fast enough to ignore her and keep walking. "Yes," he said, slowing indecisively. "Look," she said, holding up her notebook in evidence, "we are English class. We study for go to America. You help us?" He didn't reply, but he did stop walking, which was all the girls needed. The solicitations of the one who spoke changed from interrogative to imperative. "You help us. Is good friendship, is good America with Chinese. Only talk, is fun. We buy you tea, is Chinese custom. Very happy, very thank you. Where you from, Mister?"

His answer, "Boise?," set off another string of questions from the more talkative of the two girls: "Boise? Where is Boise? Is near L.A.? near Hollywood? Tea shop have many map of USA, you show us Boise? Boise have many many peoples, like Shanghai?" They'd sprung from the bench as soon as he'd stopped walking, and each had taken one of his arms. He'd stopped because he was lightheaded, he told himself, and he was lightheaded because of the humidity and because he hadn't been eating well. Both girls were petite, so as the one spoke to Delicate they both looked up, eyebrows raised. They smiled and giggled and smiled some more. Their eyes were large. Their teeth were white. Dizzy or not, Delicate knew something about this was wrong. He couldn't remember the last time a woman had taken his arm, and never ever had he walked even a single step with a woman on each arm. As they walked, their shoulders rubbed against his ribs, their hips bumped his thighs. The short-haired girl, the one who'd asked the first question, kept talking, kept asking him things. How you say this, How you say that? The three of them never turned around, but somehow they ended up leaving the park through the same gate Delicate had passed through to enter it.

The tea shop, not a block from the park, was tended by a white-haired woman in traditional dress who brought the tea mechanically, without otherwise acknowledging them. She said nothing, made no eye contact, took no order from them, merely set a thermos and three small, chipped porcelain cups on the table, as if only by coincidence had she set the tea here just when the three of them arrived. With swift shell-game movements, the girls rearranged the teacups to make room on the table for their notebooks, which they opened. The talkative one kept up her questions to Delicate. "You like Chinese tea? You drink tea in Boise?" "Yes, oh, of course we drink tea. Sometimes. But Americans usually drink coffee. Or more coffee than tea. Or I do, anyway. I think most people do. Not just in Boise. Everywhere in America, really. Denver, Salt Lake, everywhere. Lots of coffee. I really should be going home. I just meant to go for a short walk." "We learn about America, is fun, yes?" the talkative girl asked the quiet one, the one Delicate thought prettier, who smiled broadly and nodded in a way that made her black hair shimmer. "We learn talk like American, we visit you in Boise, yes?" "Yes, sure." Delicate blushed. He'd answered the talkative girl, but was still looking at the quiet one. He tried to think, but couldn't quite. Delicate was still trying to construct a courteous way to excuse himself when first the prettier girl then the talkative one went to the restroom. No sooner had the second stepped away than a man appeared at the table and presented Delicate with the check. The man was not tall, but his hands were large, thick enough that his knuckles were dimpled.

"600 Yuan for a pot of tea?" Delicate realized his voice had gone high as he reached the end of the question. He looked around the room, wanting to complain to the old woman who had served the tea, but she wasn't there. The burly man said nothing, just glared. Probably he spoke no English. What need had he? Another man the same size—they could be brothers—stood in the doorway. Without taking his eyes off Delicate's eyes, the first man tapped one thick finger on the check. Delicate sat for a moment, hoping the woman would reappear, or one of the girls. He grasped the situation reluctantly, like someone adjusting to sudden sunlight. But he *did* adjust. He pulled out his wallet, was relieved to find he had enough cash, and paid. When the man smirked and crossed his arms instead of picking up the bills, Delicate had for a moment a mental picture of Martin Strapp, whose voice he heard commenting, "Now *that* was a *de*licate gesture." Delicate stood to walk out. He tried to cross his arms authoritatively, but couldn't walk that way, so he put his hands in his pockets. The man in the doorway moved aside just enough to let him pass.

At first Delicate went the wrong way along the walk, so he had to turn around and walk back past the tea shop. He kept his eyes on the sidewalk, but he imagined all of them—the woman, the girls, the two toughs—jostling in the doorway to watch him walk past, laughing and joking with one another in Chinese. Probably the prettier girl's shoulder rubbed the burly man's ribs. Only now he realized that she, the smaller of the two girls, the one with especially slender thighs and tiny fingers, had not spoken at all.

The things to be thrown away after his mother's funeral were mostly hers, of course, but did include fragments from the model train set Delicate had built in high school. It had started in just one corner, on a card table with legs rusting at the base from the dampness, but over time had come to occupy the whole basement of his parents' house. A narrow path led from the bottom of the stairwell to the furnace, but to reach anything else, even the water heater, entailed crawling underneath the plywood sheets that over time he'd carefully leveled and hammered into place not quite seamlessly. The water heater rose through an opening in the landscape, an alien imposing structure.

He'd started with an HO gauge set he'd been given one birthday: a small loop of track, an engine and four cars. Soon, though, he retired that set and moved to N gauge, the smaller scale of which allowed him to make a more complex layout in the limited space. It wasn't the trains themselves that interested him: their movement through the landscape was incidental. The trains were only the occasion for imagining the place. He had a name for the small country he created: Pearl Valley. He seldom spent money on other things. He bought houses and people and trees from mail-order catalogs. He special-ordered a *Welcome to Pearl Valley* sign, hand-lettered. When Pearl Valley needed space, he added another sheet of plywood, and nestled another cabin among more trees. The stations between which the trains moved were an excuse for the hideaways by which they passed, to each of whose eremites he gave a name. Better names, he thought, than Dale. In the basement, under cover of the noise of the trains, he could say out loud to himself the things he imagined each miniature Thoreau saying to himself.

Pearl Valley had grown piecemeal, and over the years must have come down that way. A few plywood panels taken out to make a path to the pilot light on the water heater, more to give the workmen space when his parents had to replace the old furnace. Most no doubt thrown out years ago, but a few stacked there still at his mother's death, to be toted off by Estes, who understood that he was being paid in part not to smile or comment.

Delicate and the not-quite-right man stared at each other across GongHeXin through a whole cycle of the traffic lights. Cars passed, people passed, now ignoring both men. Now not only could Delicate not move his legs, he couldn't move his head, either, to avert his eyes from the strange man's unsettling gaze. In his head he called the man across the street "the not-quite-right man," but he knew the other man had adequate cause, better cause probably, to think of him, Delicate, as not quite right. Sentences began to say themselves in Delicate's mind. He did not know the not-quite-right man's language, but maybe neither did the man himself. The Mandarin of his interior monologue might be as malformed as his forehead, as mangled and malapropped as his legs. "Paralisect why no shufflestreet? Bagbag stopstill."

Delicate well knew that none of this made sense: not the sentences passing through his head, not his attributing them to the misshapen man, not his standing so long stock still at a stoplight in Shanghai. His only relief from the repeating loop of nonsense sentences was the recognition that from now on, he would not choose his actions, his path through the world, but that things would happen to him. His mind would grow disconnected from reality thought by thought, velcro pulled apart. From now on, men with bulbous foreheads and erratic eyes would stare at him across intersections; traffic in the street would race past faster than he could process it; his legs and his will would go separate ways; his thoughts would wash gullies through his muddy mind.

Delicate never slept well, but here his sleeplessness grew worse. At home, sleep was compromised by his body. His belly felt heavy, pressing on his lungs. His stomach churned. He had to pee two hours after peeing last. His back pinched him, sent pain through his extremities. His eyes burned, his ears buzzed. His legs and feet went numb. Sometimes too his arms and hands. Here, jet lag magnified everything. In the day, his head would hardly stay up, at night his eyes hardly close.

He'd been sent as a kind of courtesy to the Chinese company with whom his company had established a relationship. He was the human equivalent of a thank-you note. There was nothing for him to accomplish while he was here, no agreement to reach, no deal to broker, no contract to get signed. He was to eat with his hosts, smile when they smiled and bow when they bowed. That was his boss's only instruction: "Just bow when they bow." He was to say whatever he could discern of what they expected him to say, knowing that whatever he *did* say would be corrected by the translator to fulfill their expectations. The Chinese company was growing at fifty percent a year. They couldn't build new offices fast enough. Chances were that the managers with whom he exchanged surface courtesies at the beginning of his time would be promoted up the ladder and replaced by others by the end of his two weeks. Delicate and his corporation, in contrast, were two of a kind: aware of their own decline, but helpless to stop it, working only to slow it down. This wasn't a perk or a junket, a bone thrown him by the higher-ups; he'd been sent to

Shanghai because he was someone the home office could spare for two weeks.

His breasts and belly and ass now all sagged enough to be defined by creases. When had this happened? He had not always been this way, and there was no one point at which it had suddenly occurred, but there it was. There *he* was, more of him than there should be, more than he could manage. He should cut back on cheese and beer, he should exercise. But he had never been athletic, even in school. While others were at football practice or out running track, he had been arranging plastic forests on a model train layout in his parents' basement. Now what? Was he supposed to jog along the sidewalk, to let leaner people in passing cars wonder whether they were making fun of a fat-assed old woman or a fat-assed old man? Join a gym and struggle under ten-pound dumbbells in front of trim blonds with their ponytails swaying side to side as they firmed their slender thighs on stairsteppers?

The not-quite-right man stood staring long enough, heavy head askew, that Delicate expected him to cross back to the median to offer help. Eventually, though, he proved right enough at least to lose interest, knowing that there was nothing he could do. He turned and shuffled off, casting back one last quick glance, but leaving Delicate to his own resources. For his part, Delicate stood alone in his reckoning. The soul, he now knew, need not wait until the body's death to yield. The yielding imposed no pain, but it was sudden, surprising as a bandage yanked off, exposing a wound almost, but not quite, beautiful.

TODD COLBY

Can You Feel It?

In an effort to induce you
I ran my hand over the back of your leopard
and you shivered a bit and said more.
When I felt the tip of the nuisance on your lap
a pink umbrella opened under the yellow canopy.
Things got hazy as we wrestled.
Now the layers of grime are sparkles
like blue glitter held with Elmer's glue
on a kid's art makes the outline of a pony pop
off the page. Well, you are popping
through the living room with an instrument
you play with your middle finger
like an organ but rounder
and softer. Something really great
is just about to happen
can you feel it?

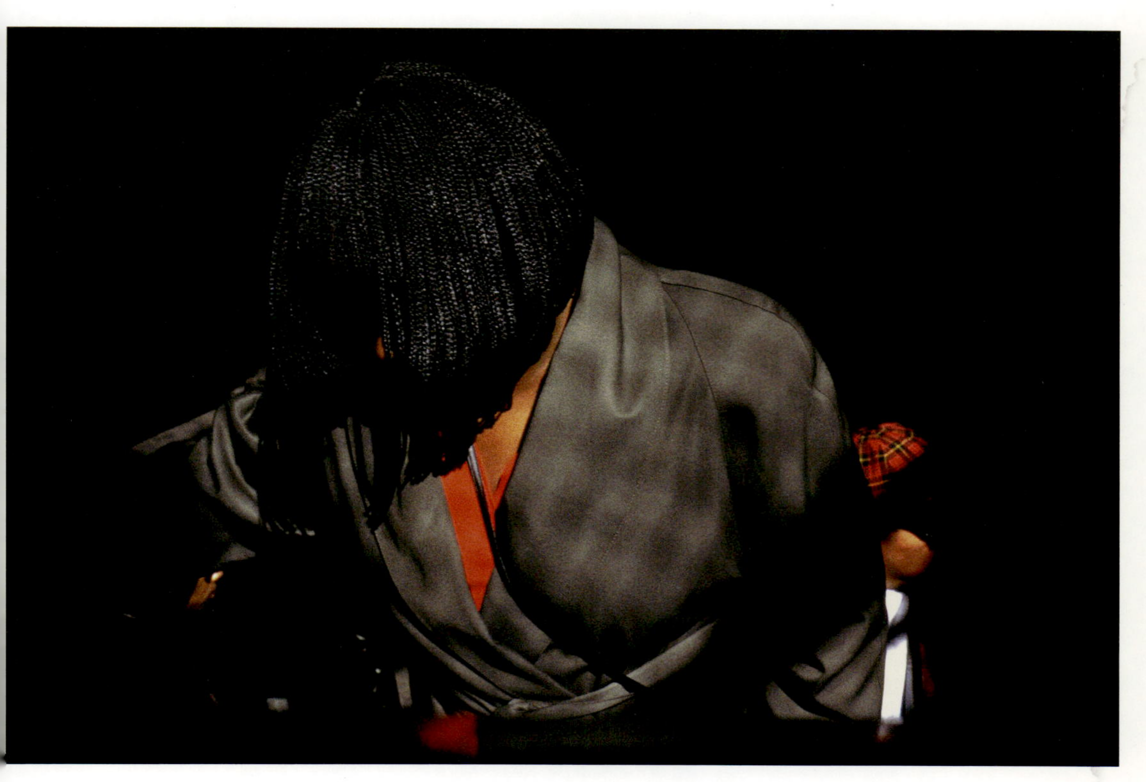

CHRISTOPHE AGOU

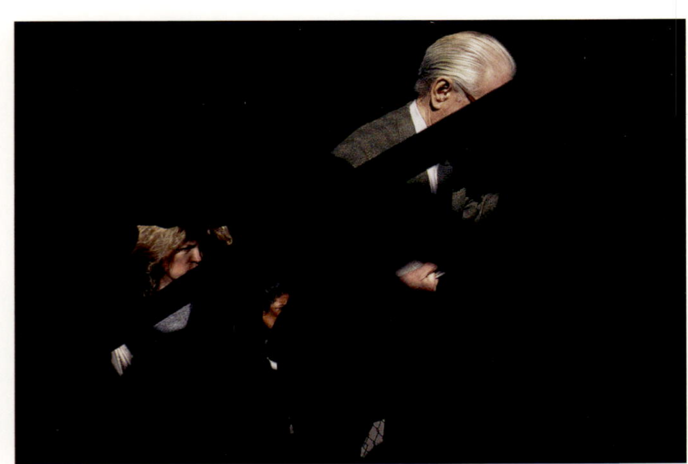

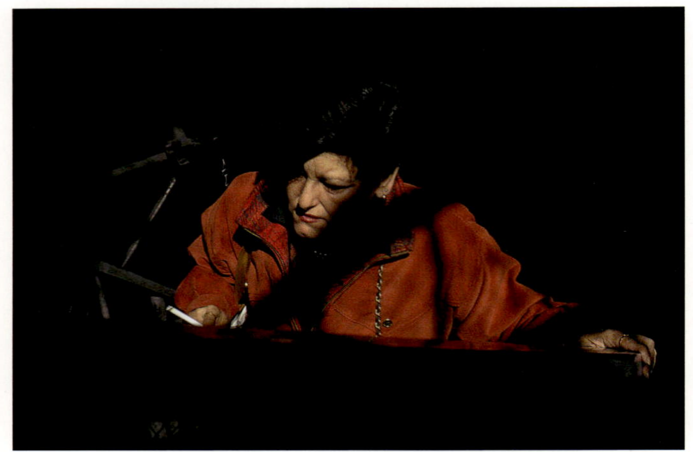

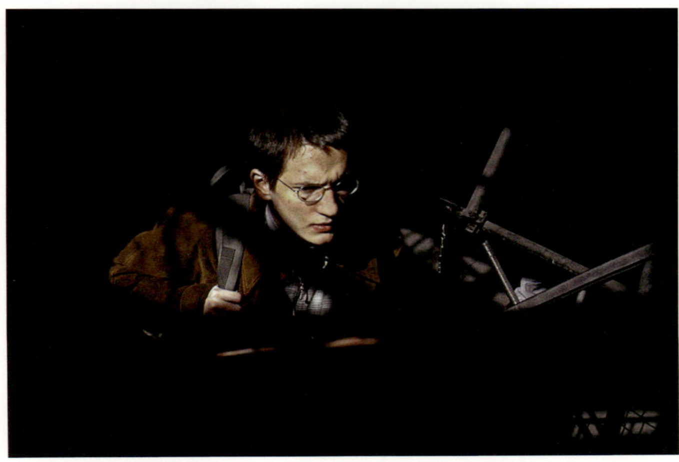

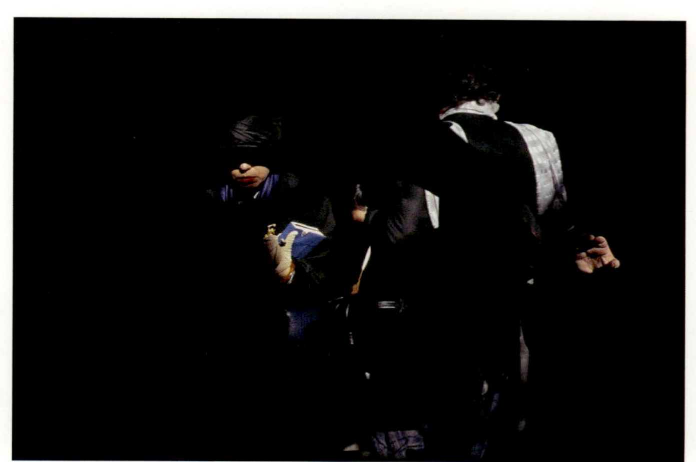

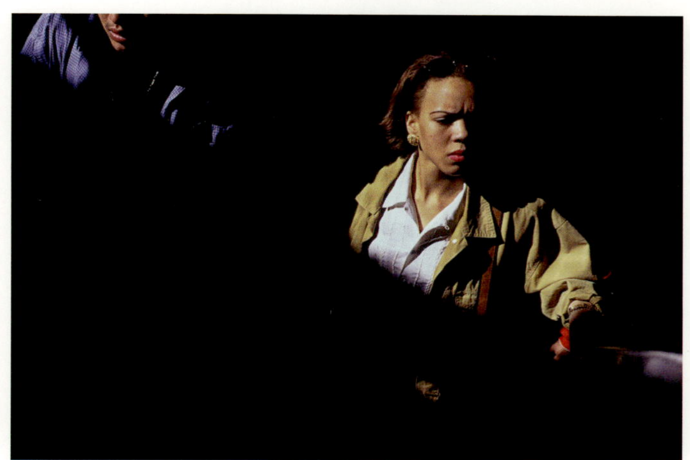

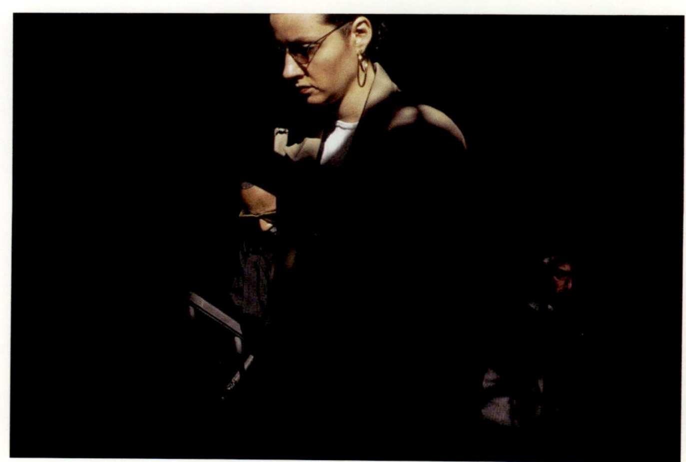

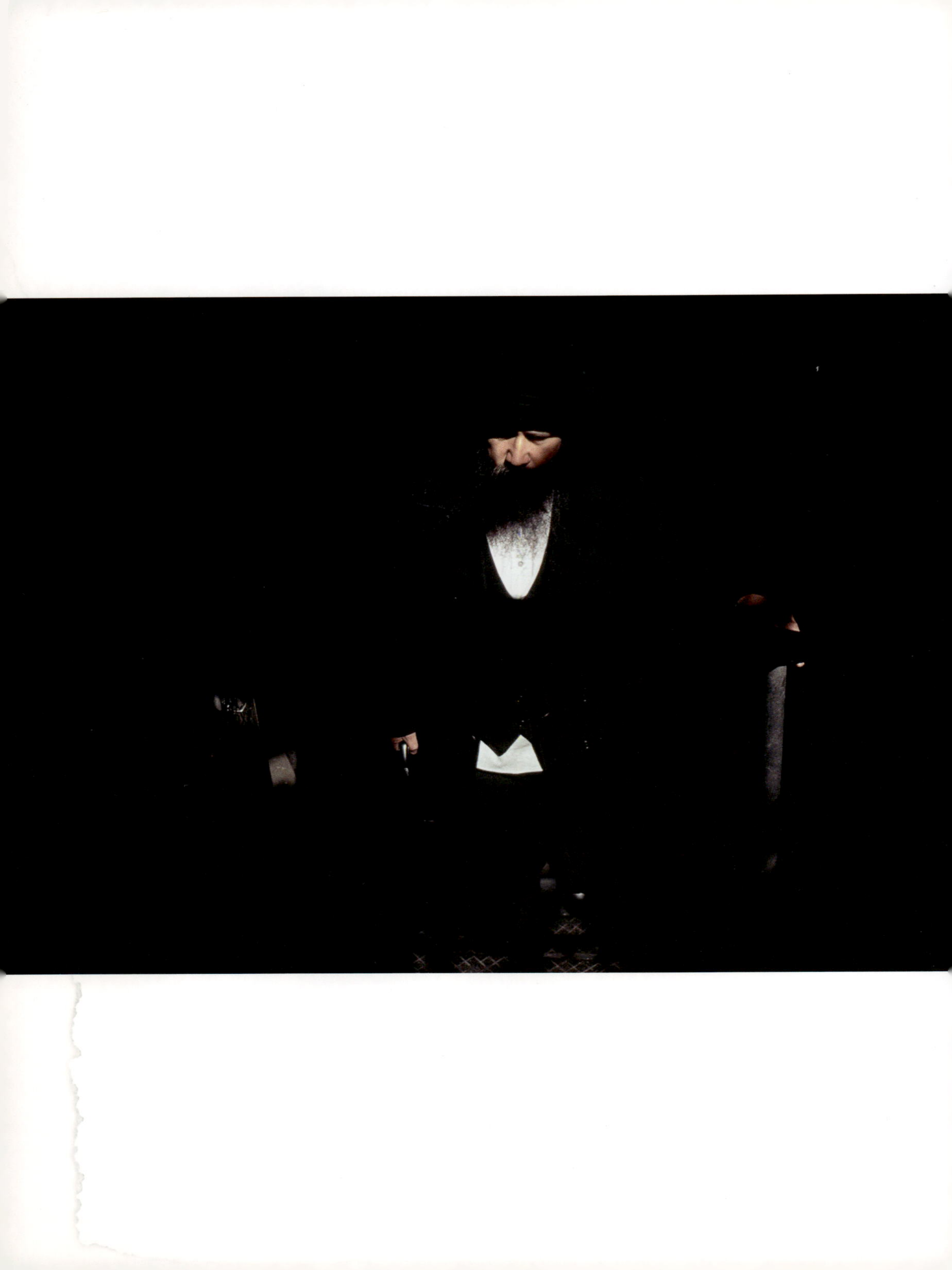

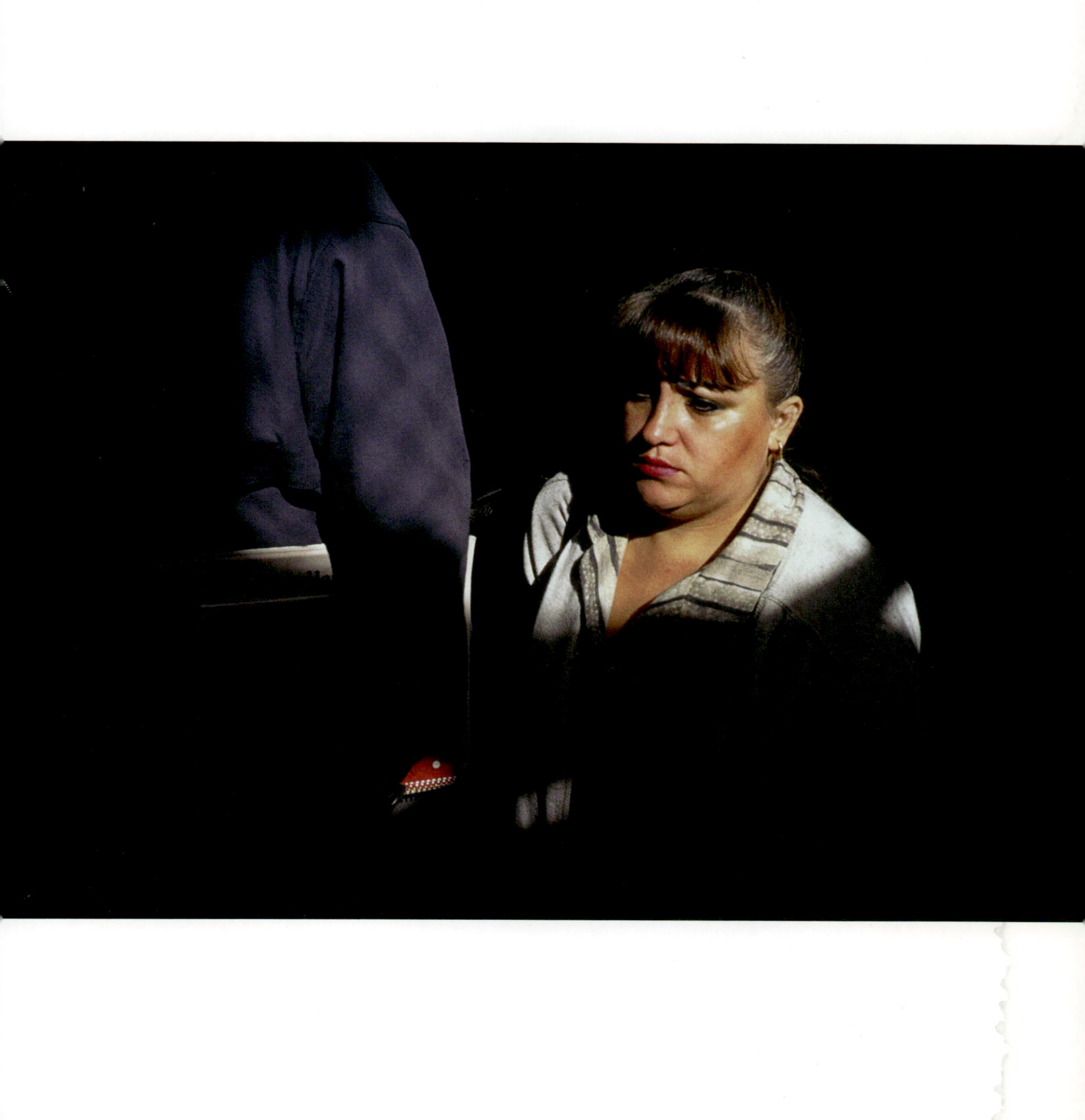

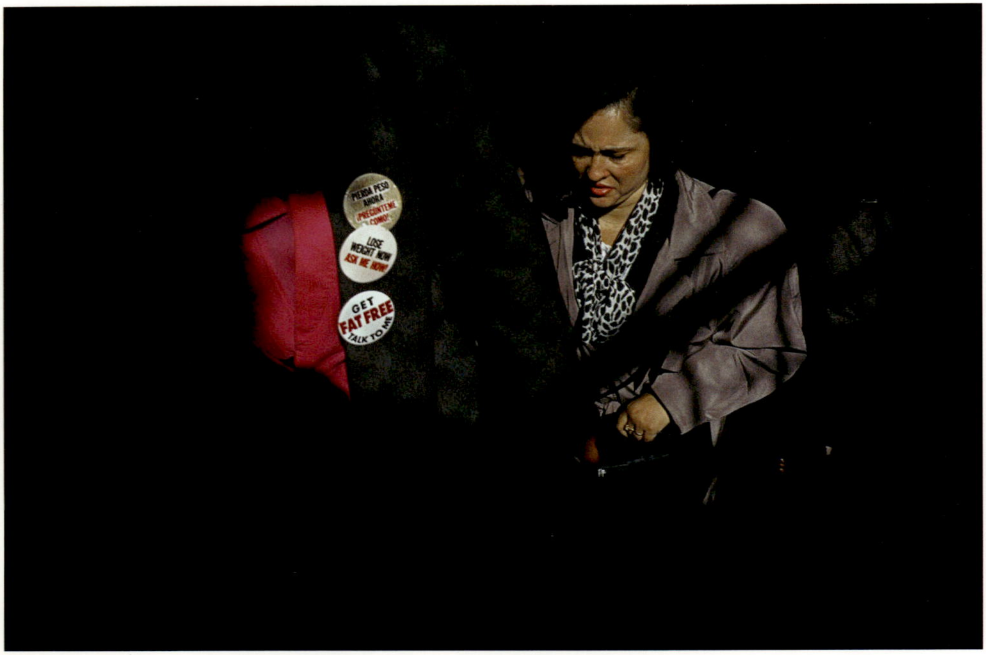

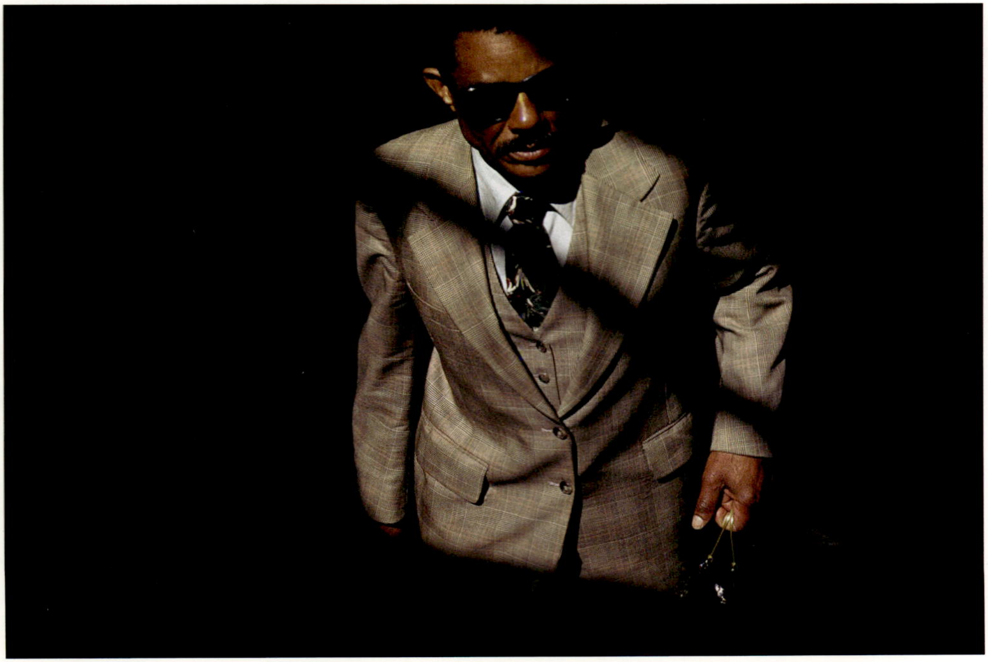

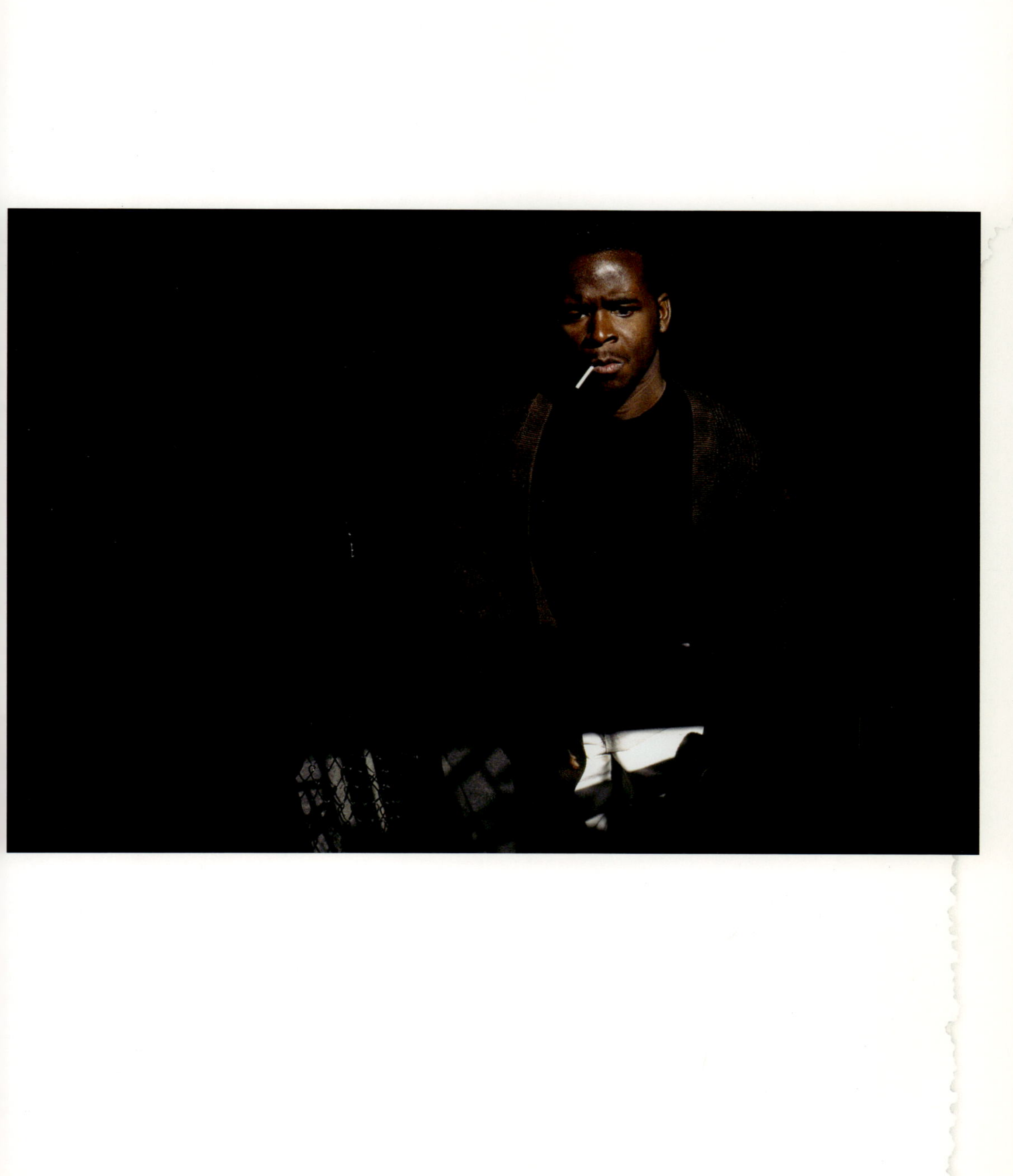

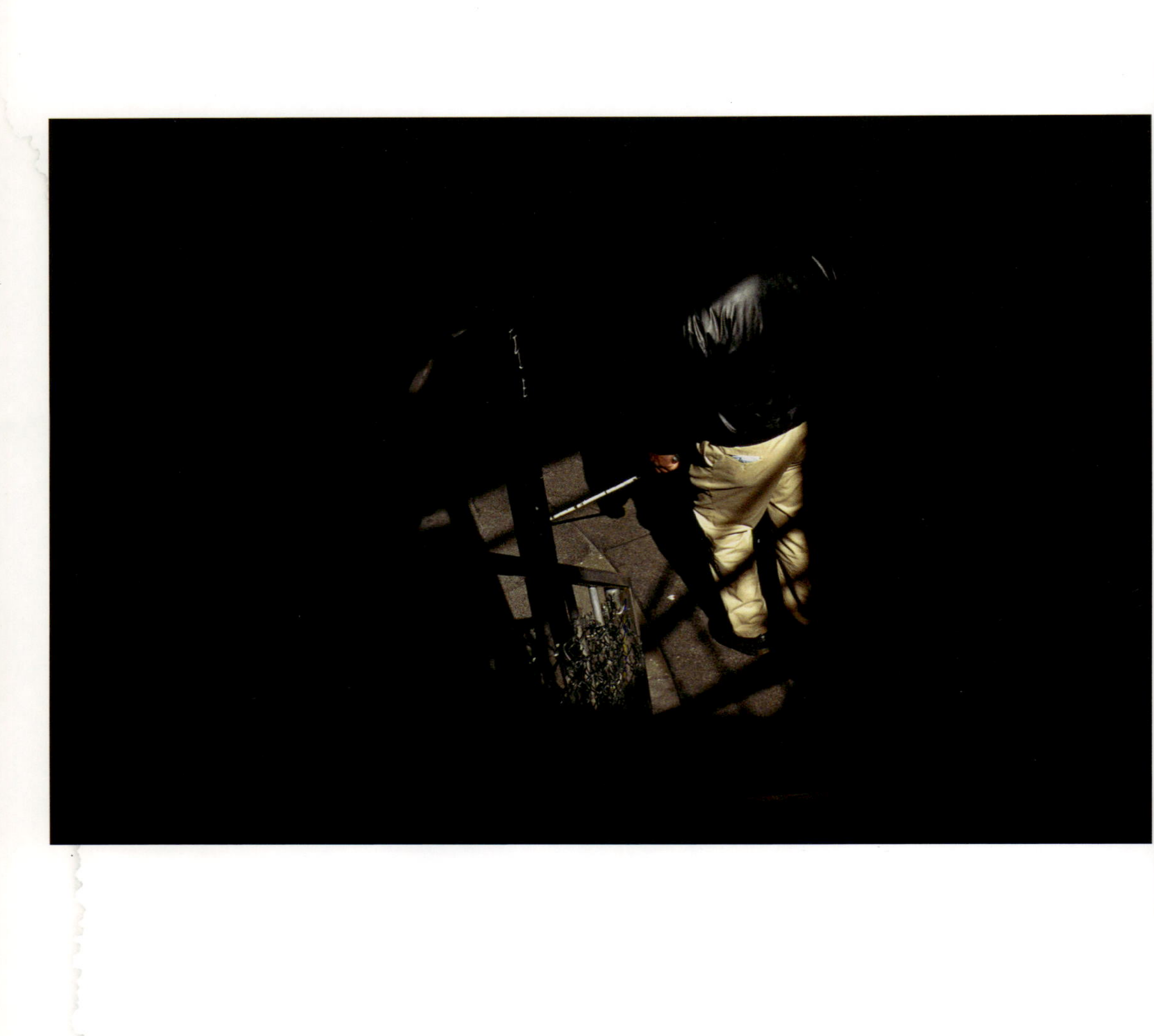

LILIAN HEEHS

Descriptions of Flowers

Legs crossed in mess of sunlight through

winter
          window.

motioning of lips   to say.

a thing   or two   ("a thing   or two")

from the arm rest
               the hole in the plush of your elbow

a scything
          unrest.   you ottoman the apartment.

sweep

          again under ankles but. okay   some description

in morse code a tap tap flower

a pair of
shoes in the front hall. a smear of semen   and,

          light on baby toe.

some description

of the way it smells   the texture of shower gel

"clean"

some watermarks or the sheets on Sunday

friend. with a rainbow in her shoebox
writes "panic" on her forehead.

takes a picture.   in the mirror.   two carafes and a ballpark
later

hop the fence and break beer bottles   for fucks sake   to animal collective and

the horseradish lingers all day

which brings us back to feet. clean dimpled toes

toenails unpainted   hanging Mona Lisa in the foreground

of lover   in the classroom. in tone : hallmark   22 River 150-77

New York City   all proper nouns

allthesesmokerspile up aroundhere
and whats left   in that suitcase   of flowers   depicted

from the window is break beats.   the ones that smell

{cinnamon and windex}

television colored.

lets go to the movies. or drive around   convertible top less

and wild. doing "it"
dotting below fourteenth street with peony sunstreaks and Lou Reed hyhpotheses

raising skinny wrists and lowered eyes

to strangers caught in the concept of traffic

there the spokes of some painted bicycle   "click"

in daisy
soundtrack and shoeless feet lift legs

protesting all description.

Room 8

She was the girl
in room 8 in the tower on the ocean;

when
we ran naked,
screaming, through the Lower East Side.

(On July 4th, 2006), no one could hear us
because no one was not sleeping.

There was a tower of sleep and we were driving,

lost over the Williamsburg

like two people who lost their Marquez

and had to create their own fiction.

In pyjamas,
the next day

we built sand castle and
stripped to the sound

of silence.

The emptiness lay there between us but both of us
were petrified

to touch it
fearful that it might collapse.

The implosion occurred in Room 8.

That girl up there rose and

fell,

a balloon in a shock of ozone.

Someone said her

        name

                and we both died in hideous recollection

of what we had made alive and

                how it had blossomed and

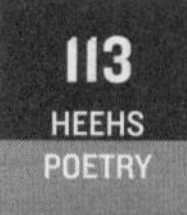

because we had made it live,
only we

were responsible
for its death.

Cowboy Killers

television again today-

perhaps

no princess

found

standing there. between the infomercials and news prints.

or record. why this disorder

puts so much order in the lives of men.

but, upon awakening to

expensive toiletries better sleep

than beauty.

or dead.

this fiction gets expensive

but really the tsunami waves

were brunette, not burlesque

and the archetypes smelled like cheap wine

not gallery - that strange women, familiar through

similar ingestion of some stomach flu

a daugher.

woman[1] some reconciliation with her fertility

in the hospital where the girl – thirteen –

gets her period

for the first time her

poetry gets darker

as petrol goes higher

Man pays higher prices. for surplus

interpretations of his death. moon rising,

head rising, thousand count sheets, virgo,

swastika,

a psychic,

charges extra, to hold the line. while later, in the kitchen

---

some version of baking   catalogs

found in the food section of the New York times. psychic says:

“please do not poetize

the fashion world

or pay that much for a pair of socks,

while eating a third world recipe

for dosa at second world prices.”

but then again developing insulin resistance

is no less insulting

to the thirteen year old candy striper   talking to her supervisor,

than her first boyfriend   holding the phone

holding a paragraph,   in the palm of his hand, She.

eats chocolate and begs her breasts

She

grows back to paradise size.   the developing world,

the news, some fiction,   this is the work

of the daugher.

the old man whose laxatives

she stirs in grapefruit juice.

mixing up his name with his diagnosis.

because of the wheezing in the lungs -

Girl's

poetry gets darker. a whisper

to a child. some vampire. constellations

she goes

out of cell phone range. to

appropriate the wilderness

and god, would she kill for a taste of that Marlboro

billboard

she says. her voice lost in reception.

Short phrases.

the way he holds her. the way he touches her breast. the sounds they make. the people listening. not listening. the flowers in the vase. the shawl coming off the shoulder. the weather. outside the windows. be it hot or cold. the intelligence of sleep and how dogs know. all this contained in her cycle, some gift on her laptop. from the moon. she wears it on a shirt. eating popsicles and wishing something could be seduced. the sidewalk. linoleum. tree.

eating an egg. or a popsicle. the derangement of words. the hysteria of silence. and boredom. this body used, again.   to escape. the boredom. inside a nail salon or a can of soda. her girlfriend's boyfriend's paintings. the two girls faces in the mirror. how stoned they look. inside the paintings. how they are not her own. how the music is not her own. but the hum of the refrigerator. the radiator, alone at night. the eggs in the morning and the icons on her laptop. these things belong to her. belong. something so alien to belong. better be like bees.

the friend, a descendent buddhist master. a young female, as well. a princess
of clouds or something called a lineage. her mother, a bulimic and
meditation queen. bees. the cost of jelly. or somehow learning to love
the smell of one's own. higher religion. this religion has
five plus senses. this is not a religion. this is a photograph of the
daughter. touched by a juniper branch when she was three. and the
space between her then and this her singing a Lakota song
with a Lakota drum, to me.

but regardless of. the way he looks up there. the smoke is smoking. there is a
croissant wafting needlessly from a nearby bakery window. in which the girl
can see his reflection.
the darkness of sky. a city where non-ness of memory rules. in entities and
cigarette smoke. those ghosts have evaporated. leaving stories and garbage
piles.

this one sitting up there and reminded of the gargoyles perched. so forever.
intense loneliness and that boy will never be more than the flop in his hat.
all, we. accessories as communication. graffiti the way he stands. paint it. the
flag. and all we. him. is a bite of peach. some mention of samsara,
here. on the grafitti. in the bathroom.

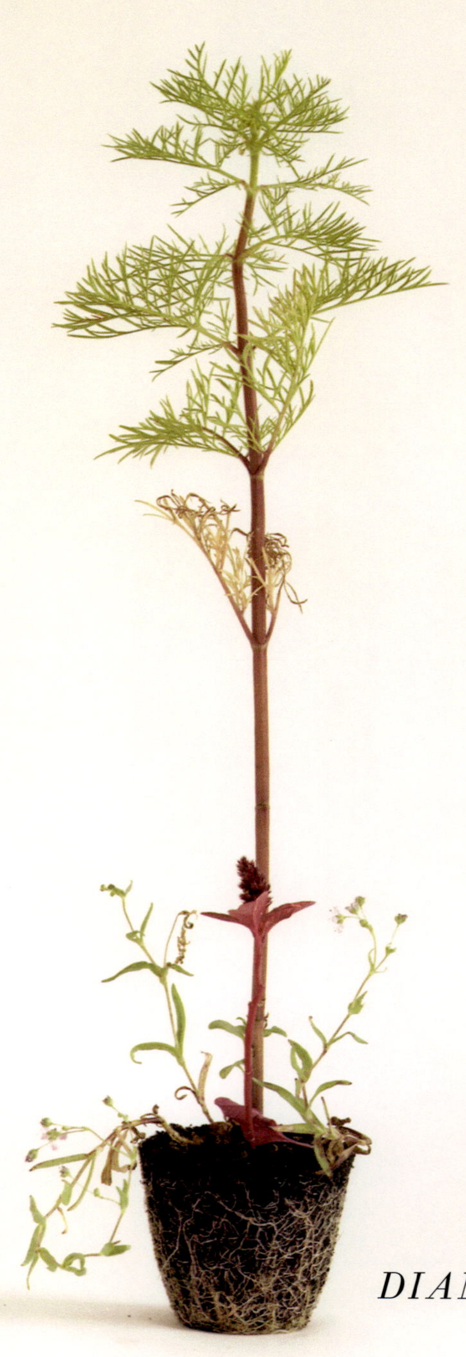

DIANA SCHERER

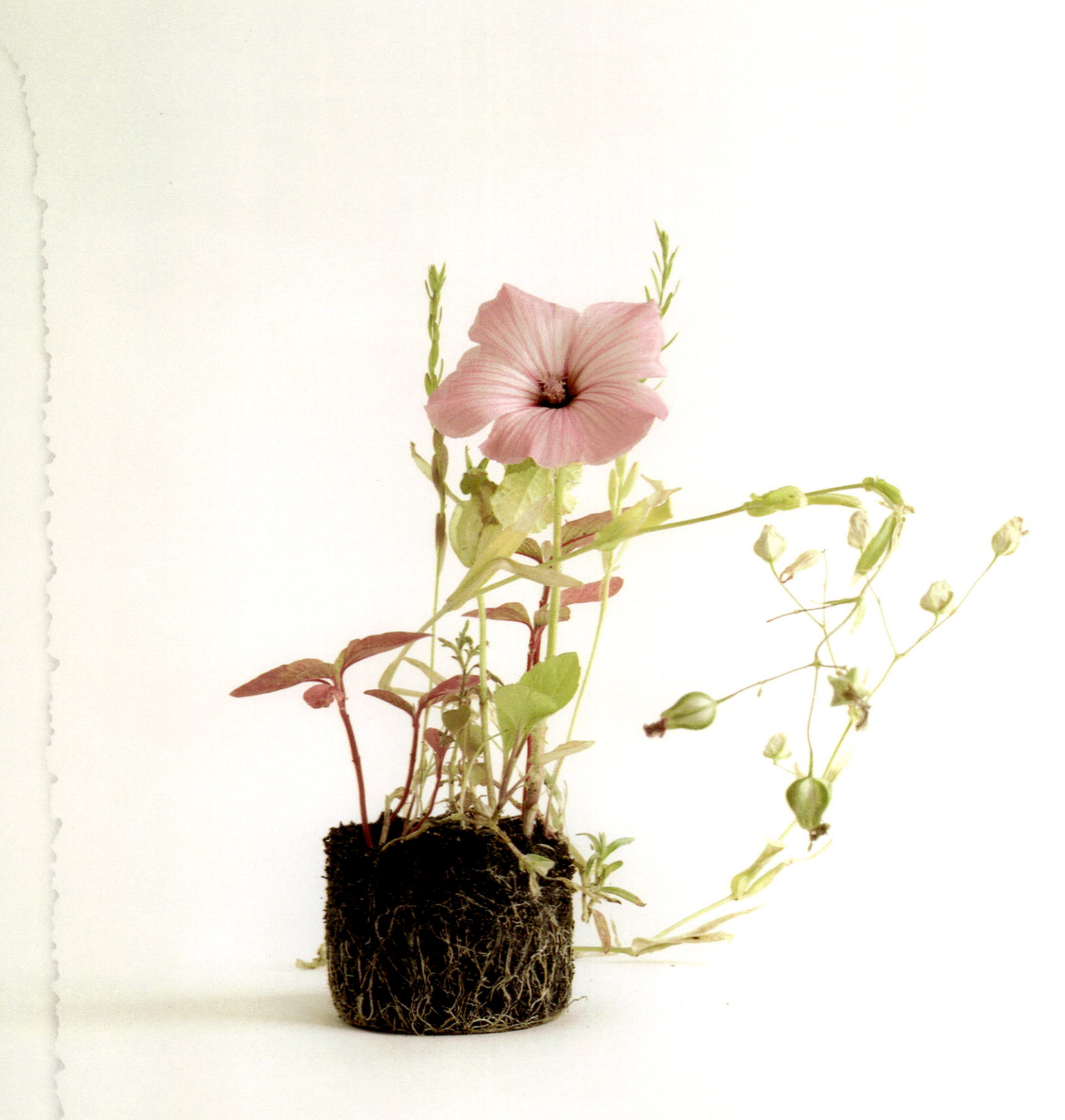

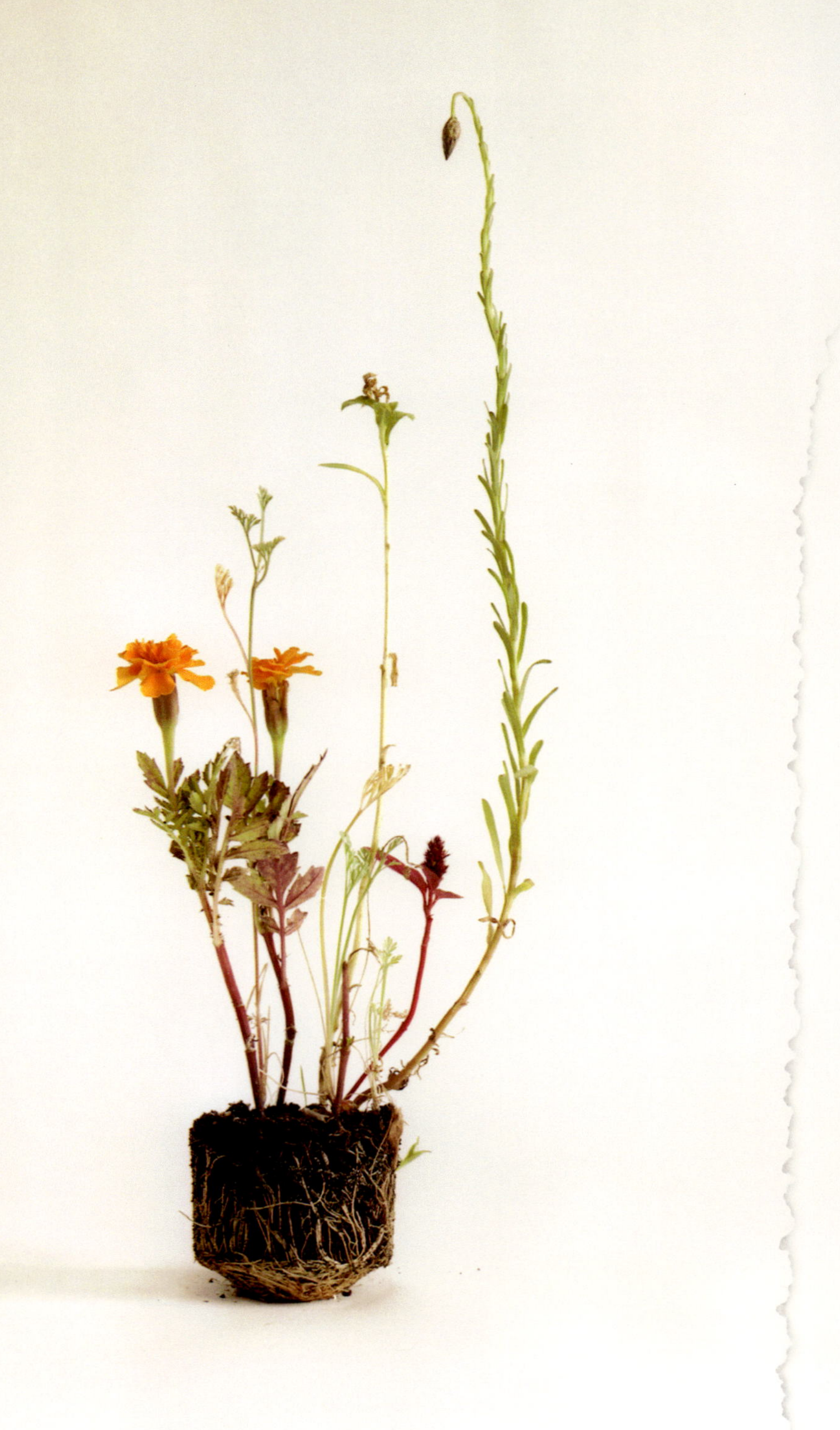

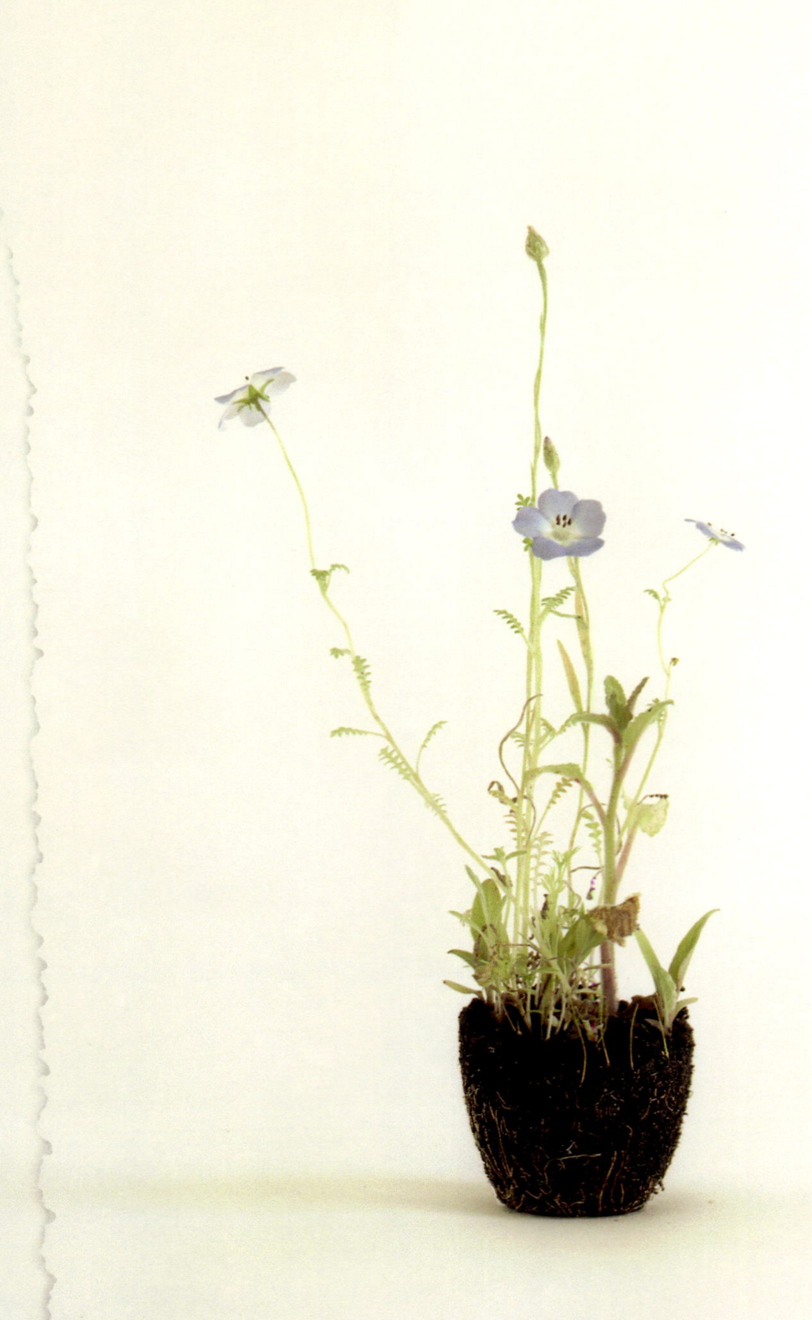

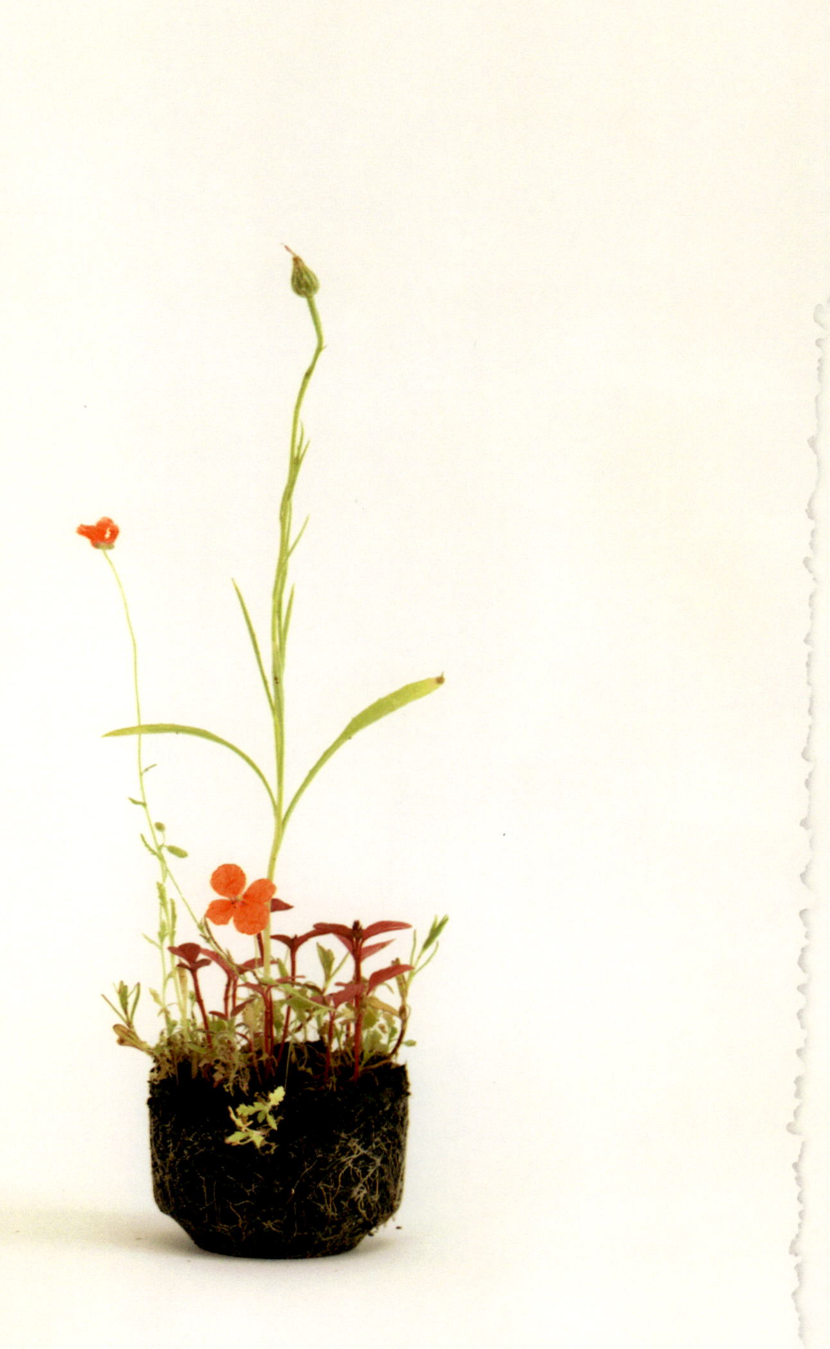

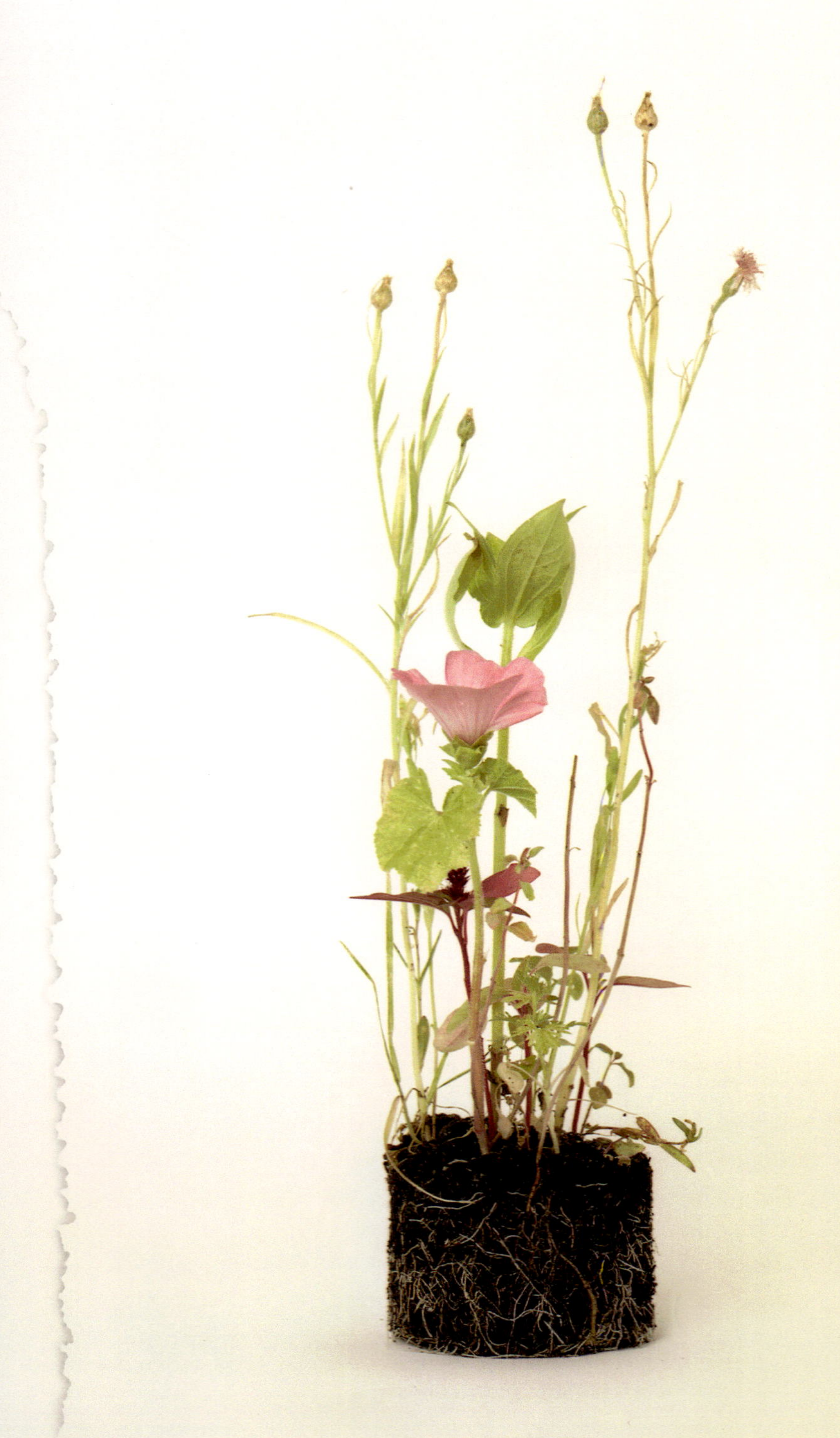

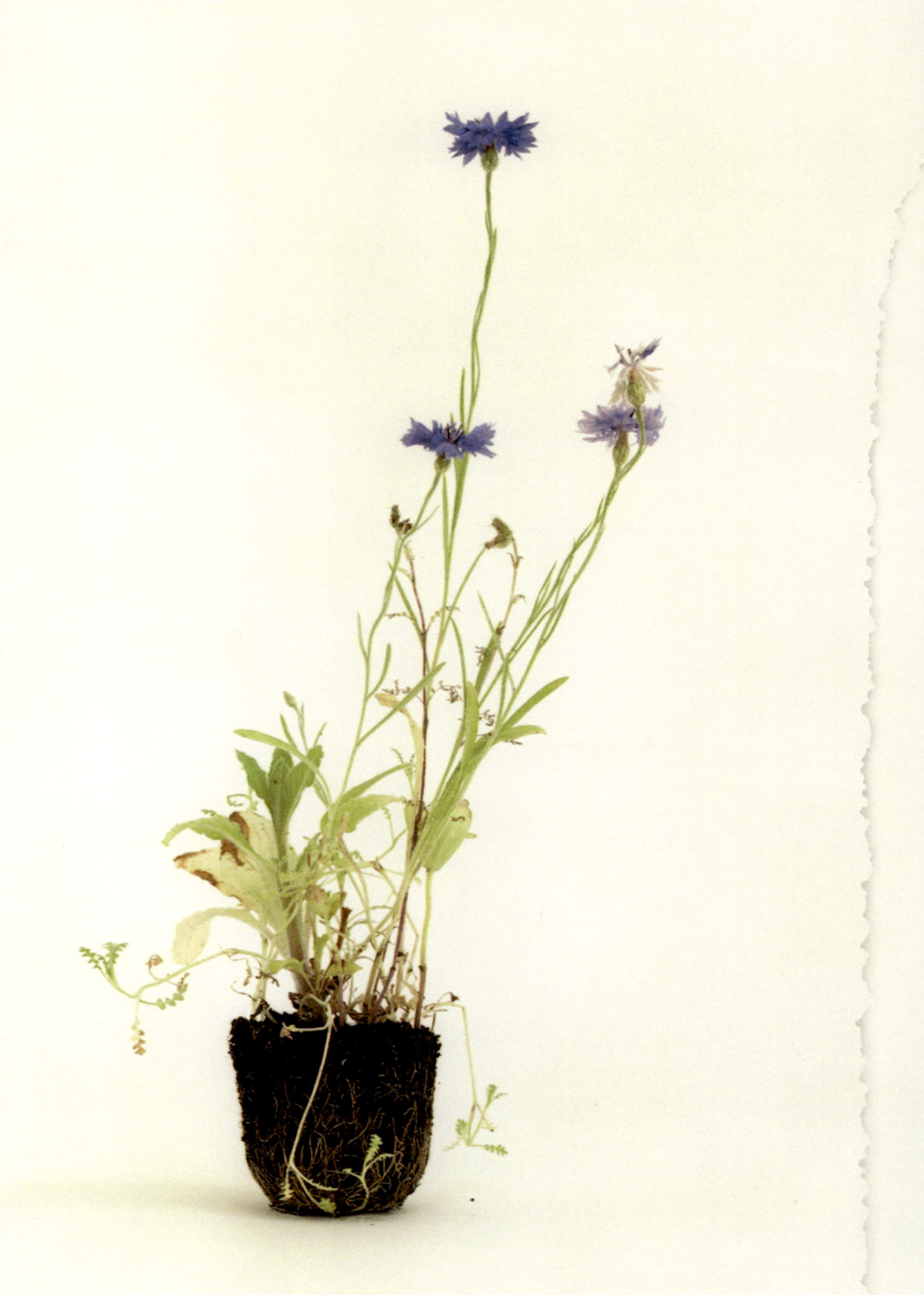

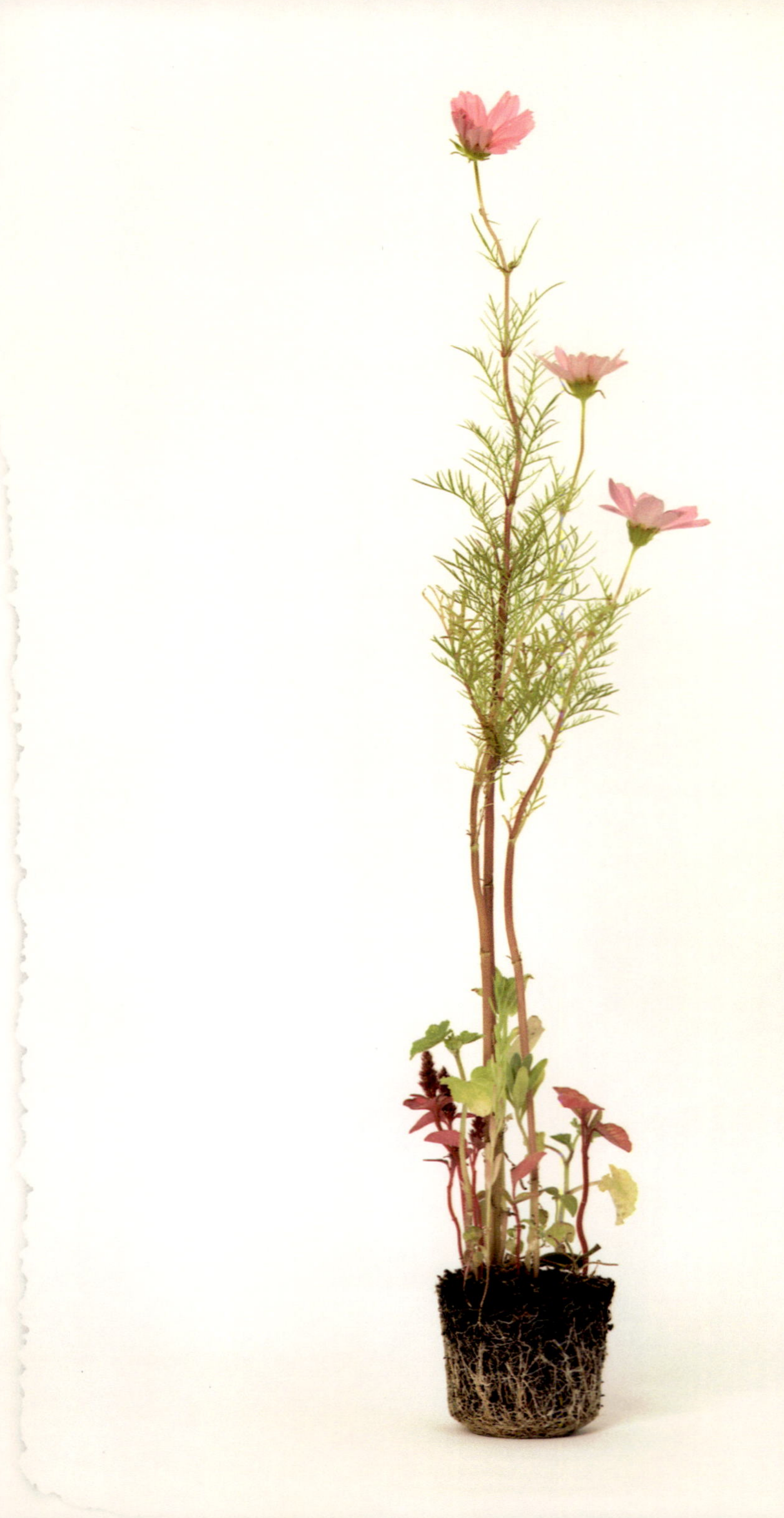

NATHANIEL RICH

DOCTORS

Manual for New Residents at Mercy General Hospital's Department of Neurology

Dear Resident,

Welcome to Mercy General. Having completed your medical school training, you may be familiar with much of what I have to tell you. I hope you will give me your attention nevertheless. In my thirty-year career I have found that one can only learn so much from textbooks. I have profited greatly from the wisdom of my teachers, and in this manual I hope to pass on their lessons to you.

Chapter One: The Diagnosis

I begin with my least favorite part of the job. Nothing you learn in medical school can prepare you for the difficulties of "breaking the news" to a patient you have diagnosed with a grave illness.

In recent years it has become fashionable in American medical circles to work hard at one's "bedside manner"—to coddle the patient as much as possible. I consider this a troubling development. I don't suggest that you be rude or aloof. I just believe in the importance of keeping a professional distance. When making difficult decisions about a course of treatment, it is crucial not to be ruled by one's feelings of affection for a patient. Often the most prudent medical action is not pleasant, and it may lead to suffering. Were we to let our emotions dictate our actions, it would be impossible to function as professional doctors. A brain surgeon who gives too freely to his emotions is likely to botch his operation. The "coldhearted" approach, I believe, should be adopted all the way down the line, whether you are a neurosurgeon or a pediatrician.

To illustrate my point, I'd like to share with you a recent example of a diagnosis session gone wrong. I hope the mistakes made by myself and my colleagues will be instructive. You never know when someone like Jason Fogg might walk into your door.

It seemed a routine case at first. Fogg had visited his general practitioner, Dr. Jenkins, with a complaint about headaches. Dr. Jenkins asked Fogg whether he had experienced any mood swings or personality changes. Initially Fogg answered in the negative, but under scrutiny he admitted that he had been short with his wife in recent days. He shrugged this off, blaming workplace pressure, but Jenkins, to his credit—he is a master of the trade, God bless him—arranged for Fogg to see a neurologist.

A Dr. Watts on the Upper East Side, after administering a range of neurological exams, informed Fogg that a brain tumor could not be ruled out. Fogg, horrified, immediately asked for a second opinion. Dr. Jenkins recommended me, which is how Fogg came to Mercy General.

Fogg was anxious from the beginning—not an unusual condition. He was particularly alarmed when I mentioned to him that we'd inject a blue dye into his arm in preparation for his brain scan. I explained, very calmly, that this was normal practice, that the dye was a contrast material that, once it reached the brain, allowed us more easily to detect abnormal tissue. Because the procedure was not particularly comfortable, many patients chose to be anesthetized.

I should say here that I hadn't worked very much with Dr. Watts, but Dr. Jenkins assured me he was qualified. Young, yes, but competent. Still, Watts might have prepared the patient better for the possibility of a brain scan. In retrospect, I realize that this was the first indication that Watts had done a poor job.

Nevertheless, everything at this point appeared to be on schedule. Fogg enthusiastically expressed his desire to be anesthetized. I sent him to our radiologist, who conducted the procedure three days later.

The following afternoon, once I received the results, I invited Fogg to meet me in my office. He was joined by his wife, Mrs. Fogg. I have mentioned my lack of bedside manner. Dispensing with formalities, I began the meeting with a straight diagnosis: brain tumor, an anaplastic ependymoma near the spinal cord. I showed Fogg the transparency, carefully prepared by the radiologist and his staff, showing the tumor. They had done good work. The tumor was clearly demarcated. Fogg held it up to the light. He seemed unable to understand what he was looking at, but when he passed it to his wife, she saw immediately the tumor, a white mark slightly smaller than a pebble. I explained that we would have to begin treatment right away. It would be expensive, I said, but the cost would be at least partially defrayed by his health insurance. Mrs. Fogg burst into tears.

Fogg's response did not surprise me, at least not at first. We expect denial; we prepare for it. But we didn't expect this.

"Hold on," he said. "I have no cancer in my family. I'm a fit person. I go to the gym every morning. I eat a healthy diet. I don't even use a cell phone. My brain works well. I have excellent memory. Helen, tell them. Don't I have a great memory?"

Mrs. Fogg's head was in her hands. She was sniffling.

"We don't know why tumors develop," I explain. "It can happen to anyone."

"You didn't even look at the scan," he said. "At least, not closely."

"Of course I did. As did our radiologist and his team."

He took the transparency in his hand and examined the section where we had indicated the tumor.

"You can barely see it."

"We can see it."

"But surely it's not serious. I'm a fighter. I can beat it."

I nodded. I tried to maintain my expression of stolid concentration.

"I've always had strong will power," he continued. "When I want something to happen, it happens. This will be no different. You know what? I'm already starting to feel better. My headache is gone."

"We will have to conduct a biopsy immediately."

"What does that mean?"

"First we remove part of your skull. Then we extract, with a needle, a section of your brain. We analyze the tissue for cancerous cells."

"Hold on." Fogg raised his hands, as if to halt an oncoming car. "Hold on! Shouldn't you do other tests? Perhaps there was an error."

"There was no error," I said, pointing to the mass I had circled with my marker on the transparency. I was growing exasperated.

"Are you sure it's my brain? Maybe you mislabeled it?"

I paged the radiologist. He arrived within a minute, his nurse by his side. I handed him the brain scan transparency. He pretended to study it for several seconds.

"Yes," he said finally. "I conducted the exam, and delivered it directly to this office. It was the only scan I've done in the last week. Besides, you can see on the bottom of the printout that the date and time of the image match that of your appointment. And that's my nurse's signature. Isn't it?"

"It is," said the nurse, nodding a bit too quickly.

Fogg placed the transparency back on the desk.

"But the other brain doctor—Dr. Watts—he told me that, based on my symptoms, if I did have a tumor, it would be a glioma. That if anything, the early tests pointed to a glioma. Not an anaphalactic..."

"An anaplastic ependymoma."

"Right. He said my symptoms were consistent with a glioma, not an anaplastic ependymoma."

The radiologist and his nurse exchanged an anxious glance.

"An ependymoma can be called a glioma," I began. "It's a question of semantics, you see—"

"But he said it would be located in my frontal lobe," said Fogg. I noticed he had begun to grit his teeth. "Not the spinal cord. In the front of the head—not the back!"

At this Mrs. Fogg raised her head for the first time. Her eyes were pink and wet, hopeful.

"Is that so?" I said. "Well. You may have misheard Dr. Watts."

"I did not mishear him. I was taking notes. I have it all written down."

He began to remove a crinkled piece of paper from his pocket.

"I will talk to Dr. Watts," I said. This couldn't go any further. "Perhaps he had a momentary confusion. The bottom line is that the tumor is there, inside your head."

Fogg reached across my desk and, to my astonishment, handed me the sheet of paper.

"See! It's right there." He was pointing at the paper. "Glioma!"

That was when things turned for the worse. You will learn that no matter how much you prepare for an appointment of this nature, it can never be enough. For just one moment I lost my composure, but it cost me. What did I do? Nothing egregious. I didn't let the cat out of the bag, as it were. But I showed my hand slightly, ever so slightly. That is to say, I smiled. I didn't mean to, but it happened, no doubt a symptom of my anxiety. I smiled.

Fogg, seeing this, rose sharply from his chair.

"You despicable, despicable man," he said. His face, blossoming with color, quivered horribly. "How dare you?"

"Excuse me?"

"You did this to me. You."

"I'm sorry, I don't know what you're talking about. Would you please sit down?"

"You implanted the tumor! You gave this to me."

"I know it must be a shock—"

Fogg turned to the radiologist and pointed his finger in the poor man's face.

"During the brain scan, you thought I was asleep, but I wasn't fully gone and I heard you whispering to her." He spun and faced the nurse. "Something about 'preparing' the 'implant.' What was this implant? Was it the tumor? The tumor that you were implanting into my brain?"

"Jason!" said his wife. "Jason!"

"You sick bastards. You put the tumor into my brain just so you could operate and make some money."

"I will not have you address us in this manner," I said. "We are professionals." But I knew it was too late.

"And this Dr. Watts. He didn't have any reason to order an MRI. All I did was complain about headaches. He was a little quick to act, wasn't he? People get headaches all the time. That doesn't mean they have brain tumors!"

"Dr. Watts was simply taking every precaution," said the radiologist.

"I get headaches every few years, always during periods of high stress. Only this time I decided I should go see a doctor about it. A doctor." He said the word like a curse.

"Listen," I said. "It could be worse. There are ways to beat this thing. But it takes your cooperation. Denial won't serve you well. Nor wrath."

"You sick, sick bastards," said Fogg. His knuckles were white on the desk. "I will get to the bottom of this. And you will pay."

He began walking around the desk, toward me, his fists clenched. Fortunately his wife rose and grabbed him around the waist. Pleading, sobbing, she pushed him against the wall. Fogg appeared suddenly fatigued, drained. Heaving, he rested there and sank into a crouch. They sat together there for a few moments. Then she led him out. It was over.

I ordered the nurse, who was quite shaken, to lock the door. She rushed to do it and when we heard the lock click, I admit we all shared a sigh of relief. We had done our best to remain unflustered but in cases like this, it would be inhuman not to feel some sense of alarm.

"Jeez," she said. "He almost swung at you."

"We need to get Dr. Watts on the phone," said the radiologist. "Completely unprofessional. If he told the patient it would be in the frontal lobe, he should have told us too!"

Of course the radiologist was correct—Dr. Watts had been negligent, and he would have to be reprimanded. I never worked with him again, in fact. But I knew that the radiologist had other motivations. He was hoping to shift the blame onto Dr. Watts, when in fact he himself had committed a far more serious error. Evidently he had miscalculated how much anesthetic to give Fogg before the brain scan. As a result, Fogg had remained conscious during the initial stage of the operation. He had heard a discussion between the radiologist and the nurse and jumped to a conclusion.

Given your medical school training, you have by now probably realized that this radiologist had made a second mistake. During such a delicate operation as tumor implantation, one must take great pains to speak in code—even if the patient is believed to be unconscious, you cannot know for certain what they are able to perceive. No one should have ever used the term "implant." If it weren't for this moment of carelessness, the patient wouldn't have concluded that we had implanted the tumor inside his brain. He would likely seek a second opinion now, and a third, and we would be at great pains to debrief neurologists at other institutions, so that none of them would make the slightest mistake when confronted by Fogg and his suspicions. Another slip-up, and we'd be in a real mess. Our entire profession could be implicated.

There was a light knock on the door then. I asked the nurse to unlock it. Mrs. Fogg was standing there, alone. I invited her back into the office. She was pressing her eyes with a balled-up piece of tissue paper.

"I don't need to sit," she said. "I just came to apologize."

I nodded, and waited for her to continue.

"I'm so sorry. I've never seen him like that. I wouldn't want you to refuse to treat him because of the way he's acting. I know that you're the best in Manhattan."

"Of course we will continue to work with you and your husband." I gave her a reassuring smile. "Denial is a common response. The news must have upset him."

"Do you think that the tumor might be pressing on a part of his brain that regulates his violent impulses? Or on a part of his brain that affects his reasoning ability? Because he doesn't normally behave like this. He's a peaceful, sensible man."

"That might be it," I said. "You may be right."

"I hope you can help him. I assure you he will be a model patient from now on. Just please try to help him."

"We will do everything we can," I said. "The best thing now would be to help him complete the insurance forms. My secretary will answer any questions you might have."

"Thank you." She shook my hand with great feeling. "Thank you."

The following week I filed a complaint with the hospital about the radiologist. He was fired immediately. As he should have been. Mercy Hospital—really any hospital—can hardly afford to tolerate such sloppiness. The medical trade is a business like any other, and we cannot worry about having one employee's lackadaisical behavior endanger the entire firm.

This, however, is not the moral of the story. What is most important, particularly in the diagnosis phase, is to keep one's composure. Don't let the patient's reaction—whether it be wrath, confusion, or denial—affect your behavior. Professionalism is not taught at medical school. It is something you have to learn. But we would never have hired you if we didn't think you were capable of great things.

Chapter Two: Implanting the Tumor

JAMES GUIDA

NEITHER HERE NOR THERE, NOR THERE

Ideally there would to be two lives: one to live, and the other for magazines.

•

The belief that you have no illusions – least attractive, least fruitful of illusions?

•

We can't be reminded enough that it's the oyster that creates the pearl, rather than another pearl doing it.

•

Very easy now for someone to say "I'm tired of life," and just mean "I'm tired of the net."

•

He's no misanthrope, but he does sometimes enjoy rolling that cigarette for others.

The man had kicked all the addictions except one: he still depended on that most powerful of drugs, the sensation that "things are happening."

•

Nietzsche advised that deep thoughts should be treated like cold baths – quick in, and quick out. Whatever the case may be, I can't help but notice their resemblance to free food, which is so often pounced upon by the young, and circumspectly navigated by the old.

•

It's extraordinary how so many people seem designed to have a set amount of friends, and of specific kinds of friends. This man is a kennel with room for one loyal occupant, while this other has an extensive network of channels and cavities inside him, there's always room for more dwellers. Here's an elaborate bird feeder, beckoning a variety of flitting visitors, all looking for some specific end... And over there's a tree that does little to deliberately attract others, but supports the few who discern her charms.

•

Reading for hours online, I imagine myself as like one of those turtles who's swallowed a plastic shopping bag, having mistaken it for a jellyfish.

•

Were it possible to get a handle on fingernails, which at times demand trimming though we seem to have done so only a day or two ago, and at others seem not to need cutting for weeks or months on end, and which, at a certain point, just make it confusing as to whether an itch really exists, or only seems to because we have fingernails long enough to thoroughly scratch one – well, then one could probably master one's entire life.

Great precision is so alien to our normal mode of conversation as to often appear fantastical.

•

Self-awareness is very often as accurate as our sense of a pain in the body, where a region can be found instantly and with uncanny precision. How we appear to others is more like a crumb stuck in your teeth: though felt surely, obsessively with the tongue, damned if our fingers know where it lies!

•

In arguments with certain people, if not with ourselves, we would like to be able to give them a little shake, turn them over, pat them down, find their cool side -- as if they were pillows.

•

The marriage of content and style in literature tends to be idealized in the way actual marriages used to be. Symmetry is exaggerated, the element of convenience overlooked.

•

Even with people who have no problem making small talk, the temptation to withhold and take the challenge of everyone's mutual silence often runs rampant. It's like looking into an abyss, feeling at once terrible and thrilled to be getting accustomed to it moment by moment. You begin by thinking "I can wait just as long as you," and end by saying anything at all, with the urgency of a diver coming up for air.

Much like novels, romance seems to rarely endure without a strong beginning.

•

"My dilettantism against yours – en guard!"

•

So people complain that she's distant, and spends too much time in her own head. Having seen a little of her imagination, however, I don't really blame her.

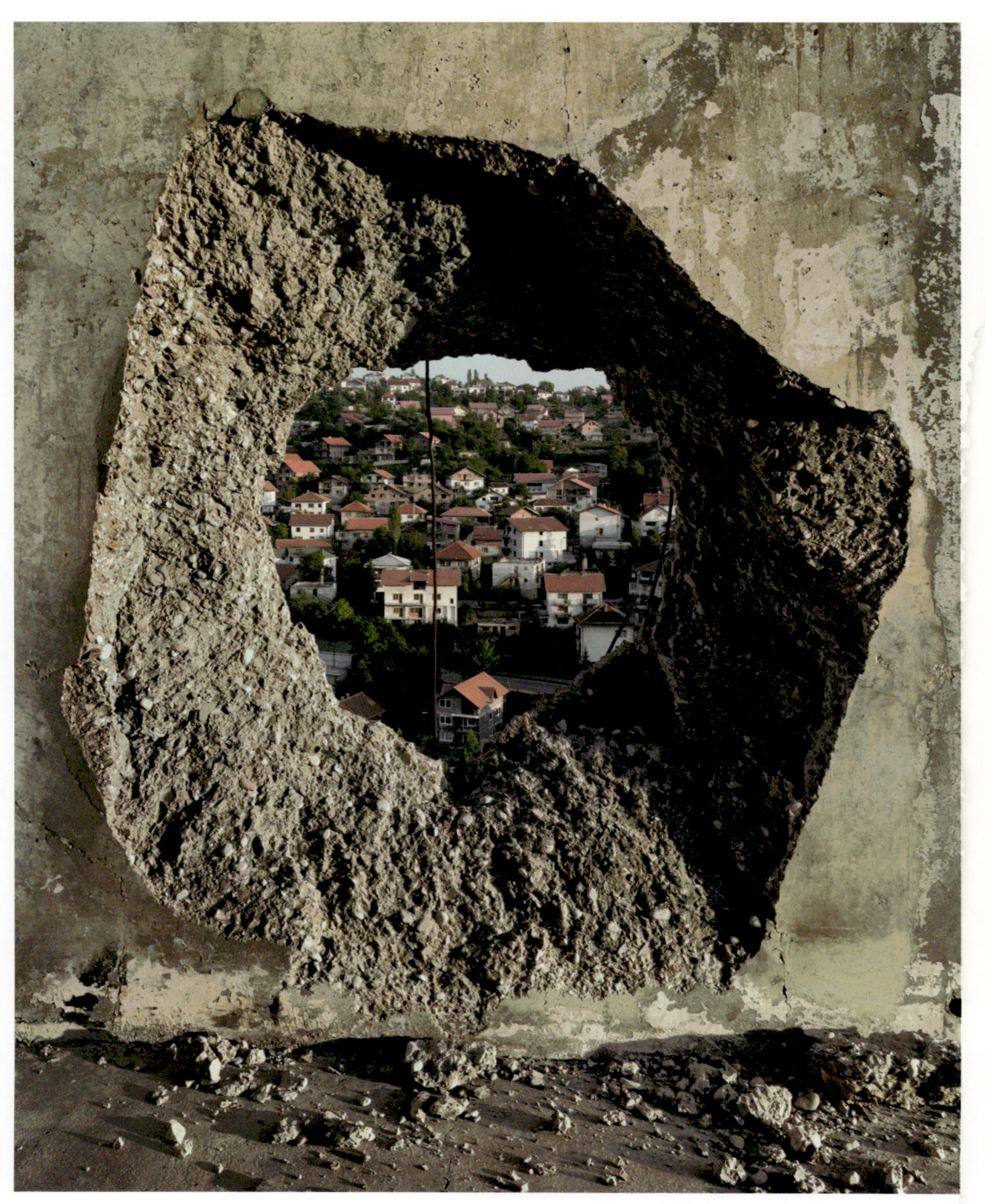

ANDREW MOORE

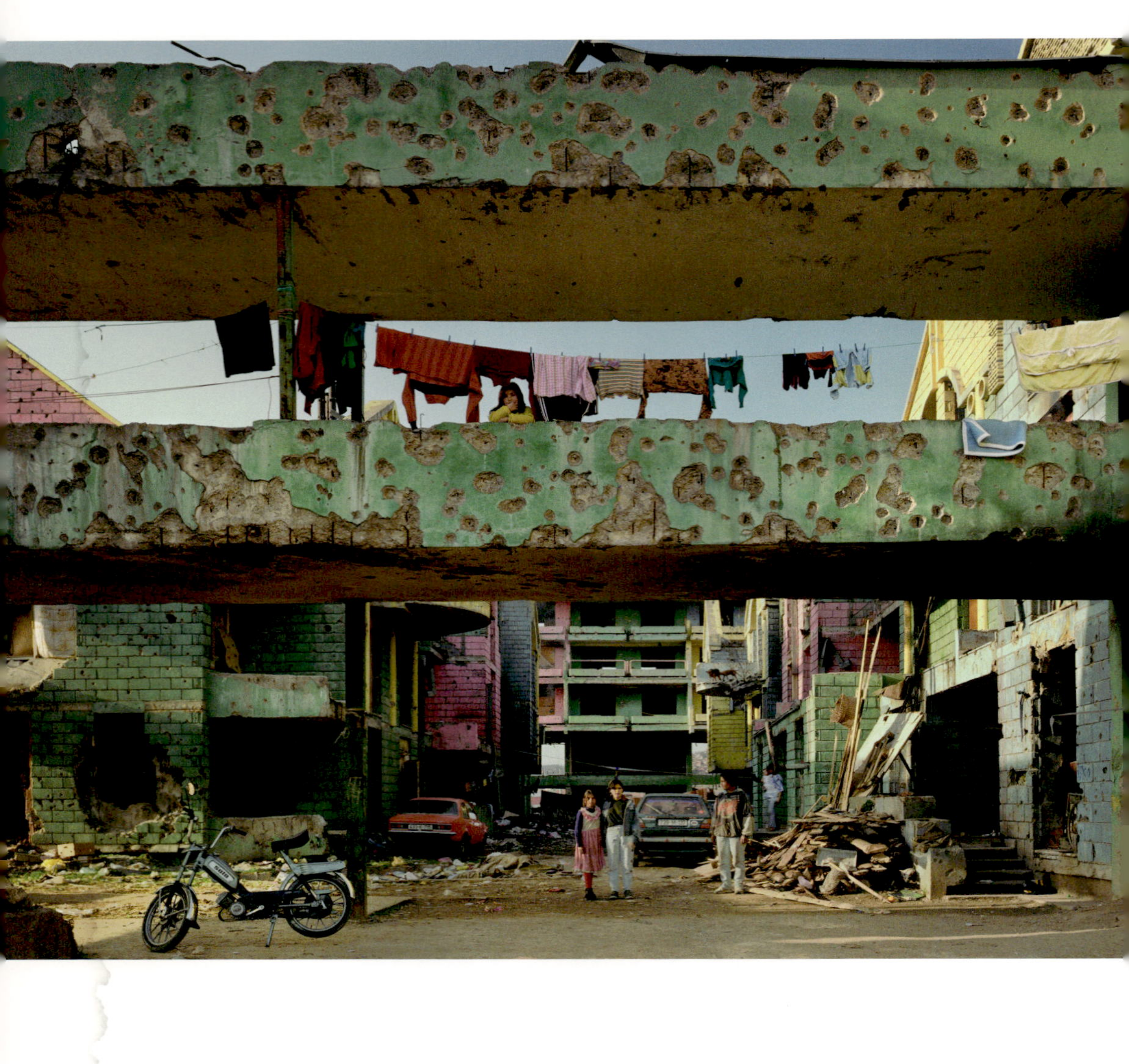

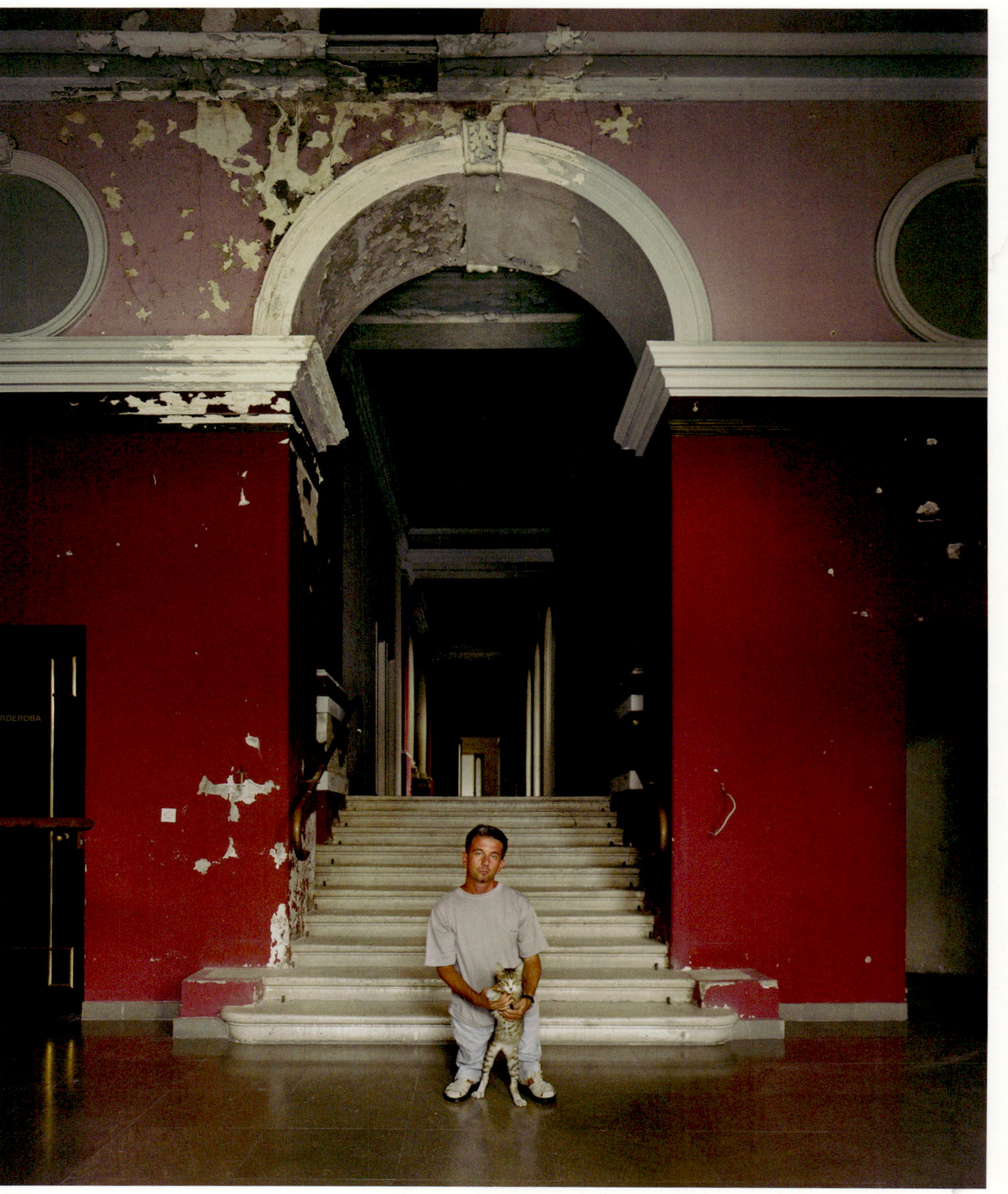
ARDEROBA

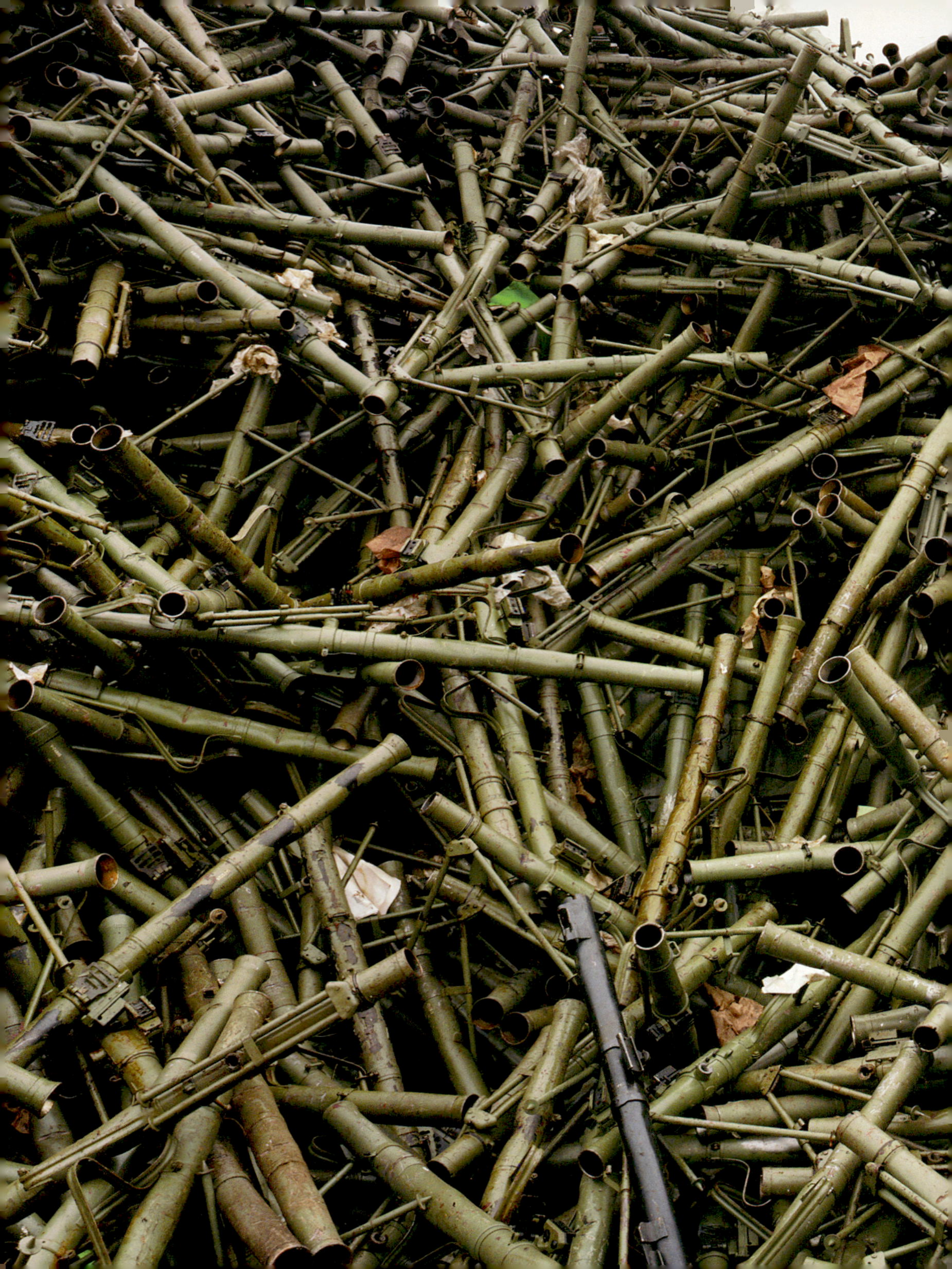

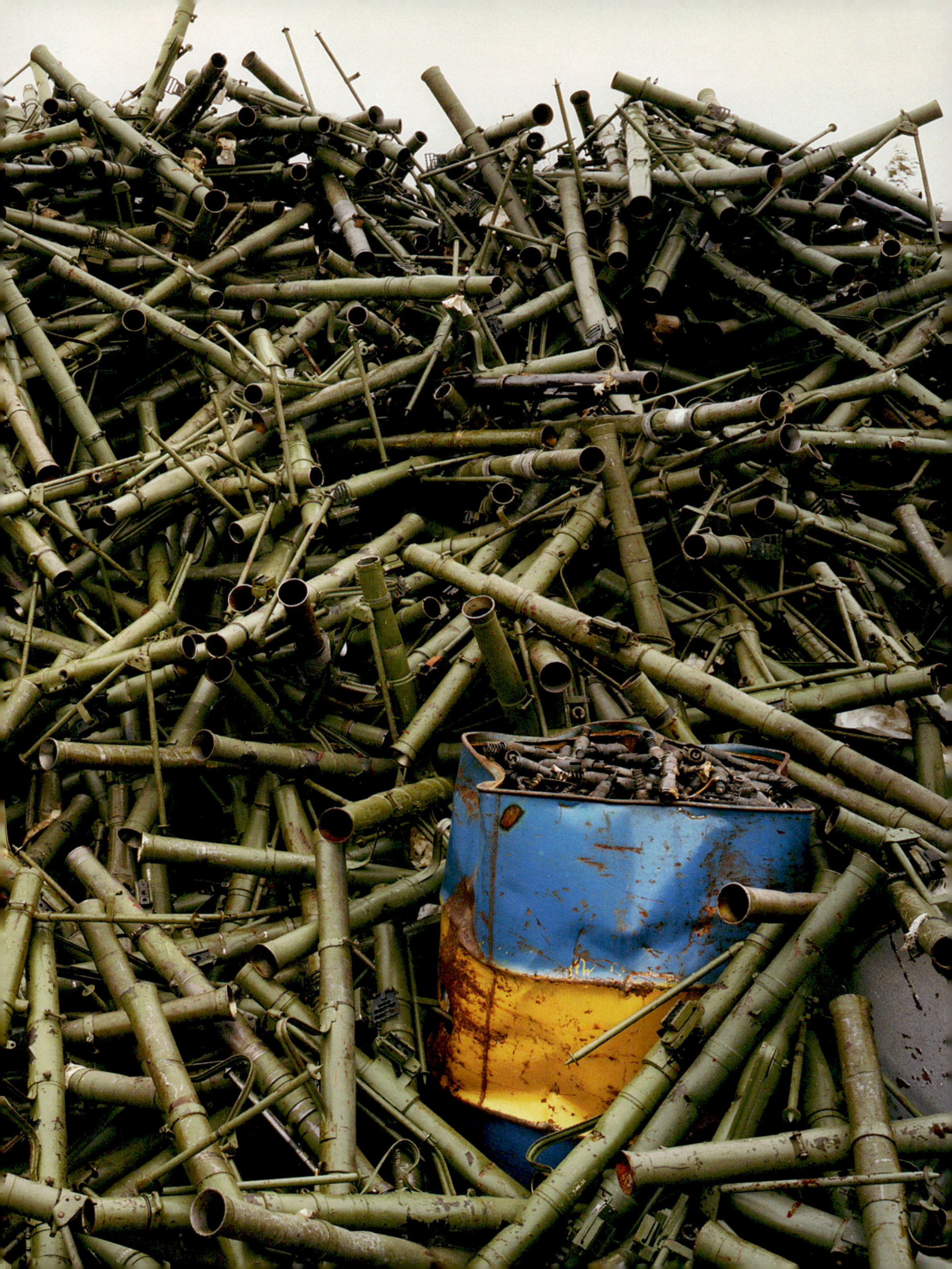

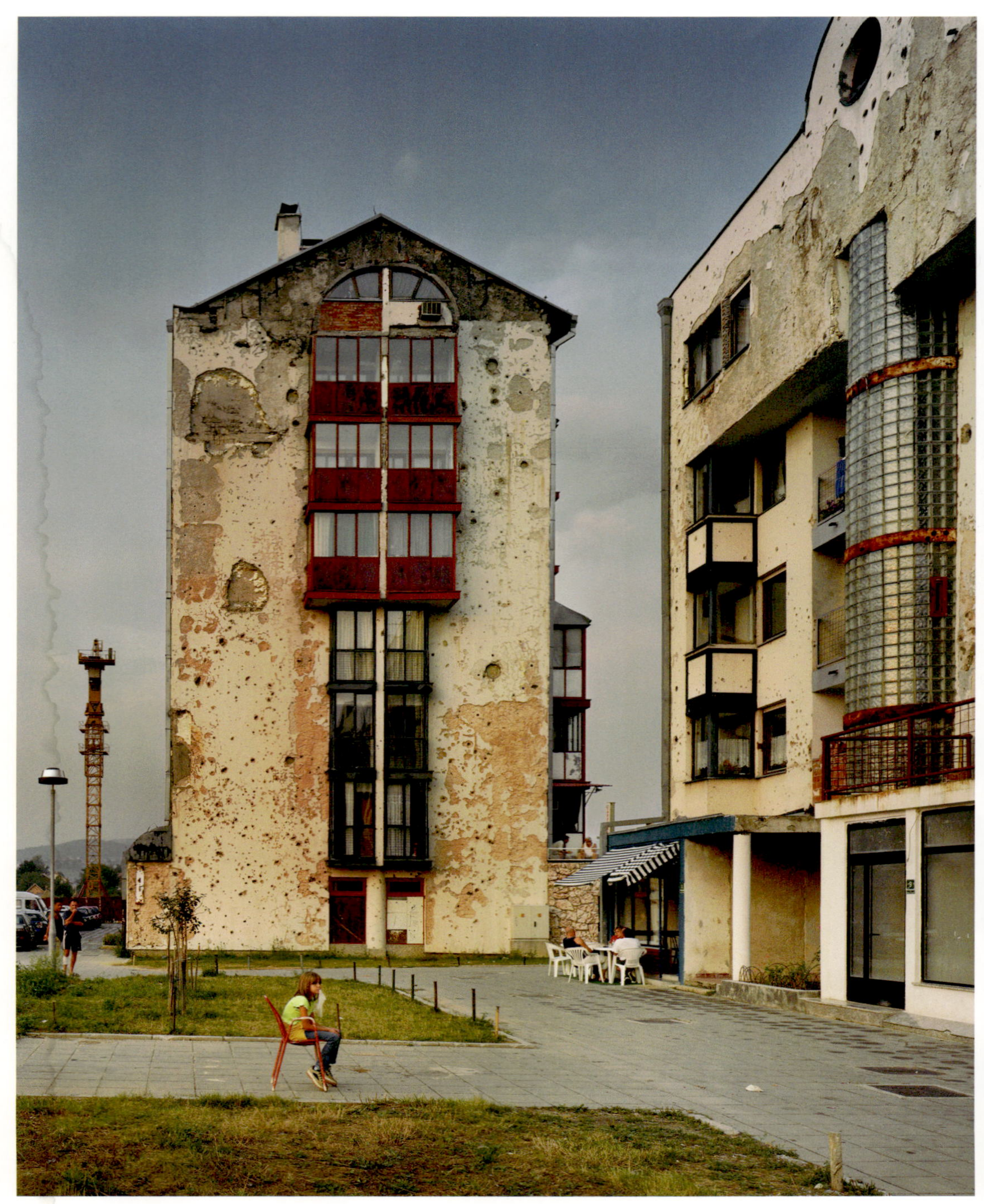

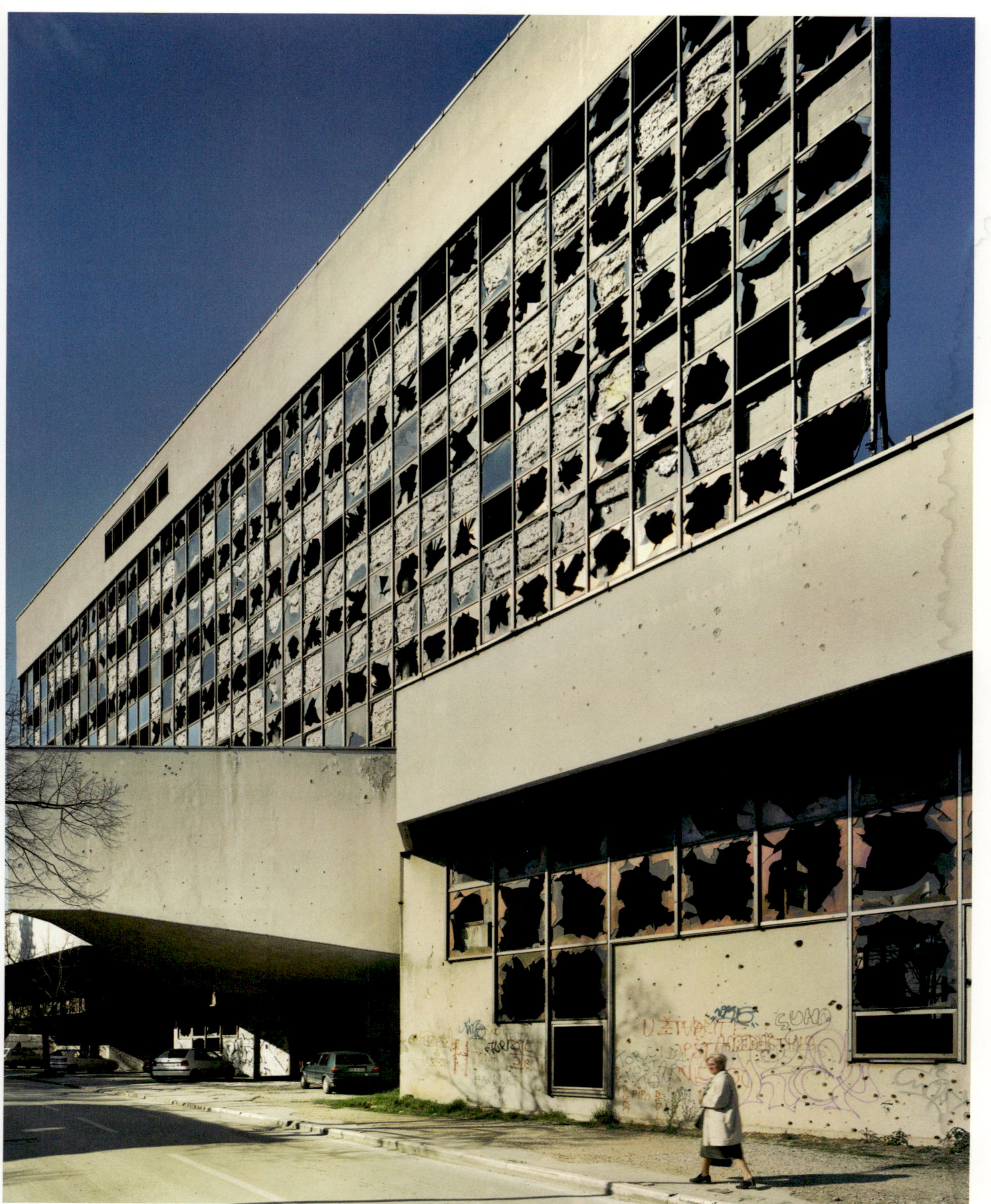

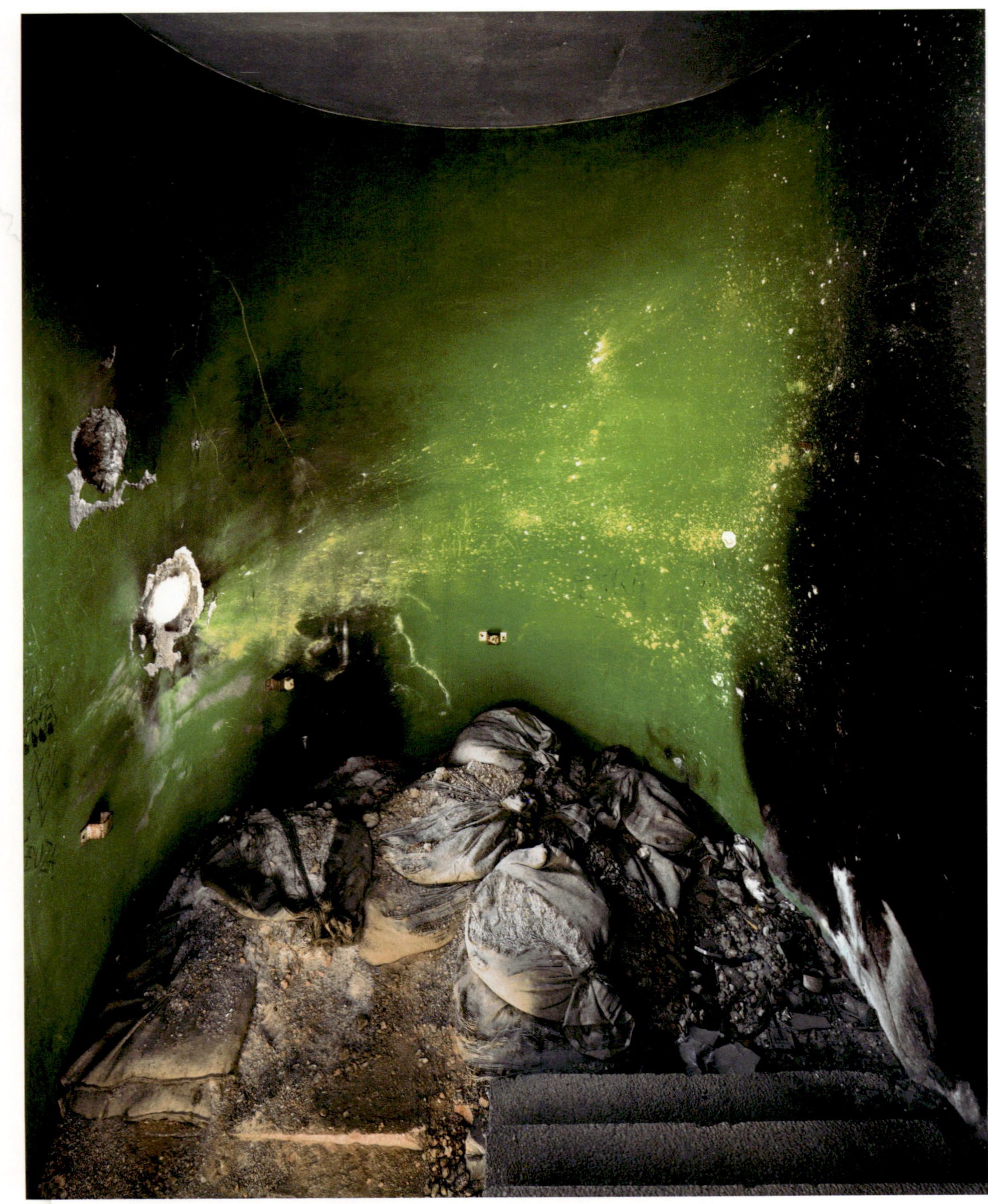

ARTHUR BRADFORD

RESORT TIK TOK

A friend had returned from Thailand and informed me that one could rent a hut on the beach there for one dollar per night, meals included. I was struggling to pay the rent on my studio apartment while holding down a shitty job as a hotel desk clerk. I'd work the night shift and, when things got slow, try to write short stories for publication. A few of my stories had been sold to magazines and though the payment was meager, I figured if I moved out to one of those shacks in Thailand I could make things go a lot farther.

The only issue was the airfare. I didn't have it. To solve this problem, I enrolled in a medical study where they deprived us of sleep for 24 hours at a time and then made us walk quickly on a treadmill while reading aloud from a book. The book was made up of slogans and stupid phrases repeated over and over and many of us got frustrated. If we stopped reading, the treadmill sped up and we had to start from the beginning. Eventually we all tripped or vomited, except for this one fellow named Frank who had incredible stamina. He made it to the end of the book. When we finished with the treadmills, we had to drink some bitter orange liquid and then go into a room and masturbate into a cup. It was very difficult, given the fatigue. Only two of us could produce a sample. I was one of those two, and felt proud about it, but the important part was that odd study paid me 1,200 bucks, enough to get me to Thailand.

My friend had written out directions to a particularly remote Thai island, and I arrived there after several days of rocky travel. While jetlagged on the streets of Bangkok, I'd been approached by a young boy who handed me a pamphlet promising a "Girl with Baboon" show at a nearby bar.

"No cover charge!" he assured me.

Who was I to turn down such an offer? I went over there and sat through several unenthusiastic "Girl with Girl" acts and a "Boy with Girl" act which should have been billed "Fat Man with Tired Person."

"Well," I thought, "at least there's no cover charge for this."

But then they brought me the check for the two beers I'd consumed, and it was sixty-five dollars! Two months' rent!

"I refuse to pay," I told them, but they locked the door and no more acts appeared on the stage. I found myself in an uneasy standoff. The beer was gone and I wasn't even going to get to see the baboon. Or maybe they'd release him to kick my ass. I'd heard baboons were very strong animals, capable of ripping humans limb from limb. Or was that chimpanzees? I decided not to chance it. I paid the sixty-five dollars, a serious dent in my finances, and left that bar unsatisfied.

The island was very nice though, once I got there. Ah, yes! It was just as I hoped: beautiful white sand beaches, palm trees, smiling Thai locals, and packs of European hippies wearing little or no clothing all day long. I felt good there. The lodging was not quite as cheap as I'd been led to believe, but I did find a set of huts perched on some rocks away from the beach where I was able to bargain for a reasonable monthly rate. The place was called Resort Tik Tok and I gave them eighty US dollars in advance for a proposed two-month stay.

Most of the beachfront huts were run by cheerful Thai hosts, but Resort Tik Tok was run by a Swiss couple named Rudy and Greta. Rudy was a ornery bear of a man, about forty-five years old, with long, thinning hair and a deep growl of a voice. Despite the idyllic surroundings, he seemed always to be in a foul mood. His wife Greta was a knockout though, and I began fantasizing about her almost immediately.

Greta was a classic Swiss mountain girl with long brown hair and the body of an Olympic shot-putter. I'm not kidding about this. She could have been on the cover of *Swiss Female Bodybuilder Magazine,* if such a publication existed. She must have been fifteen years younger than Rudy, at least. The thing that really got me about her was her insecure, imperfect smile. She had one little fang tooth on the side which stuck out from the rest and you could tell she was self-conscious about it. It looked great though. She could have been a supermodel; at least that's what I thought.

Rudy and Greta had a young daughter, a small tank of a child named Trudi who all day long ran across the sharp rock cliffs of Resort Tik Tok with no shoes or clothing. One time I saw her trip and tumble thirty feet down the rock ledge and land in a bush. Then she got up and ran along on her way. No tears or even a whimper! She was amazing, that Trudi, but it was her mother I was most interested in.

My plan had been to hole up inside my seaside shack and write for hours and hours each day. I'd build up a portfolio and then take the publishing world by storm. I got little writing done during my first month there, however. Knowing I'd likely be without electricity, I had made what I thought was a very clever purchase back in Bangkok: a solid little manual typewriter with stylish metal keys. It sat unused for weeks though, gathering dust on a table inside my hut. All I could muster on that island was a few weak sentences scribbled in pencil in a wrinkled notebook which I later lost in a cafe. Whatever motivation I'd had to write or generally work for a living had ebbed away. I was reasonably content to pass my days simply lying in the hot sun watching Greta chase Trudi around in her bathing suit.

Rudy, I feared, had caught on to my admirations, but they had few paying customers and he tolerated my presence with cautious reserve. Rudy had some Chinese characters tattooed to his forearm, and one day I asked him what they meant.

"Peace," he told me.

"That's it?" I said. There were four or five different characters there. I thought they must say more than that.

"That's it," said Rudy. I watched him walk away, this angry hulking Swiss man, and tried to picture the young hippie he might have once been, the man who wooed beautiful Greta, and asked to have "Peace" carved into his arm.

I had been there nearly a month and accomplished nothing. Then an attractive Israeli woman checked into the resort with her French boyfriend and they quickly got in a bickering fight. He left the next morning and she proceeded to smoke hashish and drink rum punch all day long out on the veranda. I joined her in the afternoon, and by nightfall we were both naked rolling around on the single cot in my shack. She was a wet kisser and kept calling me "Jacques," the name of the boyfriend who had just left her. I tried to imagine that she was Greta but it was no use. I awoke the next morning terribly hungover with the Israeli woman sprawled asleep on the sandy floor below me.

I watched her sleeping there for a little while. She really was quite pretty, and sophisticated too, despite the way we'd spent the previous day. Back home, such a woman would have avoided the likes of me, but the rules were different here on this island. Her eyes opened and she looked at me.

"What's your name?" I asked her. If she'd ever told me, I'd forgotten it instantly.

"Malka," she said. "My name is Malka. Who are you?"

"We met yesterday," I told her. "My name is George."

She rubbed her eyes and looked around. Her body heaved and she jumped up and made for the doorway, where she puked outside on the rocks. Little Trudi happened to be playing nearby and laughed at this.

Through the thin walls of my hut I heard Greta's gentle voice. "Shhh, Trudi," she said. "It's not nice."

Malka stuck her head back inside my shack and said, "I'll see you later."

I'd assumed I wouldn't actually be seeing Malka later, but in fact I did. She was eating an omelet at one of the small restaurants down on the beach and asked me to sit with her.

"You feel better?" I asked her.

"A little," she said.

We became friends, me and Malka, bonding over the mutual failures that mired us at Resort Tik Tok. Later I confessed to her my longing for Greta.

"That woman is a lesbian," she told me.

"No, she's married to Rudy," I said. "They have a daughter."

Malka gave me a pitying look.

"Why do you think Rudy is so upset all the time?" she said. "He married a lesbian."

I thought about this and could see that Malka had a point. There appeared to be little chemistry between Rudy and Greta. On the one hand this realization made me happy, because it meant the Greta didn't actually love Rudy, but one the other hand it made me sad, because now she wasn't going to end up loving me either.

Malka and I fell into a routine, sleeping together until late in the afternoon, eating omelets, and then getting drunk throughout the evening. We were both trying to avoid something, me with my writing, and her with whatever was going on with Jacques, that Frenchman who'd left her there. I chose not to ask about it, and in turn, she didn't mention the dusty typewriter on the table.

One afternoon, we were lying asleep on my cot and something crashed into the outside of my shack. It was Trudi. She got up, of course, but then Rudy started yelling at her. He shouted out vile German curse words which I couldn't understand, but made Trudi cry. I got up and stuck my head out the door just in time to see Greta come along, scoop Trudi off of the ground, and give Rudy an angry look.

"Shame on you," she said to Rudy. And then she added a few words in German which made him blow his top. Rudy's face turned red, and he picked up a wooden bench and hurled it down the rocks where it splintered apart and landed in the ocean. He screamed and spit flew out of his mouth as he rattled off German insults at his wife. Greta appeared unmoved.

That night at the resort restaurant Greta cooked a fish for Malka and I, and we ate it with a bottle of cheap white wine.

"I'm running out of money," I told Malka. "I haven't planned well. I thought I could stay here and write for months, but I'm nearly broke already."

"Well, you're not writing anyway," said Malka.

"I know," I said. "I know that, thank you."

When we were through eating, Greta came for our plates and Malka said to her, "That fish was delicious."

"Thank you," said Greta.

Malka put her hand on Greta's and left it there. Greta stared down at her and smiled.

"You'll join us this evening?" said Malka.

Greta nodded and walked away.

"What just happened?" I asked.

"She will be joining us," said Malka.

"Us? Where?"

"In bed: At your hut."

I couldn't believe it. Malka had never discussed this possibility with me. My heart began to flutter and my throat got tight. Greta! A threesome!

After dinner I hustled back to my shack to get things in order. The little cot would not do. I flipped it over, pushed it against the wall, and spread blankets on the floor. Then I lit some candles and decided to do some push-ups. I was excited. I felt I needed to get my blood flowing properly, perhaps puff up my pectoral muscles so as to appear more attractive. Malka walked in as I was doing this and told me to stop.

"Don't be an idiot," she said.

Greta arrived at the shack around midnight. I was surprised to see that she was carrying Trudi in her arms. The little girl was asleep. Greta lay her down in the corner and looked around at my candles and the overturned cot.

"Okay," she said.

We drank some Thai beer and smoked hashish with tobacco and everyone tried to relax. Finally, Malka leaned over and kissed Greta on the lips. Right before it happened Greta gave this little smile, flashing the crooked tooth. She kissed Malka back tentatively and I sat there watching. What was I supposed to do?

Malka removed Greta's shirt and then took off her own. I felt stupid watching them and considered leaving the hut, a coward's move I knew, but I'd be damned if I was just going to sit there and watch them like a monkey. Then Malka grabbed my leg and pulled me closer. Suddenly we were three people all groping one another, a desperate pile of humanity. I couldn't tell whose hands were doing what. We all got naked and Malka began licking me. I looked over at Greta and she smiled again. I ejaculated on Malka's face. It was terrible timing. I couldn't help it.

Malka wiped herself off and turned her attention back to Greta. They looked amazing, the two of them gliding against each other in the candlelight. Greta began to moan and then Trudi woke up.

"What are you doing, mother?" she asked.

Greta said, "Shhhh…" and Trudi lay back down to sleep.

I joined back in with Malka and Greta but it was hard to find my rhythm. I wanted to be with Greta, yet I suspected she wanted to be with Malka, and Malka, I knew, would have preferred her man Jacques over either of us. Eventually we all feel asleep in a confused heap.

In the early morning twilight I felt a hand brushing slowly across my stomach. It was sturdy and different from Malka's. I was scared to open my eyes. I slid my hand over and touched Greta's firm side. Greta! We rolled together slowly and began to kiss. I couldn't believe it. She grabbed hold of me and I ran my hands all over her muscled back and wonderful Swiss breasts. Oh yes! We lay together side by side, trying not to wake the sleeping bodies around us.

I remember telling myself, "You must savor this moment. It will not last or happen again."

I let out a sound, a groan or a grunt, and woke Trudi up. She stared at us with wide, calm eyes and again I ejaculated at an inopportune moment.

"Your daughter's awake," I told Greta, once I had caught my breath.

Greta wrapped herself in a blanket and picked Trudi up off the floor. They left the shack.

Malka lay asleep against the wall. Perhaps she was just pretending to sleep. I wrapped my arms around her and dozed off.

That next day it was cloudy. It had been sunny and hot for thirty straight days, and now it was cloudy and cold. Malka and I walked to get our omelet and as we ate, she told me it was time for her to go.

"I've waited here long enough," she said.

She went back to pack her bag and I hitched a ride to the post office over the hill. When I got there I found a small bundle of mail waiting for me. Two letters from friends, a book which I'd ordered, a bill, somehow forwarded to me all the way out here, and finally, a check. It was from a magazine. Five hundred dollars. I could live another three months on that, at least. I flipped the check over and over in my hands, making sure it was real.

When I got back to Resort Tik Tok, Malka was gone. She'd left a note on my cot. As I began to read it, Rudy burst through the door and socked me very hard in the face. I felt a crushing pain in my skull, blacked out for a second, and woke up with him standing above me, his two huge fists ready for more.

I rolled myself up into a ball and said, "Please stop."

"You took Greta." he said to me.

"I didn't take her," I replied. "I didn't take her anywhere."

"You took Greta," he said again and kicked at my ribs. This time I did not reply.

Rudy picked up the rickety cot leaning against the wall and threw it down upon me. I let it stay there as a frail shield. Then he took all my clothing and flung it out the door.

I thought of something clever to say at that point, still hiding under the overturned cot.

"Hey, what about Peace?" I said, pointing to his tattooed arm.

Rudy grabbed my manual typewriter from the table and slammed it against the wall. Then he stomped upon it, crushing several of the keys.

"Fuck you," he said to me, and then he left.

I had this urge to just go to sleep, to just stay there on the ground and sleep for a long while, but my head throbbed and there was blood dripping from my lip. A couple of my teeth felt loose. I got up and examined the typewriter. It looked like a wounded animal, a creature run over by a car. Several of the

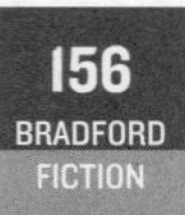

little letter stamp hammers were bent out to the sides. Most of the keys still worked, though. I could still make words with them. I found a blank piece of paper, rolled it inside the mangled machine, and began to type. I typed out a letter to a friend back home, the person with whom I'd left my belongings for when I returned. In the halted language of that messed up typewriter, I told my friend I'd be staying in Thailand for a while longer and he didn't need to hold onto my belongings any more.

"ZEll my Ztuff," I wrote to him, "or don8tE it plEEZE. The RRiting'Z REllly coMMin Elong now..."

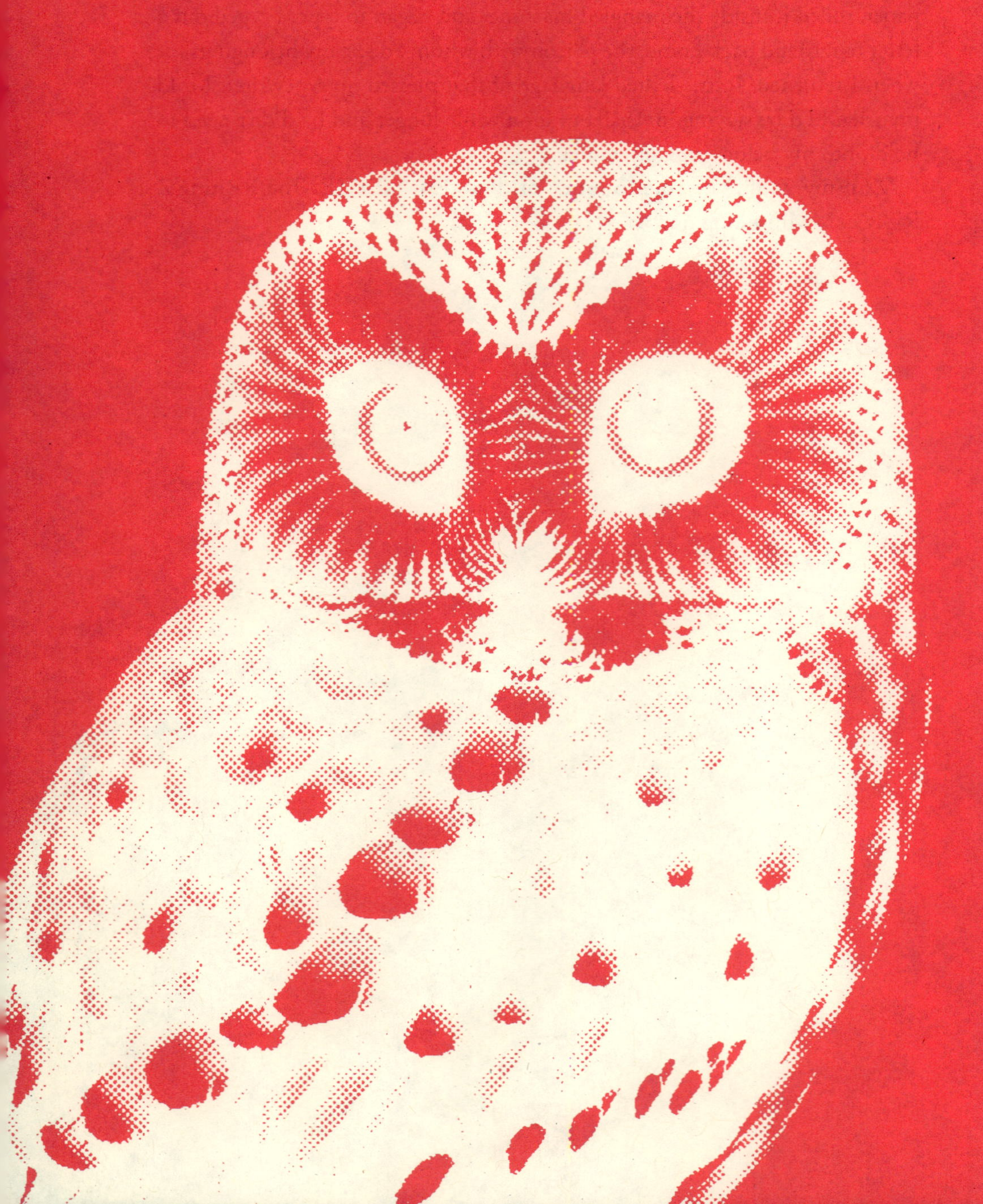

ANDREW GORIN

Argument

the genus of the place invites the she defends by addresses the night in the
obscura   love explodes all stars   morning and evening skies   the earth's
animal visits   phosphoric lights   luminous   discovery   gunpowder
applied   water-engines   electric   halo round the heads of saints
death draws.

Dear One Thousand Friends

In another life, I would call you to tell you not to worry about my monied past.
Our dogs died in the same year and probably ate the same death.
It is also a dream I have.
I dream sex with each one of my plants
then I shoot myself out of the tree house of her love.
I built the treehouse.
I had always wanted it;
accent snakes, plasma, velour.
It is still intact, though the furniture has been lost.
And there were pests, horrible horrible pests!
which I am just now beginning to understand.

All My Enemies

I gave a little blood today and made the park grow metallic skin.
Three dimensional portraits of the situation revealed plotters to the north.
In the woods, they were reenacting nos. 1 through 7 of my fatal flaws.
(Number 8 requires a cast of ice continents and some lazy ass bears.)
I spoke with an understudy and ended up signing his gun.

All my enemies watch me from the dugout as I click through hairdos
to thwart my enemies. All my enemies terrace the future with
thank-you notes, camp on intimacies, plant death blossoms
in terrible night. My enemies and I eat enantiomorphic sandwiches
and call hotlines, and try to think historically about sex.

Last week one of my enemies called to say that he was leaving town.
Black feathers fell out of his bag.
We went for burgers and he interpreted my beard.
It's only coitus if you know you're free, he said.
I sleep and I sleep and I sleep.

Rest Assured

We will keep you updated about the urn situation.
Know that in this one horse town, everybody plays Jai Alai.
Just now a man walked by palming a coconut at his side like a concealed knife.
He seemed to be trying to understand.
Here is the real trick: getting the rabbit to wear the hat.
It was a ridiculous gift.
Meanwhile, I am making a study in con and arabesque:
The palm, the cesta, and the pelican's beak.
I enter the clearing, only to discover a strange color tampering with my van.
This is a game no foreigner will comprehend.
One horse is all we can stand.

God Anymore

this photographer
will forgive you

with somewhat
flat

windiness, or,

of speech,
with articles

unsegmented as
the tapeworm.

COMIX BLOCK

SPRING
2011

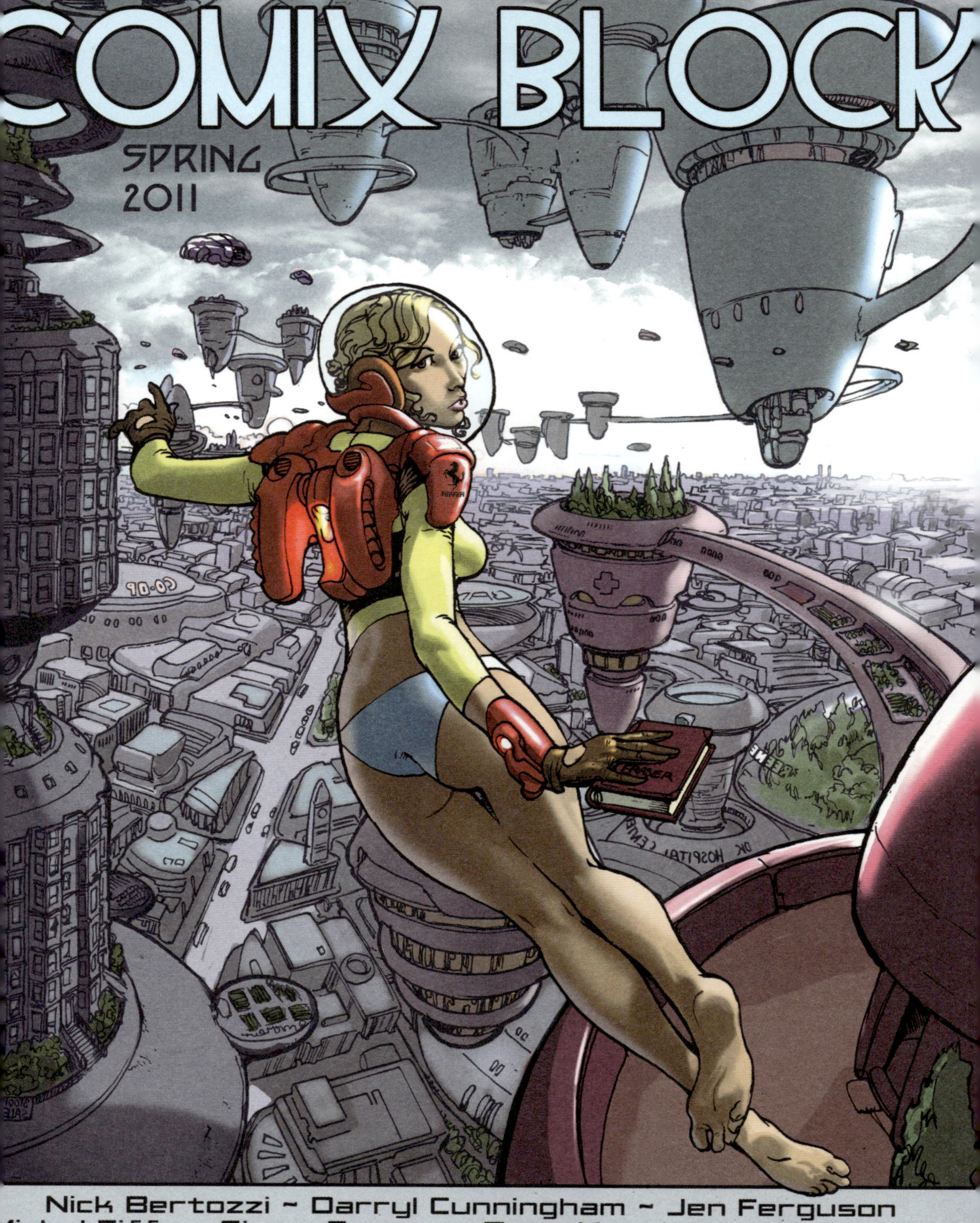

Nick Bertozzi ~ Darryl Cunningham ~ Jen Ferguson
Michel Fiffe ~ Simon Fraser ~ Dean Haspiel ~ Josh Neufeld
James Smith ~ JG Thirlwell

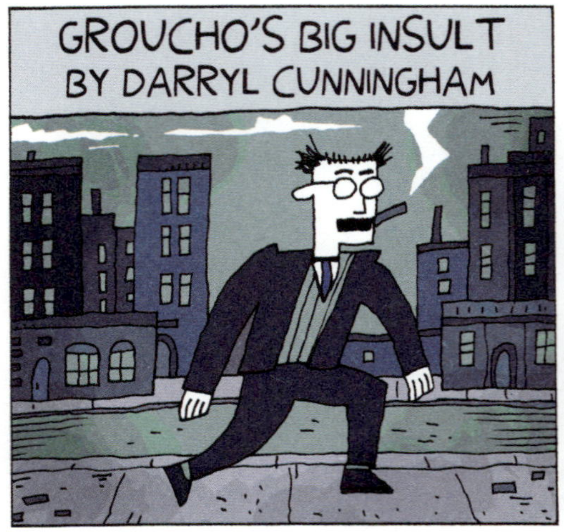
GROUCHO'S BIG INSULT
BY DARRYL CUNNINGHAM

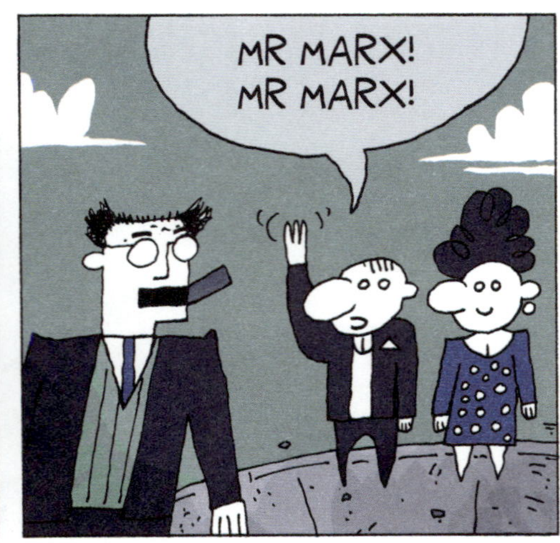
MR MARX!
MR MARX!

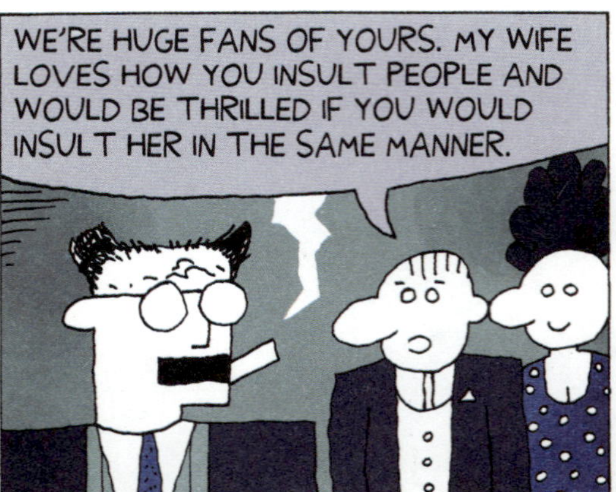
WE'RE HUGE FANS OF YOURS. MY WIFE LOVES HOW YOU INSULT PEOPLE AND WOULD BE THRILLED IF YOU WOULD INSULT HER IN THE SAME MANNER.

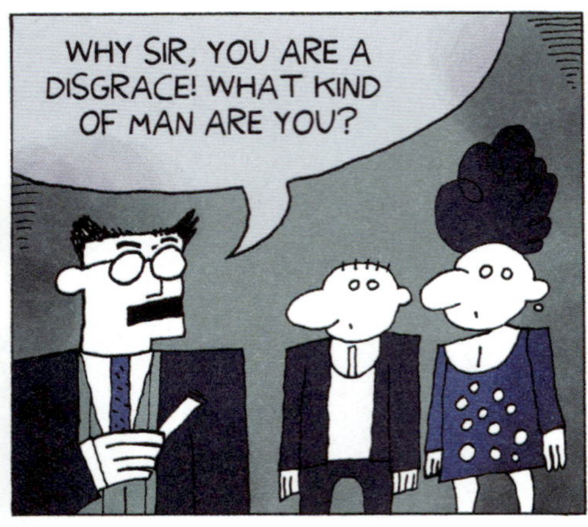
WHY SIR, YOU ARE A DISGRACE! WHAT KIND OF MAN ARE YOU?

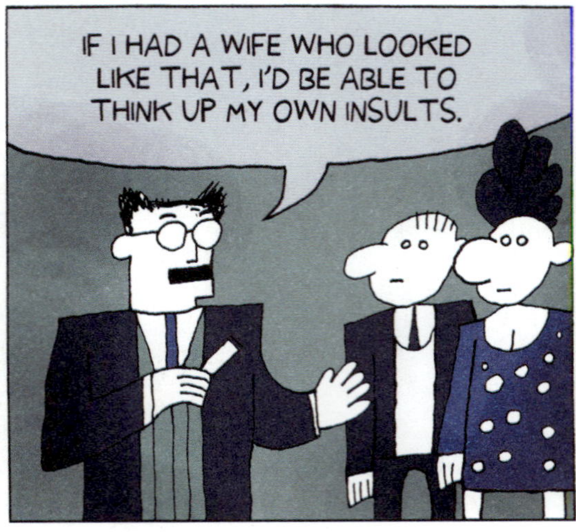
IF I HAD A WIFE WHO LOOKED LIKE THAT, I'D BE ABLE TO THINK UP MY OWN INSULTS.

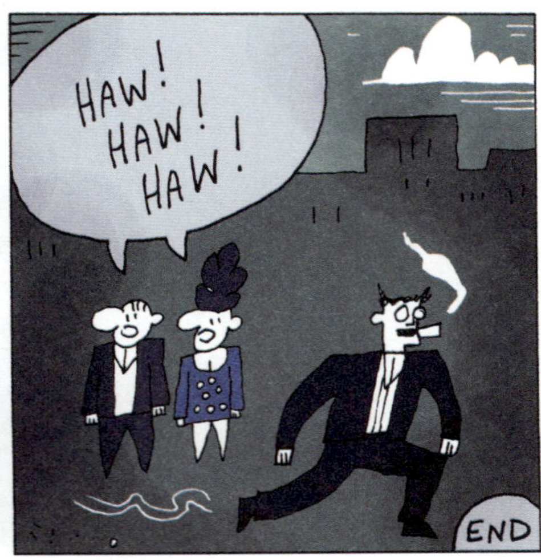
HAW! HAW! HAW!
END

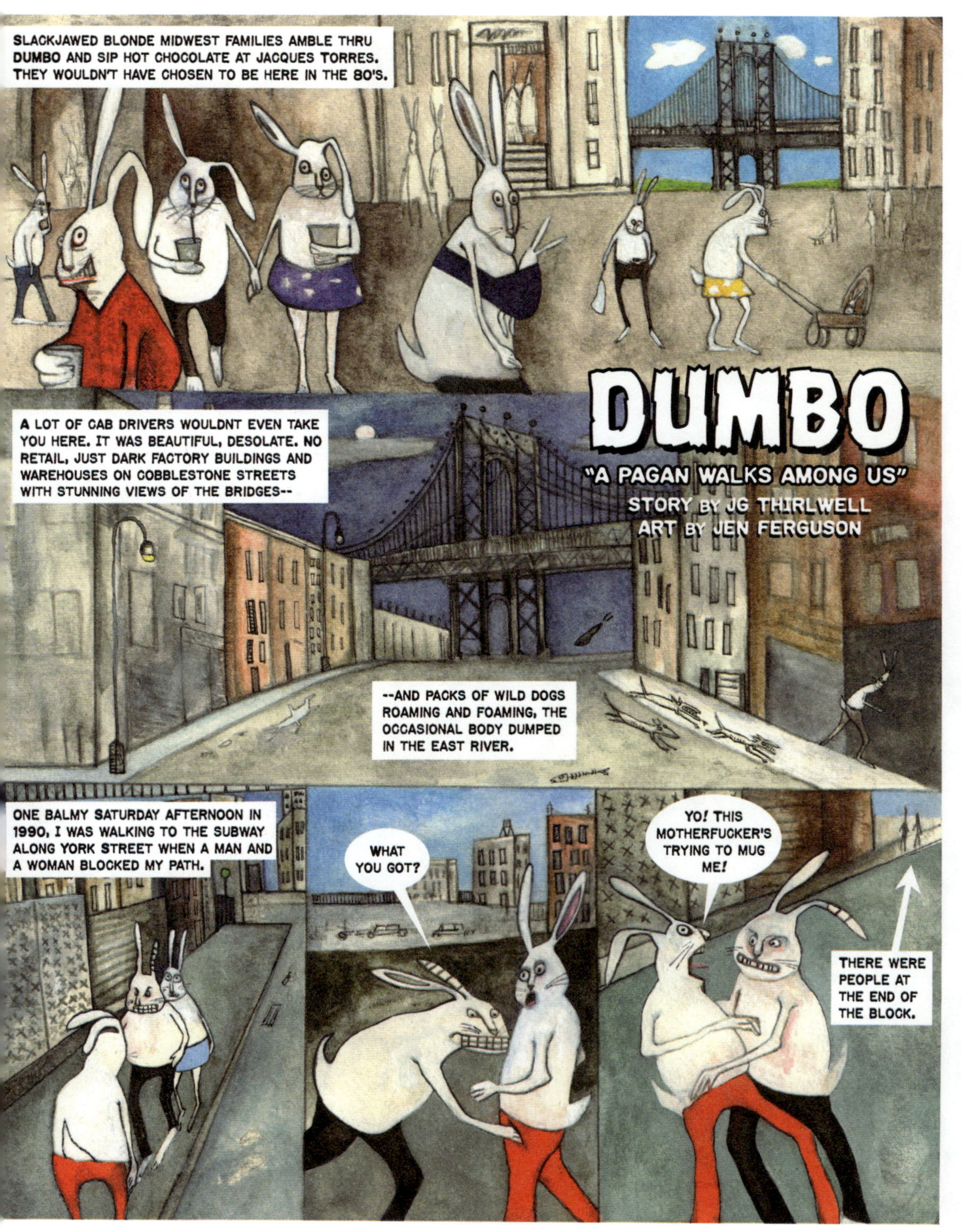
SLACKJAWED BLONDE MIDWEST FAMILIES AMBLE THRU DUMBO AND SIP HOT CHOCOLATE AT JACQUES TORRES. THEY WOULDN'T HAVE CHOSEN TO BE HERE IN THE 80'S.
DUMBO
"A PAGAN WALKS AMONG US"
STORY BY JG THIRLWELL
ART BY JEN FERGUSON
A LOT OF CAB DRIVERS WOULDNT EVEN TAKE YOU HERE. IT WAS BEAUTIFUL, DESOLATE. NO RETAIL, JUST DARK FACTORY BUILDINGS AND WAREHOUSES ON COBBLESTONE STREETS WITH STUNNING VIEWS OF THE BRIDGES--
--AND PACKS OF WILD DOGS ROAMING AND FOAMING, THE OCCASIONAL BODY DUMPED IN THE EAST RIVER.
ONE BALMY SATURDAY AFTERNOON IN 1990, I WAS WALKING TO THE SUBWAY ALONG YORK STREET WHEN A MAN AND A WOMAN BLOCKED MY PATH.
WHAT YOU GOT?
YO! THIS MOTHERFUCKER'S TRYING TO MUG ME!
THERE WERE PEOPLE AT THE END OF THE BLOCK.

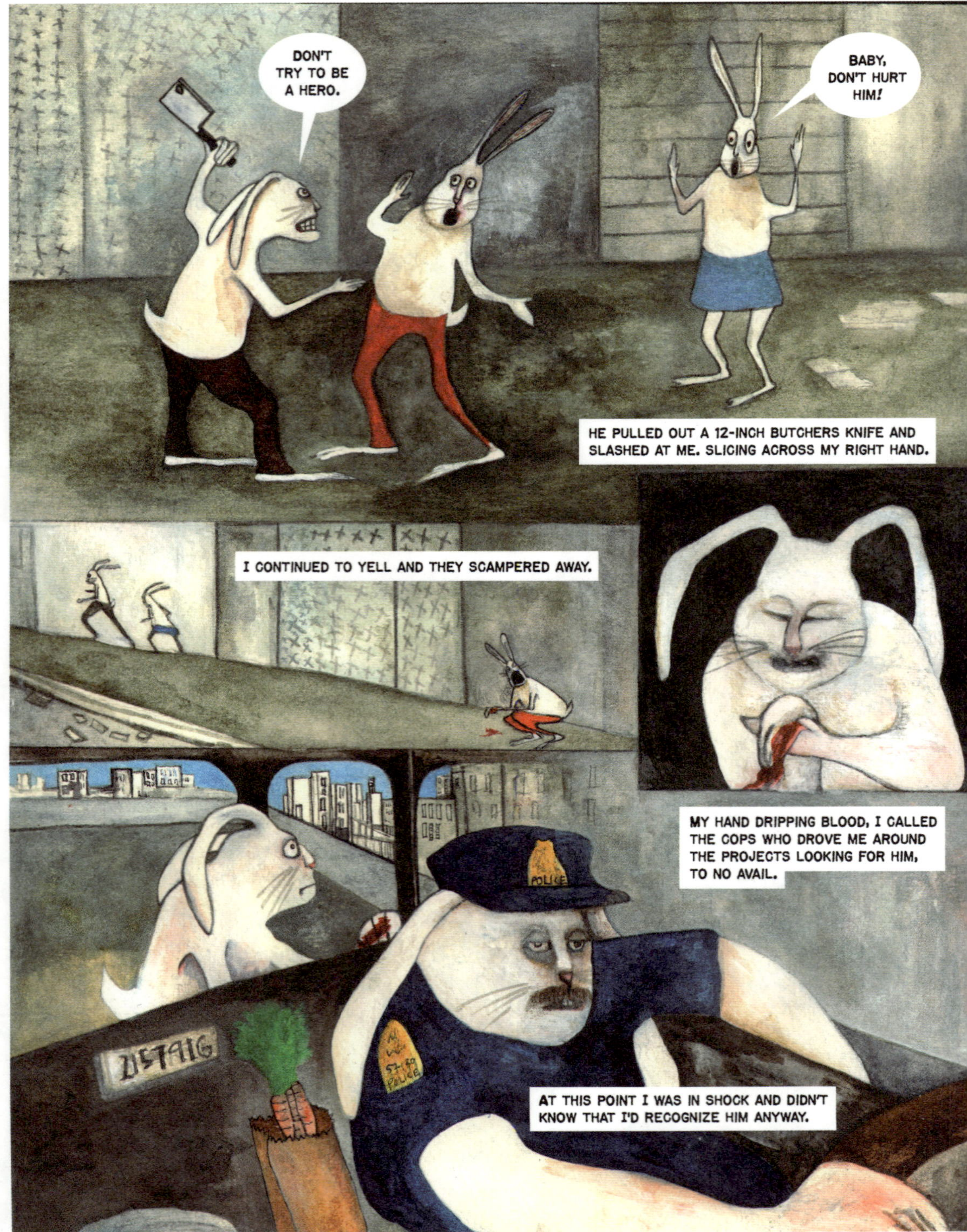
DON'T TRY TO BE A HERO.
BABY, DON'T HURT HIM!
HE PULLED OUT A 12-INCH BUTCHERS KNIFE AND SLASHED AT ME. SLICING ACROSS MY RIGHT HAND.
I CONTINUED TO YELL AND THEY SCAMPERED AWAY.
MY HAND DRIPPING BLOOD, I CALLED THE COPS WHO DROVE ME AROUND THE PROJECTS LOOKING FOR HIM, TO NO AVAIL.
POLICE
AT THIS POINT I WAS IN SHOCK AND DIDN'T KNOW THAT I'D RECOGNIZE HIM ANYWAY.

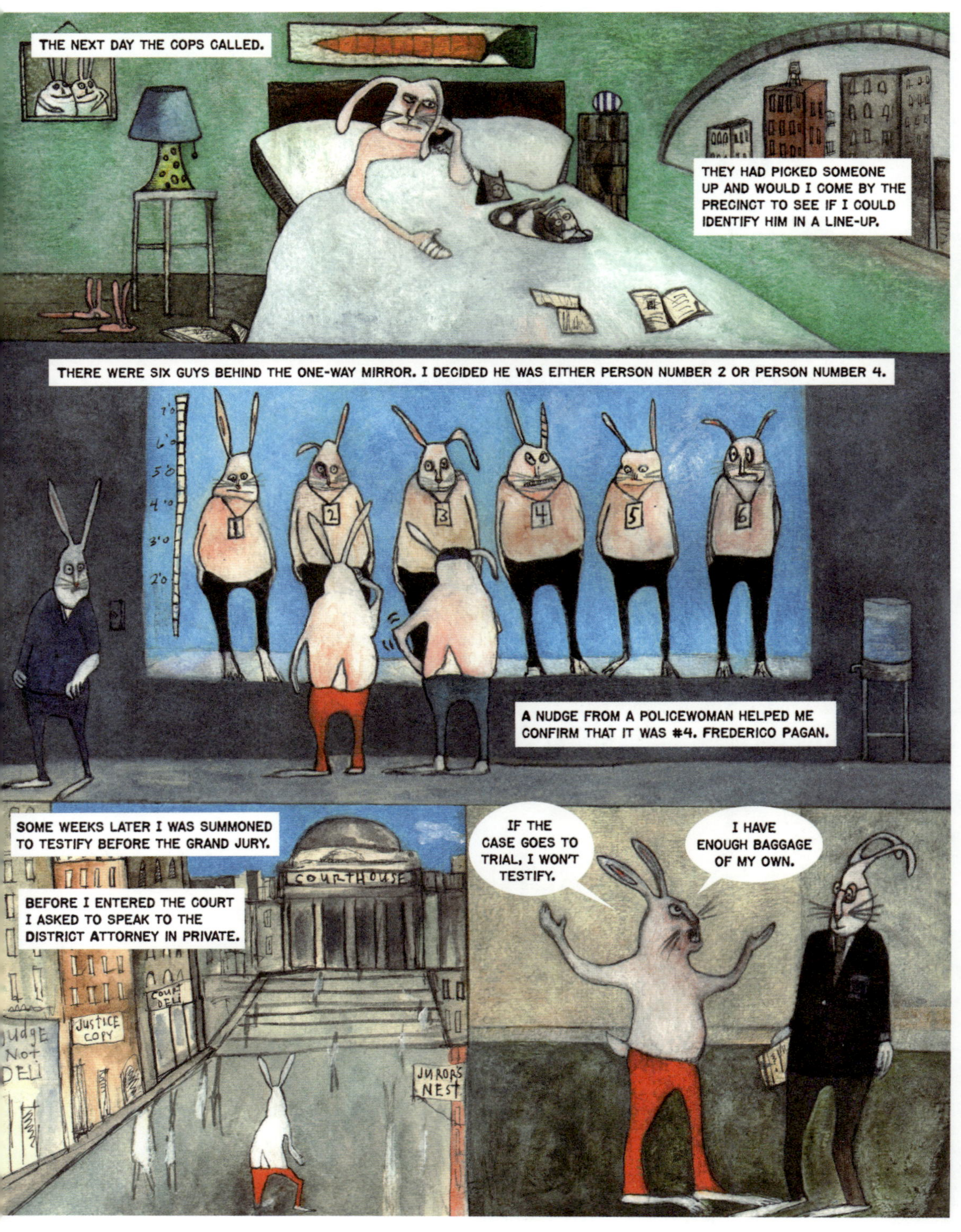
THE NEXT DAY THE COPS CALLED.
THEY HAD PICKED SOMEONE UP AND WOULD I COME BY THE PRECINCT TO SEE IF I COULD IDENTIFY HIM IN A LINE-UP.
THERE WERE SIX GUYS BEHIND THE ONE-WAY MIRROR. I DECIDED HE WAS EITHER PERSON NUMBER 2 OR PERSON NUMBER 4.
7'0
6'0
5'0
4'0
3'0
2'0
1
2
3
4
5
6
A NUDGE FROM A POLICEWOMAN HELPED ME CONFIRM THAT IT WAS #4. FREDERICO PAGAN.
SOME WEEKS LATER I WAS SUMMONED TO TESTIFY BEFORE THE GRAND JURY.
BEFORE I ENTERED THE COURT I ASKED TO SPEAK TO THE DISTRICT ATTORNEY IN PRIVATE.
COURTHOUSE
COURT DELI
JUSTICE COPY
JUDGE NOT DELI
JUROR'S NEST
IF THE CASE GOES TO TRIAL, I WON'T TESTIFY.
I HAVE ENOUGH BAGGAGE OF MY OWN.

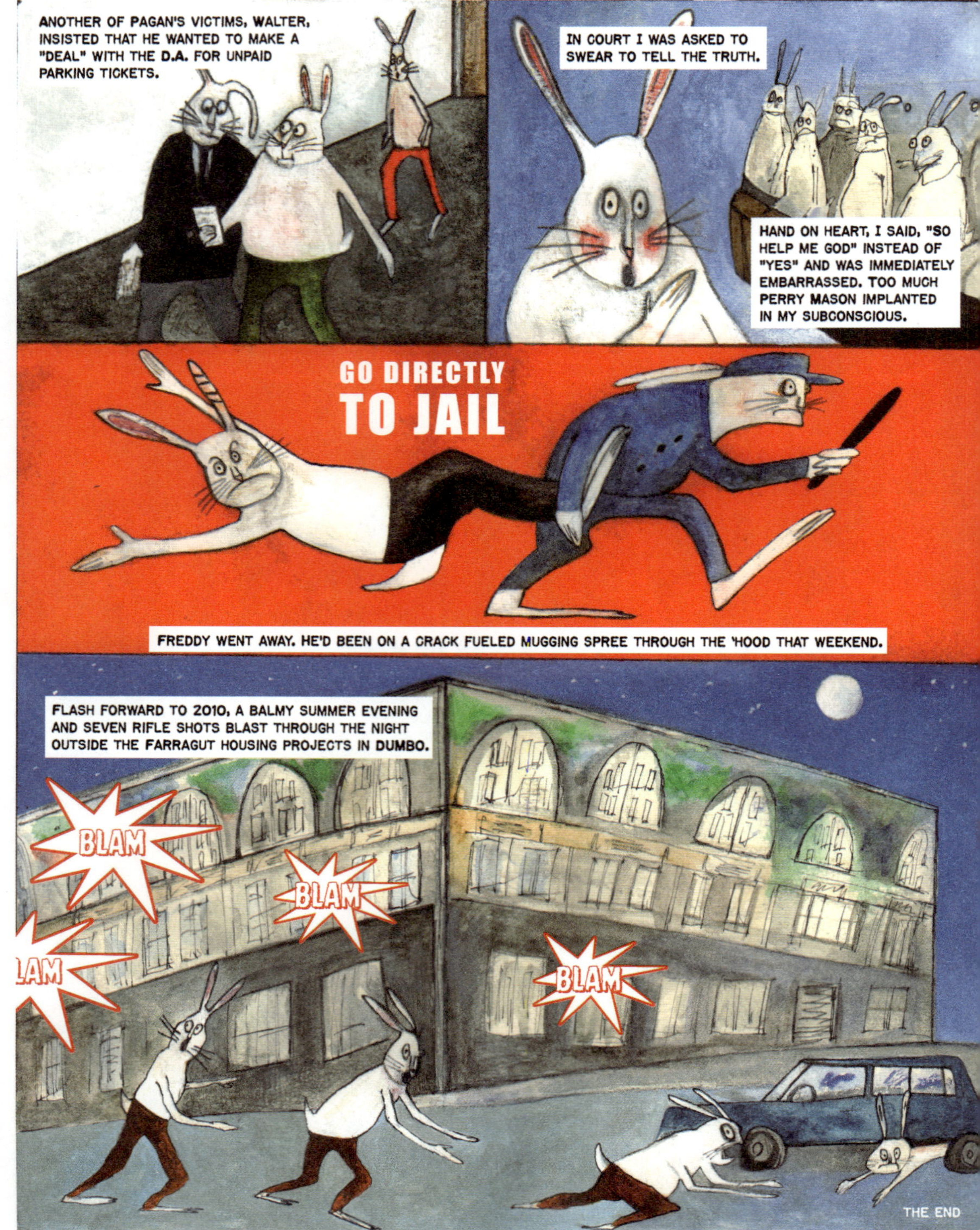
ANOTHER OF PAGAN'S VICTIMS, WALTER, INSISTED THAT HE WANTED TO MAKE A "DEAL" WITH THE D.A. FOR UNPAID PARKING TICKETS.
IN COURT I WAS ASKED TO SWEAR TO TELL THE TRUTH.
HAND ON HEART, I SAID, "SO HELP ME GOD" INSTEAD OF "YES" AND WAS IMMEDIATELY EMBARRASSED. TOO MUCH PERRY MASON IMPLANTED IN MY SUBCONSCIOUS.
GO DIRECTLY TO JAIL
FREDDY WENT AWAY. HE'D BEEN ON A CRACK FUELED MUGGING SPREE THROUGH THE 'HOOD THAT WEEKEND.
FLASH FORWARD TO 2010, A BALMY SUMMER EVENING AND SEVEN RIFLE SHOTS BLAST THROUGH THE NIGHT OUTSIDE THE FARRAGUT HOUSING PROJECTS IN DUMBO.
BLAM
BLAM
LAM
BLAM
THE END

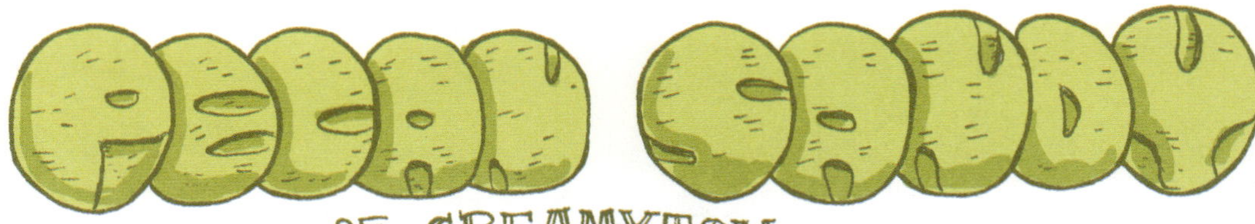

OF CREAMYTON

by NuB

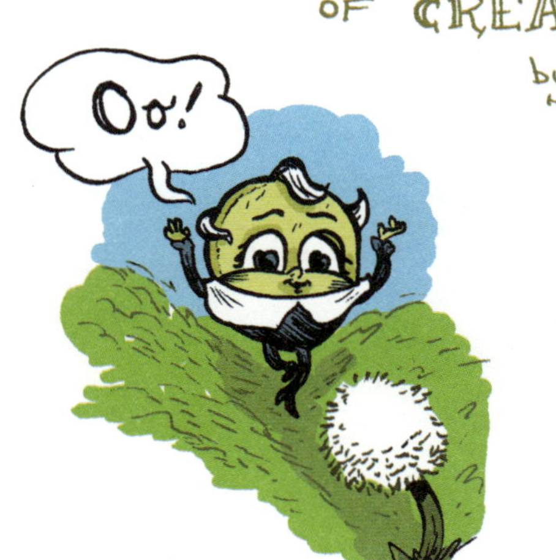

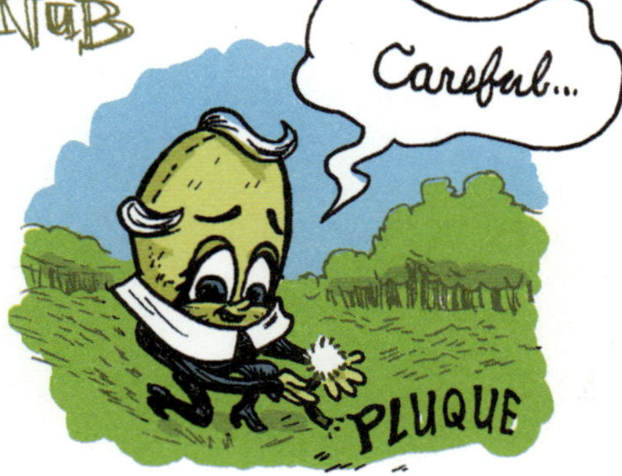

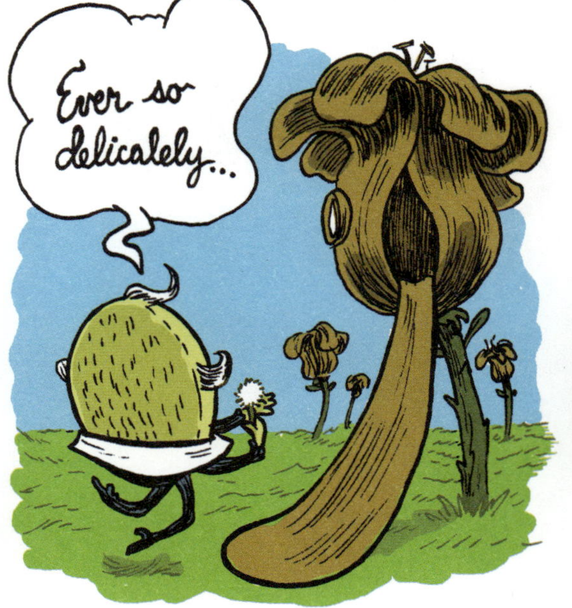

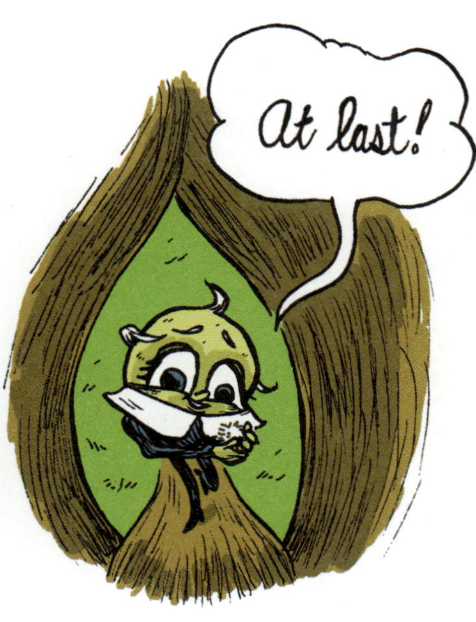

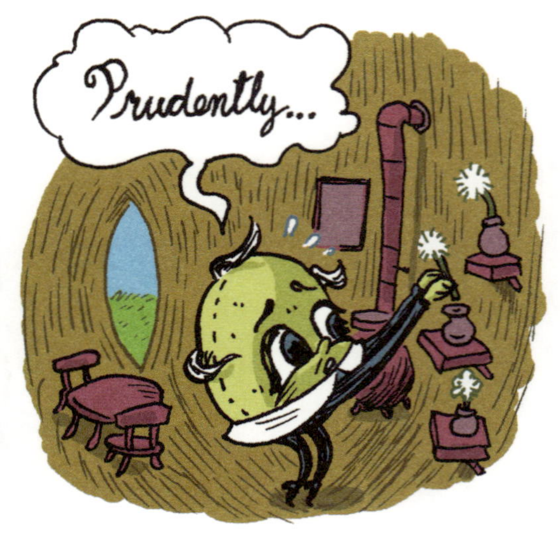
Prudently...

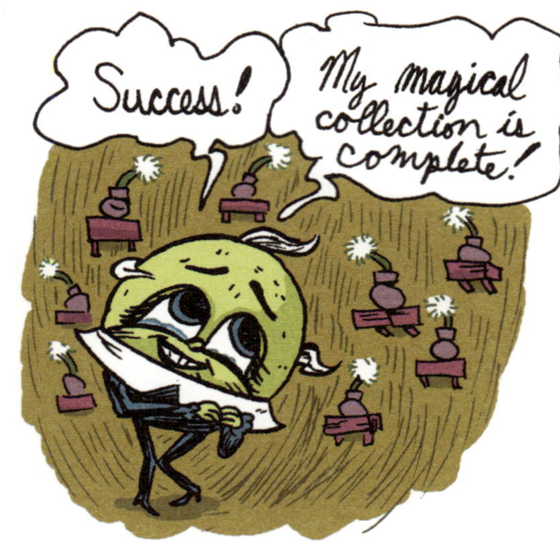
Success!
My magical collection is complete!

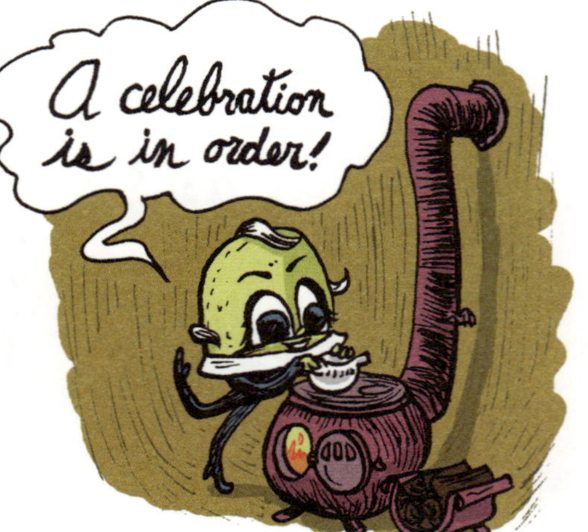
A celebration is in order!

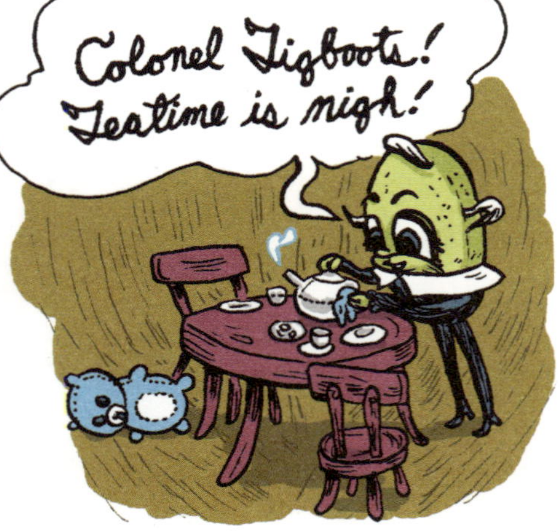
Colonel Jigboots! Teatime is nigh!

Have you *EVER* seen a more perfect domicile, Colonel?

What's the matter, Colonel? Isn't the camomile to your liking?

You're being **MOST** disagreeable, Colonel!

Do finish your tea!

I declare: it seems as though you **want** to provoke me--

HARK!

That sound...

Ssss

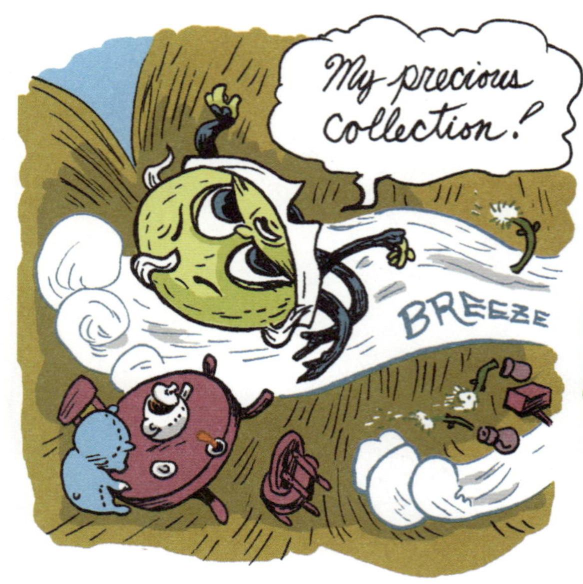
My precious collection!
BREEZE

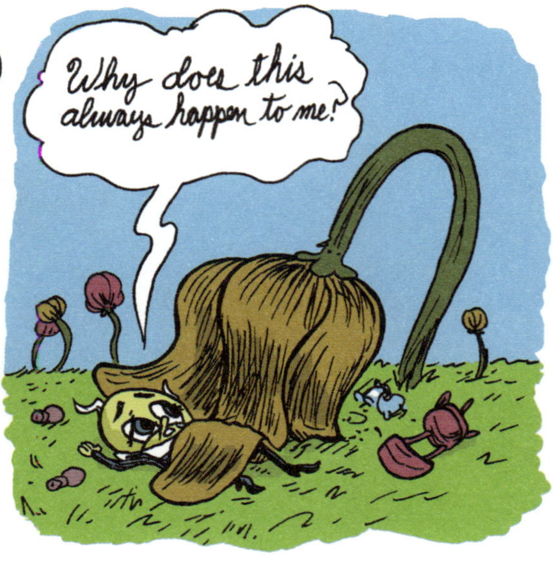
Why does this always happen to me?

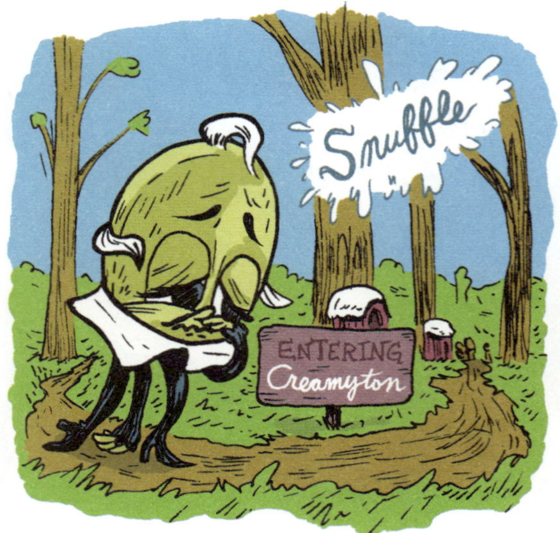
Snuffle
ENTERING
Creamyton

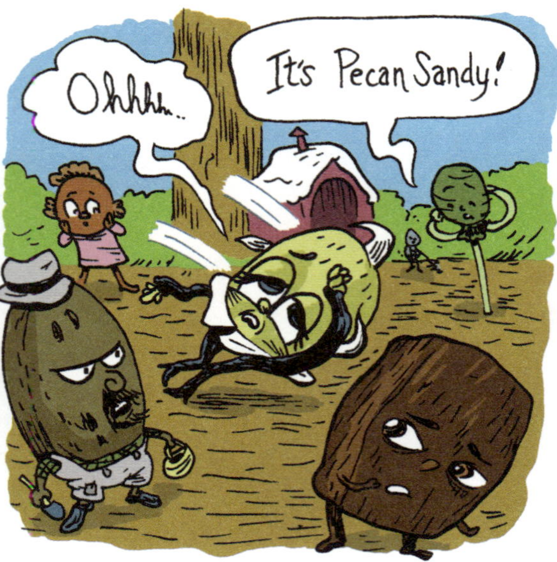
Ohhhh..
It's Pecan Sandy!

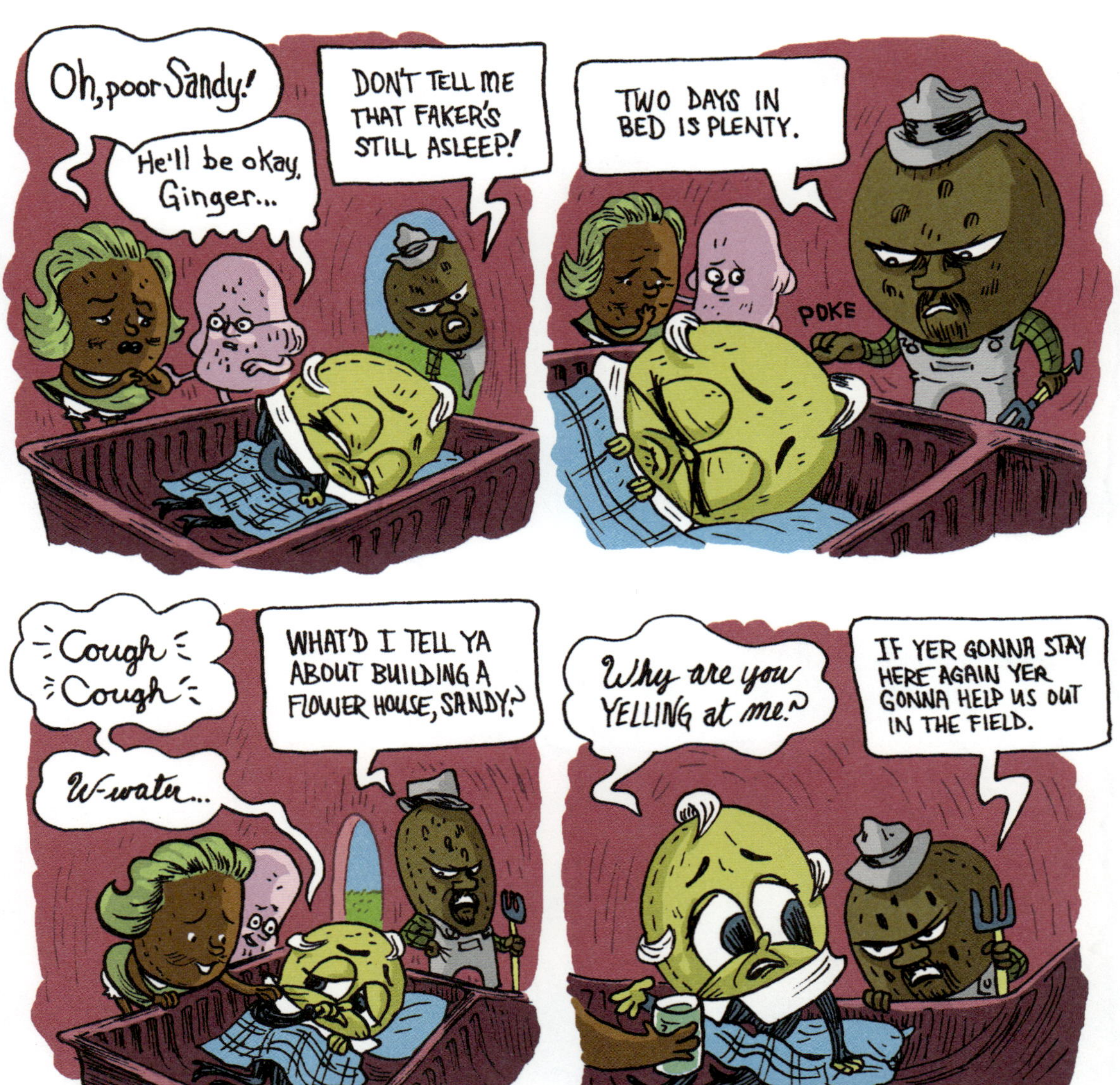
Oh, poor Sandy!
He'll be okay, Ginger...
DON'T TELL ME THAT FAKER'S STILL ASLEEP!
TWO DAYS IN BED IS PLENTY.
POKE
Cough Cough
W-water...
WHAT'D I TELL YA ABOUT BUILDING A FLOWER HOUSE, SANDY?
Why are you YELLING at me?
IF YER GONNA STAY HERE AGAIN YER GONNA HELP US OUT IN THE FIELD.

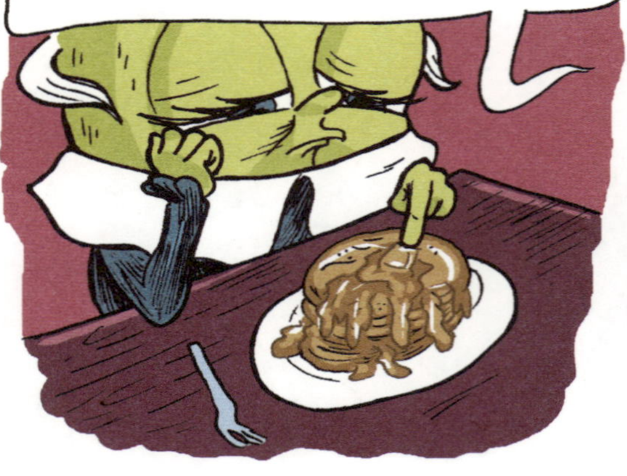
You're not hungry, Pecan Sandy?

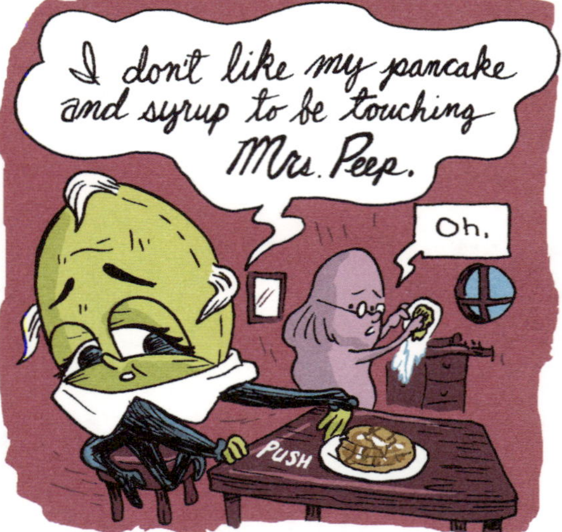
I don't like my pancake and syrup to be touching Mrs. Peep.
Oh.
PUSH

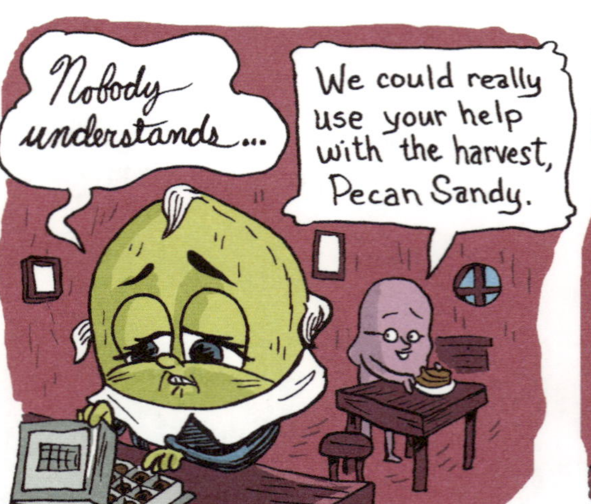
Nobody understands...
We could really use your help with the harvest, Pecan Sandy.

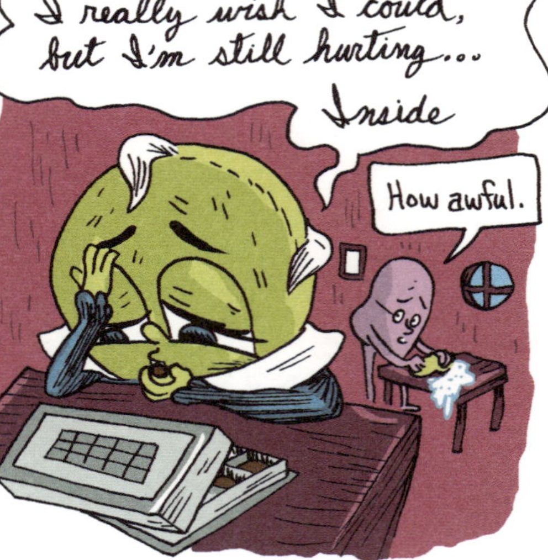
I really wish I could, but I'm still hurting... Inside
How awful.

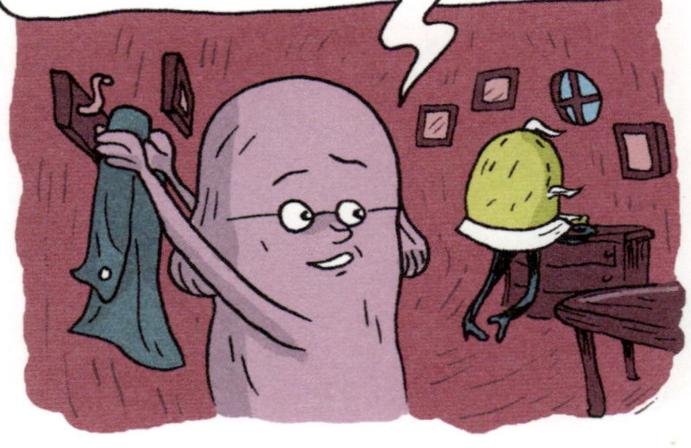
You know, Pecan Sandy, I think the camraderie of the harvest could do you a world of good.

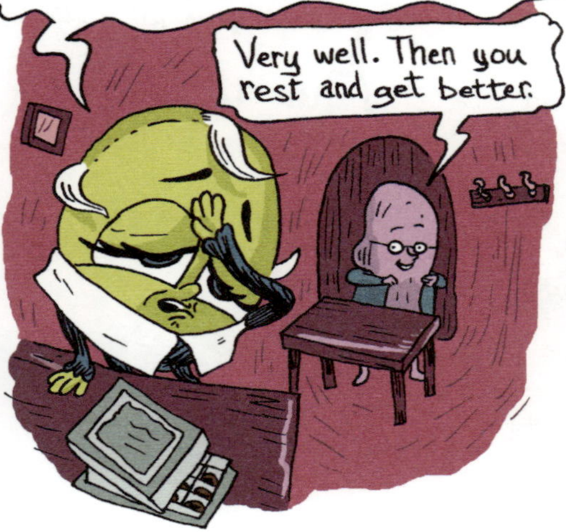
I'm simply too traumatized...
Very well. Then you rest and get better.

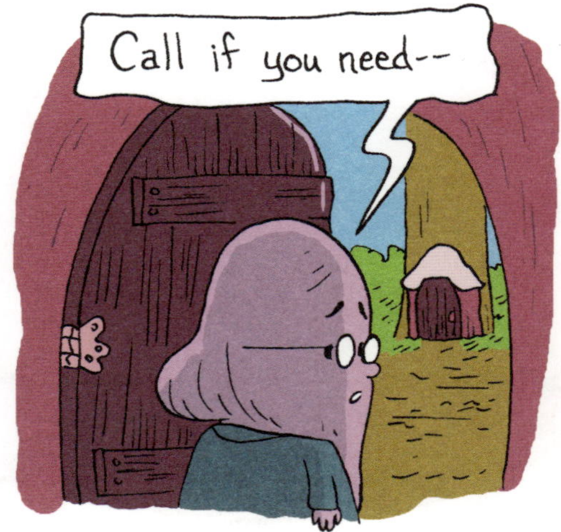
Call if you need--

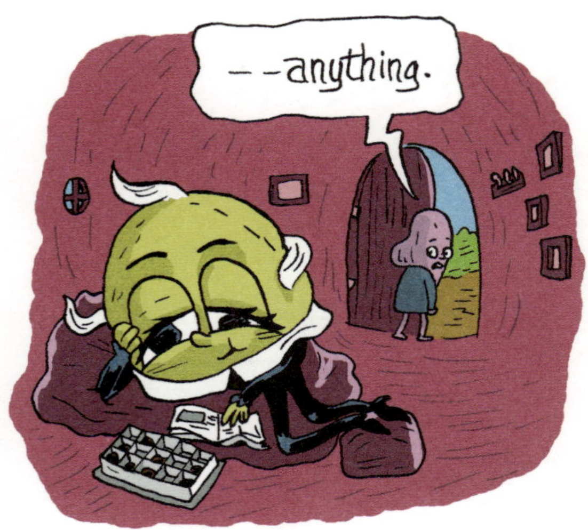
--anything.

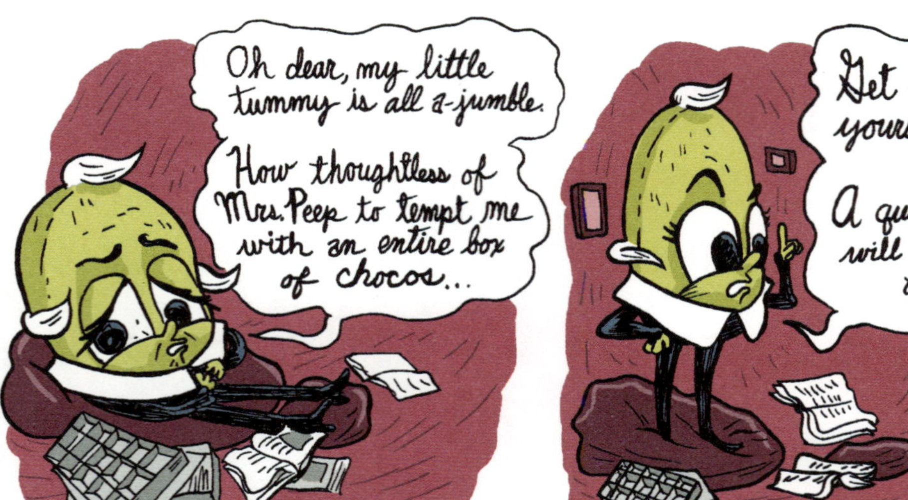
Oh dear, my little tummy is all a-jumble.
How thoughtless of Mrs. Peep to tempt me with an entire box of chocos...
Get ahold of yourself, Pecan!
A quick constitutiona will set things aright!

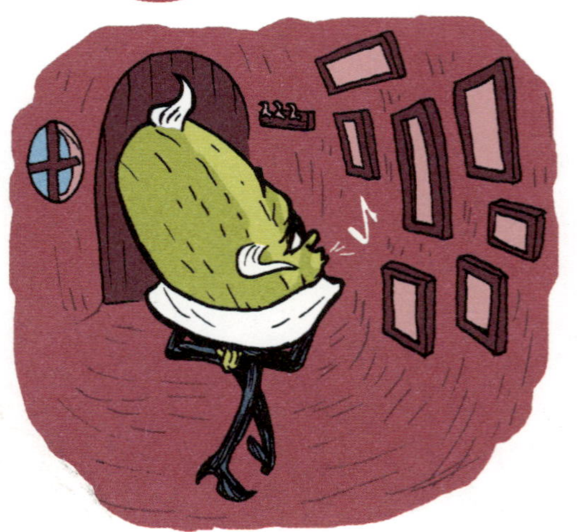

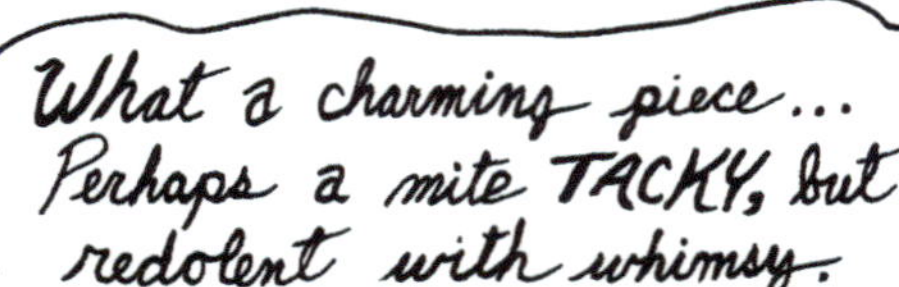
What a charming piece... Perhaps a mite TACKY, but redolent with whimsy.

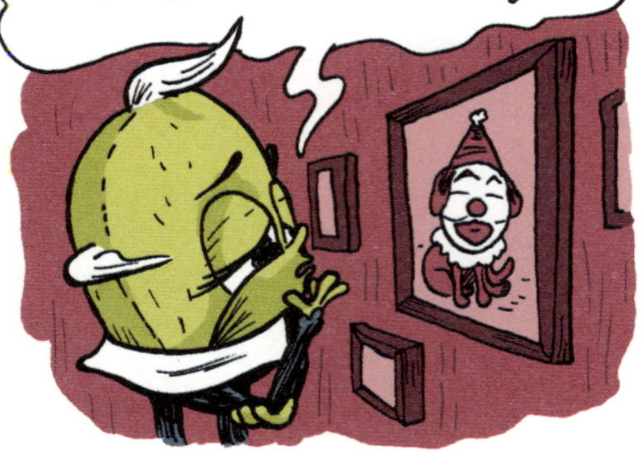

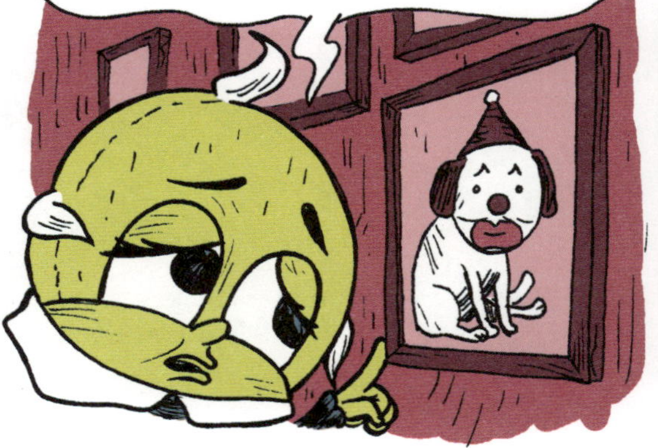
I wish I had a fine collection like this...

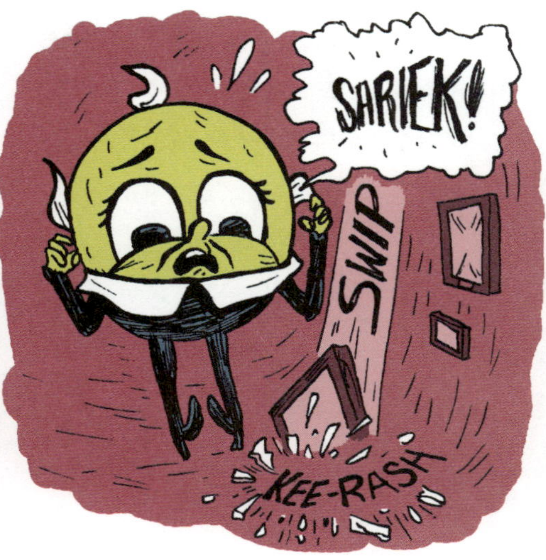
SHRIEK!
SWIP
KEE-RASH

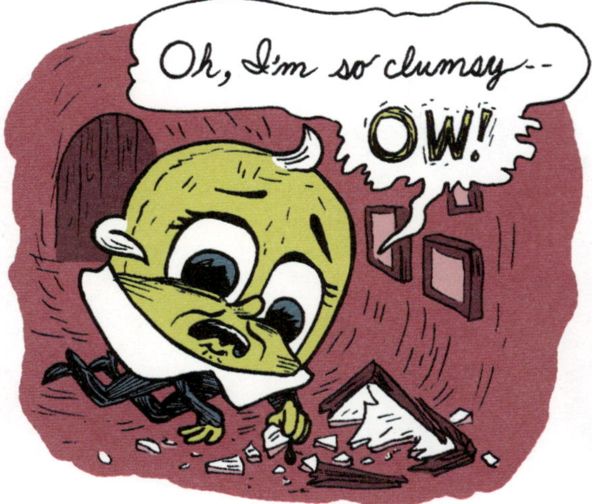
Oh, I'm so clumsy--
OW!

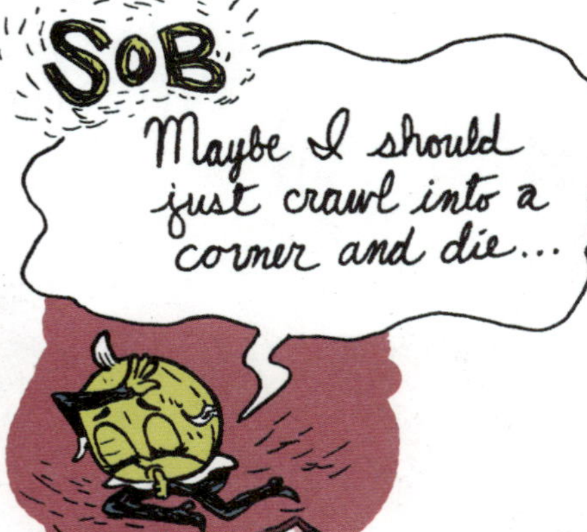
SOB
Maybe I should just crawl into a corner and die...

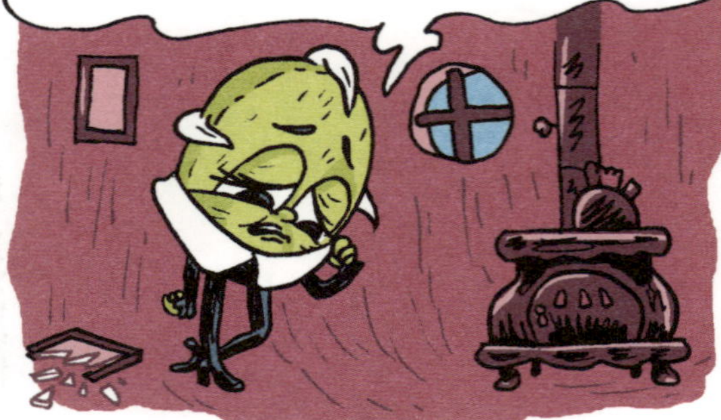
I should just make a cup of camomile and wait for the end...

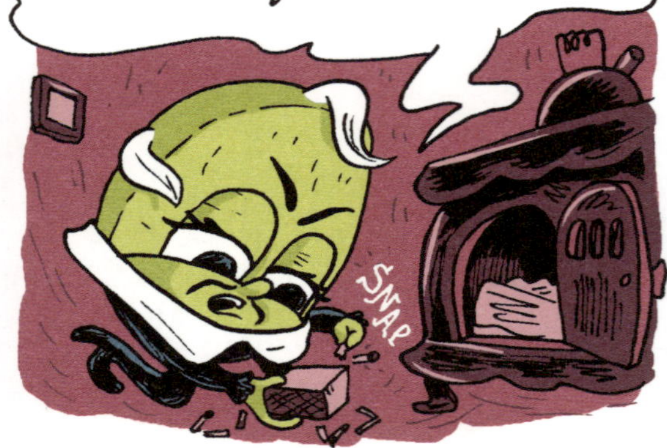
UGH! I can't do these ones! They're too hard!
SNAP

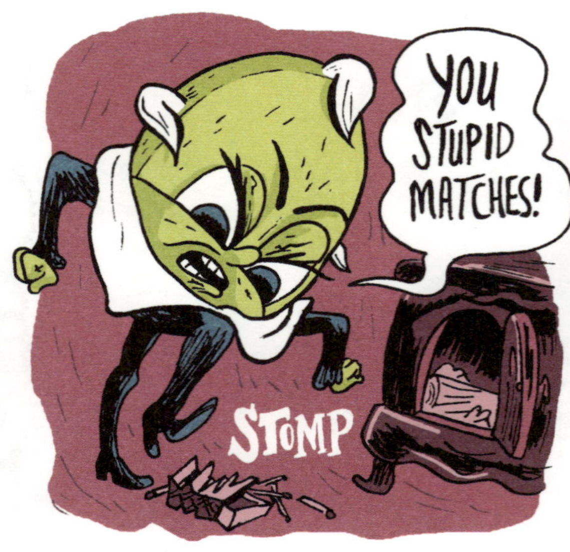
YOU STUPID MATCHES!
STOMP

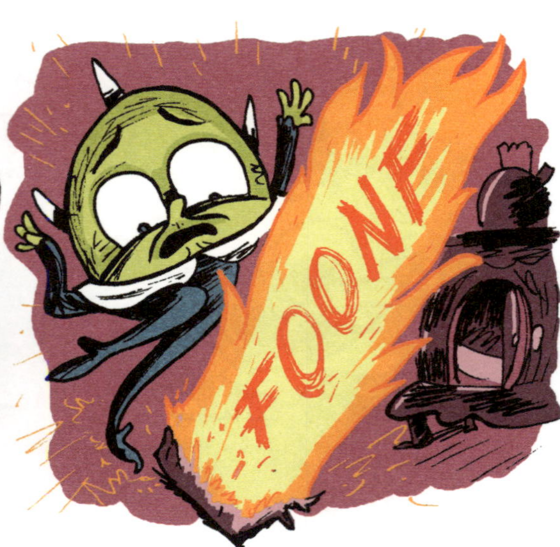
FOOMF

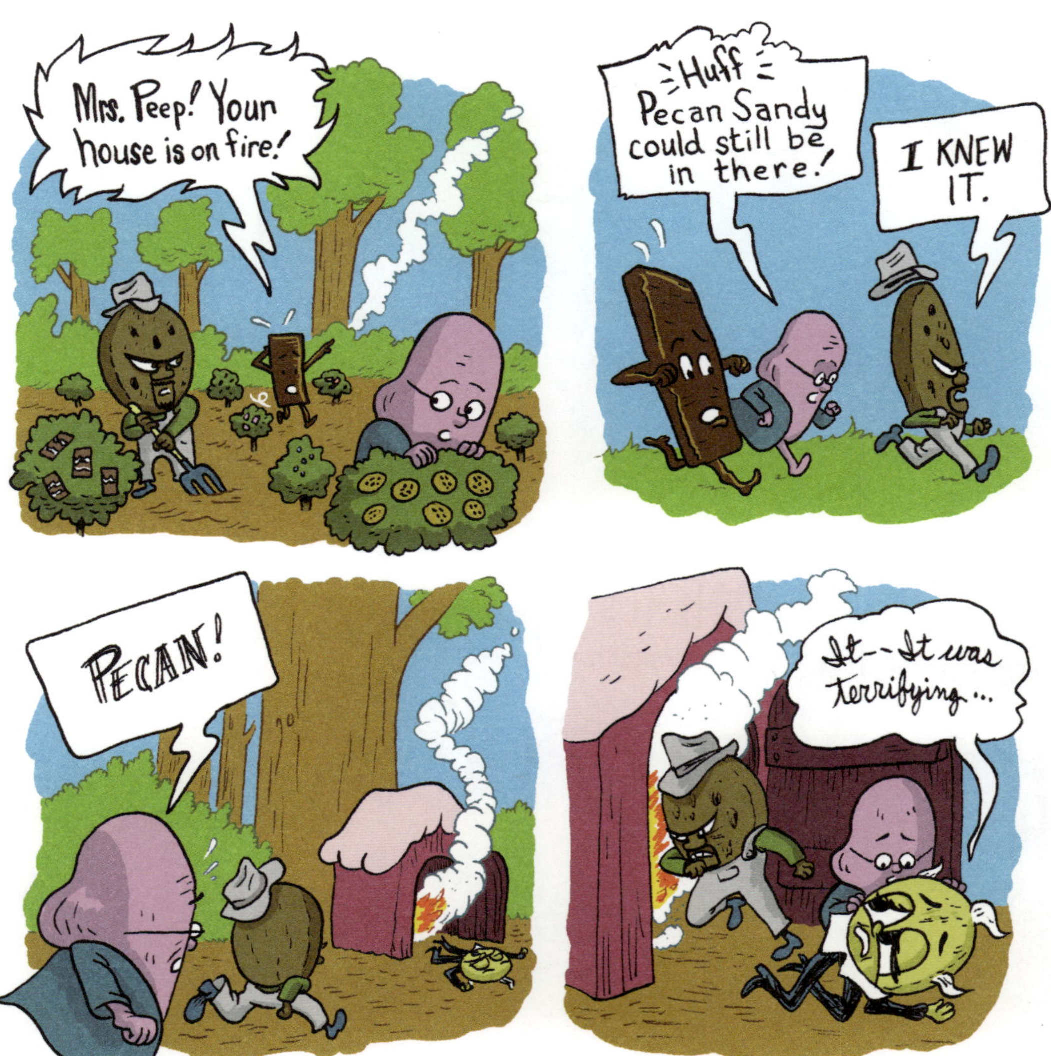
Mrs. Peep! Your house is on fire!
Huff
Pecan Sandy could still be in there!
I KNEW IT.
PECAN!
It-- It was terrifying...

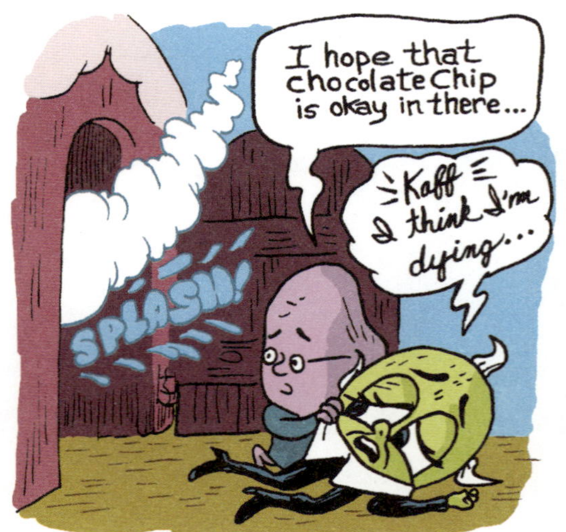
I hope that chocolate Chip is okay in there...
SPLASH!
Kaff I think I'm dying...

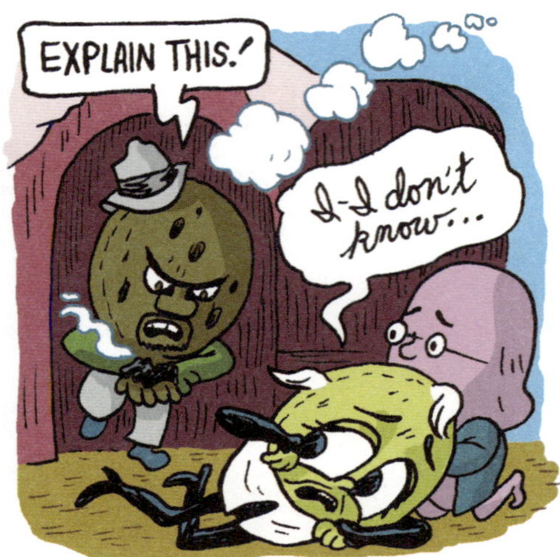
EXPLAIN THIS.!
I-I don't know...

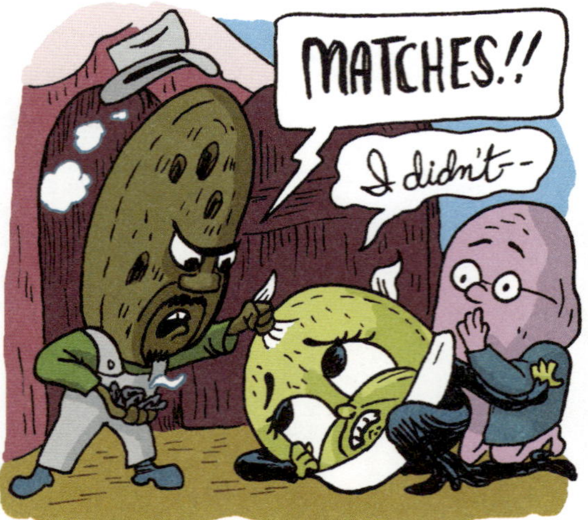
MATCHES!!
I didn't-

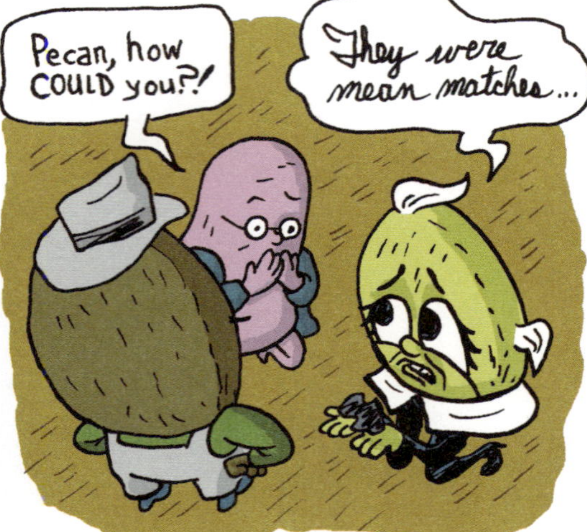
Pecan, how COULD you?!
They were mean matches...

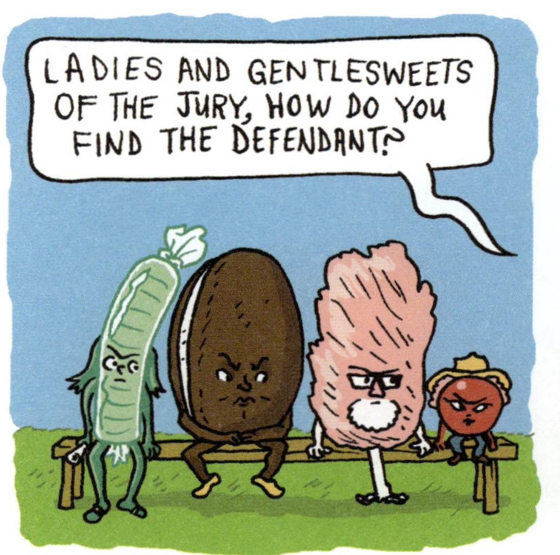
LADIES AND GENTLESWEETS OF THE JURY, HOW DO YOU FIND THE DEFENDANT?

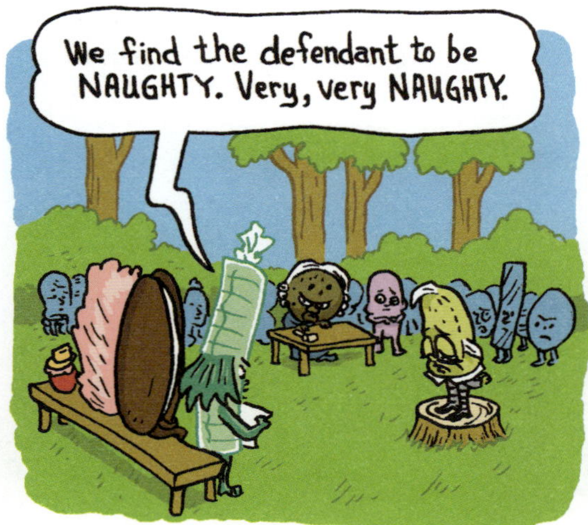
We find the defendant to be NAUGHTY. Very, very NAUGHTY.

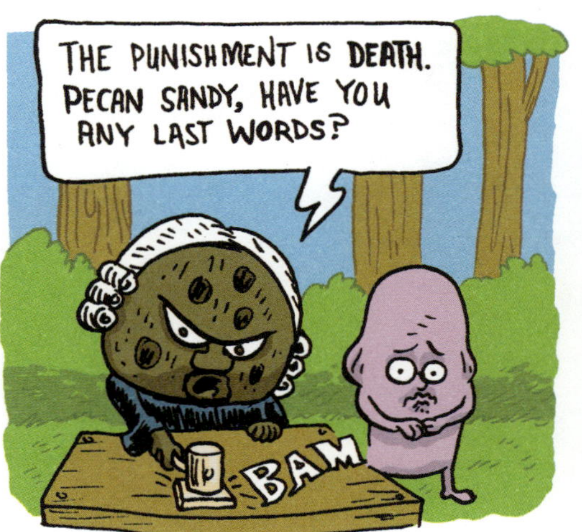
THE PUNISHMENT IS DEATH. PECAN SANDY, HAVE YOU ANY LAST WORDS?
BAM

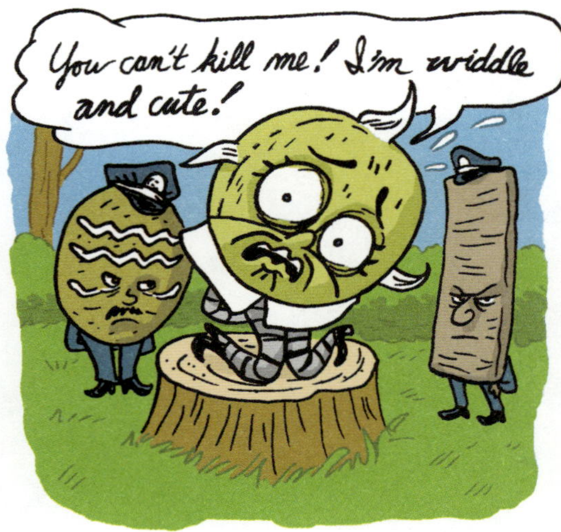
You can't kill me! I'm widdle and cute!

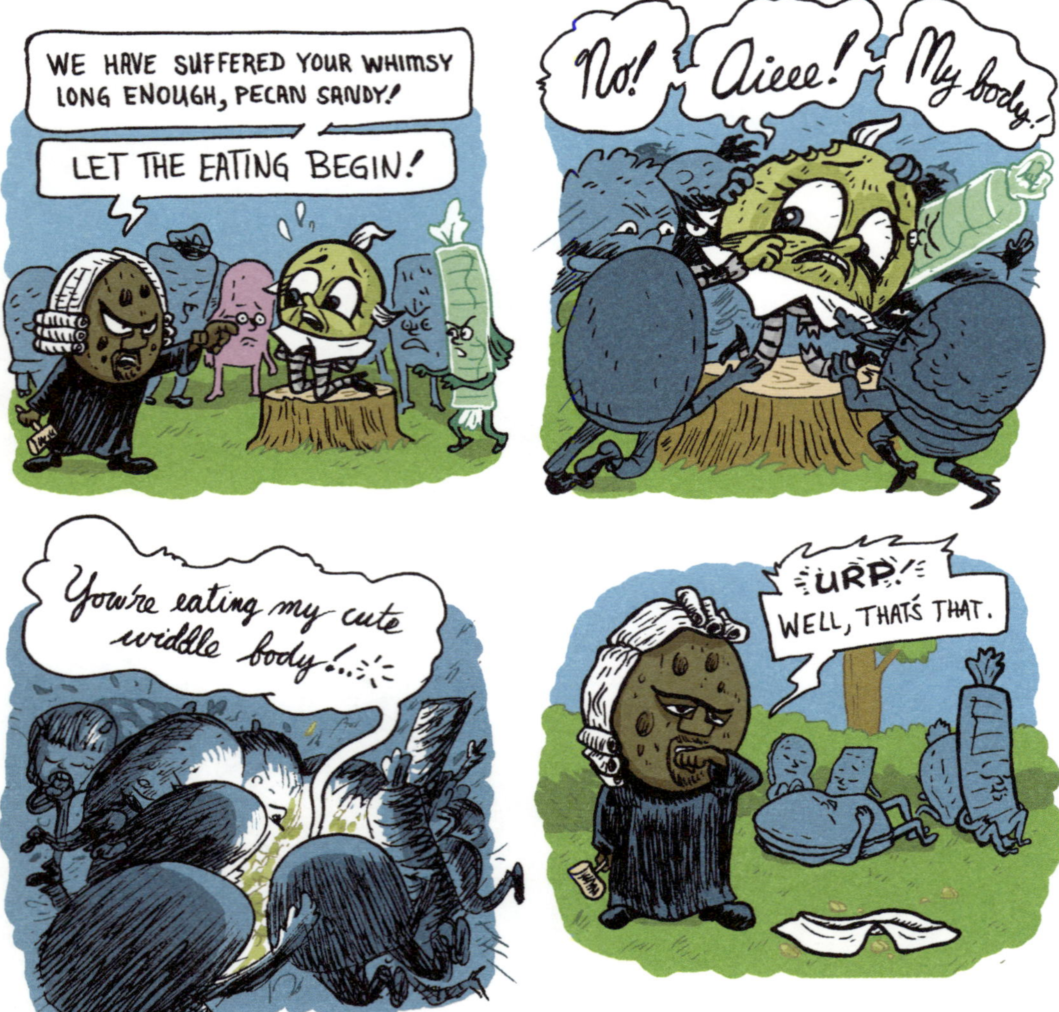
WE HAVE SUFFERED YOUR WHIMSY LONG ENOUGH, PECAN SANDY!
LET THE EATING BEGIN!
No!
Aieee!
My body!
You're eating my cute widdle body!...
URP!
WELL, THAT'S THAT.

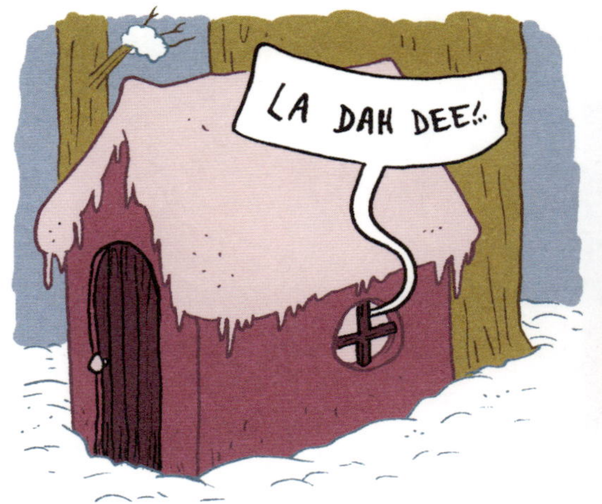
LA DAH DEE!..

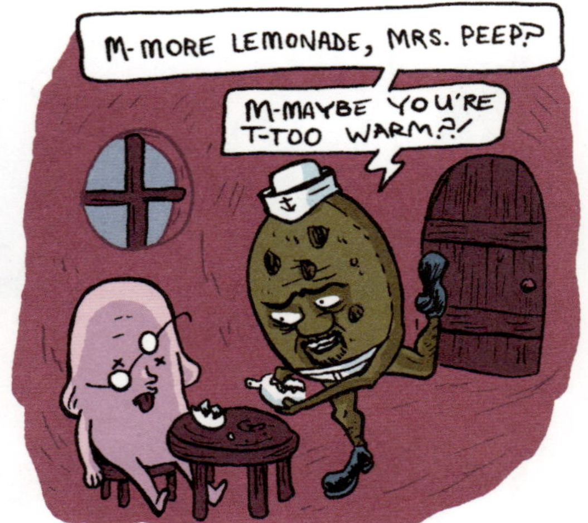
M-MORE LEMONADE, MRS. PEEP?
M-MAYBE YOU'RE T-TOO WARM?!

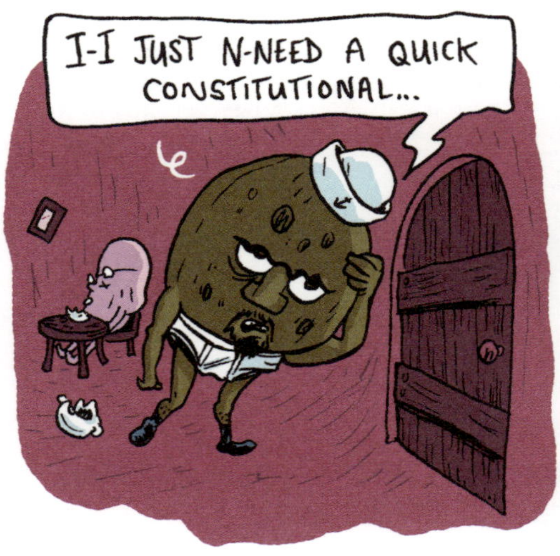
I-I JUST N-NEED A QUICK CONSTITUTIONAL...

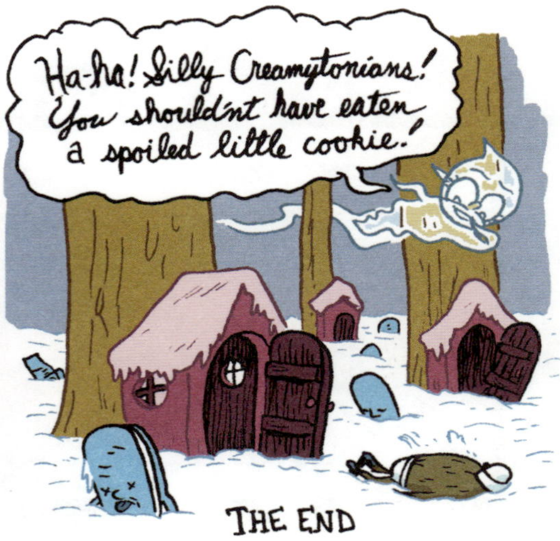
Ha-ha! Silly Creamytonians! You shouldn't have eaten a spoiled little cookie!
THE END

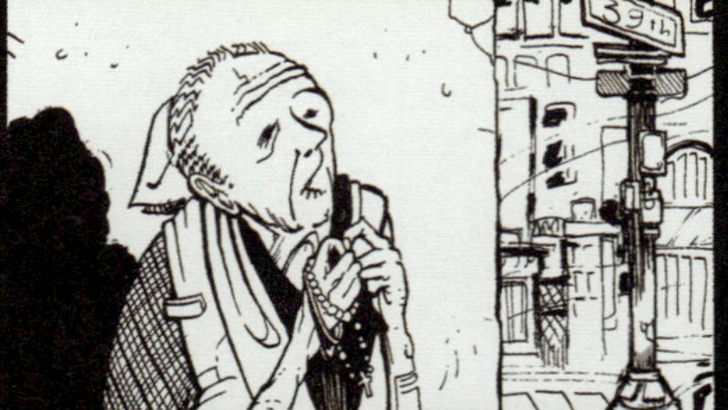

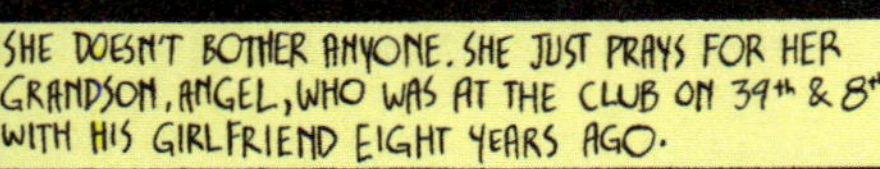

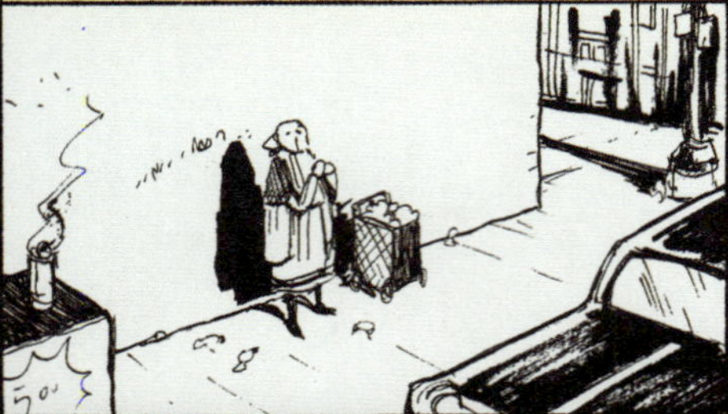

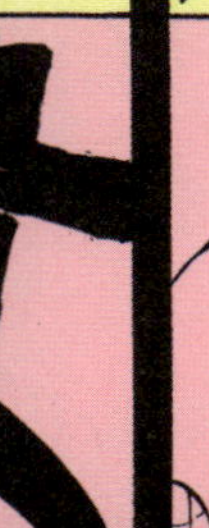

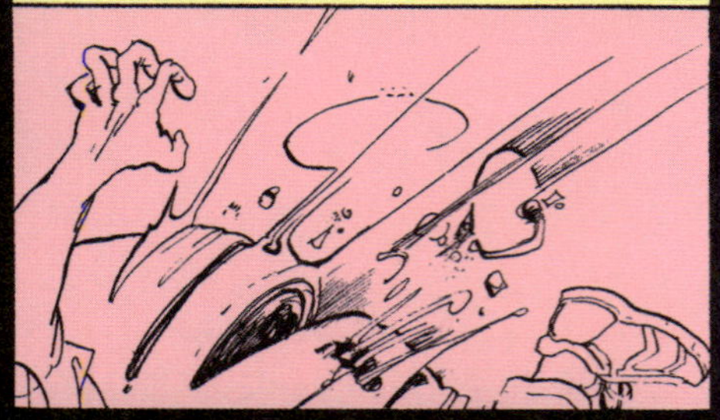

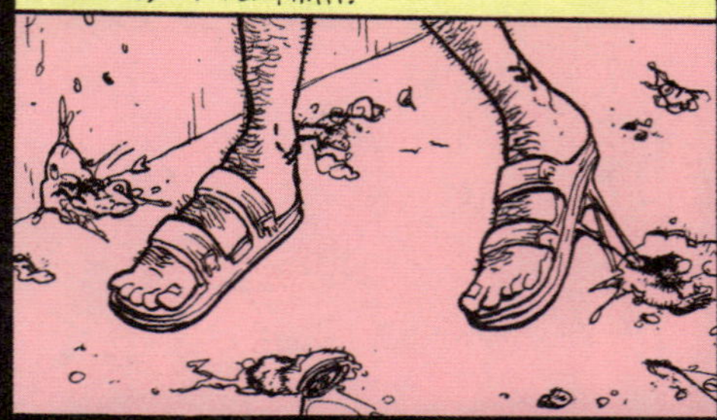

NO MATTER HOW MANY COATS OF PAINT ARE APPLIED, THEY STILL CAN'T GET THE STAINS OFF OF THE WALL.

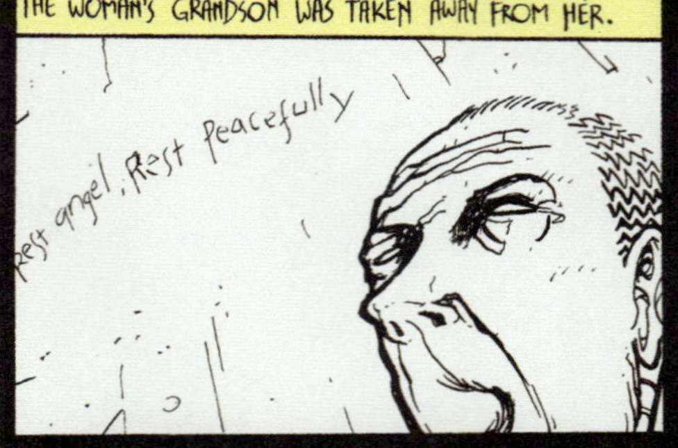

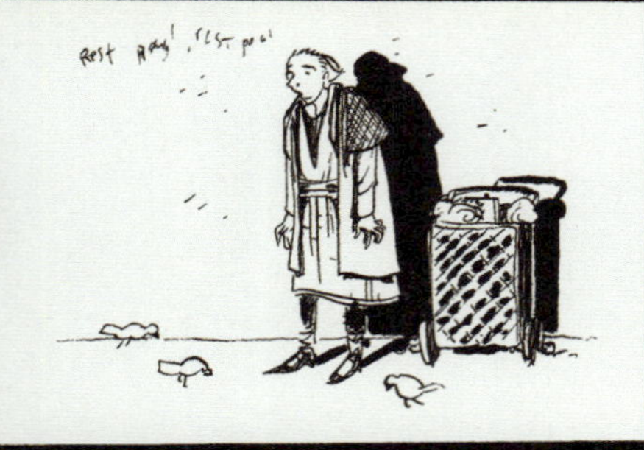

"39th & 8th" FIFFE

SOMETIMES YER HAVING SEX WITH A GIRL, RIGHT? AND YOU'VE ...UM... *FORGOTTEN* TO WEAR A CONDOM AND YOU SUDDENLY REALIZE IT.

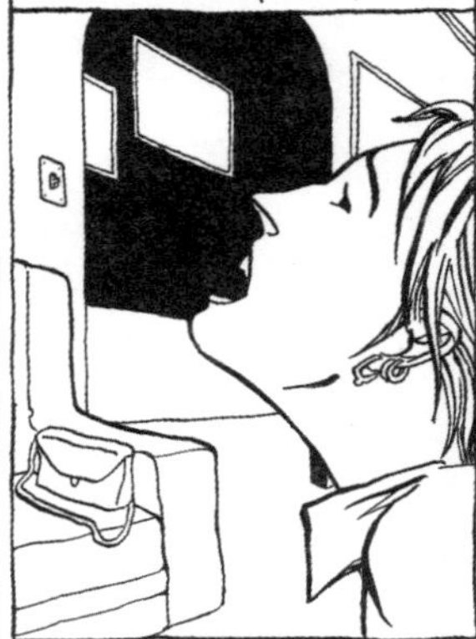

AND ALL THIS STUFF IS GOIN' THROUGH YER MIND LIKE: "I'M DYING OF AIDS RIGHT NOW. I'M SCREWING THIS CHICK AND SHE GAVE ME AIDS SO I MIGHT AS WELL FUCK THE HELL OUTTA HER CUZ I'M DYING."

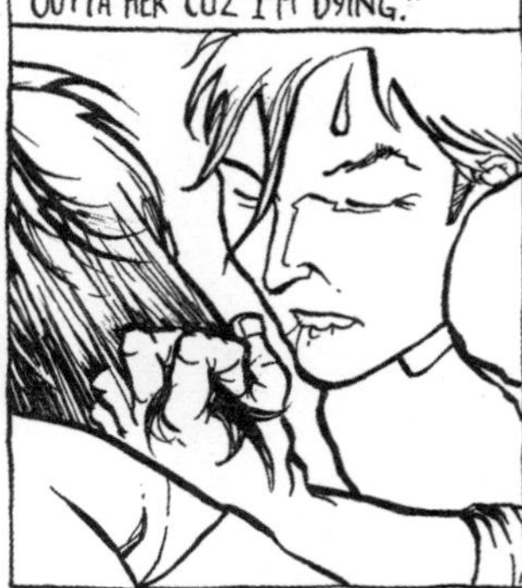

OR..."WHAT IF SHE'S A RIGHT WING NUT AND DECIDES TO *NOT GET AN ABORTION* IN CASE I KNOCK HER UP?"

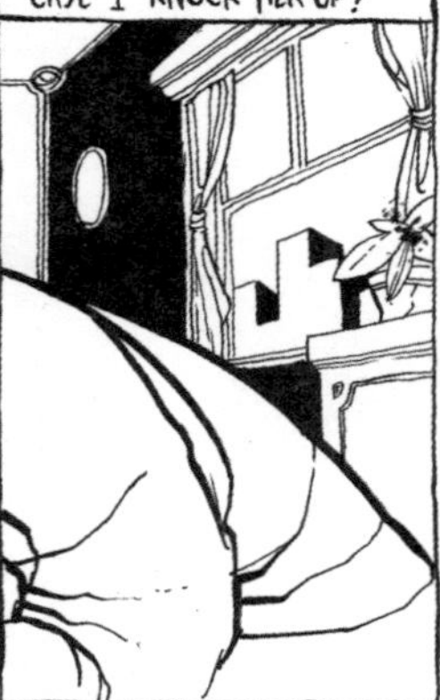

THEN THERE'S THE TYPE OF GIRL WHO YOU WOULDN'T MIND IF SHE DECIDED TO KEEP THE CHILD. YOU'D BE ABLE TO LIVE WITH THAT DESPITE IT BEING AN ACCIDENT.

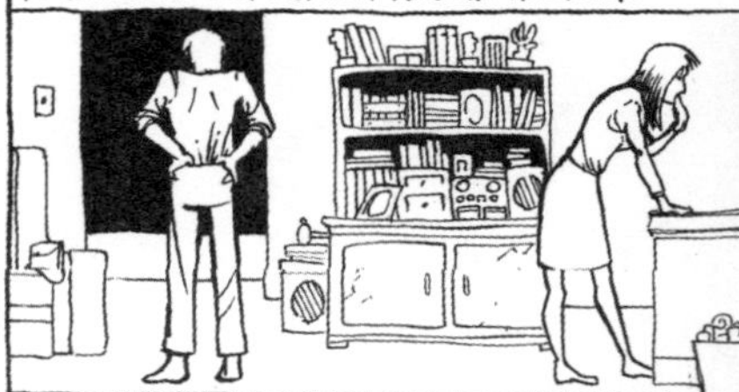

IF YOU DON'T EVEN LIKE 'ER THAT MUCH, THOUGH, AND YOU KEEP IMAGINING SOMEONE ELSE ON TOP OF YOU AND SHE GOES AHEAD AND GETS PREGGERS ON YOU...

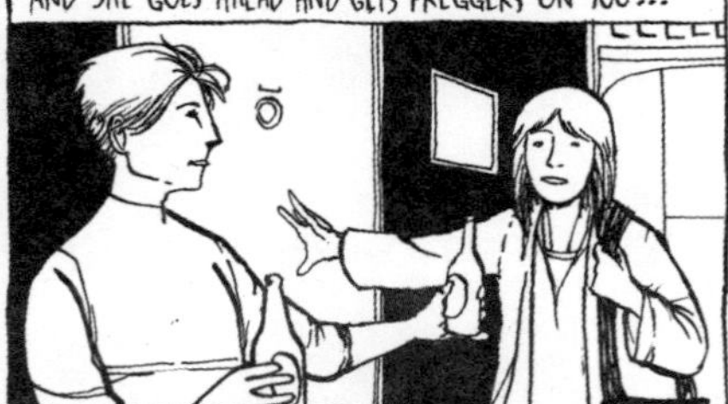

THEN YOUR LIFE IS FOREVER RUINED AND CHANGED INTO A MISERABLE SUICIDE INDUCING HELLISH TRAP ALL CUZ YOU WERE TOO DRUNK TO GET A CONDOM.

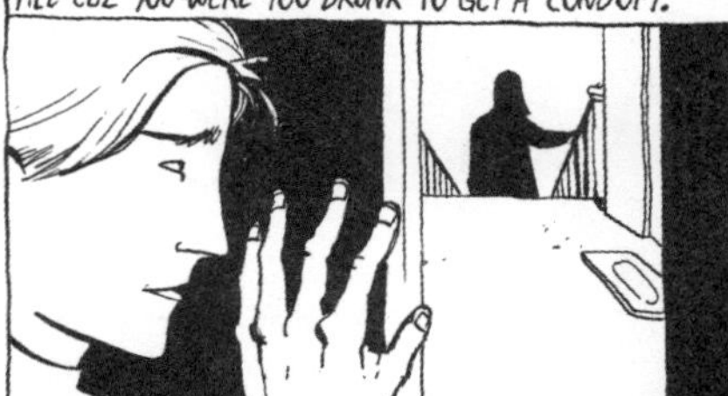

IN FACT, AT YOUR MOST STUPIDEST, YOU EVEN PREFER GETTING AIDS OVER CREATING A CHILD WITH A GIRL THAT TOOK 10 SHOTS TO MAKE HER SEEM DOABLE.

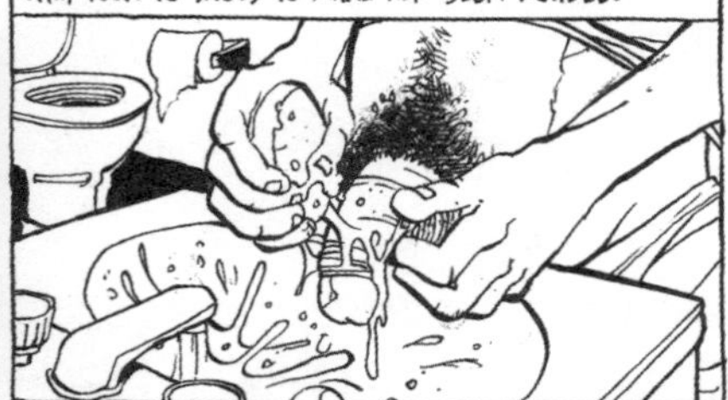

SURE YOU WERE DESPERATE AND FEELING A LITTLE EVIL AND YOUR ROOMMATE WAS OUTTA TOWN... BUT WAS IT WORTH THE EFFORT? YOU DESERVE BAD HEAD.

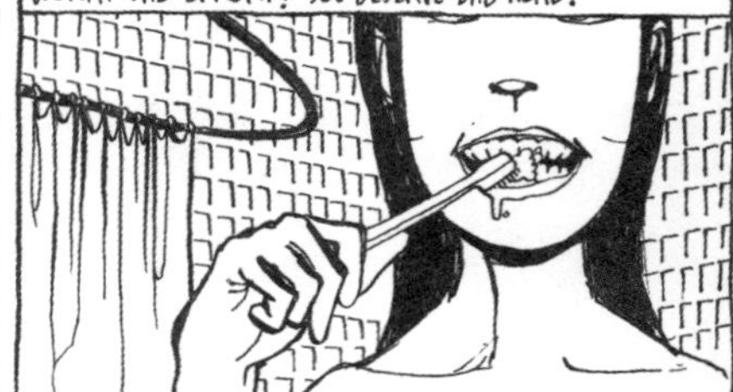

NEXT TIME THINK OF THE MORNING AFTER AND HER WARM MORNING BREATH WHISPERING, "WHAT ARE YA THINKIN'?". MAKE SURE YOU ANSWER, "AIDS.".

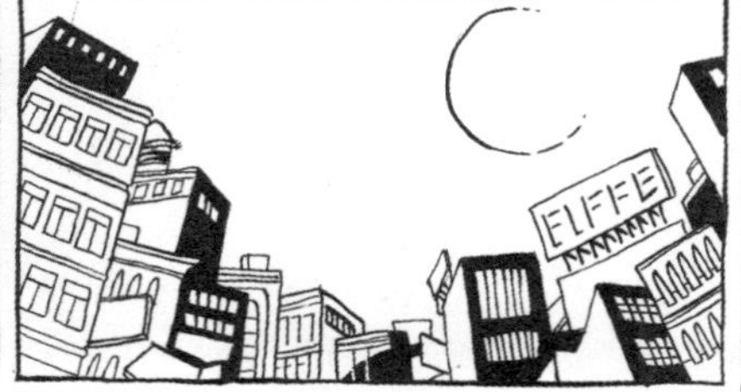

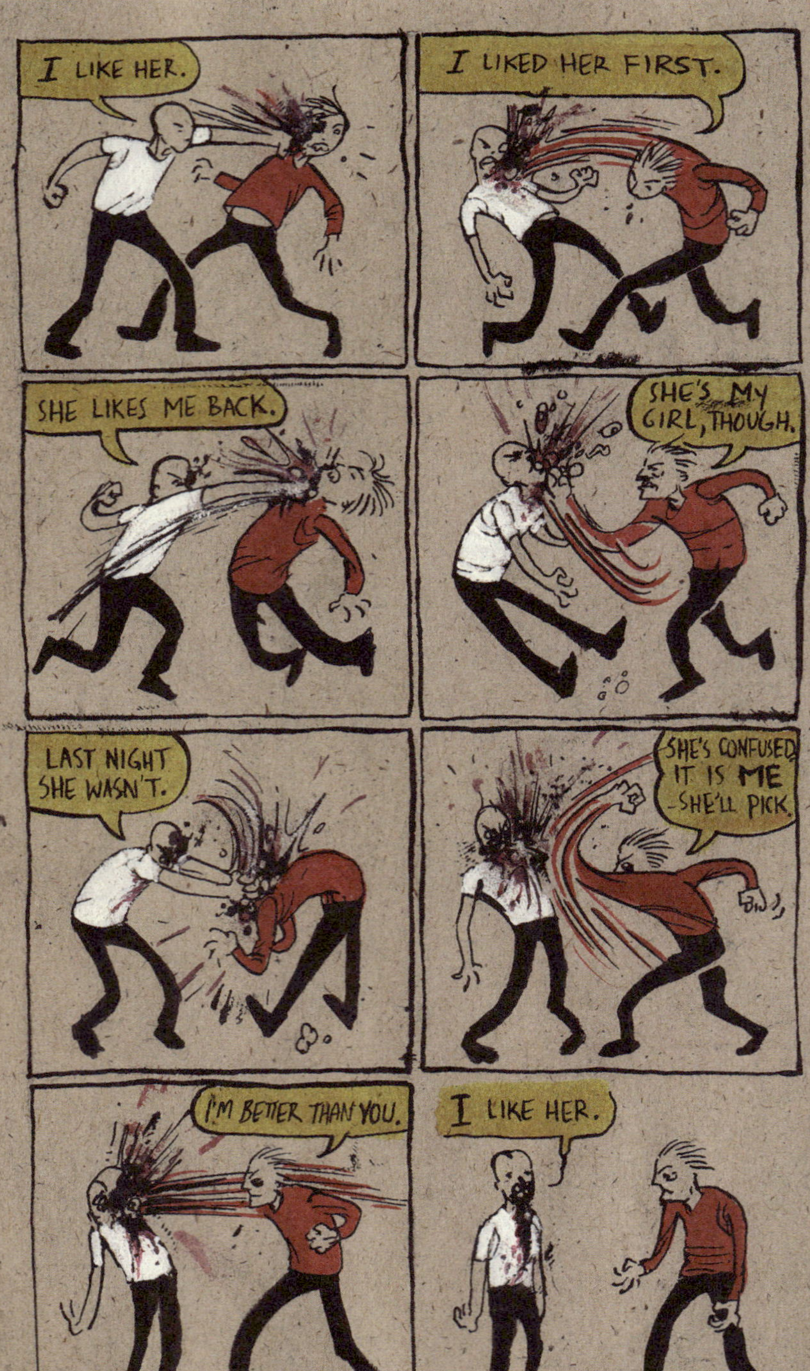
I LIKE HER.
I LIKED HER FIRST.
SHE LIKES ME BACK.
SHE'S MY GIRL, THOUGH.
LAST NIGHT SHE WASN'T.
SHE'S CONFUSED. IT IS ME SHE'LL PICK.
I'M BETTER THAN YOU.
I LIKE HER.

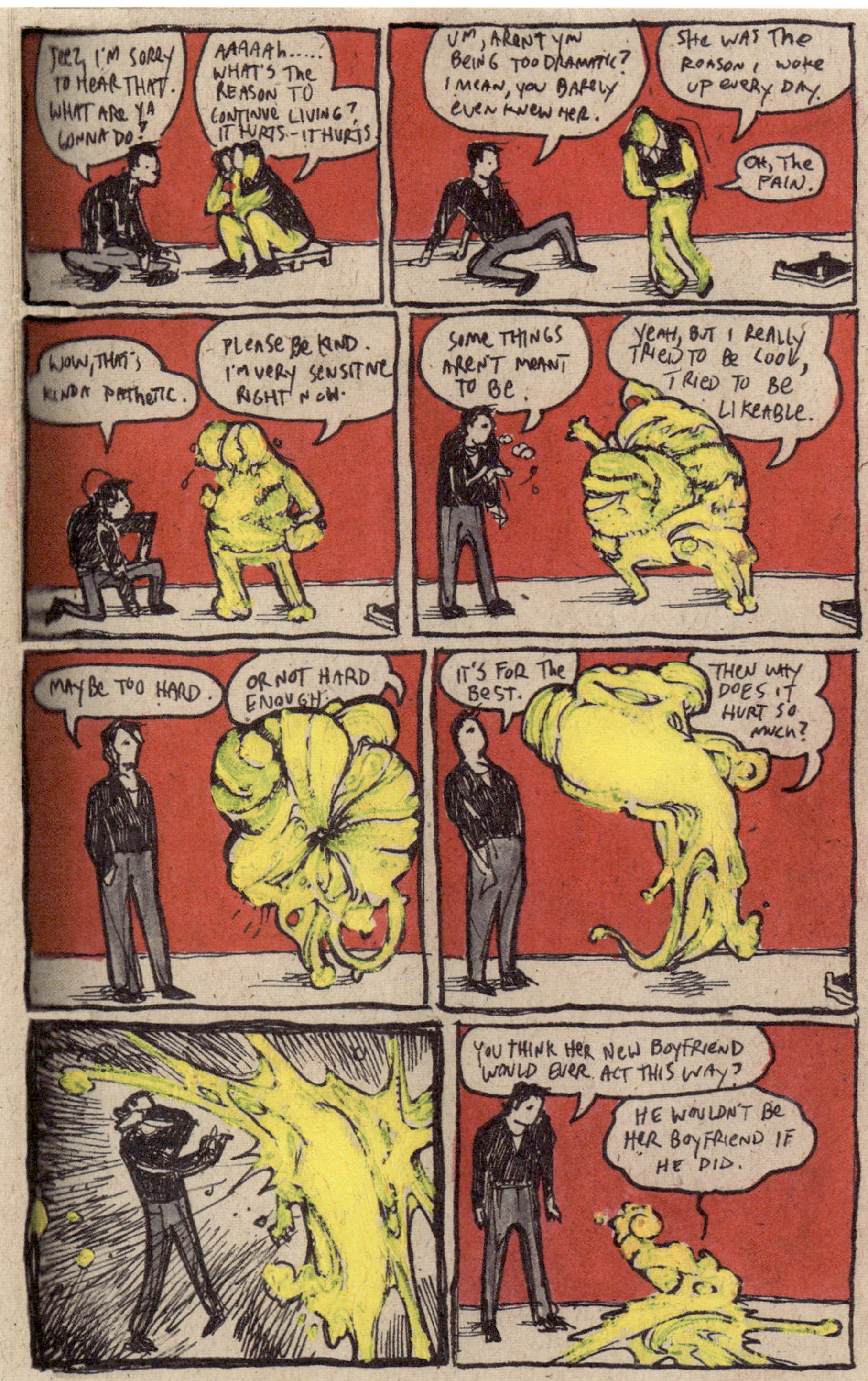
JEEZ, I'M SORRY TO HEAR THAT. WHAT ARE YA GONNA DO?
AAAAAh..... WHAT'S THE REASON TO CONTINUE LIVING? IT HURTS - IT HURTS
UM, AREN'T YOU BEING TOO DRAMATIC? I MEAN, YOU BARELY EVEN KNEW HER.
SHE WAS THE REASON I WOKE UP EVERY DAY.
OH, THE PAIN.
WOW, THAT'S KINDA PATHETIC.
PLEASE BE KIND. I'M VERY SENSITIVE RIGHT NOW.
SOME THINGS AREN'T MEANT TO BE.
YEAH, BUT I REALLY TRIED TO BE COOL, TRIED TO BE LIKEABLE.
MAYBE TOO HARD.
OR NOT HARD ENOUGH.
IT'S FOR THE BEST.
THEN WHY DOES IT HURT SO MUCH?
YOU THINK HER NEW BOYFRIEND WOULD EVER ACT THIS WAY?
HE WOULDN'T BE HER BOYFRIEND IF HE DID.

SPRINKLES

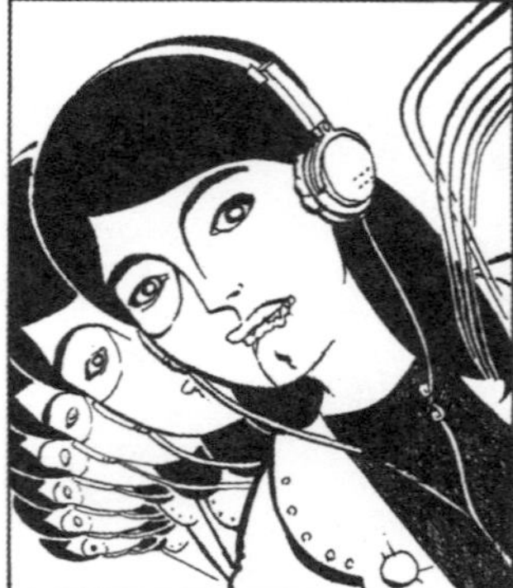

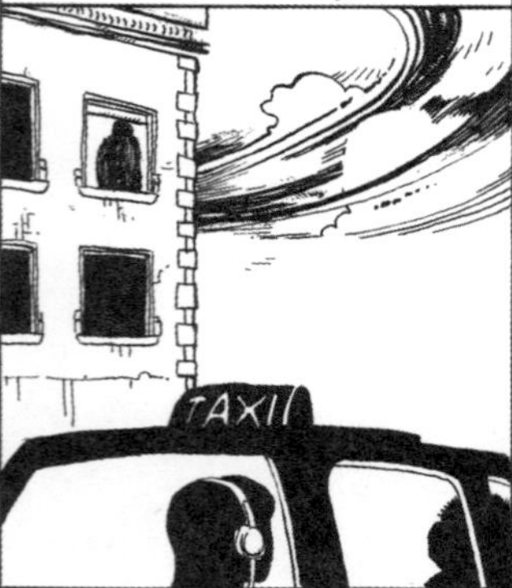

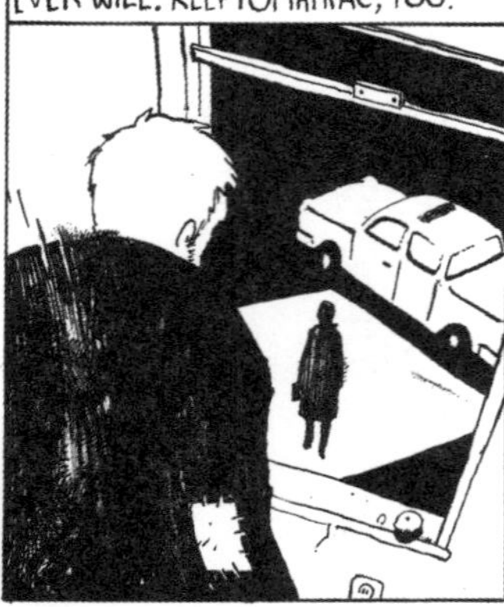

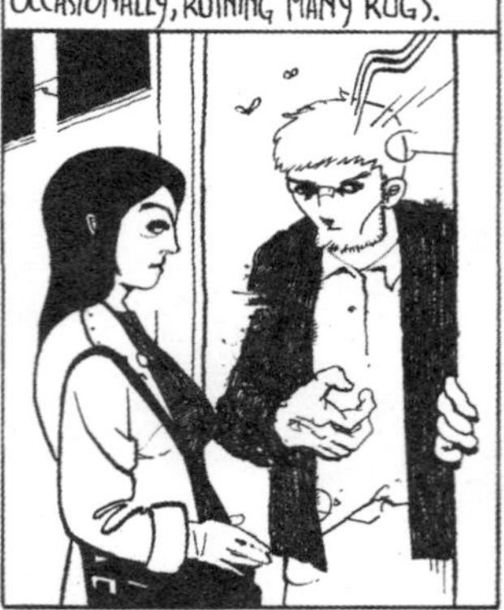

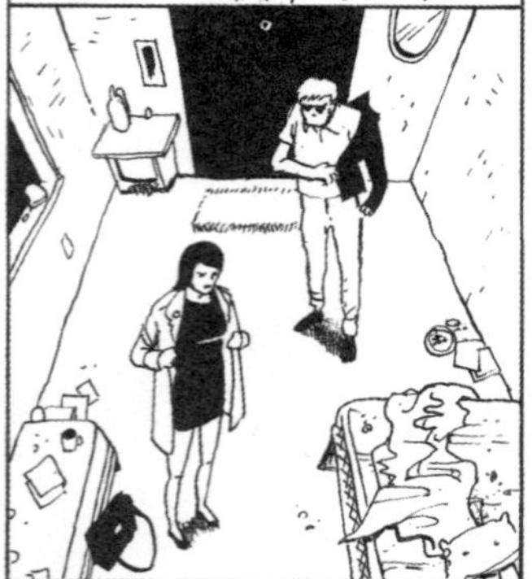

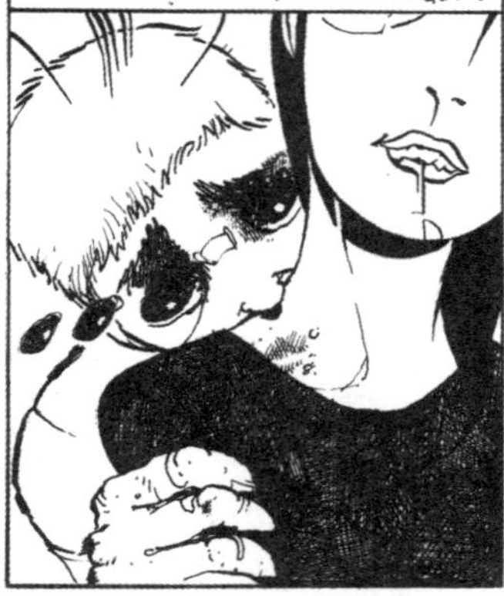

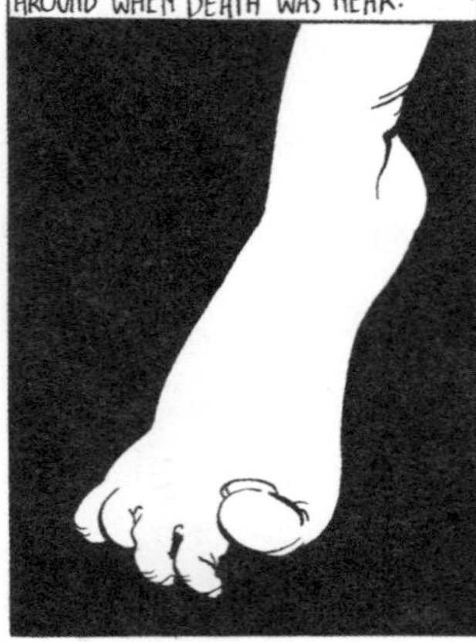

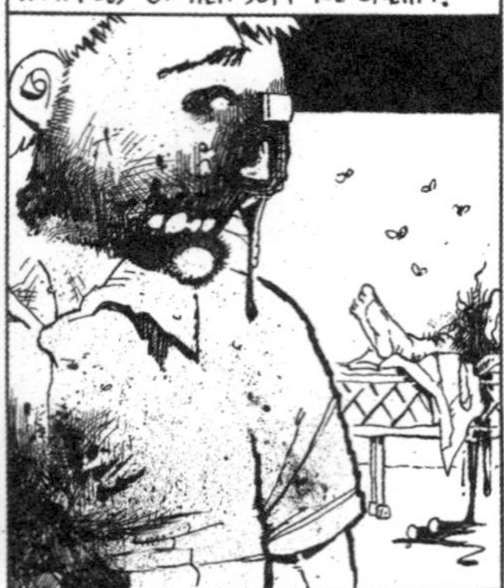

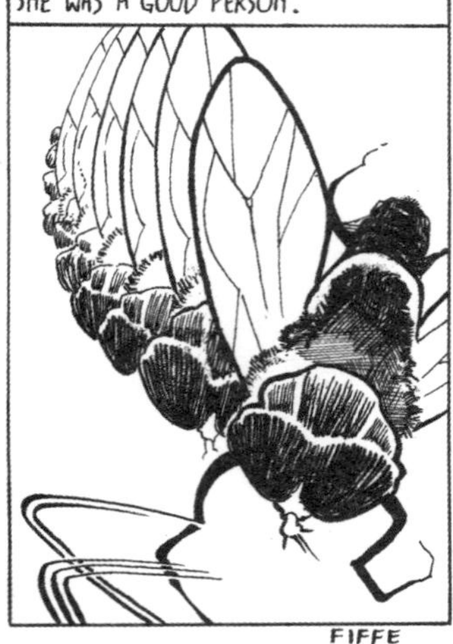

FIFFE

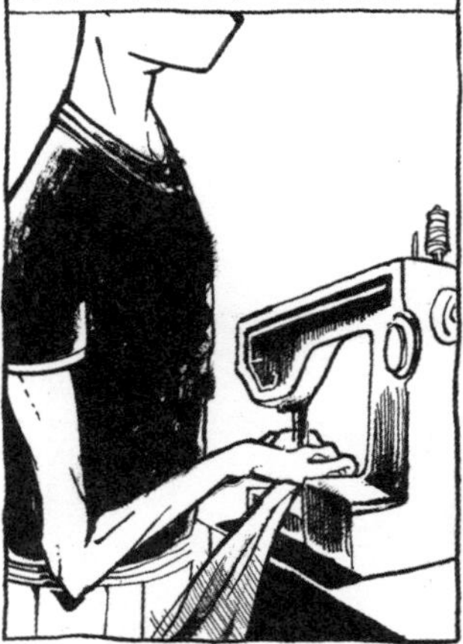

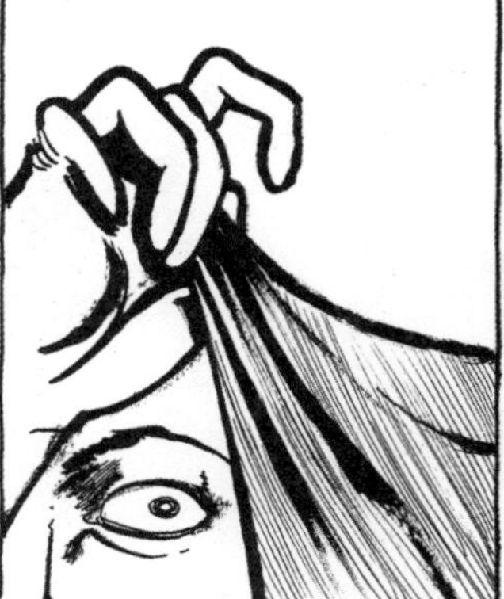

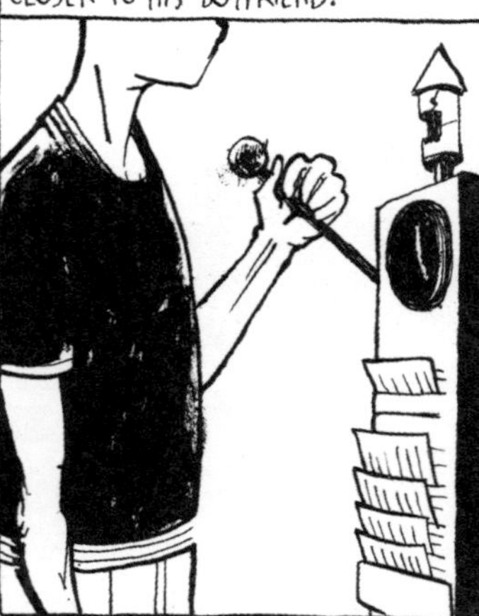

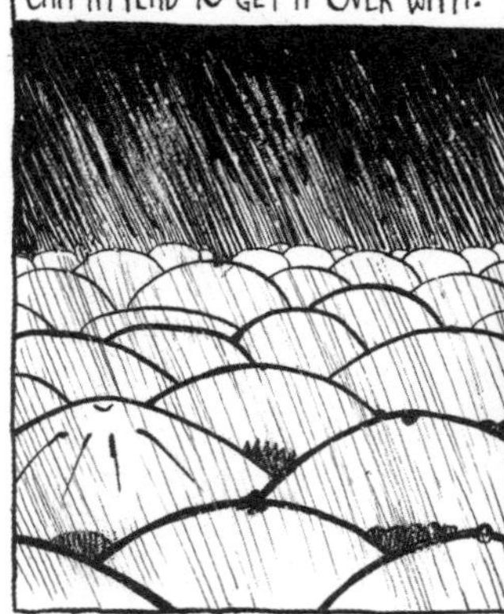

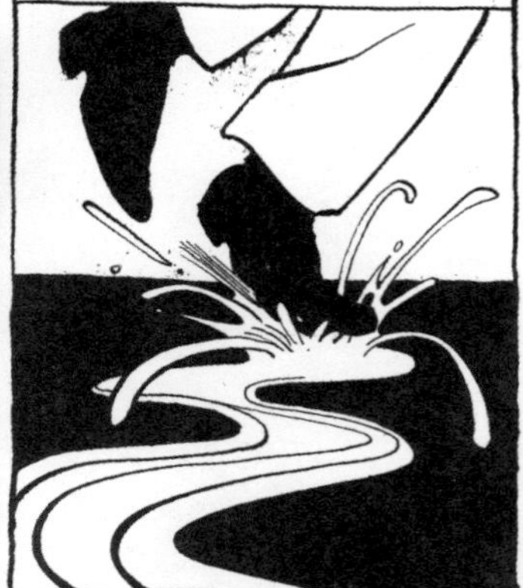

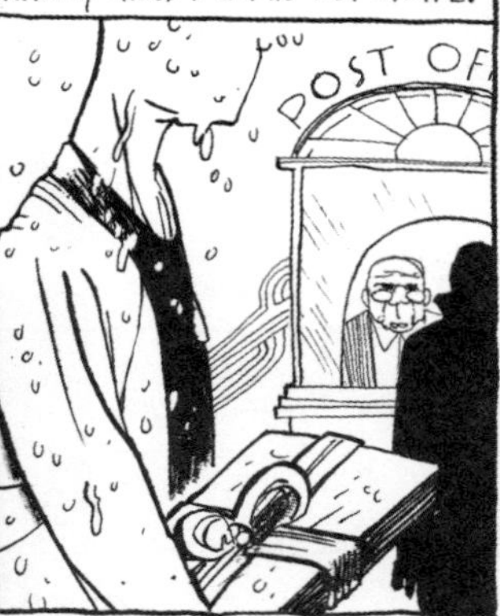

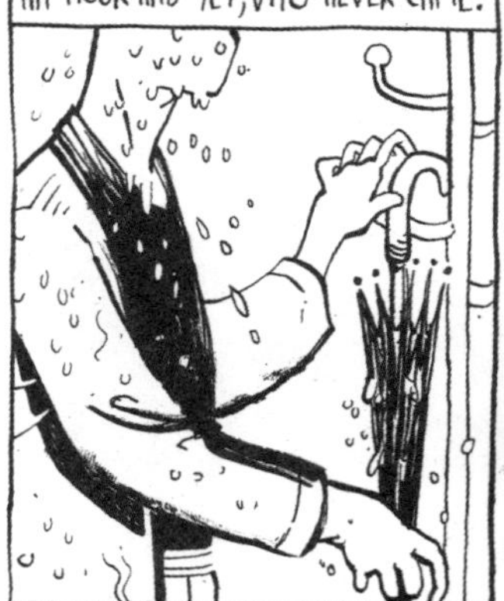

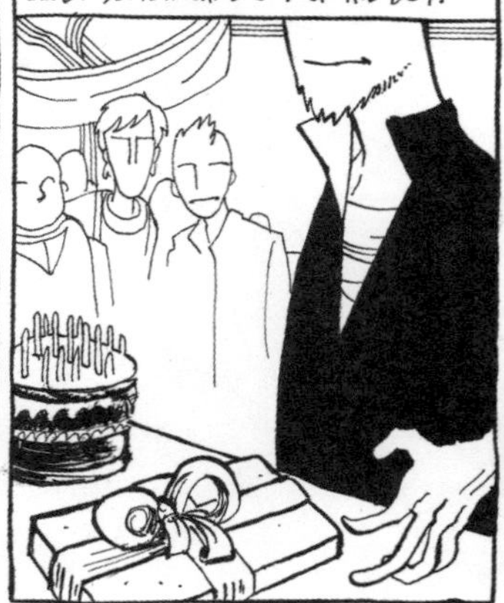

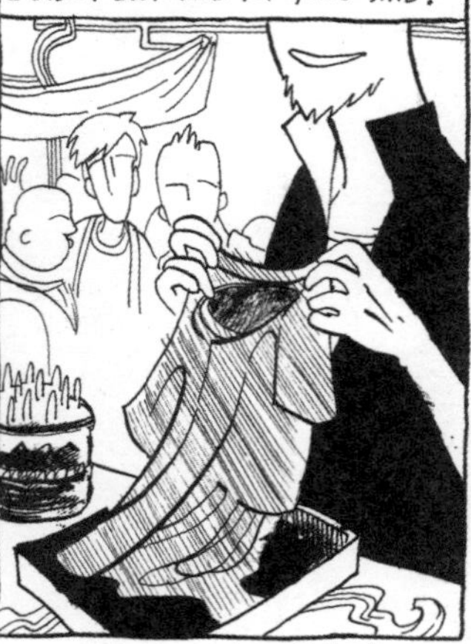

UNTITLED by FIFFE

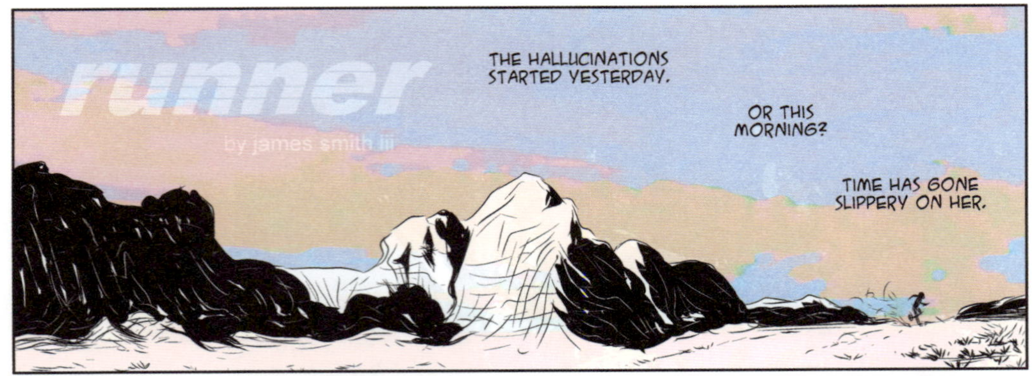
runner
by james smith iii
THE HALLUCINATIONS STARTED YESTERDAY.
OR THIS MORNING?
TIME HAS GONE SLIPPERY ON HER.

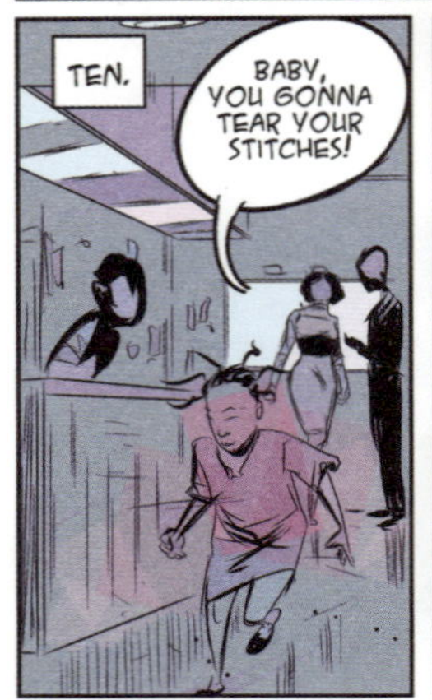
TEN.
BABY, YOU GONNA TEAR YOUR STITCHES!

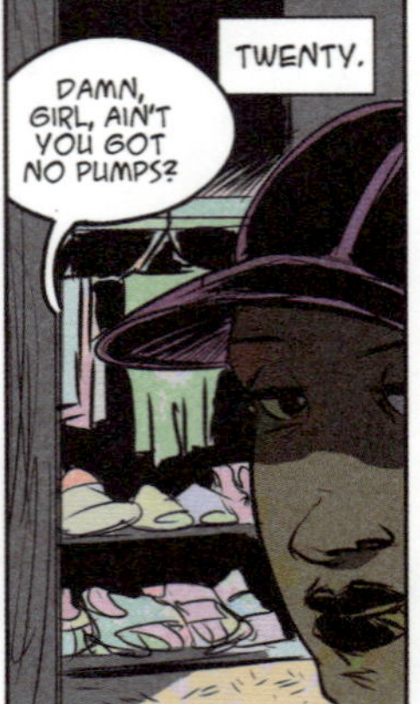
TWENTY.
DAMN, GIRL, AIN'T YOU GOT NO PUMPS?

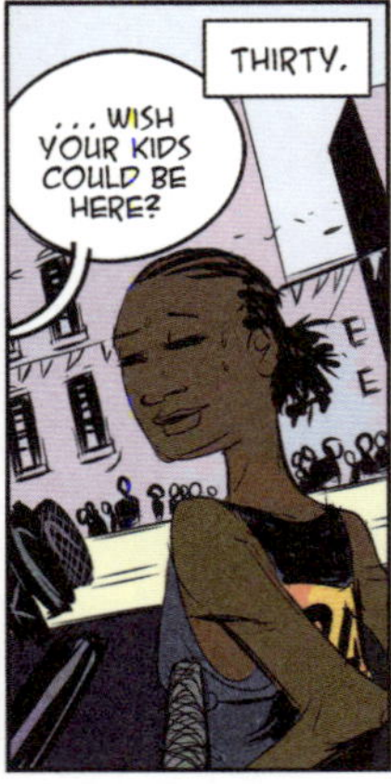
THIRTY.
. . . WISH YOUR KIDS COULD BE HERE?

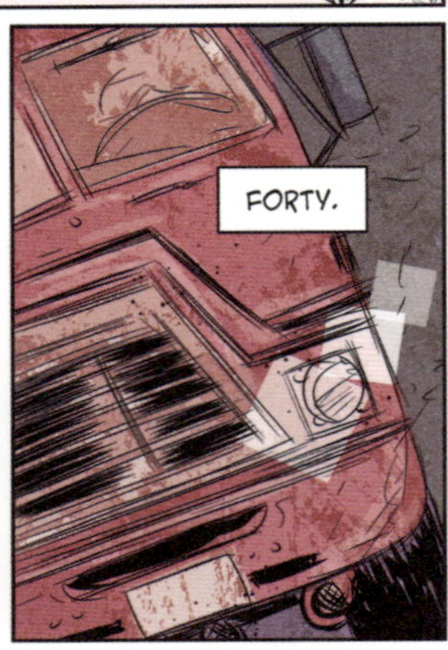
FORTY.

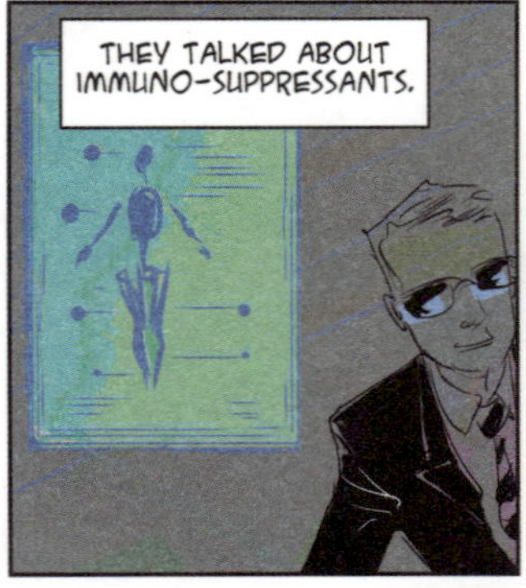
THEY TALKED ABOUT IMMUNO-SUPPRESSANTS.

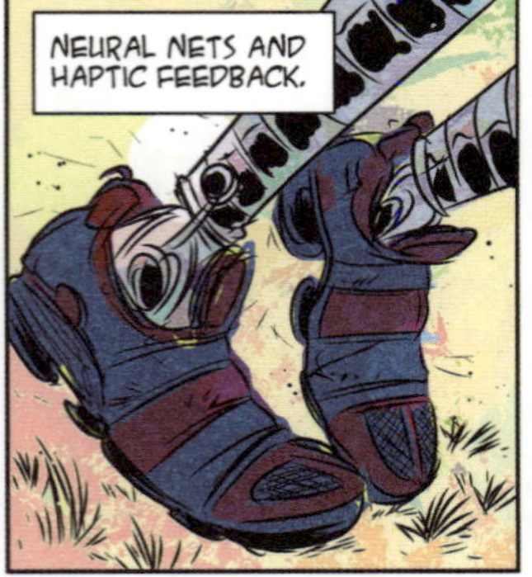
NEURAL NETS AND HAPTIC FEEDBACK.

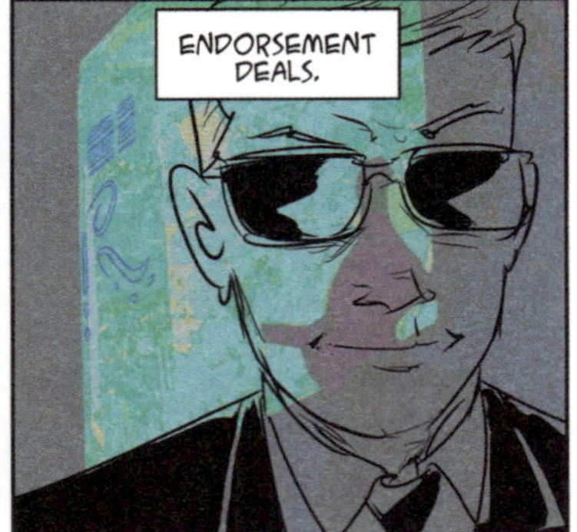
ENDORSEMENT DEALS.

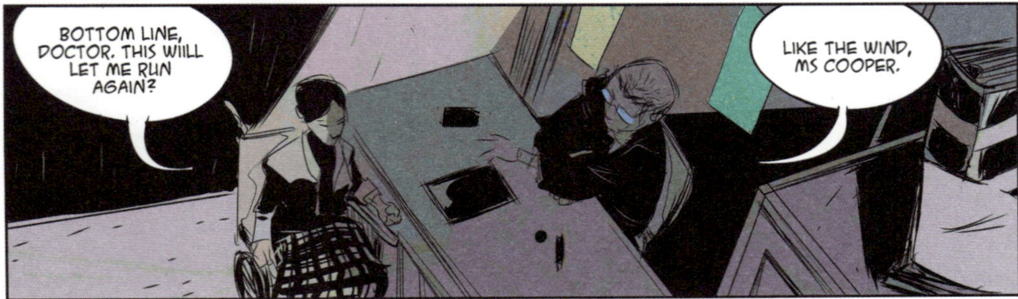
BOTTOM LINE, DOCTOR. THIS WIILL LET ME RUN AGAIN?
LIKE THE WIND, MS COOPER.

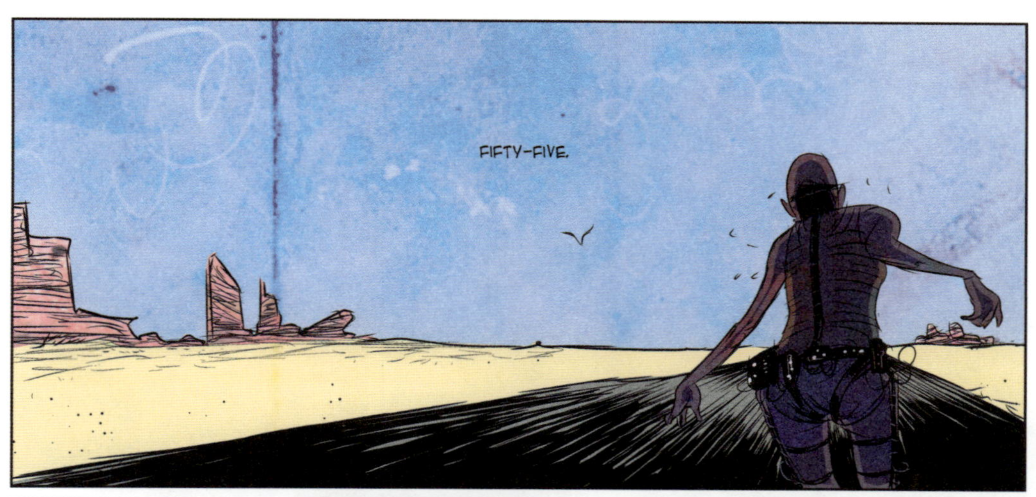
FIFTY-FIVE.

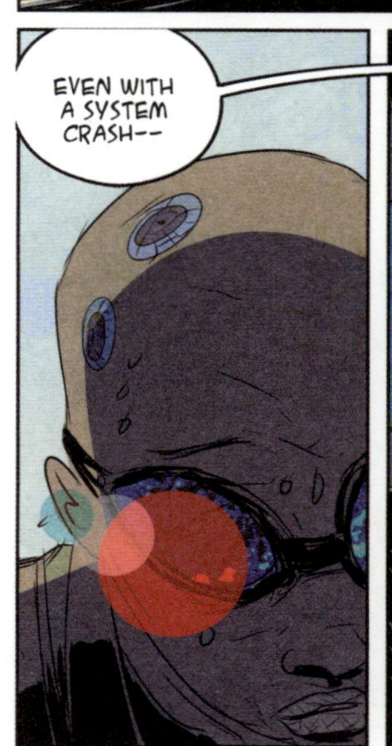
EVEN WITH A SYSTEM CRASH--

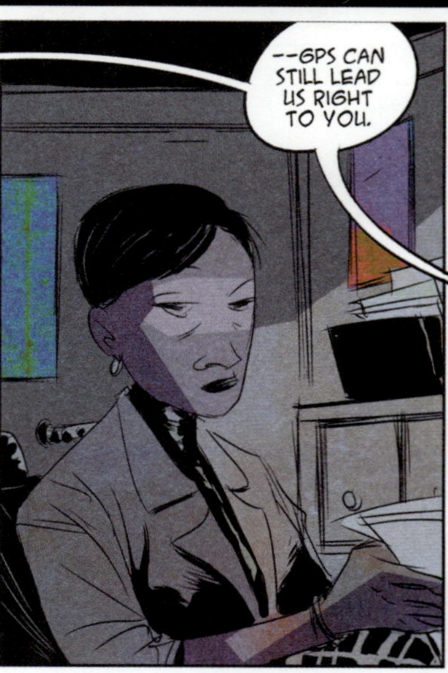
--GPS CAN STILL LEAD US RIGHT TO YOU.

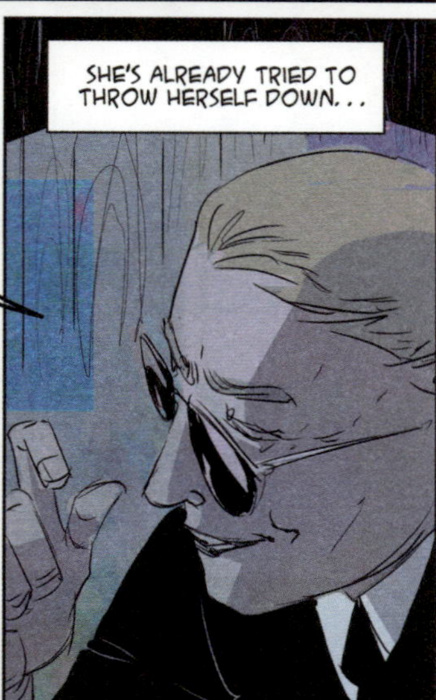
SHE'S ALREADY TRIED TO THROW HERSELF DOWN. . .

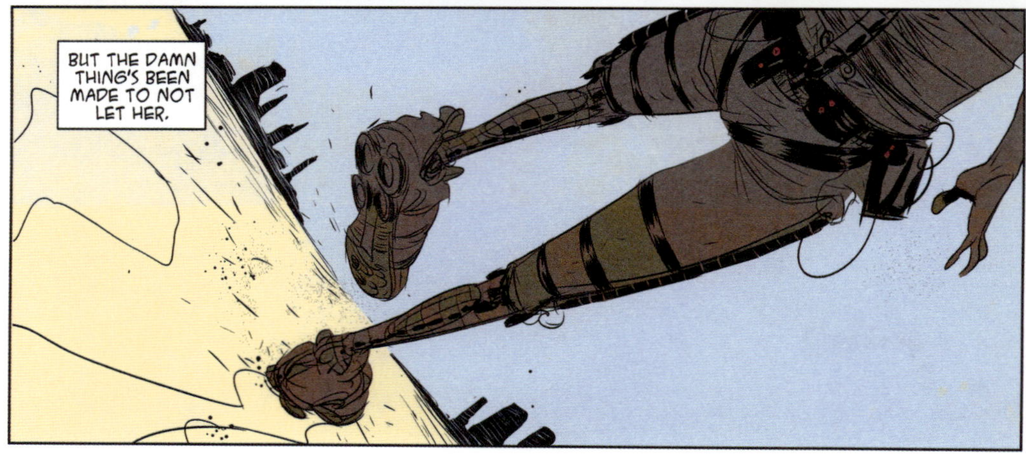
BUT THE DAMN THING'S BEEN MADE TO NOT LET HER.

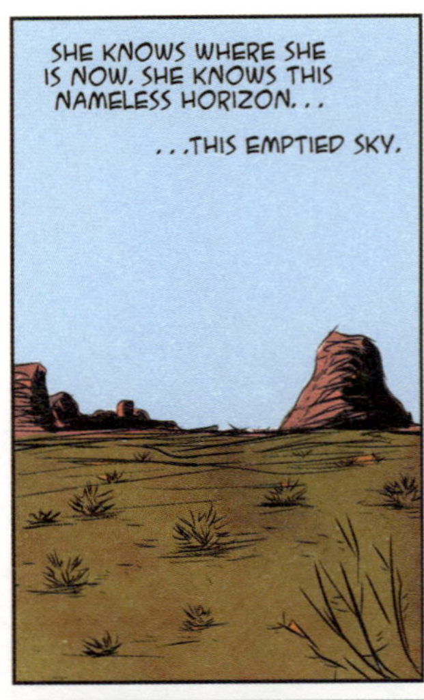
SHE KNOWS WHERE SHE IS NOW. SHE KNOWS THIS NAMELESS HORIZON. . .
. . .THIS EMPTIED SKY.
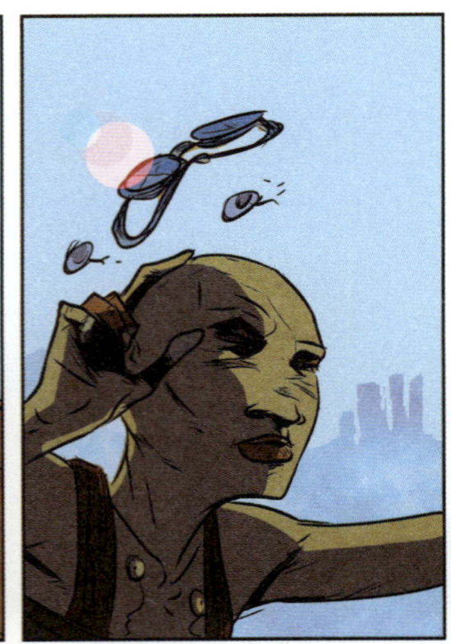
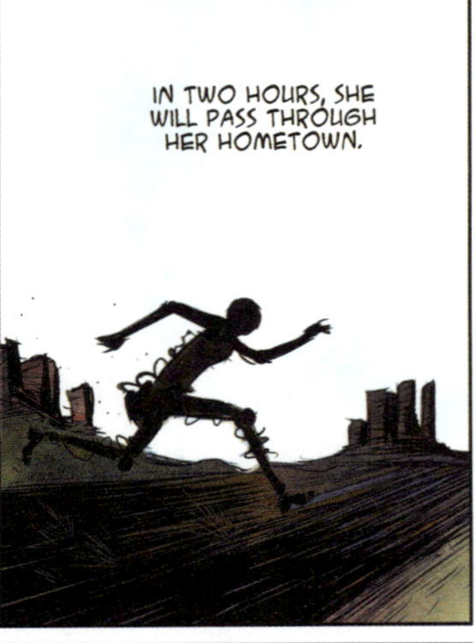
IN TWO HOURS, SHE WILL PASS THROUGH HER HOMETOWN.
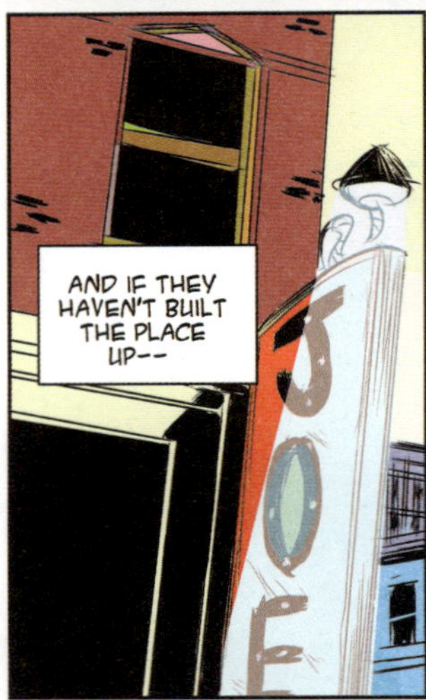
AND IF THEY HAVEN'T BUILT THE PLACE UP--
JOE
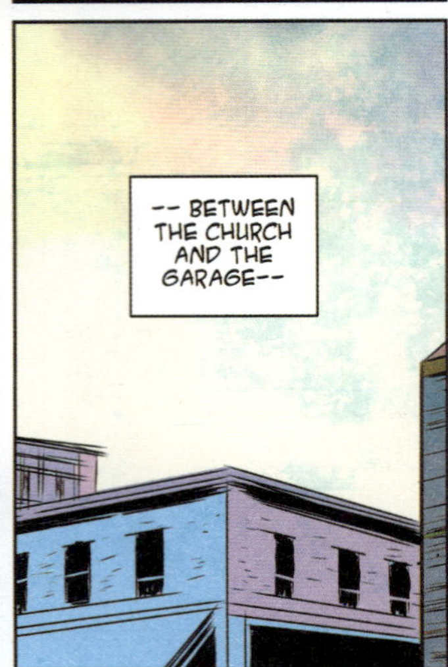
-- BETWEEN THE CHURCH AND THE GARAGE--
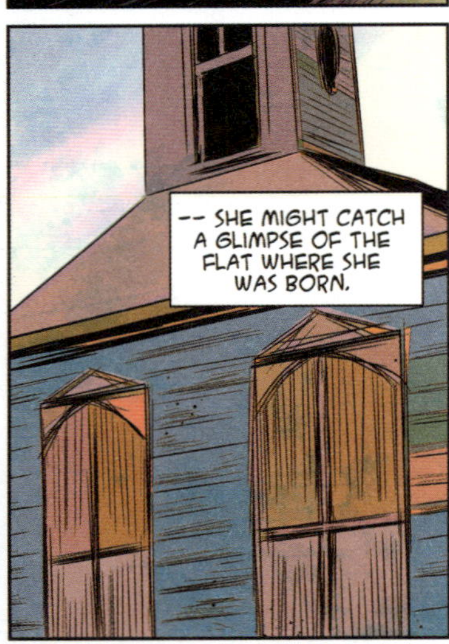
-- SHE MIGHT CATCH A GLIMPSE OF THE FLAT WHERE SHE WAS BORN.
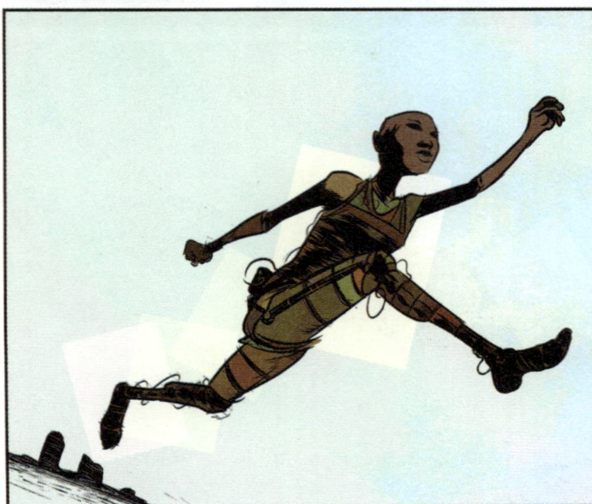
AND THEN SHE WILL BE THREE HOURS FROM THE SEA.

Post-Traumatic Skyscraper Anxiety

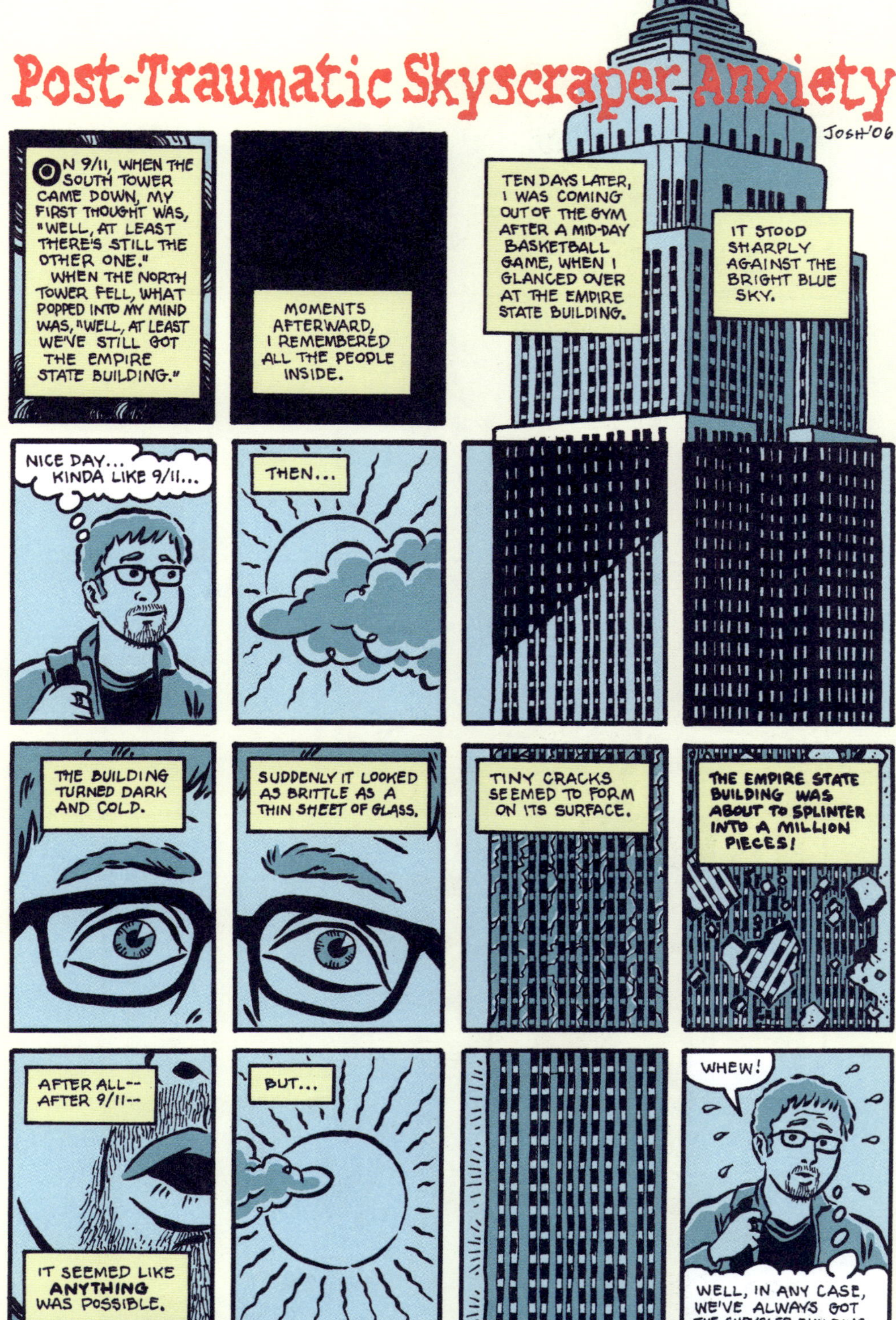

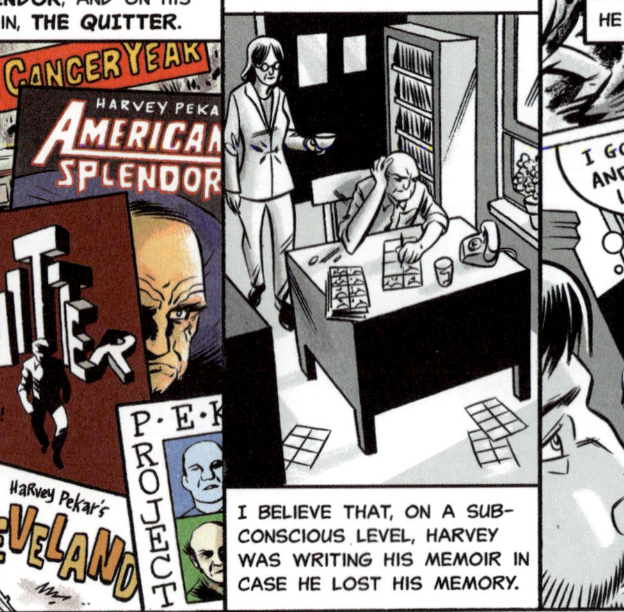
HARVEY PEKAR
OCT. 8, 1939 - JULY 12, 2010
BY DEAN HASPIEL
A PIONEER OF THE AUTOBIOGRAPHICAL COMIC BOOK, HARVEY PEKAR TAUGHT ME THE POWER OF OBSERVATION SANS JUDGMENT. OUR MAN NOT ONLY LENT AN EAR BUT KEPT ONE, TOO.
I GOT LOOPY...
SEE, COMIC BOOKS BOIL STORIES TO THEIR NARRATIVE CORE WHERE IMAGES ARE TEXT, TOO. BUT IN HARVEY'S COMICS, THAT WASN'T ALWAYS THE CASE.
INSTEAD, HARVEY WROTE IN A SPIRITED STREET-SPEAK AND REVELED IN THE MUNDANE, FURNISHING GENERATIONS WITH THE VERISIMILITUDE OF A FUNNY, ALBEIT CRANKY, JAZZ-LOVING, WORKING-CLASS JEW.
I WAS HONORED TO HAVE BEEN ONE OF A SELECT GROUP OF ARTISTS WHO SERVED HARVEY'S TALES, INCLUDING HIS GROUND-BREAKING SERIES AND MOVIE, AMERICAN SPLENDOR, AND ON HIS ORIGIN, THE QUITTER.
OUR CANCER YEAR
HARVEY PEKA
AMERICAN SPLENDOR
QUITTER
Dino!
P·E·K
PROJECT
Harvey Pekar's
CLEVELAND
LATER, I LEARNED HARVEY'S PARENTS DIED HAVING SUFFERED FROM ALZHEIMER'S DISEASE. SUDDENLY, ALL THIS STUFF ABOUT DOCUMENTING THE QUOTIDIAN MOMENTS OF HIS LIFE MADE SENSE.
I BELIEVE THAT, ON A SUBCONSCIOUS LEVEL, HARVEY WAS WRITING HIS MEMOIR IN CASE HE LOST HIS MEMORY.
AND, DESPITE HIS UNTIMELY DEMISE, HARVEY PEKAR WILL NEVER BE FORGOTTEN.
HE CAN'T BE.
I GOT LOOPY AND I'M TAKING LOOPY HOME.

ERNESTO QUIÑONEZ

THE MAN MAMI NEVER LOVED

I saw the man mami never loved at the bodega. I was buying ramen noodles and collected my change quickly so as not to be spotted. But I dropped a quarter and it rolled, crashing into his dirty sneaker.

"Tito?" he said, looking up. "Dag you big. Last time you were like this high," and he bent down and picked up my coin.

"Thanks," I said to the man mami never loved.

"Hey Tito, how's your mother?"

"Oh, she's fine," I said and he just stood there and waited as if I was going to tell him more. I clutched my styrofoam cups, one shrimp, the other chicken noodles, and left him looking at his shoelaces.

"Ma," I said when I got upstairs, placing the groceries and the change down on the table. "I saw that guy again. He was at the store."

"Did you bring the milk?" she asked, knowing full well I forget things.

"Can I get that tomorrow?"

Mami's eyes never leave her novella.

When she doesn't answer me it means, no.

So I needed to go back down and get milk.

When I came back for the milk, the man mami never loved was at the bodega sweeping the sidewalk. He was whistling to himself.

When people first pointed him out to me, I thought he owned the bodega but no, he just does odd jobs like sweep, change the cat's litter, stack cans, and kill his days there. That was all he did, jobs like sweep the sidewalk, and he'd talk with anyone who passed by.

"You back, pa'," Carlitos says to me.

"Yeah, I forgot something."

"Yeah, I forget stuff too. Lissen, how's your mother?"

"Okay." I shrug and go inside the store and bring the milk to the counter, only to remember I left the money upstairs.

"Can you give me credit?" I tell the bodegero because I don't want to go back up and face mami again with no milk.

"Credit? No way, papi."

"But I never asked for any, so give me a break. I'll pay you early tomorrow before I go to school."

"Your family never needed credit, isn't your father the janitor at that school you go to?"

"Yeah?"

"Yeah, so ask your father for some money."

I put the milk back in the store's fridge and stepped outside. The man mami never loved is standing on the sidewalk, resting his arm against the broom like a crutch as he smokes a cigarette.

"How did you get this job, Carlitos?"

"What job, Tito?" he says, taking a puff.

"This job, sweeping the bodega."

"Oh, yeah, I guess it's a job," he says, smiling a little at me.

"So how you get it?"

"You know Tito, I don't know," he says, shaking his head. "I just started hanging around the bodega and next thing you know," and his eyes pointed towards the broom.

"I'll be back, I forgot something," I say.

"Dag, you big," he says, and as I start walking he yells to say hi to my mother.

My father was home and he wanted to talk to me, something about my grades and I had told them that the teacher had said that I needed to watch this series on the History Channel but that mami didn't want to miss her novella. So I flunked that class.

"Don't you know," my father yells, "that I'm trying to be your school's custodian?"

"Yeah, I know," I say.

"How am I 'spose to get that job when you're flunking classes."

And I don't answer him because I know it won't matter.

"What am I 'spose to do now? Take my belt off and whip a fourteen-year-old?" He stares at me.

Mami's novellas are in commercials. So she is free to talk. "Did you bring the milk?"

"Nah," I say, looking at the floor. "I forgot the money."

My father throws his arms out, up in the air.

"What are you good for?" he asks the ceiling or the sky or God.

"Go get the milk," mami says, returning to her soap.

This time I take the leftover money from the table and go outside. I pass by my father who sucks his teeth at me, holding my report card in his hands. He signs it and then gives it to me to take back to school the next day.

"Do better, or you're going to do this whole family in," he says to me and I nod. I put the report card in my school bag so I won't forget it the next day. Then I step out to get the milk.

The man mami never loved is putting the bodega's trash inside plastic bags and piling them outside by the parking meter. He sees me coming and smiles at me.

"Tito, you play stickball, right?"

"When they pick me," I shrug, "sometimes, I get picked."

"Man, I got these brooms here," and he showed me these old brooms with frizzy heads. "These are good."

"Really?" I say, taking them and looking at them with suspicion. "They're pretty ugly."

"Nah, see pa, the older the wood, the better the stickball bat. Mops don't make good stickball bats, brooms do."

"Yeah, why's that?"

"Because," he says, "mops get wet a lot. So the wood rots. But brooms don't, so the wood is vintage." He says the last word like he just learned it, "Vinnnntagggge."

"Okay."

And I go into the store with my brooms. I get the milk and take it to the counter.

"See, you got money," the bodegero says and I smile at him. "Carlitos gave you those?"

"Yeah, I'm gonna make stickball bats."

"You know, you're both crazy," he says. "That wood is old."

"The older the wood the better," I say.

"Who told you that?"

I don't tell him.

"That only works for oak or good wood, not cheap shit wood that's used for brooms."

But I don't believe him, because I've heard the man mami never loved was the best stickball player in Spanish Harlem but I've never heard anyone talk about the bodegero being any good. People told me that the man mami never loved met my mother while playing stickball. That he hit the pink spalding into her window and broke it. When my mother poked her head out, all the kids ran but he stayed there, staring at the broken window, wondering how was he going to get the ball back. My mother stuck her head out and saw him and she threw the ball back down to him. She then lied to her parents saying that someone threw a rock. I don't know if that's true though, because mami never likes to talk about him at all. And if someone mentions him, my father sneaks a peek at my mother as if she has done something wrong and he is reminding her of his forgiveness. So at our house, I've never heard his real name. All pops says to mami is, you never loved him, you never loved him, tell me you never loved a dummy like that. And mami just nods.

I walk out of the bodega with the milk and my broomsticks. The man mami never loved is sweeping again. Inelda Flores is next to him. She sits behind me in history class and she always smells nice though she can be mean.

"That's not how you sweep, I'll show you how to sweep," she says to him.

"I know how to sweep," he says to Inelda.

"Hi," I say. Inelda smells nice.

"Another retard," she says and pokes her head forward to see what I bought.

"Just milk," I say.

"Just milk? You know that forms mucus, it's bad for you," she says. "What are those for?"

"Bats, stickball bats," I say.

"Yeah," she sways her head from side to side, "and when do you play stickball?"

"When I get picked, sometimes I get picked."

"You never get picked, Tito," she laughs, "only if they're short a guy. I know cuz I have seen the guys play and I never seen you play unless they are short."

"But they do pick me, sometimes." And I know that Inelda's window faces the street where we, when they pick me, play stickball. But it doesn't matter because I don't think Inelda would throw the ball back down if I broke her window, anyway.

"Hey, how's your mother?" the man mami never loved asks me.

"Okay," I say. "Thanks for the bats."

I leave, taking one last look at Inelda, who bends down to tie her sneaker.

At home I hear my mother and father arguing about things. I put the milk down and the change. I don't interrupt them. I check again that I did place the report card in my school bag. When I see that the yellow envelope is inside my bag, I whisper to myself, "Good." I then leave one broomstick in my room and take the other with me downstairs.

The man mami never loved is doing nothing but standing outside the bodega. He sees me coming and smiles again. I look for Inelda but she is gone.

"Can you help me make this into a stickball bat?" I say to him.

"No sweat, Tito," he says, all excited to be doing something, I think. "We need to pick out every straw and get the broom bald, see. Some people don't do that and just saw off the head but that weakens the wood. Then we need to get sandpaper to rub it down with. But most important thing is the electric tape to wrap it around at the top for a good grip."

The man mami never loved begins telling me, "When I was your age," and he goes on about how good were the kids he played with. But I know he was the best, I tell him this, because he always got picked first. I want him to teach me how to do that. "No way I was the best." He tells me that he knew kids who could "hit the Spaldeeeeen as far as three sewers, three manholes. That's three blocks, away, you know, Tito." And this makes me happy because Inelda lives only one block away from where all the kid's play. I know with practice and a good bat, I can hit her window one sewer away. I can hit her window one sewer away.

"I can do that," I say out loud and the man mami never loved thinks I'm talking to him.

"I know you can, Tito," he says as he leads me back onto the bodega to find electric tape. "I know you can. I know you can hit it even further."

TODD COLBY

ACTS OF KINDNESS

A few months ago I had this idea about killing someone with kindness. I figured it's worth trying because of the enormous difficulty of actually committing homicide with an act of kindness. I thought I'd start by killing a few ex-friends that had been a thorn in my side by calling them and complimenting them on their life choices and good fortune. I imagined that I'd be able to hear a loud pop followed by an abrupt choking sound on the other end, which would indicate that whichever ex-friend I was talking to had in fact been slain by my kindness. But at the same time I was struck by the likelihood that getting a call from me out of the blue might simply confuse some of them and create an awkward situation that would make me nostalgic for the power I'd previously held over them with my silence. I also knew that if one of the calls turned sour I'd torture myself by replaying the failure to kill them with kindness over and over again in my head. I reminded myself that there might even be several ex-friends who would hang up on me the instant they heard my voice. The bottom line is, I don't hate any of my ex-friends enough to kill them, so that really wasn't the best place to start. Then it occurred to me that I could kill the neighbors upstairs by becoming exceedingly kind to them. The next time I heard them stomping down the stairs I could open my door and say, "So, where are you two going on such a beautiful day?" The hard part would be not letting any sarcasm creep into my voice while maintaining friendly eye contact with the very people I abhor. In a sense, I would have to play the role of "The Person with Kindness" so convincingly that it would actually kill the neighbors upstairs.

One icy morning, after I'd made my decision to kill them with kindness, I peeked through the blinds and saw the woman upstairs walking her dogs out front. As she struggled to hold onto the leash connected to her two mangy gray poodles, she slipped and fell face first on the ice-covered sidewalk. It startled her dogs when she fell and they tugged harder, dragging her a bit on her face as she struggled to get to her feet. Watching her plight gave me a pleasant tight sensation in my throat. I recognized that this was a perfect opportunity to kill her with kindness, but I didn't want to help her; it was more pleasant to watch her struggle with the dogs. When she stood up, she turned abruptly and looked up at my window. Once I got a glimpse of the blood smeared on her chin, I let the aluminum blinds slap shut and leapt into bed. I spent the next few hours under the covers while I replayed the image in my head of her looking up at me with blood on her chin. I saw this incident as an indication that it was okay to try and kill her and her boyfriend with kindness.

Whenever I begin a new project, I always put isopropyl alcohol on a paper towel and rub it on the entire surface of my desk in order to kill any germs that might have accumulated there from the previous project. While the isopropyl alcohol was evaporating, I wondered what would happen if a person's entire body were submerged in a bathtub full of isopropyl alcohol for a few hours. Surely the person who was submerged in the isopropyl alcohol would have to use a long tube to breathe through, like a snorkel. If I submerged one of the neighbors upstairs in a bathtub full of isopropyl alcohol, would offering one of them a tube to breathe through be the act of kindness that would kill them, or would the cruelty of submerging them in a tub of isopropyl alcohol be the agent of death? Would the neighbor's skin eventually be dried off? Would their head and body become shrunken? Part of isopropyl alcohol's sensation of coldness on the skin is its rapid process of evaporation. And what about the eyes? Surely the isopropyl alcohol would cause enormous pain as it seeped its way into the eyes. What about the rectum? The vagina? The penis? Or any open wounds, cuts, or scrapes that my upstairs neighbors had? Surely there would be enormous stinging pain in the individual submerged in the isopropyl alcohol, which would definitely outweigh any act of kindness I could offer the person submerged in the bathtub full of isopropyl alcohol. Eventually I discarded this idea and credited myself with being much more rational than I thought I was.

A few weeks ago, when I was walking home, I thought about going directly upstairs and telling the neighbors to go ahead and stomp around and let their dogs bark as much as they wanted because I was planning to buy a set of earplugs that are designed to block out almost any noise that they could make. I had a certain bounce in my step as I walked home because I felt victorious about my new ability to block them out. It's not a good idea to get caught in the loop of hate with them, which is why I decided to tell them outright that I didn't want to get caught in the loop of hate with them, which is also why I was going to buy the earplugs in the first place. If I think about them too much it gets me in the loop of hate with them, and then all I can think about is them. If I'm in the loop of hate with them, then I can't think about observing them as they leave the building with their dogs. When I got home I found my big red marker and wrote "AVOID THE LOOP OF HATE" on a piece of typing paper and tacked it to the wall in front of my desk as a reminder. I decided not to tell the people upstairs about my plans to buy the earplugs because I was afraid I hadn't yet rehearsed exactly how I was going to phrase my announcement. I wanted them to understand without a doubt that I knew all about the loop of hate and I was doing everything in my power, and then some, to avoid getting into the loop with them. I would try to make it as clear as possible that once I purchased the earplugs, they would no longer have any power over me with their various noises. I knew that if I'd gone up there without feeling perfectly calm and self-confident about what I was going to say, then there was the distinct possibility that they would hear the stress in my voice and not take me seriously, or take me too seriously and freak out. I didn't want to be the butt of their jokes, or the agent of their fear; I simply wanted to kill them with kindness.

I thought, what better way to flatter the people upstairs than to tell them that I'm writing a book about my experiences while living downstairs from them. I thought I'd tell them that they are such fascinating subjects that they have become the central characters in my novel, which means the plot revolves around them and when it's published I will personally sign a copy for each of them. I thought I'd tell them to go ahead and do anything they want, because I'm writing down everything they do, which is why it's critically important that they act as naturally as possible with the knowledge that I am writing about them. I didn't want them to become too self-conscious about being observed because then I wouldn't be able to witness and document their genuine behavior.

That night I dreamed that I was cooking one of their dogs on a spit over a fire. I was turning the dog over and over with a lever while it cooked. Once the fur had burned off, the meat of the dog was as shiny and dark as a chunk of black marble. It was tender enough to pull off with my fingers, which is what I did, as I looked up at their window and announced, "I'm eating your dog!" When they looked outside I tugged a piece of the dark meat off the dog's carcass and stuck it in my mouth, letting a little grease dribble down my chin and shimmer by the light of the fire.

Not long ago I bought some cheap cologne called Drakkar Noir from a street vendor. I brought it home and sprinkled it on the doorknob that leads out of the building. I thought it would make the people upstairs furious because there's no sure way they could ever know who did it, nor could they ever be absolutely certain that it was done intentionally to make them wear the cheap cologne on their hands. I thought it would drive them mad having to smell it on their hands, which would only remind them of me throughout the day. The next morning when I heard the woman come downstairs with her dogs, I looked outside through the blinds. She stood about three feet in front of my window, smelled her right hand, curled her lip and spat on the ground between her dogs.

In an effort to take the smell theme one step further I decided to rub my fingers around my rectum and wipe my hand on the doorknob leading out of the building. Knowing that they would have to put their hands on my shit and possibly get it in their mouths made me positively giddy. I saw both of them getting tremendously ill as they jockeyed for position in front of their toilet. I could see them teetering around the apartment with shit and vomit spewing out both ends of their convulsing bodies until they collapsed with a deep thud while flopping around on the bathroom floor like big tuna on the deck of a boat.

What I'd really like to do right now is go up there and have a look around to see what giant piece of furniture they're moving from one end of the apartment to the other this early on a Sunday morning. I know for a fact that they'll just keep on stomping and moving things around until I go up there and take a shit on their bed. I'd knock on their door and when they opened it I'd say, "Excuse me, I'm the guy who lives downstairs and I'm going to take a shit on your bed right now." I can see myself wiping my ass with their bedspread and saying, "Don't worry, it's all gonna be in the novel."

Before I go up there I'll have to prepare myself mentally for the fact that they might have a gun. Or her boyfriend might be the type of guy who is able to sense when someone is harboring mean ideas about them. He might be waiting for me to come up there and take a shit. He might have known about my plan from the very first time I thought about it and maybe he's been preparing for me to come up there all this time that I've been thinking about it. The thought of me shitting on their bed might turn him on and give him an elaborate excuse to drop the gun and climb up on the bed with me and start fondling my ass in order to make me stop shitting their bed. Whenever I think about shitting on their bed it makes me realize that for once in my goddamn life I've come up with a plan that makes me stand out from the crowd for having the courage and tenacity to not only think it but do it.

I know these are obviously not acts of kindness but acts of meanness, and if I keep up with this line of reasoning I'll be straying from my original goal of killing them with kindness. Yet I find myself pursuing all things mean and harmful in relation to them. I feel compelled to constantly think about all the bad things that I can do to them. Every time I hear them stomping around at 5:30 in the morning, I wake up and add another item to the list of things that I can do to them that would cause them great harm. My only fear is that they're sneaking into my apartment when I'm not around, checking out my list of bad things, or reading the novel I'm writing about them so that they can anticipate certain things from me. That's why I've started hiding these things. I've even taken to hiding my toothbrush when I leave my apartment because I don't want them to do anything to it that would make me sick.

Whenever I don't think about them they're quiet, but when I think about them they're noisy. So I'm trying not to think about them, but even in the midst of trying not to think about them I find myself thinking about them. I'm not sure if they're thinking about me very much. Right now they're washing their fifth load of laundry and the spin cycle is off-balance again and it's making the whole building vibrate with its obscenely grating "thump-thump" noise. I know this is something that they've concocted in a most extraordinarily feeble manner simply to bother me. It's sad that the best plan they've come up with to annoy me is making their washing machine go off-balance by washing only one towel at a time. They're dumber than lint and I have my proof. Perhaps someday I'll talk to my neighbors about this knowledge I have of them. But one thing is certain: I must not get caught in the loop of hate with them.

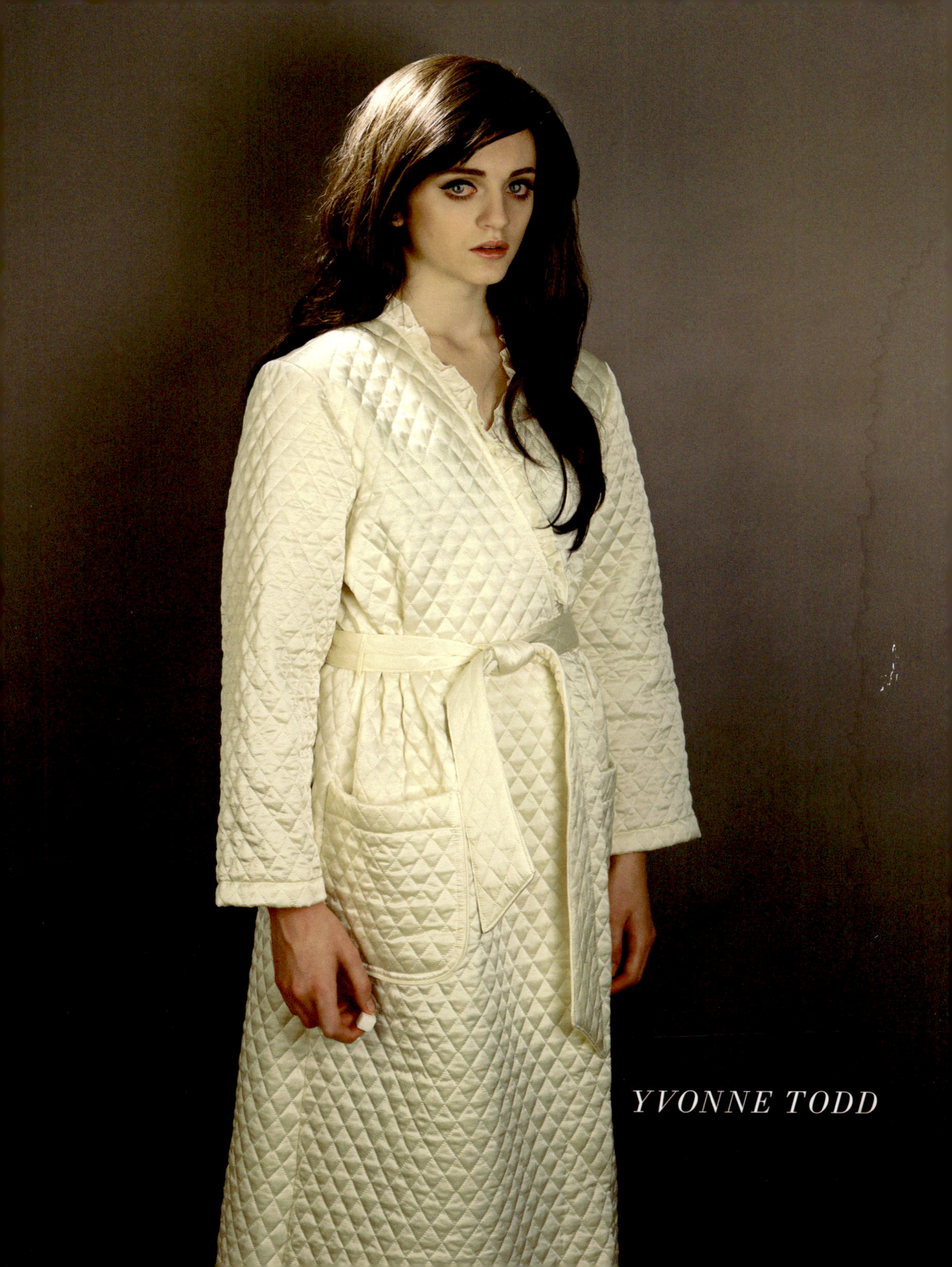

YVONNE TODD

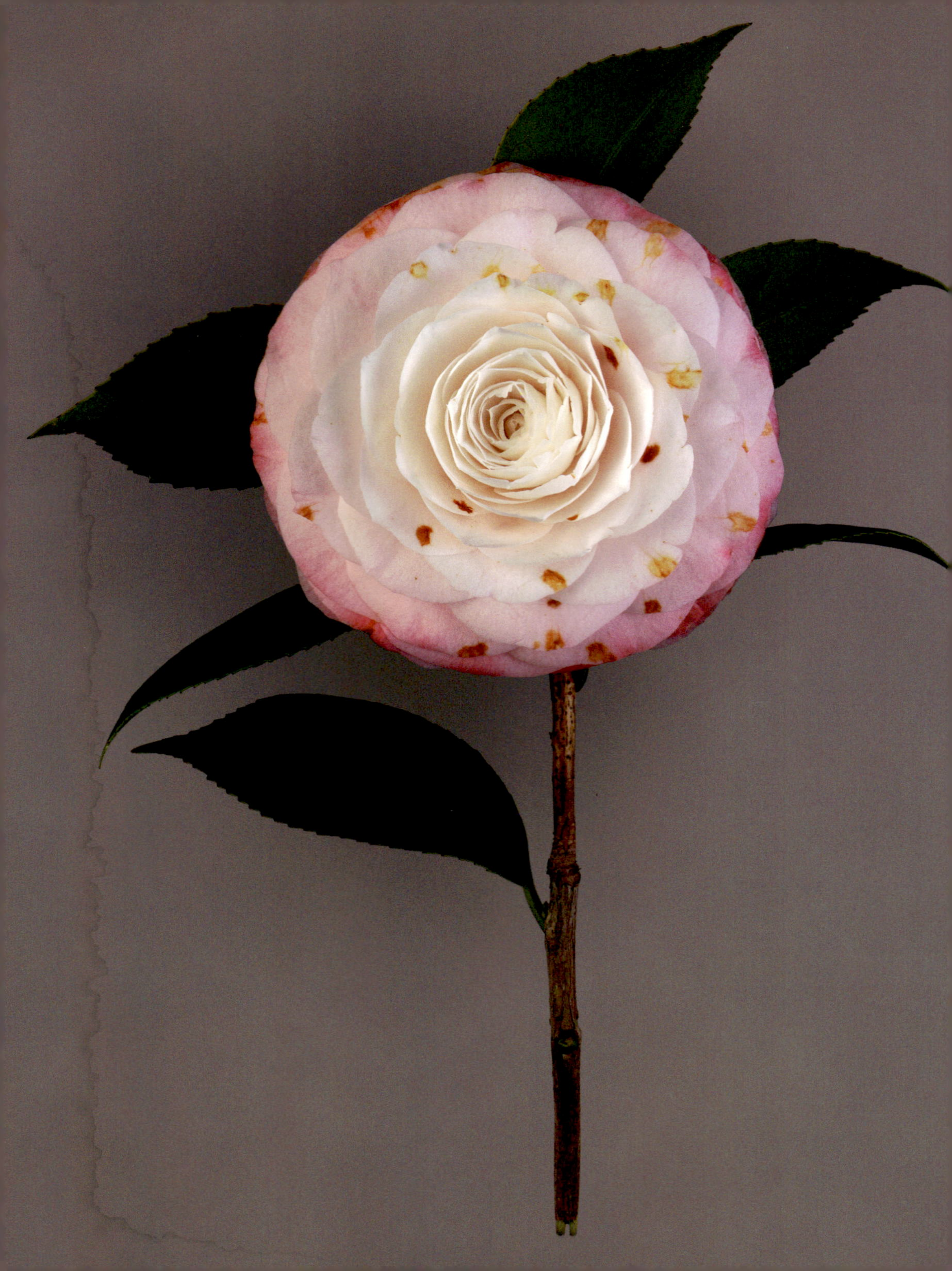

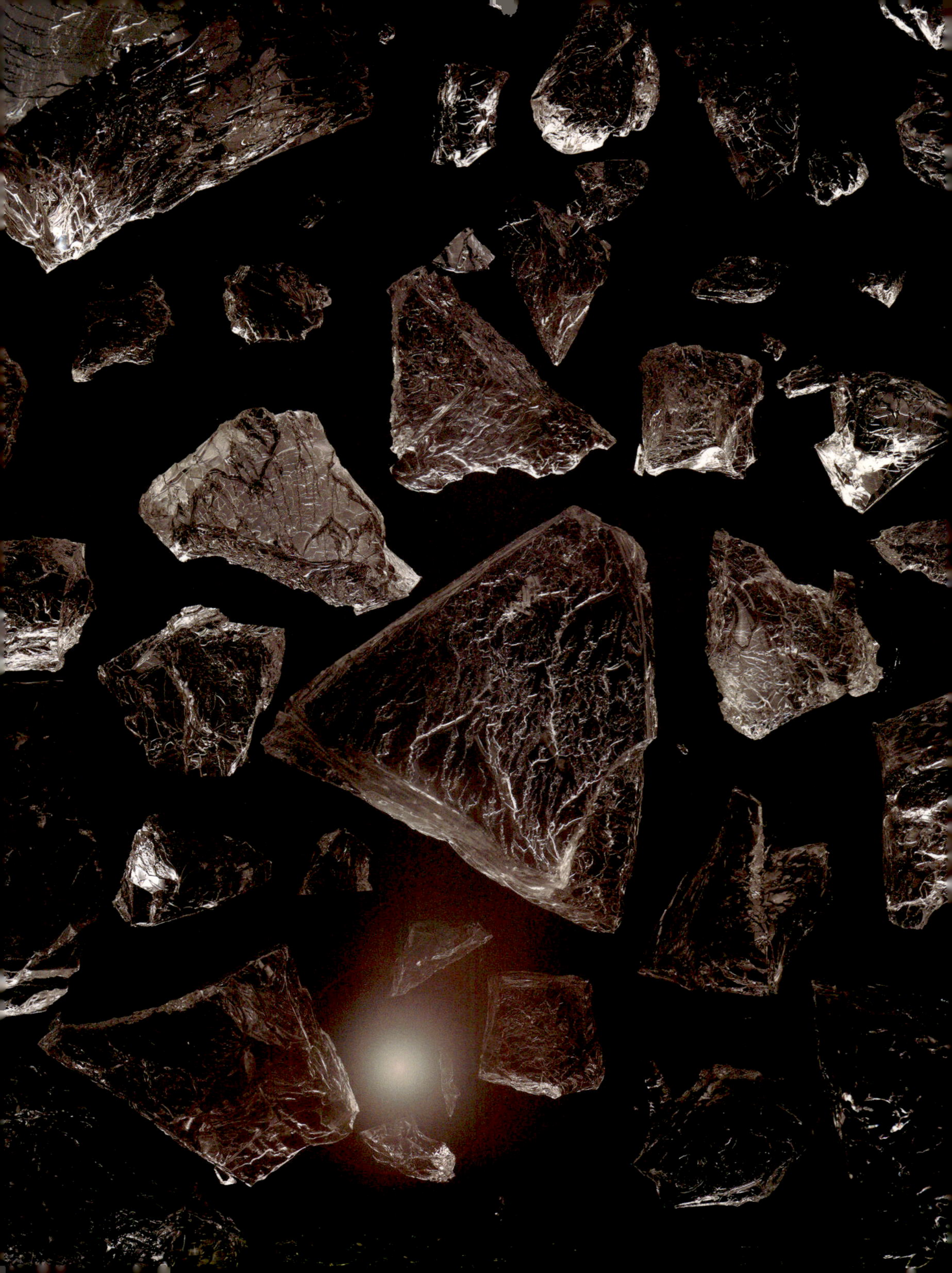

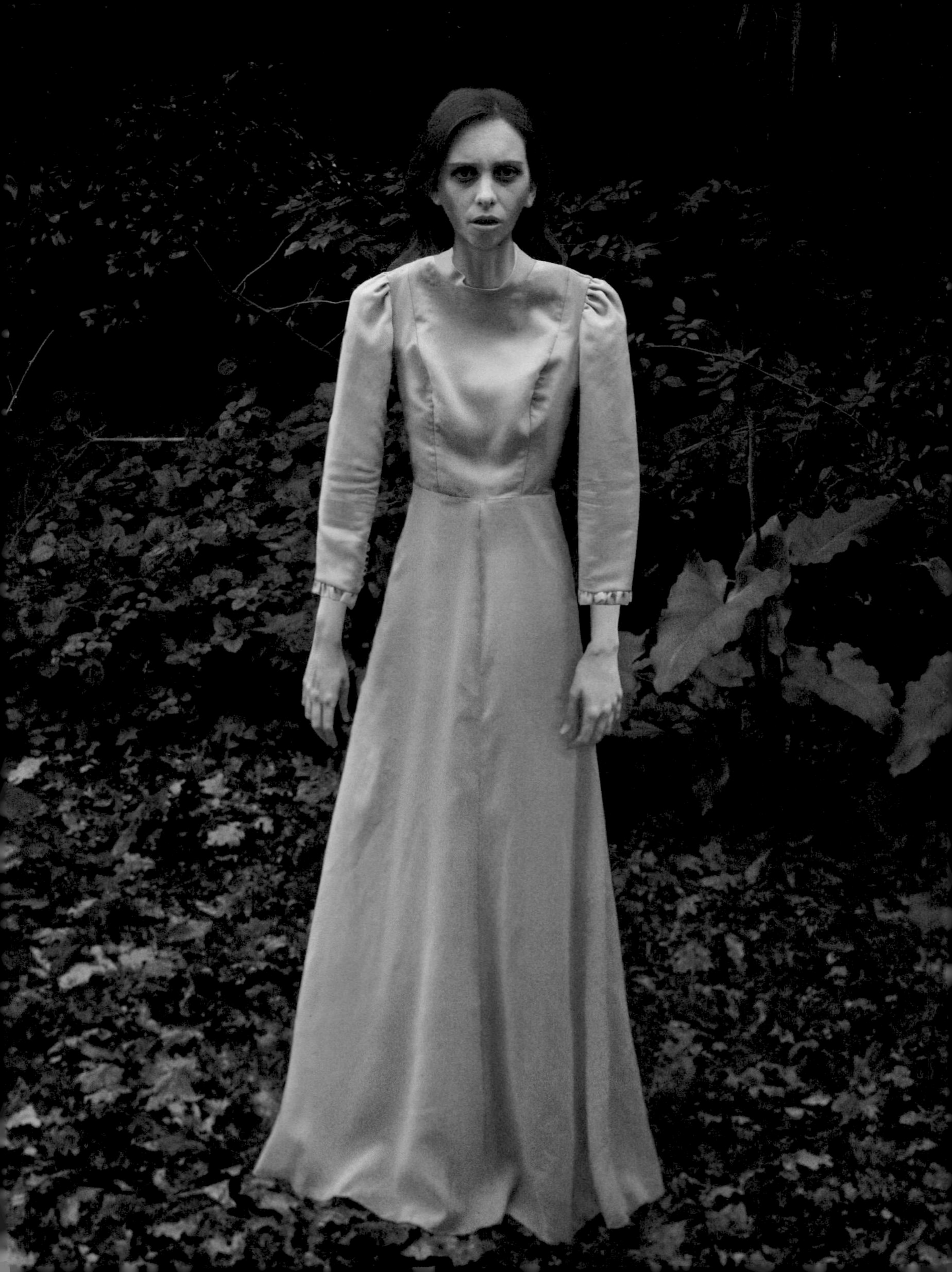

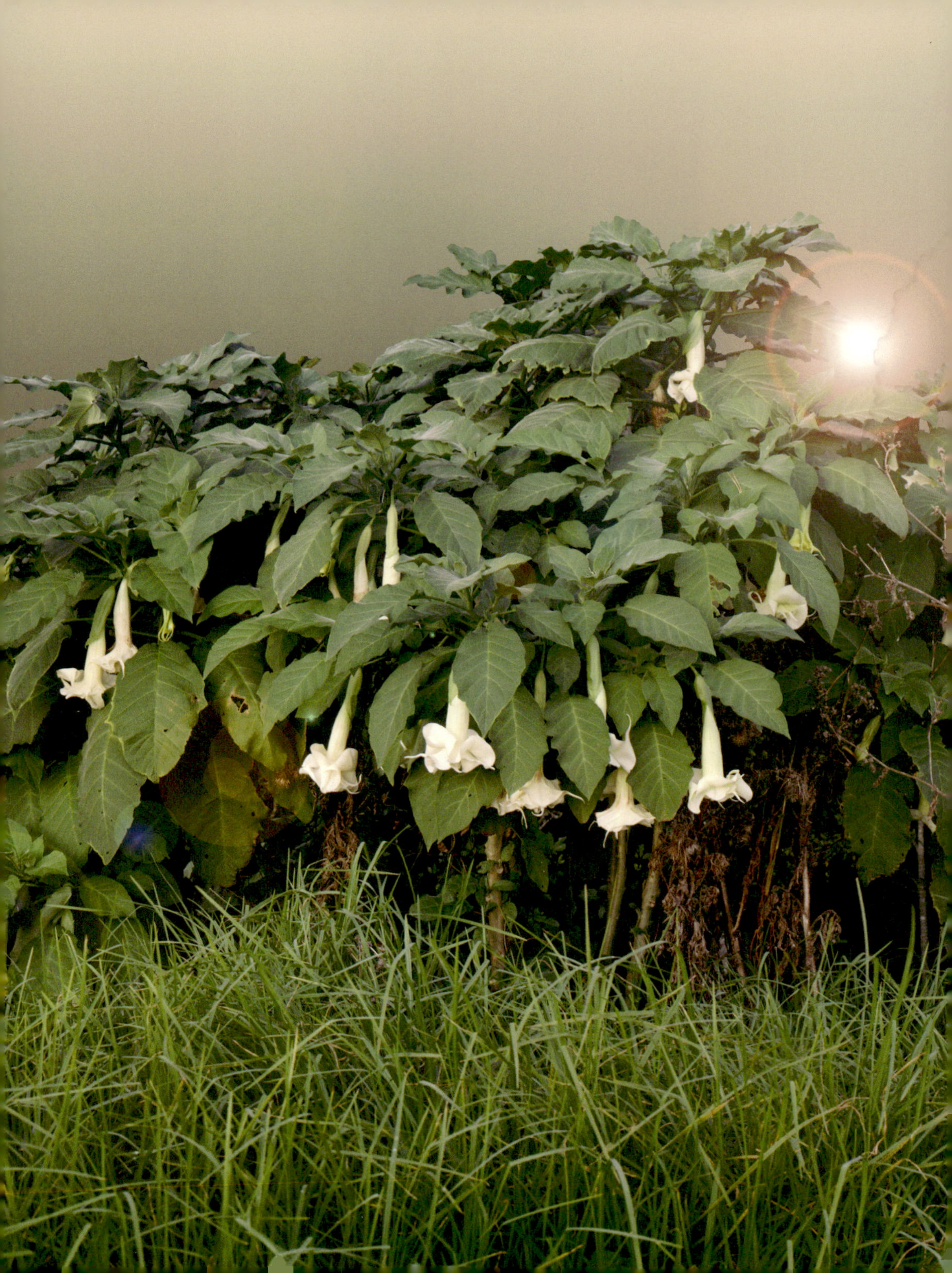

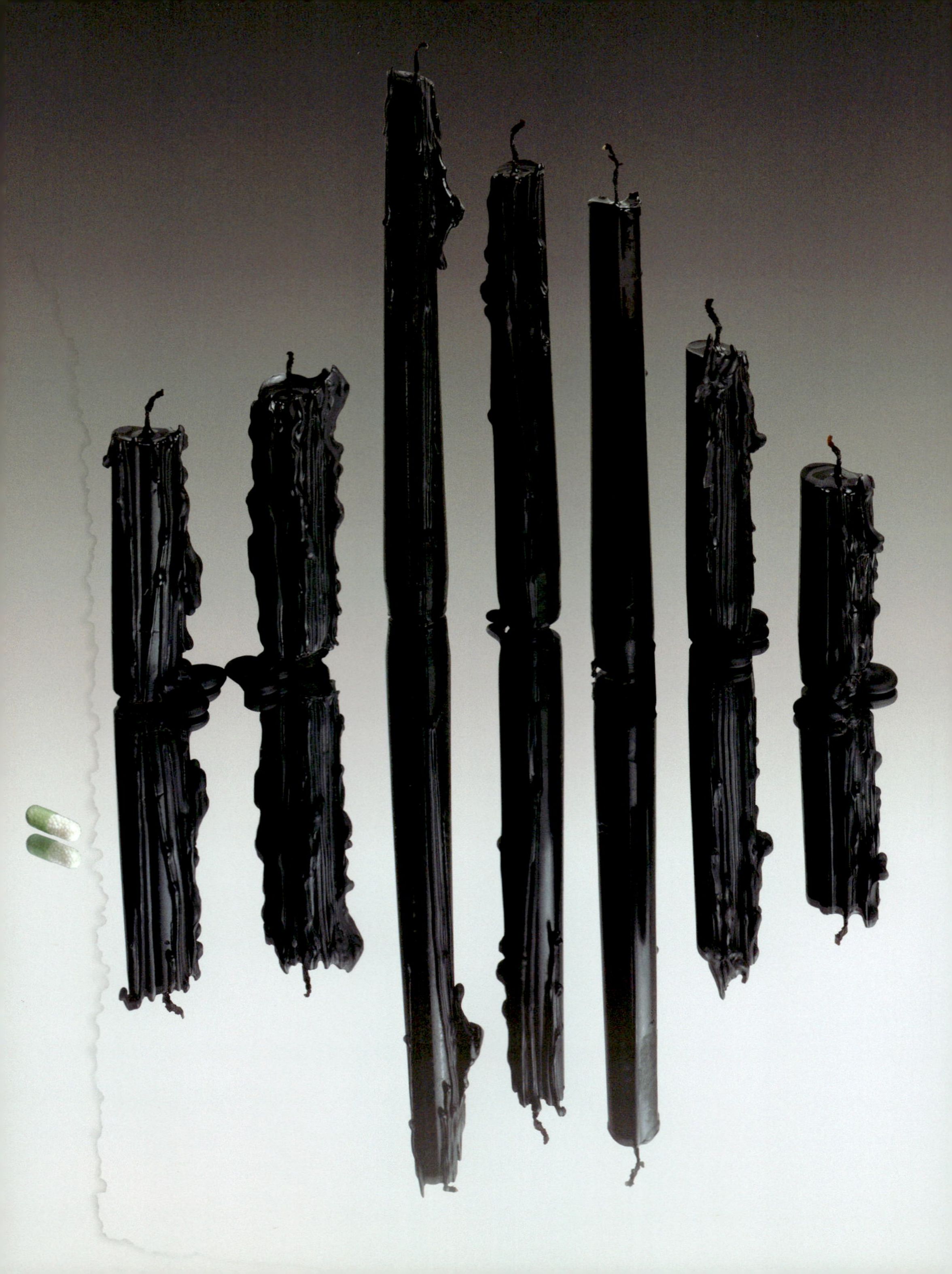

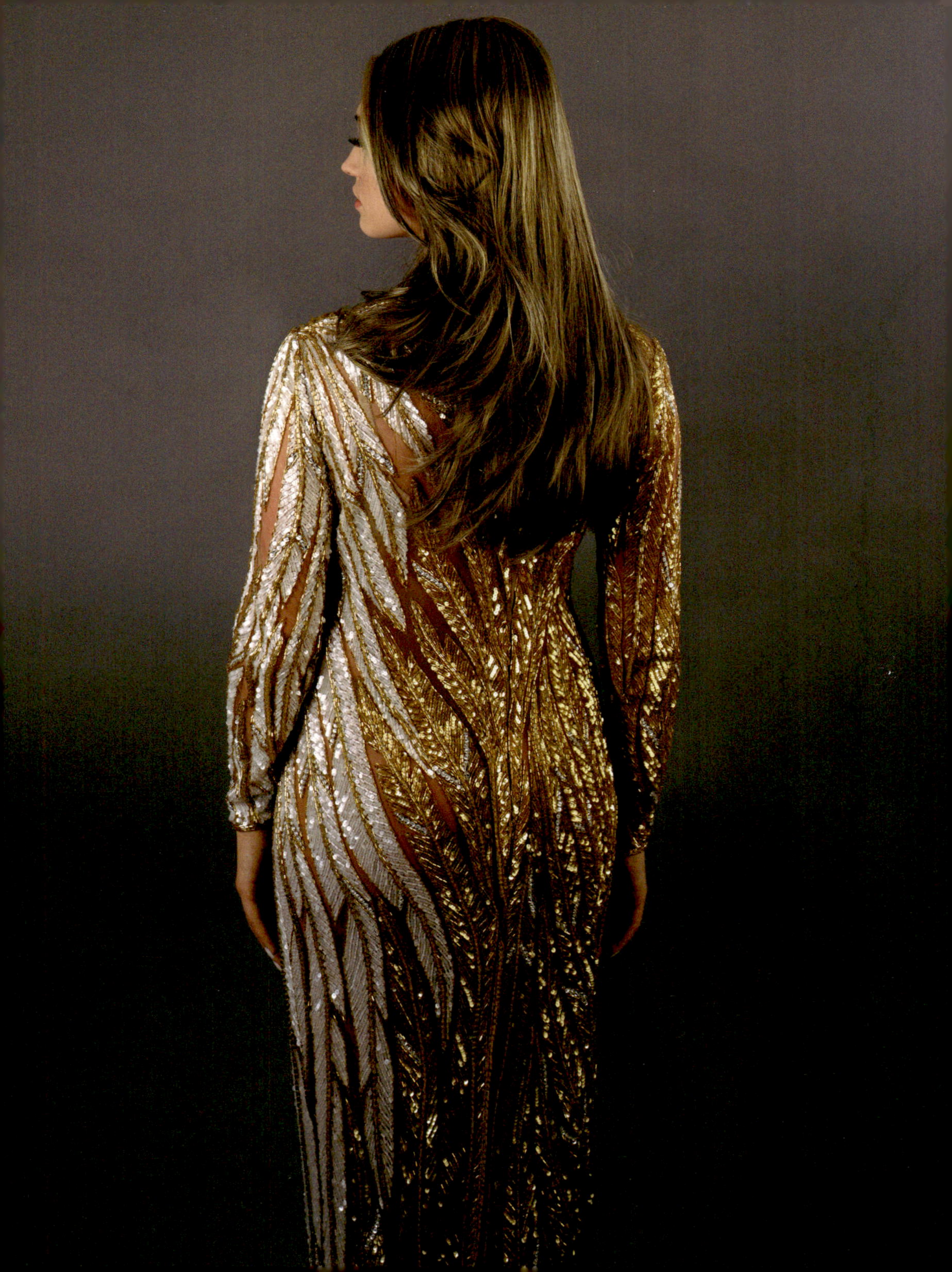

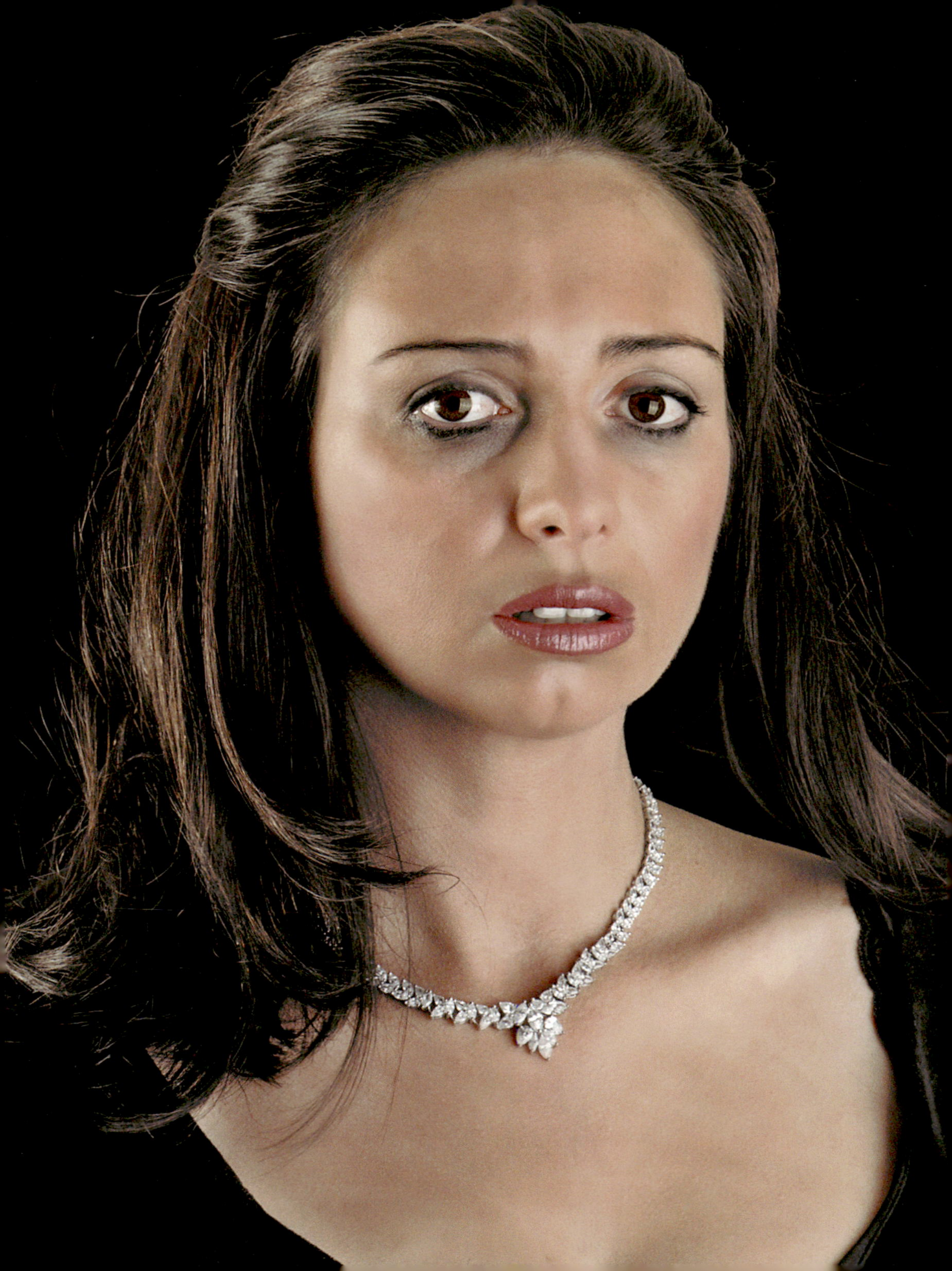

MEG ATKINSON

ILLUMINATED MANUSCRIPTS

The magnifying glass, the largest I have ever seen, is almost toy-like in its insistence on resembling one half of a pair of owl-shaped glasses. It is new and cleanish and its lens is perfectly round. I attempt to hold it steady, almost parallel to the floor, but after a while its weight causes my wrist to tire. As it droops I correct its angle. Lifting it once more, I hold it closer to my nose.

I am in the Metropolitan Museum in New York City.

My feet hurt. I am wearing sandals. My sandals—black, simple, slightly elevated—are inappropriate for standing around in. Normally I wear shoes in which I can walk long, long distances—from 93rd Street to 34th Street, let's say; or home, over the Brooklyn Bridge. But I am wearing sandals today because it is warm (almost summer) and already 90 degrees outside and because I like the sandals and almost never wear them. *And now I know why,* I think, as I attempt to peer at the illuminated scenes, the heavy, over-sized, almost toy-like magnifying glass in my hand.

The illuminated manuscripts have come from France, but because I am still thinking about my sandals I find myself ignoring their provenance. The cobblestone sidewalk, leading from work and down to the Met, had been tricky to navigate; *and yet here is where I am.*

The magnifying glass really is enormous. It takes a few seconds of minor adjustments—a little lower perhaps, a bit of an angle, closer, not too close—before I have it sandwiched at just the right interval between my own shockingly nearsighted eyes and the clear plastic covering underneath which sits protected each diminutive scene.

I peer closer. My nose is almost touching the lens. I know from having overheard the narrator in the educational video in the nook to my left that the manuscripts are parchment. Parchment, as I now know, was made from animal skins. The monks, way back when, first collected these skins, then boiled them, then scraped the hairs off. The rest of this process is still unknown to me as, having become increasingly bored with the sanctimoniousness of the narrator's tones, I have moved along. But still, animal skins! Scraped clean of hairs! *Who knew?*

I continue to peer. Looking through the magnifying glass is like looking through a wormhole. The glass is round and wormholes are round. Wormholes transport persons to faraway, nonexistent places, and, as far as I can tell, this is what I am looking at now. It, the world at which I am now looking, has soft greenish-grayish, awkwardly jutting-up mountains; a pink structure (probably a castle); a boat—its hull the exact size and shape of one half of a walnut shell, upturned and floating on a brownish turbulent sea, a pennant attached to its mast; a person, a book in hand, in the boat. That person, as I am to learn by reading the card alongside of the manuscript, is Saint Jerome. Saint Jerome, bear-like and fleshy, looks similar to all of his compatriot monks, who, like himself, sport long flowing robes and long flowing beards.

I don't really care about Saint Jerome. I am not particularly interested in him. What does interest me are the landscapes beyond: the illuminated, mysterious, karst-like mountains; the pink buildings; the dun colored-caves; the skies in which gold leaf *fleurs de lis* fill up the spaces from heaven on down. The colors are extraordinary, the handiwork intense. In some cases—I am sure of this—one or other of the artists (a Limbourg brother) has had to use a single hair on which to transport a single dot of paint. But what kind of person transports a single dot of paint via a single strand of hair? It is fantastic and peculiar. I am transfixed.

The other figures in the scenes (some of them remind me of that Botticelli-person, that blue-faced one who looks like the victim of a drowning, the one with the flowers streaming from its mouth) are fleshy, and in their stances *contrappposto.* They are mesomorphs, not ectomorphs. Which isn't to say there are no waifs in these scenes. There *are* waifs in these scenes; as are there executioners (their arms are upturned, they have long sweeping swords). And their victims—now headless—have bright warm-looking squirts of blood spurting, extruding from their lopped off necks.

In each scene a grouping of figures huddles, fully robed. The world in which these tableaux exist is insecure. Events are happening—some good, some bad—and people look harried. There are choppy seas and mud-colored waves. Storms are brewing. There are beatings, beheadings, practical jokes. . .

I continue to peer. Behind me, in the museum, are the hushed voices of the tourists. A guard remonstrates a youth for touching a fountain. "Come on," says the youth to his friend. "Let's get out of here."

I peer ever closer. Inside the museum is cool and dim. Outside, as I know, it is hot and bright. The streets are crowded. There are people milling about. There is traffic. It is a snarling, noisy and blaring kind of a place in which to be. People are catcalling, calling.

Earlier at work, when I was showing a painting to my second graders, I had successfully put out of my mind that *second* wormhole. That second wormhole, of course, is my own TV, which, even now as I am squinting through this magnifying glass at bearded and robed Saint Jerome, is available to be turned on. I shudder. I feel cold. I think about the coolness of the museum, its quietude. I contrast its quietude with the blaring of the streets.

In the morning, before leaving for work, I had not turned on that TV wormhole. And the reason I had not turned on that TV wormhole lies in the fact that that TV wormhole leads to a vision of a worse wormhole, a third wormhole, a wormhole that *even now as I am looking through this magnifying glass at Saint Jerome* is gushing black crude into the gulf of Mexico. The President of the United States has given a speech about it. Several speeches. So has the Secretary of the Interior, and so has that woman who was in charge of the country's minerals. (As if anyone could be in charge of those?) Naturally the CEO of the Oil Company has been seen and heard, too. The problem, as I continue to think about it, lies in the fact that *not a person among them knows what to do with this hole.*

I know I can go home right now if I want to. I can go home and turn on my TV and I can watch those plumes of oil as they continue to spurt from that third wormhole, the one that has been tampered with. That wormhole, the one that has been tampered with, is a natural one, a one that has lain dormant at the bottom of the sea.

I study Saint Jerome. In one scene he is robed in a woman's dress. And the reason he is robed in a woman's dress is because his brother monks have played a joke on him. They have laid out this woman's dress by Jerome's bedside the night before, knowing full well that upon his waking he will be so addled from sleep, so disoriented that he will don this dress unknowingly. And of course—you guessed it!—there is Jerome and he is wearing the dress!

I stretch. My back hurts from bending over. What a nasty, viper-filled, pitfall-filled world this is! I push the thought of the crude from my mind. No, I don't. I imagine the crude. I imagine it bubbling, gushing, foaming. I imagine the brown seas of the gulf of Mexico becoming ever browner, choppier. As the oil fills the gulf it will, I know, seep into the sandy beaches. The sand will become brown and sticky; soon it will resemble a bowl of granulated sugar into which gouts of molasses have been poured. But not as nice. And the waters will rise. The brown oozing of the waters of the Gulf of Mexico will spread. They will lap slowly, first at the marshes and the watersheds and then at the low-lying bushes. Even the coast of Maine, with its scrub blueberries and rounded boulders, will not be immune.

The spill will grow and grow. It will enter the already murky waters of New York Harbor. Boats will become stuck in it. A lone kayaker attempting to wipe the slime off his paddle will be unable to do so. The slimy waters will lap along Wall Street, mixing in with the strewn trash: the dog shit, the coffee cups, the dropped pacifiers. Floating atop this murk the trash will be borne along the sidewalks. It will besmear the ankles of pedestrians. The gunk will attach itself to loafers, bare feet, high heels. People will scurry and curse. There will be no pushing. One does not push in times of ooze. As the ooze continues to rise it will befoul the tires of the taxis and the buses, and then it will dribble compellingly down the subway's steps, where the rats, their fur slick and matted with oil, like the feathers of the waterfowl before them, will slip and slide in their attempts to get home.

As the waters rise they will meander uptown.

By now, of course, people—citizens, denizens, the Mayor—will be on their parlor floors. They will be peering out through their hand-clenched drapes at the sickening ooze, their shocked faces staring.

The waters, continuing to rise, will surge, bubble and froth up the shallow risers of the steps of the Museum.

I shift my feet. It will be odd, I think, being here now in the museum at the first sign of lapping. I continue to study through the magnifying glass the world of Saint Jerome: the castellations, the jokers, the beards and the robes. When next I shift my feet, it will have to be done gingerly so as not to slide. The ooze in which I will be standing will be slippery. Its brownness will sully the polished white floors of the Museum. Which will be a shame. Over my toes it will lap. It will lap up my shins.

Looking through the wormhole is like being enveloped by it. It sucks you in. As I continue to peer, I wonder: what did Jerome know that we do not? The answer, when it comes, comes in a flash: He knew enough, it would seem, to be worried.

MICHAEL SIGNORELLI

REPLICAS

It was Tuesday morning. Sunlight slanted over the neighborhood. The sky held a catch of clouds still cool from night. Catherine and Jeanie made breakfast in the kitchen. Vince looked himself over in the bedroom mirror, filled his pockets, and walked down the stairs. Halfway through the front hall, on his way to the kitchen, he heard a knock at the door. Just one knock, and he turned. At each window on either side of the door was a dark, sturdy-looking shoulder, as if one impossibly wide person waited on the front steps. Or, more likely, there were two deliverymen standing abreast, invoice at the ready. Vince rerouted himself, grasped the handle, pressed down the latch, and swung open the door.

"Good morning, fellas. Can I help you?"

Vince received no immediate response. The two men stood there mutely, unmoving, perhaps waiting for Vince to register the entirety of their presence, which he soon did. But first he couldn't help but glance past them to see the grass and trees shimmering with light-soaked dew, a blue-gray breeze rustling their dampness. And who were these happy visitors? Vince returned his attention to the men, and the funniest thing occurred to him: they were identical. Inch for inch, one a replica of the other. But they were not twins, not like Danny and Aaron Westlake, two middle-school kids who lived three houses down the street. These men seemed to vibrate with likeness: from their broad chests to their dense, meaty shoulders to their bloodless, gray skin. Vince looked searchingly into their faces for some explanation and met their eyes. These, he found, were different. Not from each other but from humans. They were liquid, not orbs, not tense spheroids of flesh, twitching after the world, but a kind of liquid. Not milky or transparent but metallic. As Vince saw them, they looked like backlit puddles of oil, with no rounding, no curvature exposed beyond the orbital opening. There were no pupils to speak of except for luminescent swirls that stormed round and round like trippy screensavers. The surface of their eyes—in fact, the whole constitution of their location in space—ran straight along a ray originating in the center of the earth. Vince didn't know they looked so much like that, but it is nonetheless what he saw. He cleared his throat impatiently, as if they were all about to start on some business, and said, "Yes?"

Catherine was in the kitchen pantry, putting away a box of cereal. An orange peel lay temporarily agape on the counter. Jeanie continued to rinse the recently employed dish- and silverware in the sink. Once done, she placed everything on the pre-machine drying rack. Catherine backed out of the pantry, pushing open the door with her backside. She was bent forward, holding a green bin full of aluminum and plastic receptacles. They felt busy and barely noted the front door opening.

Catherine dropped the bin over by the back door, beyond which lay a gravel path that skirted along the backyard to the driveway. Jeanie sat on a stool not going anywhere. She had ten minutes before she needed to leave for school. There was no point in being early. Her mother returned to the main square of the kitchen looking rushed and alert.

"Honey, you should get going," she said.

"I don't have to leave yet. Ten more minutes."

Jeanie figured she'd leave the moment her mother became resolved for her to go. But, seemingly satisfied with the interval, her mother asked, "So, what's happening this week?"

Two things came foremost to Jeanie's mind: Friday night and Mark Sterling. Mark Sterling, the boy who it was rumored would ask Jeanie to his Senior Prom, the boy who would be out Friday night at her friend Emma's party. Jeanie was hopeful that life would happen as she wished it to, since she could honestly tell her mother she was "just going over to Emma's," something she'd done many Friday nights before. But never before had Emma been so brazen and excellent as to invite boys, too. Wait, she thought, is that Mark at the door?

"Well, Jeanie, what's happening?"

"Nothing. I have tests tomorrow and Thursday. I think I'm going over to Emma's on Friday."

"Have you been studying?"

"I started Sunday. Yes. It's just reviews of what they've already taught us. I've got it."

"If you are so absolutely sure then."

Jeanie resisted rolling her eyes and instead moved them quickly sideways away from her mother. Then she remembered the possibility of Mark and walked toward the front door.

"Who's Dad talking to?"

The men took Vince's pause as invitation to enter. Vince walked backward. They displaced him from the space he previously occupied not by force but as a natural exchange, as a fulfillment of some presumptive will. He was back by the stairs. Vince heard Jeanie behind him. She started to ask, "Who is it?" then gasped.

Upon seeing Jeanie enter the front hall, the two men, still silent, exuded an air of delight. This was made known by Vince knowing it. He half-turned to shout.

"Jeanie, out back and to school, now!"

Squaring back to face the men, Vince noticed a change in their appearance. They seemed to have grown taller and somehow brighter, as if the threading of their clothes hummed with light. The eyes, the liquid-filled clefts in their faces, removed themselves from either side their nose holes and scrambled round their stony features in dueling figure eights.

"I want you out now!"

The men loomed taller as the breath left Vince's throat.

"Now!"

And taller.

Vince ran into the kitchen.

His wife and daughter stood wide-eyed near the back door. Catherine had a hand on Jeanie's shoulder. They both stared at Vince.

"We should go, please, now. Out the back."

"What's happening?"

"I don't even know what they could be."

"What?"

"I don't know. Two men. Very strange. They're in the house."

"Who?"

"This is crazy."

"Dad?—"

The air lurched with an awful noise. Dizzy in the new way of things, again Vince shouted, "Out the back!"

The back door would not open. A wall of light pressed against it. Nothing except white of a muted brightness could be seen out the framed glass. The men appeared at the threshold between the kitchen and front hall. Their eyes had returned to their original positions. The men had reassumed their original size. But the sight of Jeanie, and now Catherine too, re-aroused their luster. They stepped in unison. Their arms swung slack from slumped shoulders, pendular, like goons from Goonland. Vince and family inched away from the unaccountable white. They shuffled as a unit to just in front of the oven. Three meters and the kitchen island separated family from these two… what? Men. Goons. Figures. Hallucinations. The latter must be discounted, as things wouldn't be like they were with so many participants if not for some corroboration external to Vince's mind. Could they be emissaries? Freak visitors from some asteroid nation? Were they human? Projections of human elements taken form and life? How did they arrive here? How did they choose this house? What were they after?

A standstill fell upon them, a hush happened, each party remained where it was and remained still. The men seemed temporarily satisfied by their progress and leered across the distance. In the pause, Vince could hear Jeanie breathing. Air moved in and out of her nostrils. He listened and heard fear loosening the pace of her diaphragm, tripping it up, fear over fear, a shudder.

The men moved toward them, raising in sync their arms from their sides. Their movement marked only by vision of the act. They were soundless. Vince heard only Jeanie's breath quaking in tempo, then, by increments, slowing ever so, every exhale lengthening a fraction of a second, every inhale falsely sounding larger lungs; and as Vince sensed this slowing, he watched the two figures move closer, raising their arms to shoulder-height before them, lurching forward like stock monsters; and as they advanced, they too slowed as if they were being enfolded in hardening invisible matter, transfixing them in time to the petering whisper of Jeanie's breath.

Nothing moved. Not Vince, not Jeanie. Not their breath, not their blood. The men, the strangers, were leant forward, checked in step, paused. Jeanie's lips were parted a pea's width; her mouth softly gupped; her eyes wide and wet as if she were only just aware of something that would become very upsetting. Catherine's mouth was tight; her cheeks taut round her pursed lips; her eyes said "violation," "anger," "final danger." The whiteness filled the windows above the kitchen counter. It was a white of profound inertness—a sight of negation. Vince felt the stillness of time settle in his chest like a weight. It was heavier than the earth and pulled the wound chords of his soul deep into blackness. Vince braced for his jaw to be ripped from his skull, for his arms to be torn from his shoulders, for his neck to crinkle into his chest, and for the whole of him to crack and collapse through the floor, to be dragged a wreck for light years.

The fact of his bracing sprung him up. A conscious knot of him existed unharmed. But all remained frozen. The two men, not men, their motion checked, were now ready for fuller inspection: oval heads of human proportion; hairless; the eyes unsettling, their sheen reflecting light from more than these three dimensions; their clothes of a biological tailor, stitches like sinews; their thin fingers striving forward, look to be capable of swift penetration, look to be aimed at the throats of Jeanie and Catherine. Vince could see no more than that. His eyes offered him only a snapshot.

Things remained like this, as far as Vince could tell, for an unknowable amount of time. The sequential passing of moments had somehow stopped.

There was only this moment, and yet Vince's mind kept on. He was aware of time excusing itself, as if it was draining out of his body, out of this sensed scene; and, as it did, the particles of visual reality began to separate into a non-image, into something incompatible with individual consciousness. The world, his family, this danger began to disappear; either because of or precipitating Vince's waning ability to sense. But just as these particles scattered to the brink of irreversible dissolution, the gravity of Vince, the chemistry of his soul pulled himself together and so also the world. Vince was not powerless.

Again, he perceived the static present. Everything was as he remembered it—Jeanie half-crouched between and clutching him and Catherine, the two men frozen in threat—but the edges of his snapshot were dimmer and out of focus. Less of the world had returned. He felt as if he was teetering on a divide. Down one side was dissolution into nothing. Down the other was reanimation of time. Vince knew his choice would decide the balance. He could relinquish time and avoid the coming violence. He could allow Jeanie, Catherine, and the two men gnarled in action to dissolve into something inconceivable but necessarily real. He could usher them into death. But would that be death? Would that be the same as having one's body destroyed either by time or disease or abrupt failure? Would that be acceptable in the face of what was promised before today, before these visitors, before time became unlike itself? Or would that be cowardice? Suicide? To willfully avoid what's coming. To take reckless possession of a mysterious gift.

Time rolled like a ball, slowly at first, down a slight but endless grade, gathering to its terminal velocity. Air seeped into his lungs. His heart clenched to beat. The vividness of forms returned. He heard the electric whump of their time-stalled appliances. He felt the warmth of Jeanie's hand around his arm, sensed the presence of his panicked wife. He could feel the weight of them.

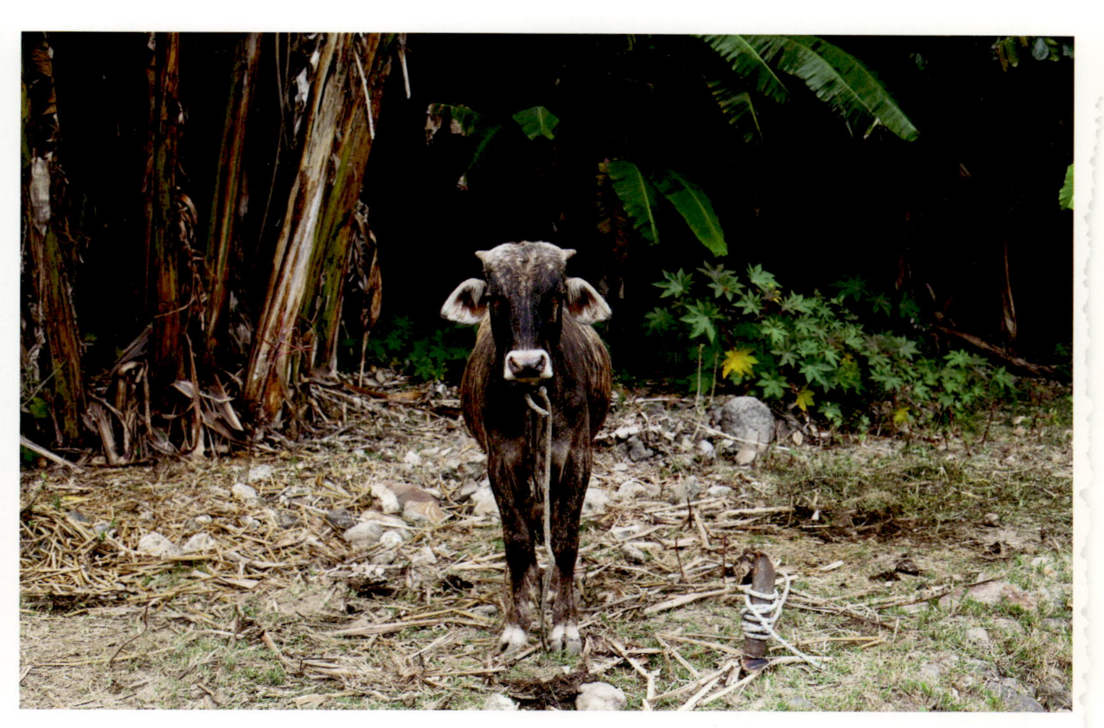

SUZANNA FINLEY

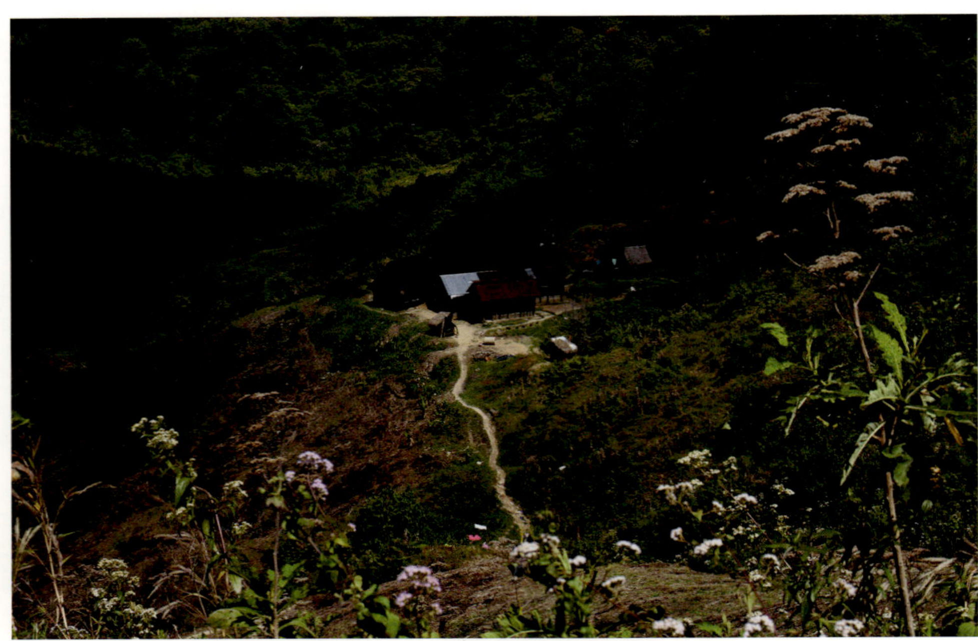

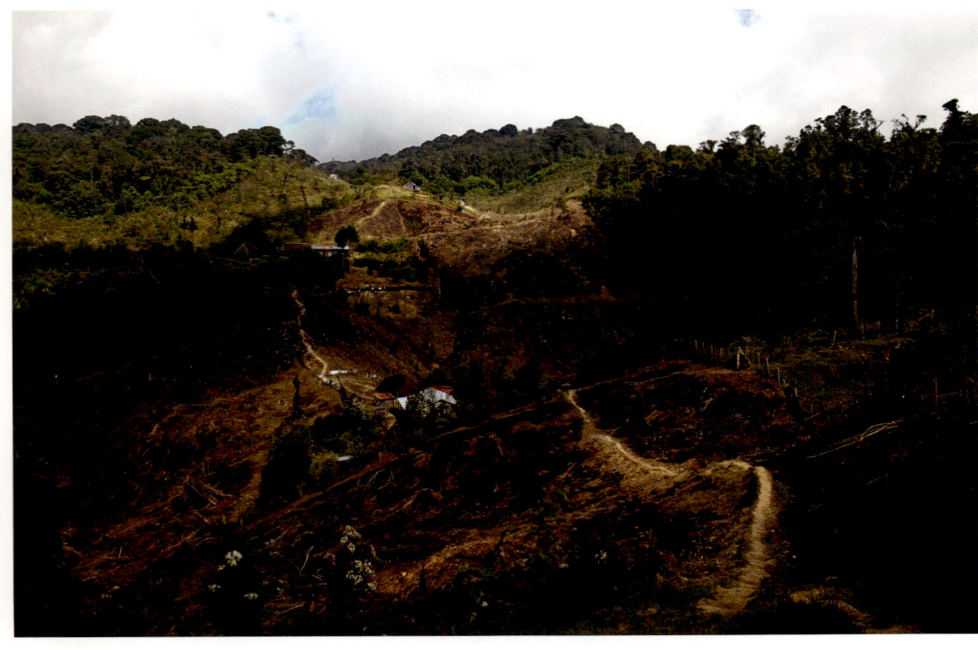

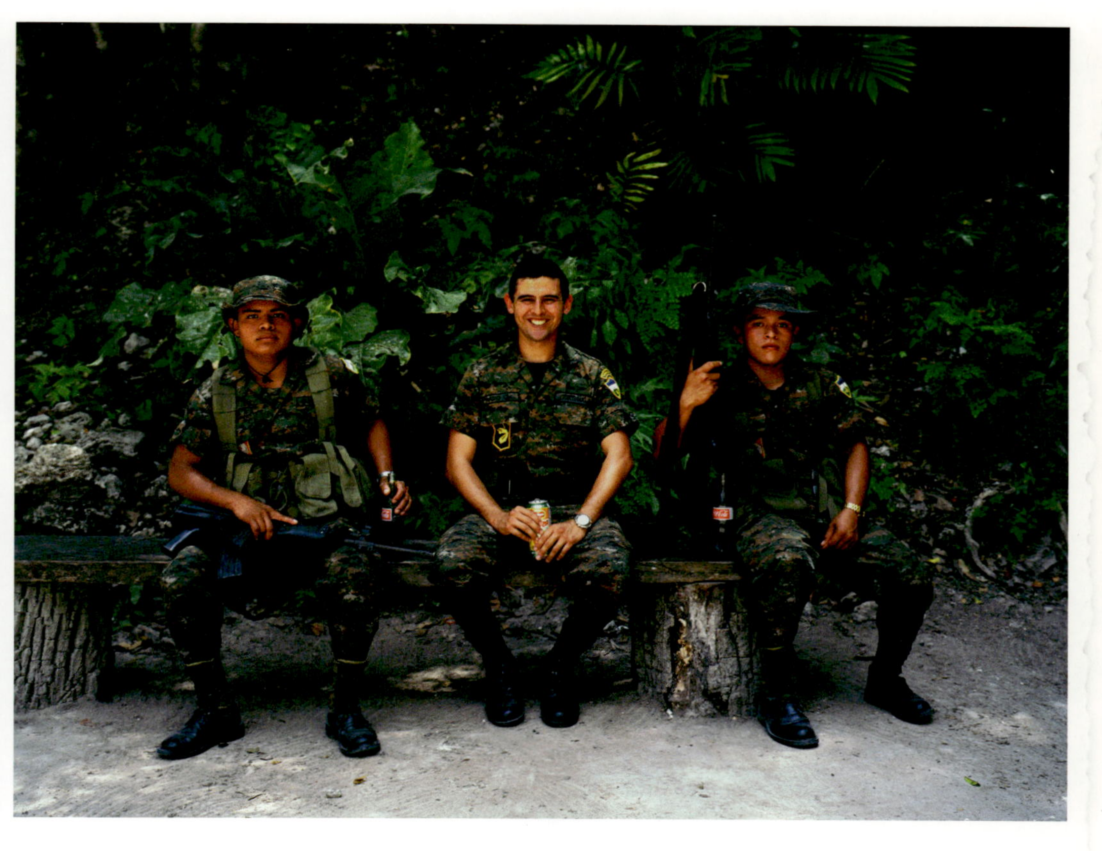

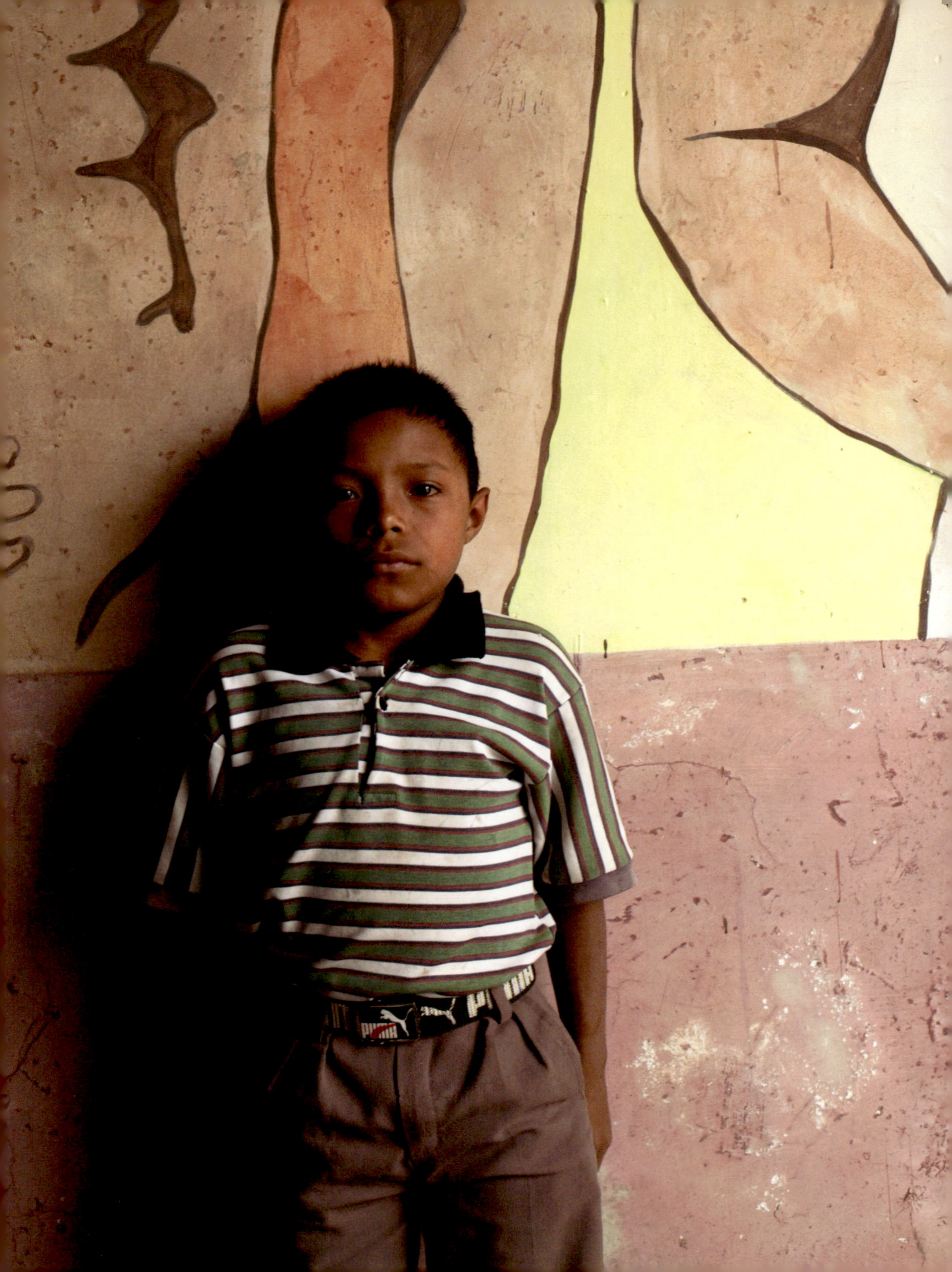
PUMA

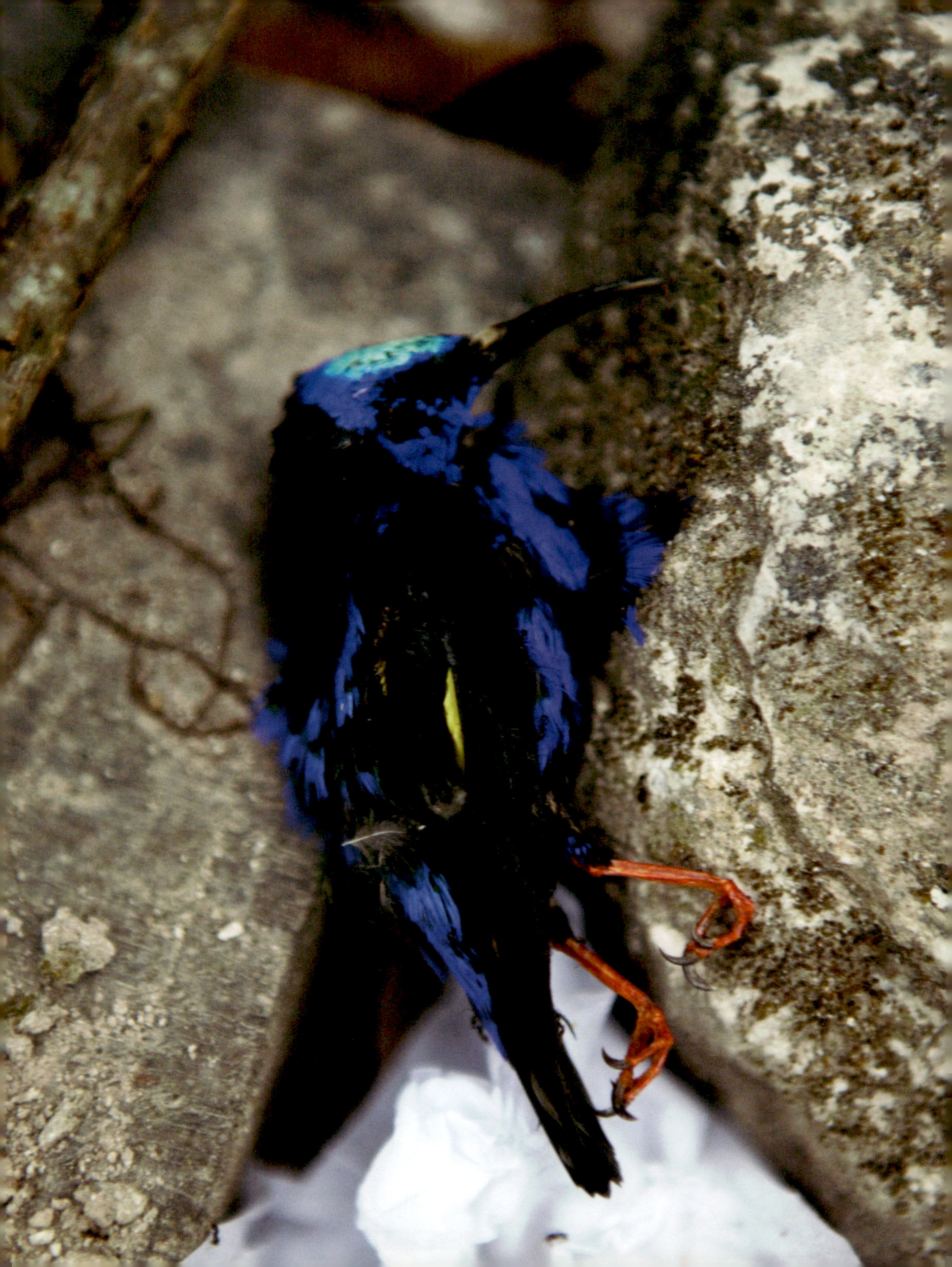

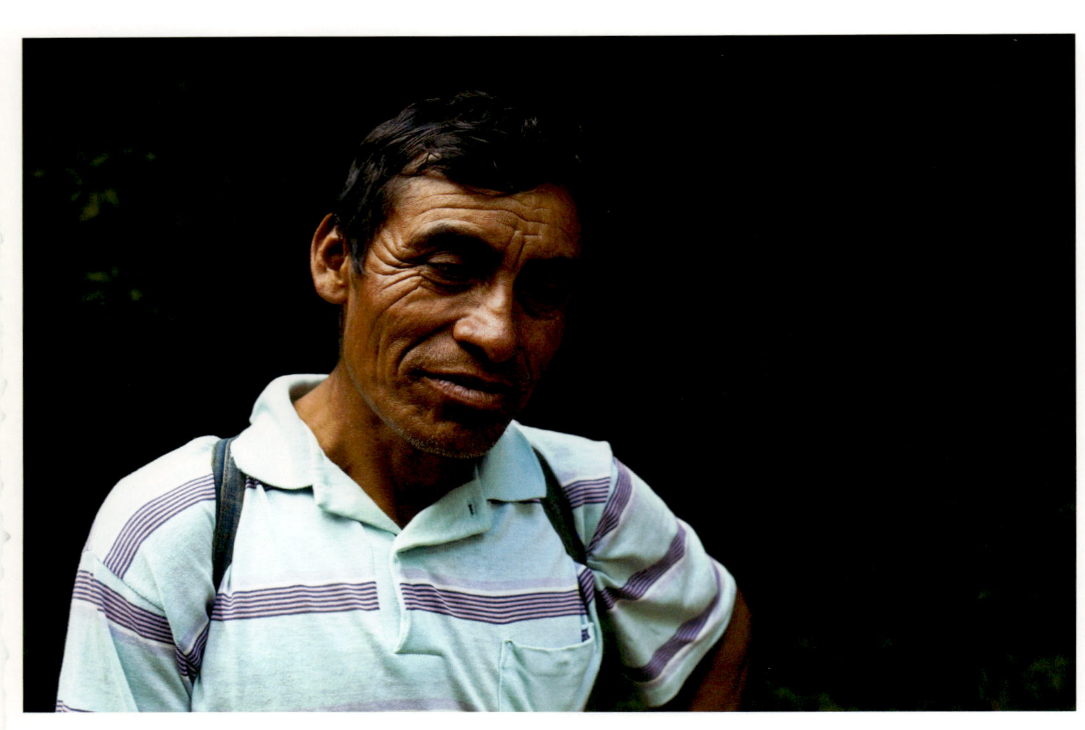

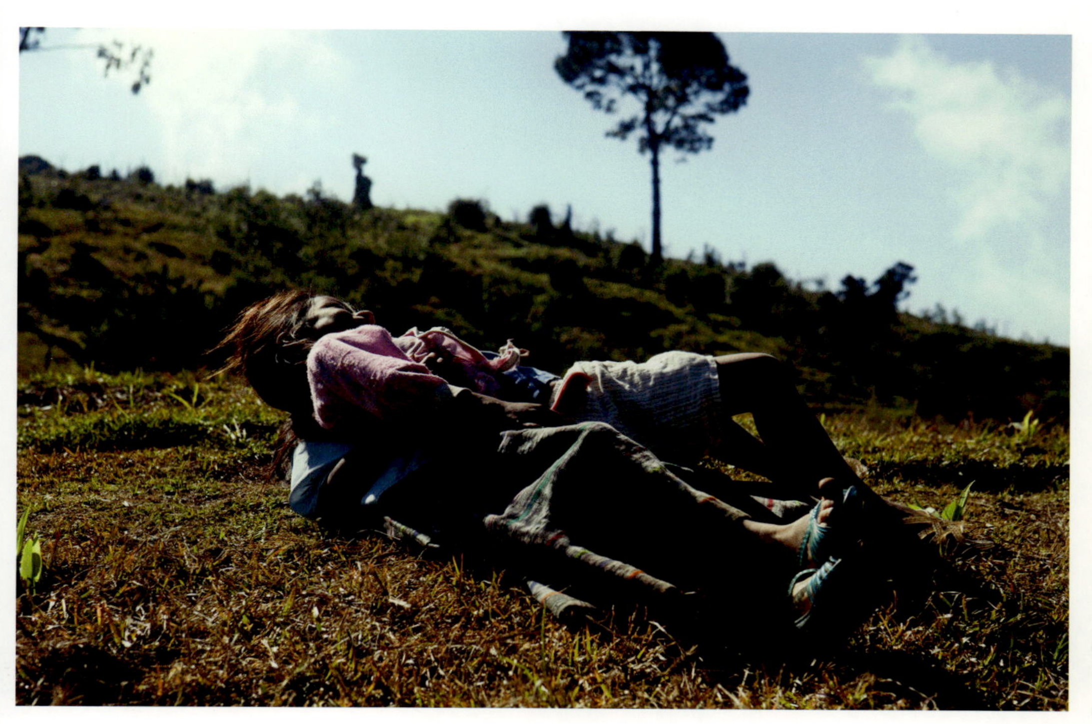

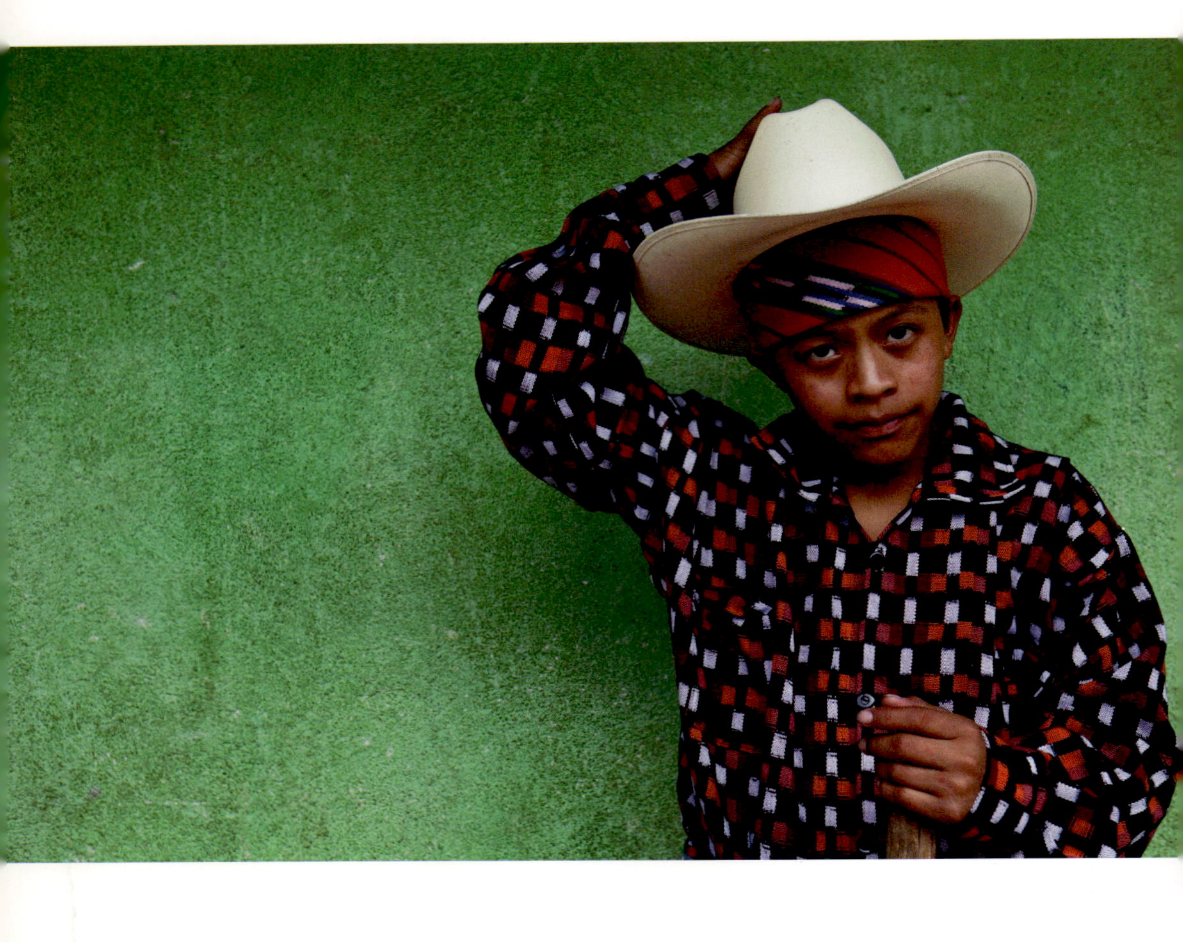

YASMINA

KHAN

REINVENTING

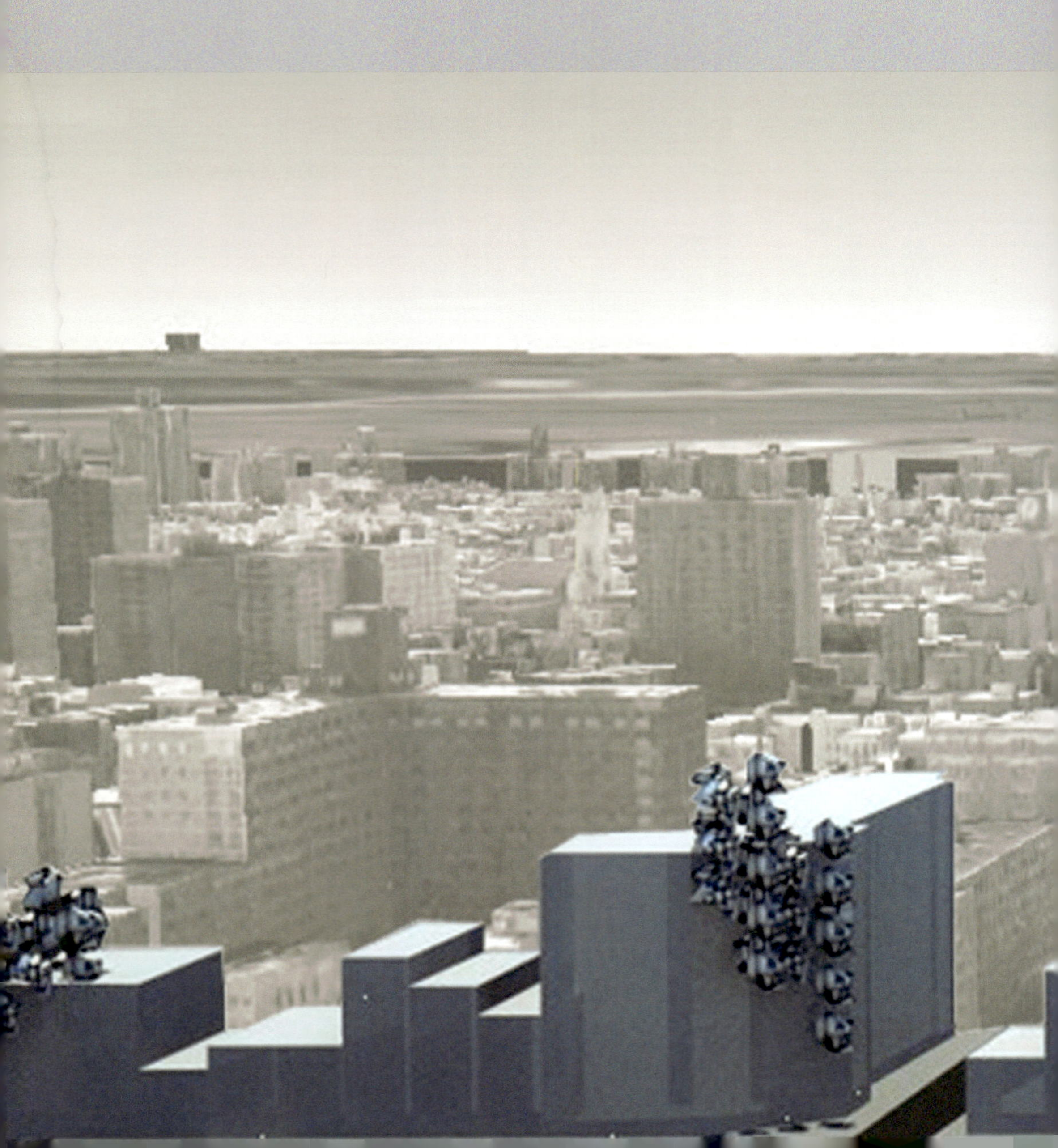

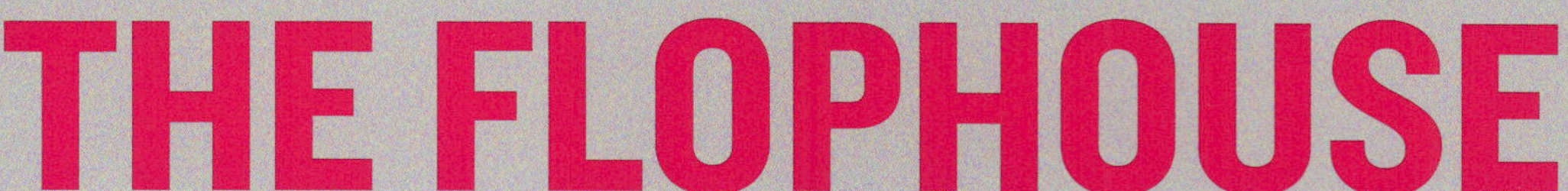

THE FLOPHOUSE

The Bowery, once home to saloons, tatoo parlors, dime museums, dive bars, and lodging houses, has gone under gradual change since the 1900s. The cheapest lodging, or flophouses has completely dissappeared. In its place are galleries, hotels and restaurants. Since the dissappearance of the flophouse there is no longer a place for cheap lodging along the Bowery. In my design intervention I explore re-inserting the original Bowery into its contemporary identity. What if the new flophouse could reflect and reinvigorate the reknown thoroughfare's transformed culture?

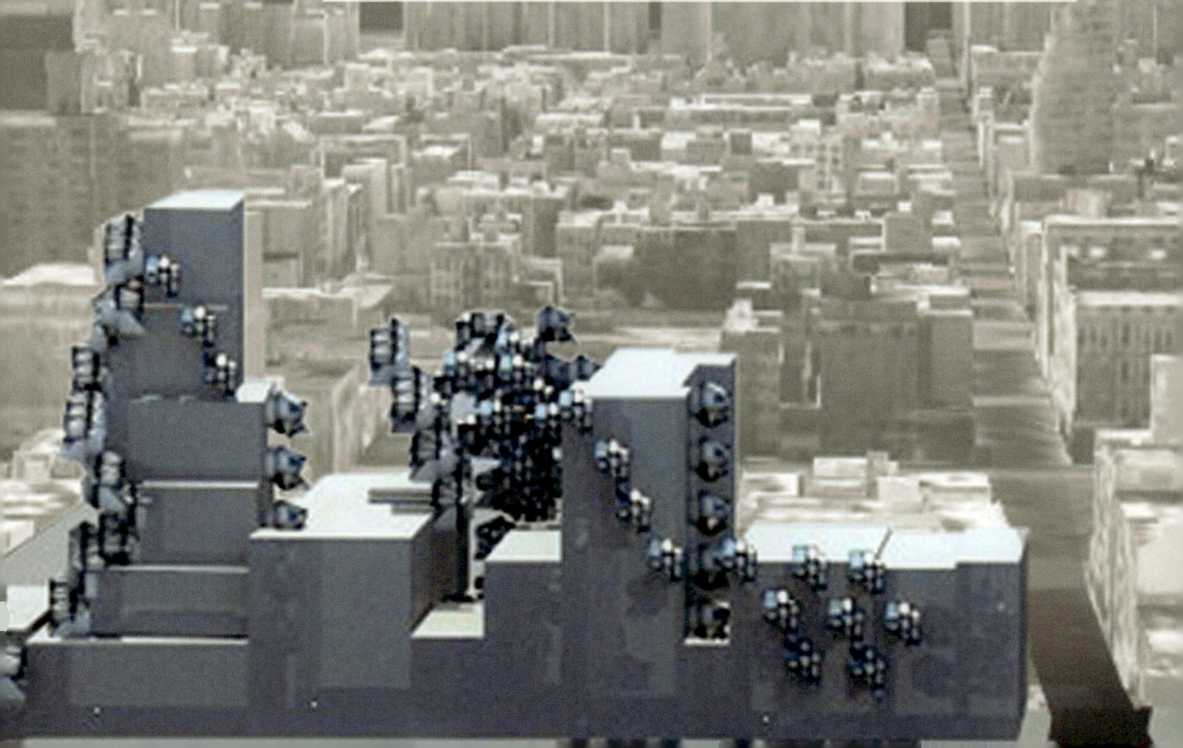

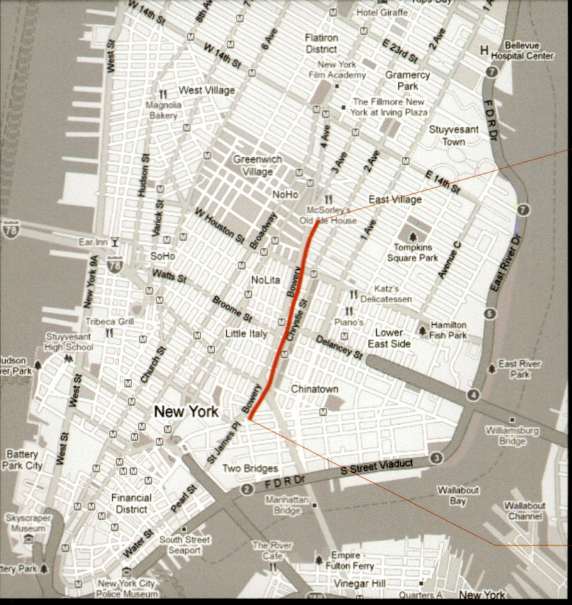

The Bowery is the oldest thoroughfare in Manhattan, it existed as an footpath used by the natives before the street grid. This accounts for the Bowery's irregular, winding shape. The Dutch settlers named the path *Bouwerij Road*, after the old Dutch word for farm. This was because it connected farmlands and estates on the outskirts of the heart of the city. It is the only street which is marked at its beginning and end by open spaces, Chatham and

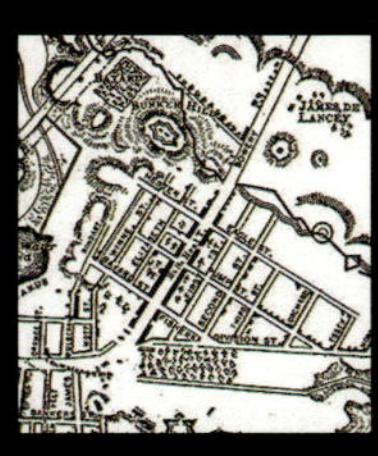

MAP OF BOWERY LANE, 1782

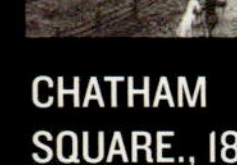

CHATHAM SQUARE., 1861

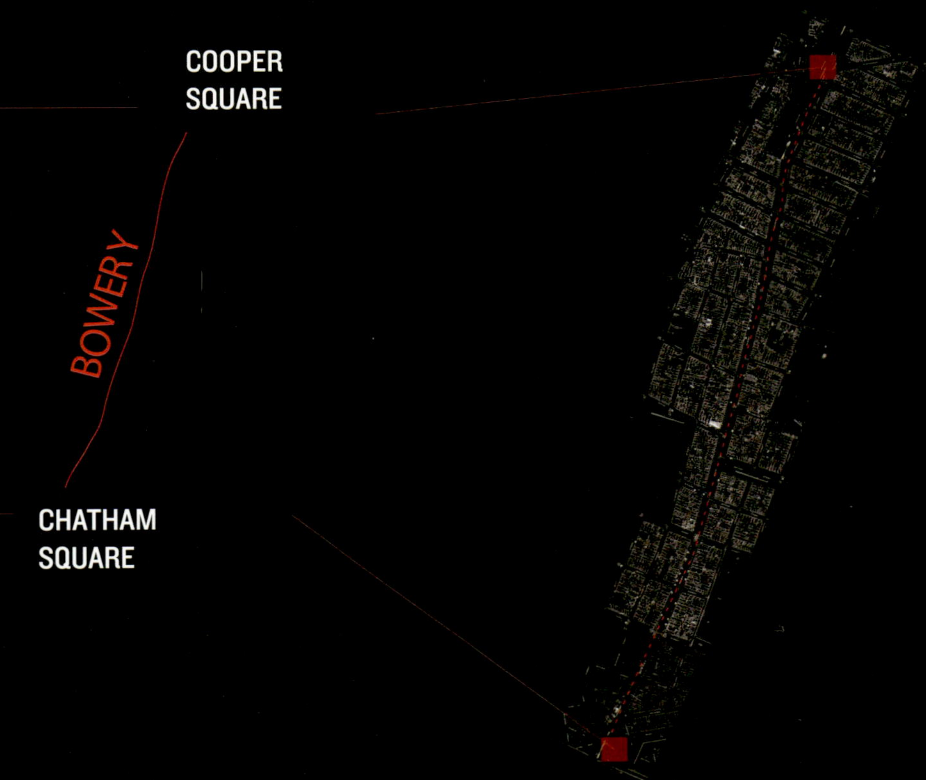

LOCATING SITE

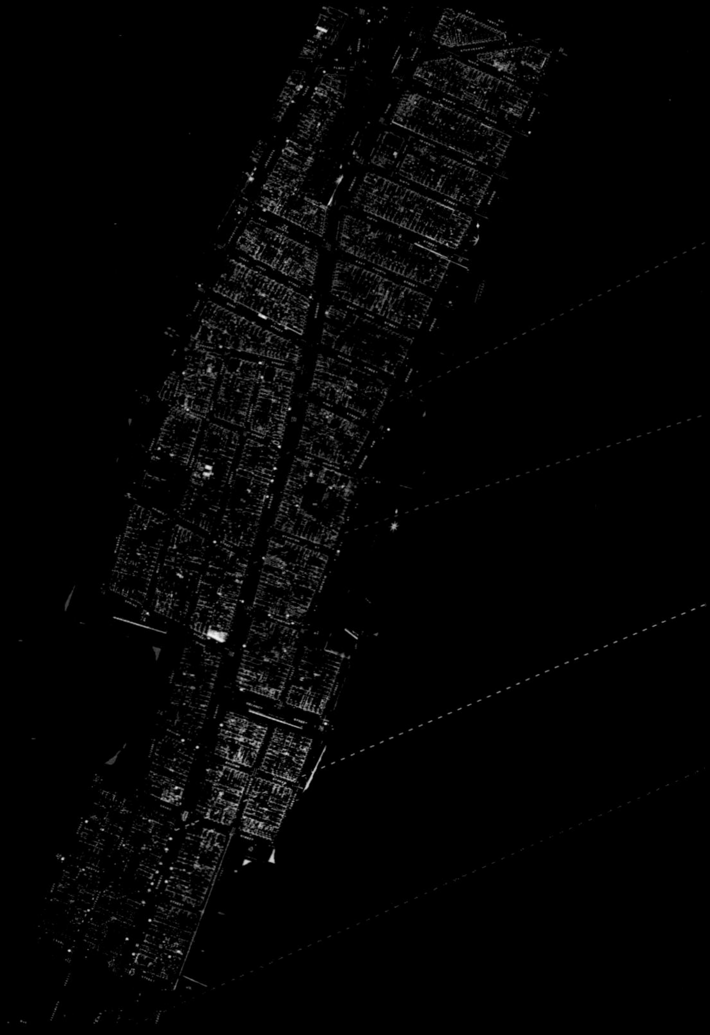

In early 1900, Manhattan became an escape for immigrants from all over the world. Many came to Ellis Island with hope of freedom and jobs. As a result an influx of immigrants populated the Bowery. However, these communities used The Bowery as a dividing line between the various populations. Even in the earlies Sandborne Maps. cartographers used the Bowery as a dividing line for their records. This fact emphasizes the rich culture surrounding the history of the Bowery, as grounds for the blending of various visitors.

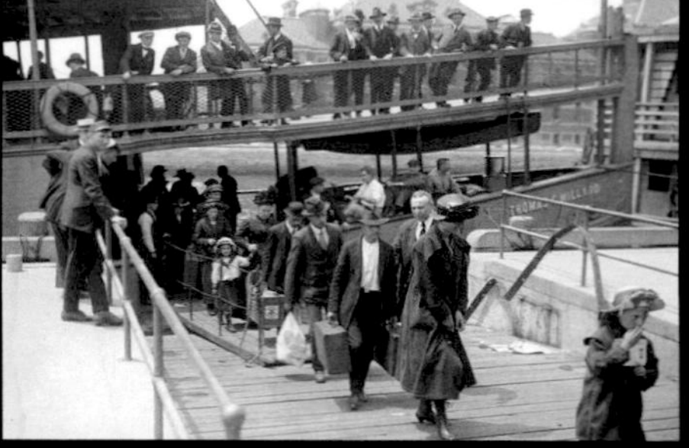

ITALIAN

JEWISH

GERMAN

CHINESE

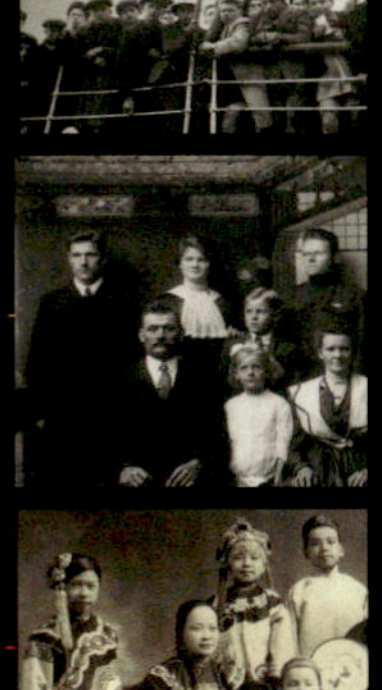

IMMIGRANT HISTORY

FLOPHOUSE

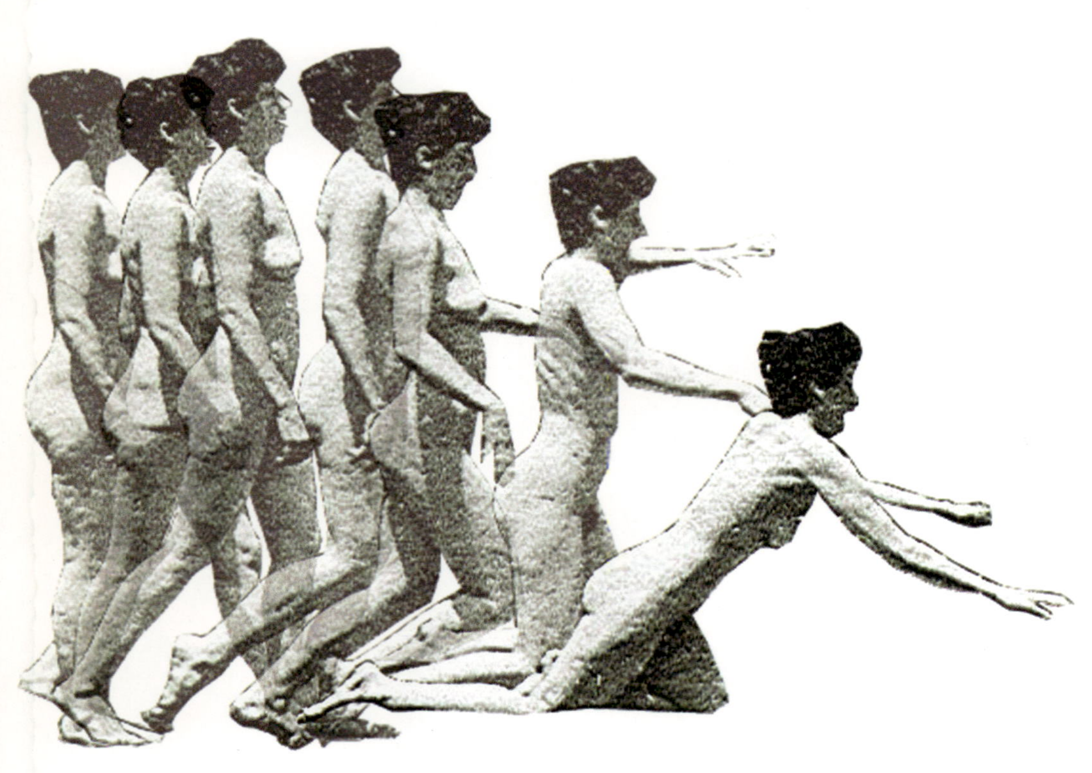

FLOP
(n.) A variant of a flap with a duller, heavier sound. To collapse or fall down heavily. To lie down for sleep.

FLOPHOUSE
(n.) A cheap hotel.

etymology

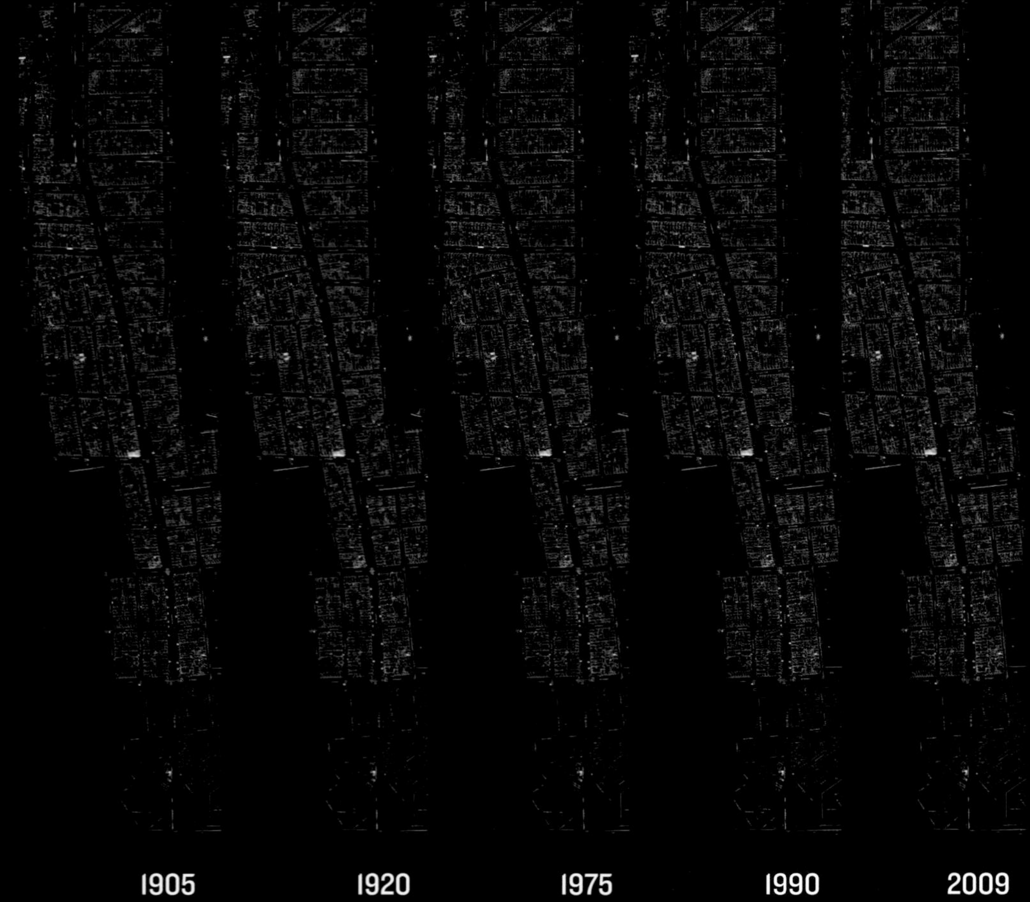

In the diagram above, the red represents flophouses on the Bowery. In the late eighties, the reknown rock club, CBGB was replaced by a high end retail store. The loss of this cultural monument was just the beginning of the gentrification on Bowery Lane. Today, the architecture of the Bowery Hotel, Avalon Bowery Place, and the Cooper Hotel have a personality that is isolated from the street's history. The variety of users and their needs are not served by these large, generic structures. With the dissappearance of the bars that once attracted immigrants, came the appearance of other programs that draw people to the Bowery. The Bowery, thus, is the blending ground for the historic old guard and contemporary culture.

COMMUNITY GARDEN

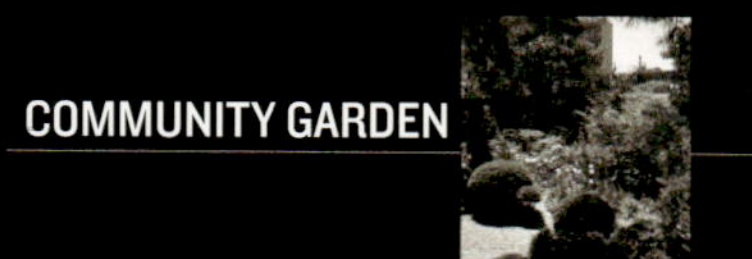

BOWERY BALLROOM

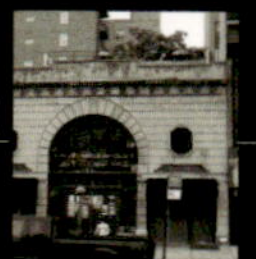

BOWERY MISSION

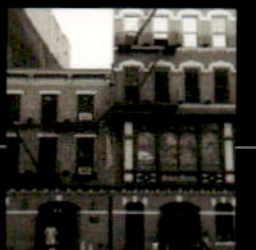

BOWERY HOTEL

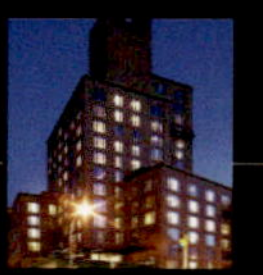

AVALON BOWERY PL.

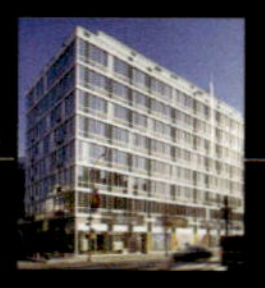

WHITE HOUSE HOTEL

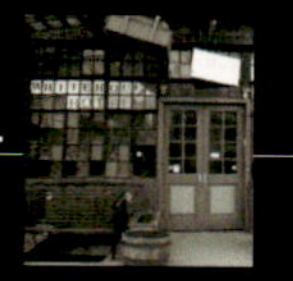

BOWERY ELECTRIC

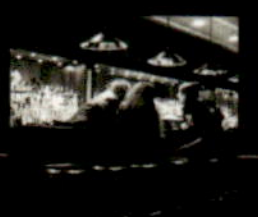

BOWERY POETRY CLUB

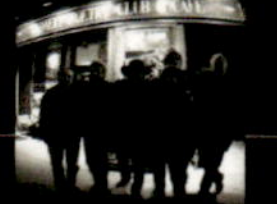

NEW MUSEUM

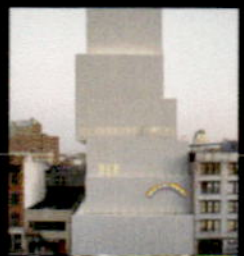

COOPER HOTEL

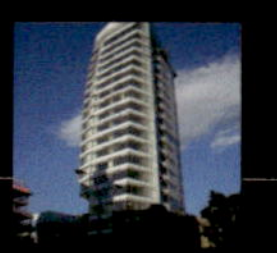

THE BOWERY CHANGES

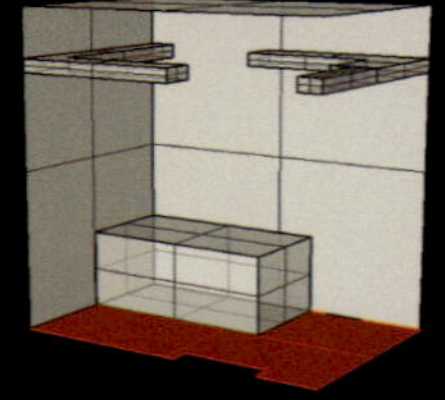

FLOOR SPACE

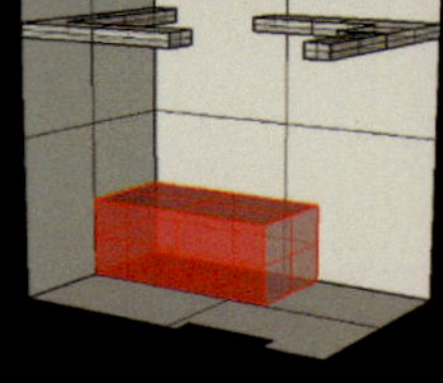

BED SPACE

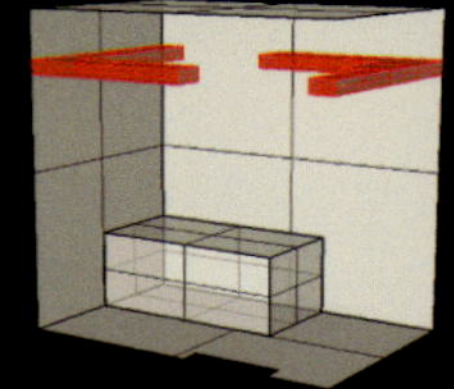

STORAGE SPACE

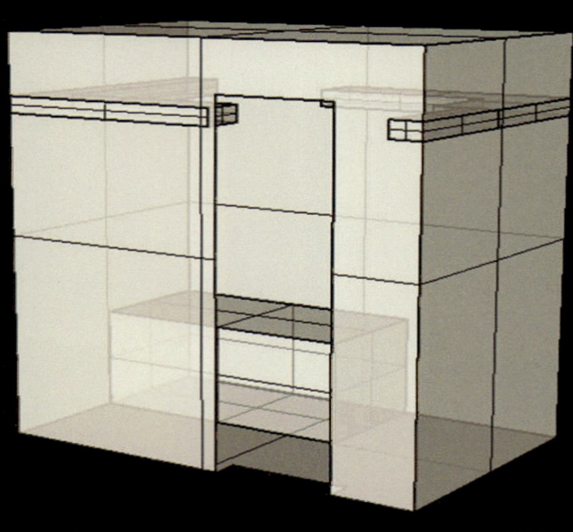

8′

3′3″

10′

The original flophouse was an extreemly constrained space. The height did not exceed eight feet and was usually topped by chickenwire, to evade building codes. These diagrams examine the dimensions of the original floophouse. Then, I compared this space to other single room occupancy spaces. Even, the minimum requirements for a single person in a state prison cell in the US exceed the dimensions of the flophouse. Though, this constrained space has a single purpose: sleep.

FLOPHOUSE configured

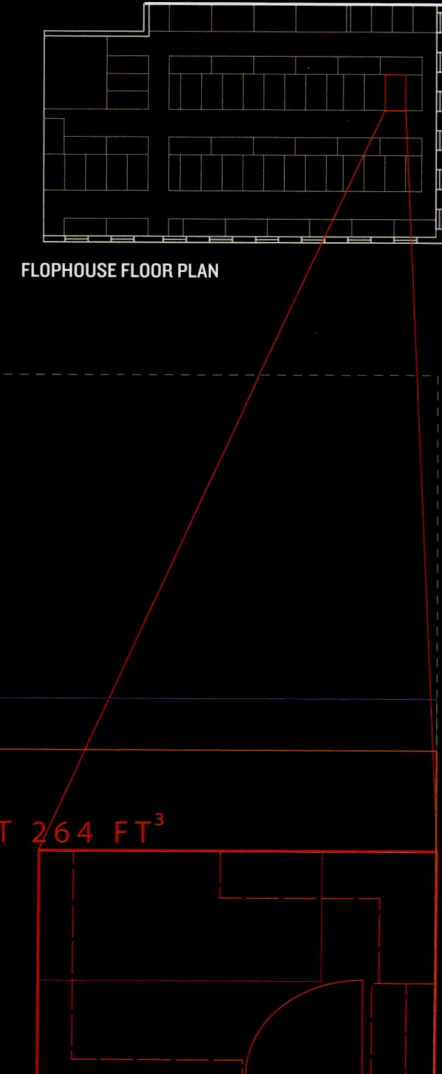

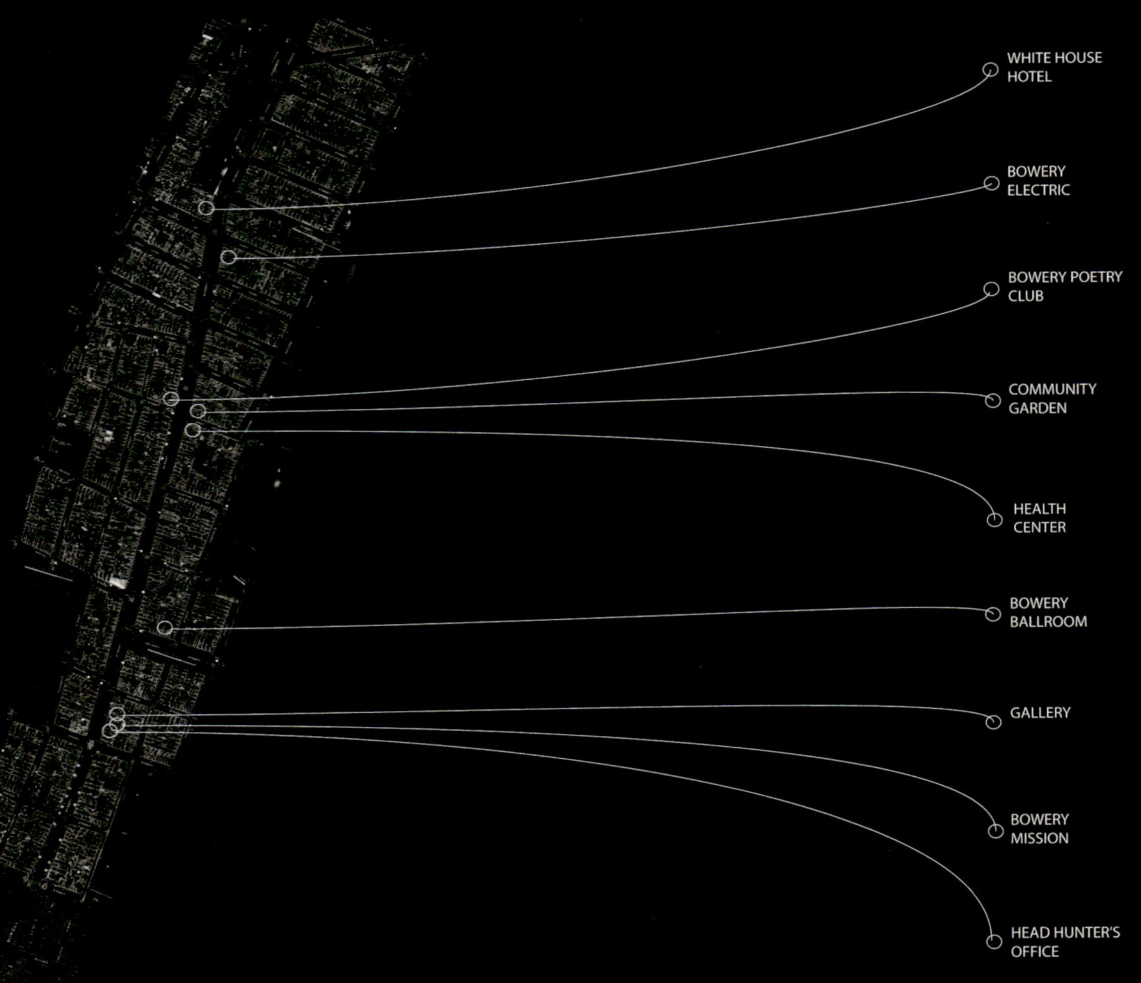

NETWORKS & THE BOWERY

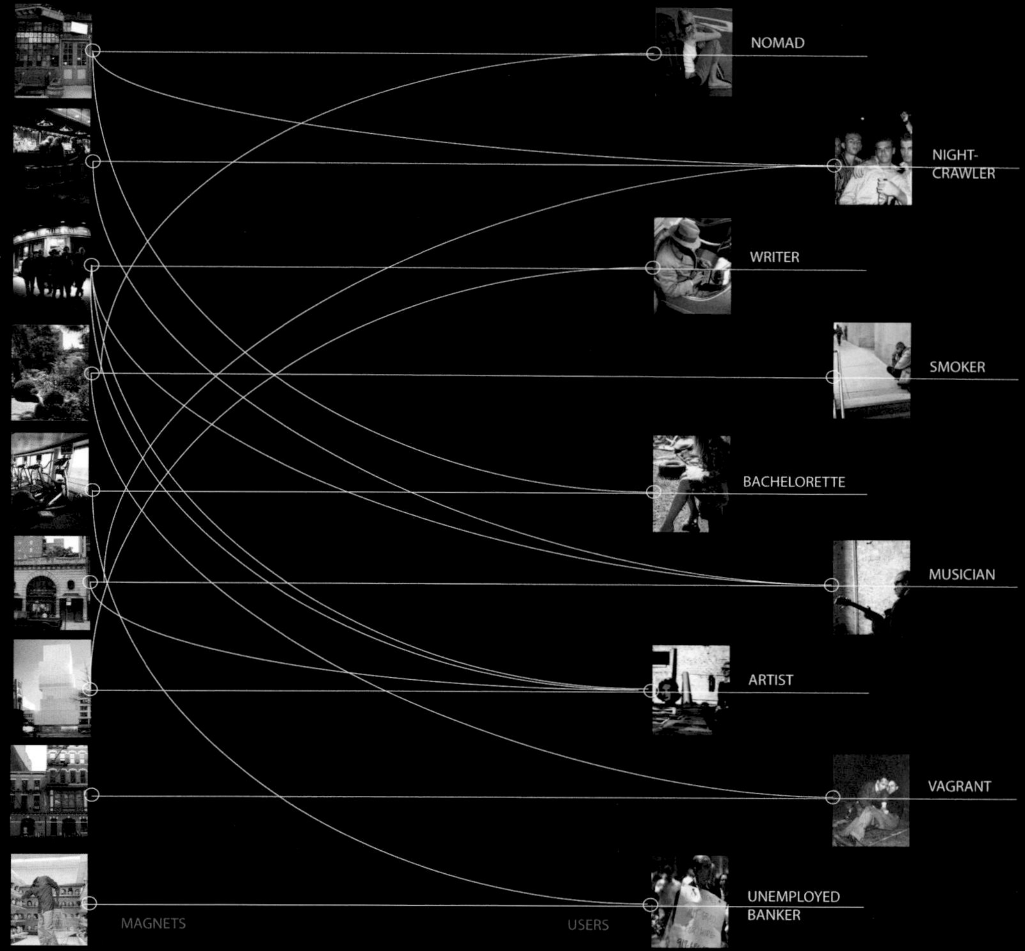

The original Bowery users settled into communites around the Bowery. Today, the change on the Bowery has resulted in a change in users. Each of these new users, in turn, is drawn to the Bowery by a particular establishment or institution. These places, or magnets, bring people to the Bowery. This results in a complex web of potential interactions and connections between both magnets and users.

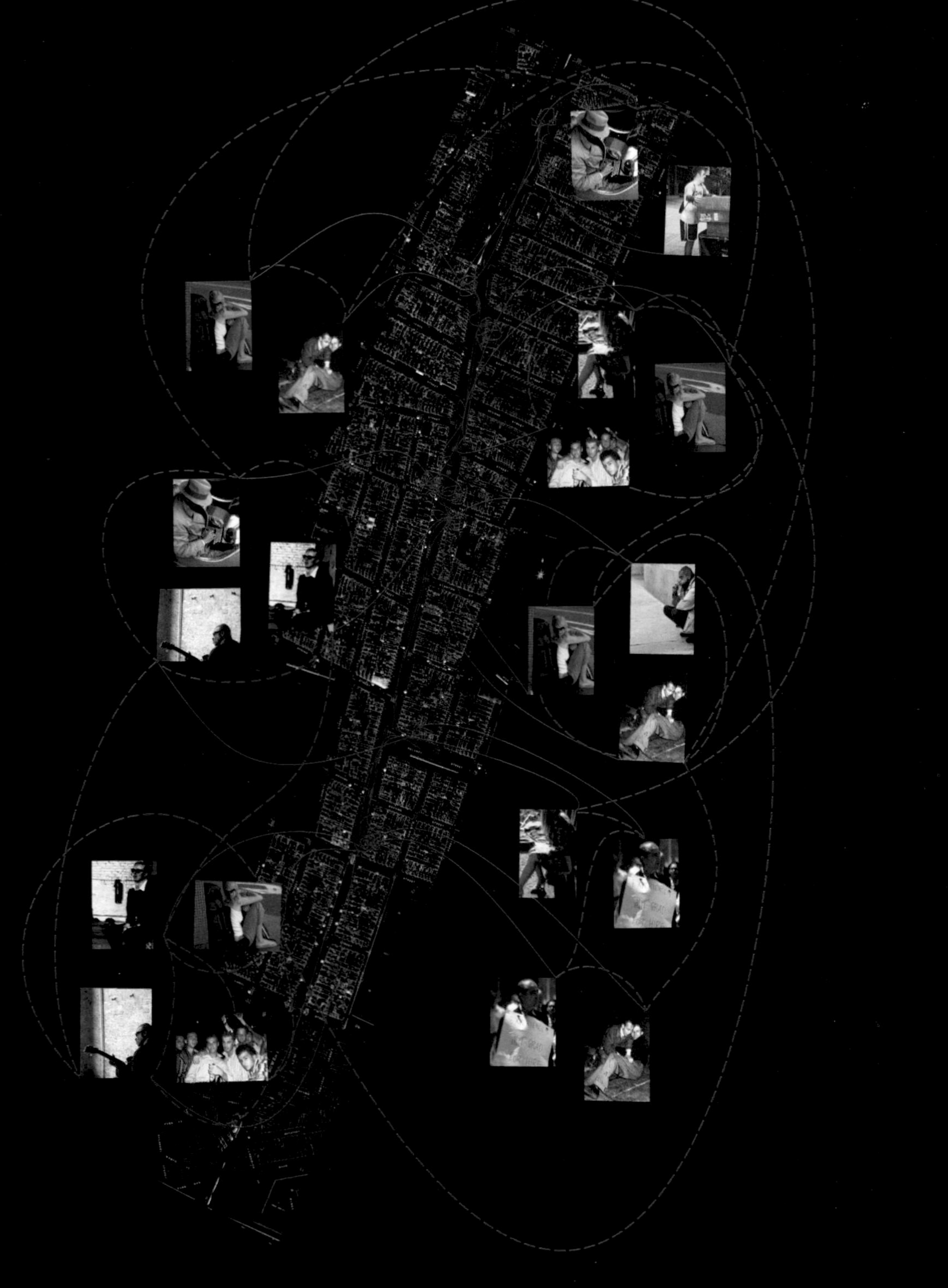

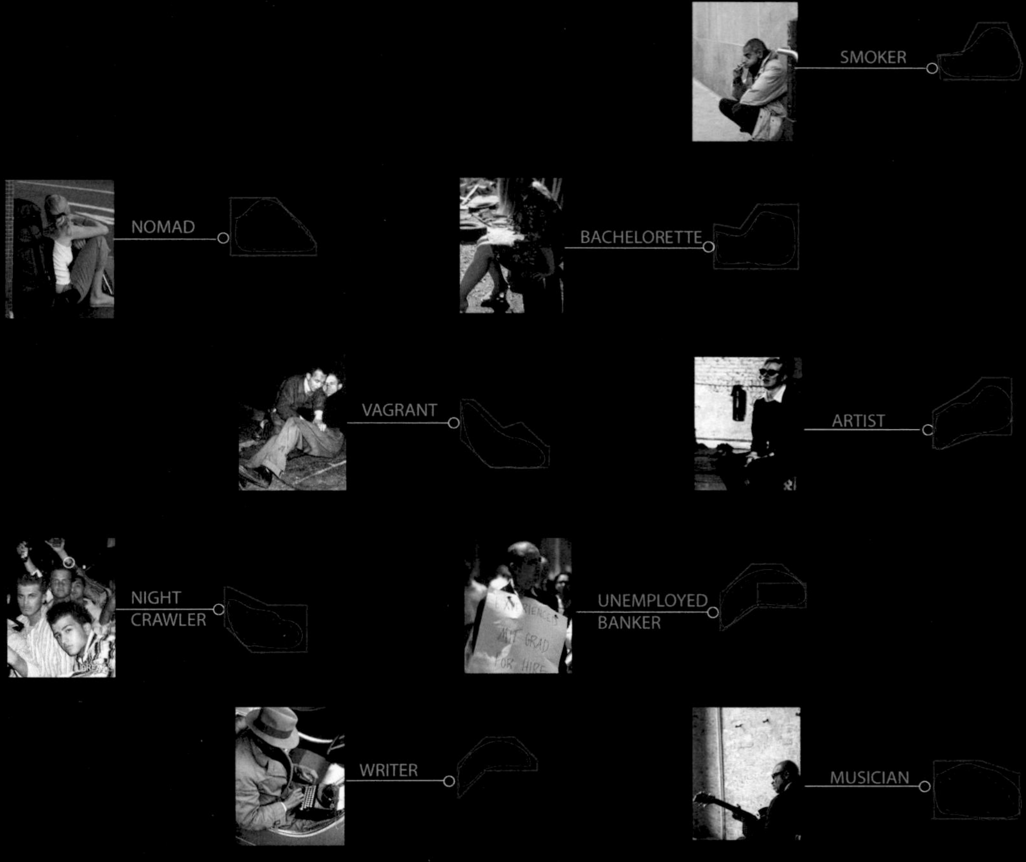

This diagram represents the complex network of Bowery users interacting with one another at various magnets. These magnets have replaced the bar, drawing a variety of people to a variety of locations along the Bowery. Each individual user requires a particular program, thus each unit is unique, tailored to a particular use.

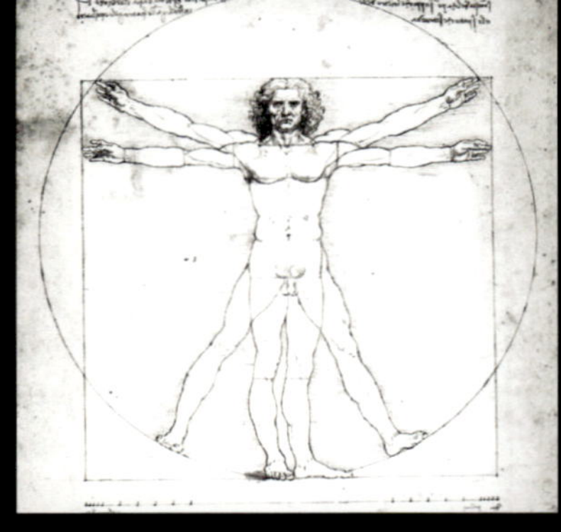

LEONARDO DAVININCI'S VITRUVIUS, 1487

HISTORICALLY, WE FIT THE BODY INTO THE BOX.

Here, Da Vinci and Lecorbusier both depict the body in the box. However, Le Corbusier's drawing of the man moving from sitting to standing begins to explore the kinetic nature of the body in space.

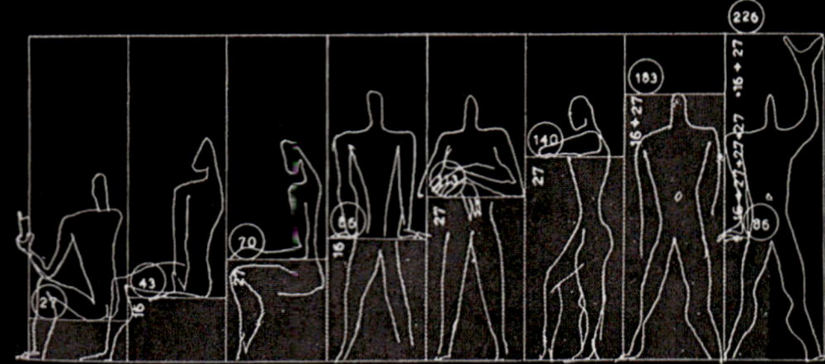

LE CORBUSIER'S MODULAR MAN, 1948

KINETIC SPACE

WHAT IF THE BOX FIT THE BODY?

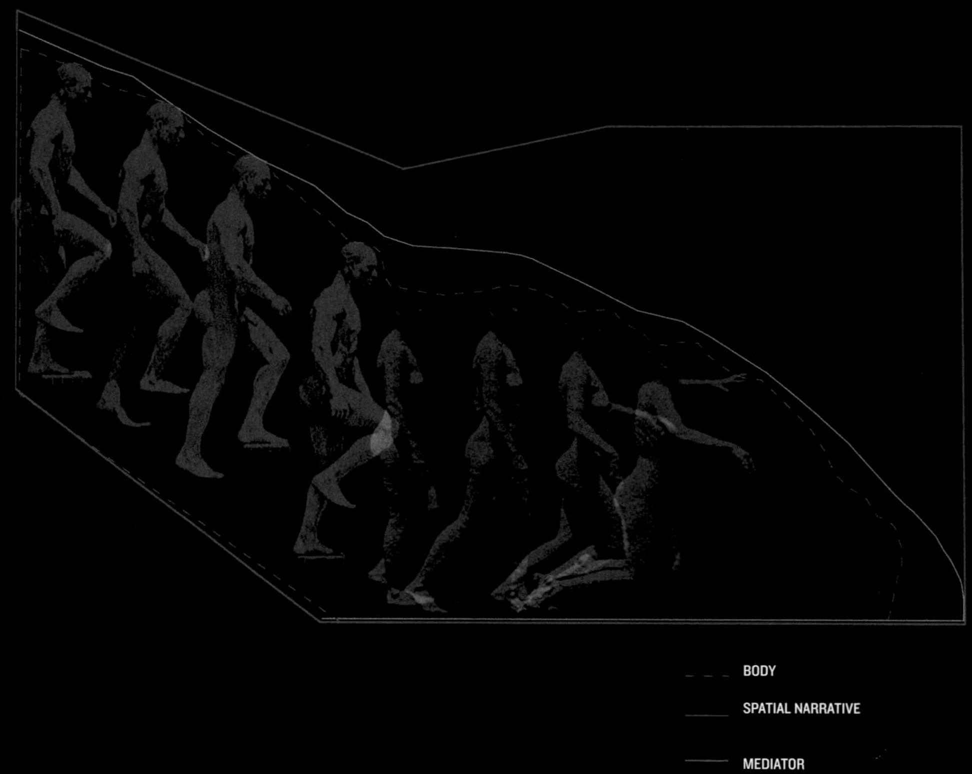

To understand how the flophouse unit could be shaped by a single purpose, I studied how the human body moves through space. Using Muybridge's photographs I defined three lines. The first dotted red line explores how the body moves closely. The blue line represents a separate spatial experience. Finally, the orange line represents a mediator between these two lines, and represents a transparent insulating membrane that reacts to the body's movement in space, while letting in light where needed.

USERS
profiled

UNEMPLOYED BANKER

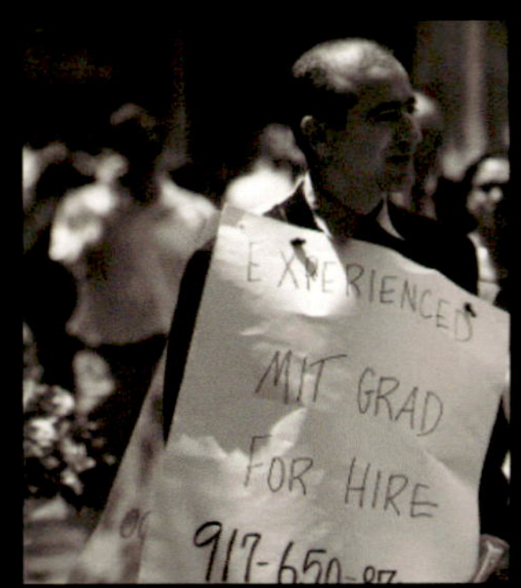

contemporary vagrant

PROGRAM:

- WORK SPACE
- SLEEP SPACE

NEEDS:

- BED
- DESK
- CHAIR

VAGRANT

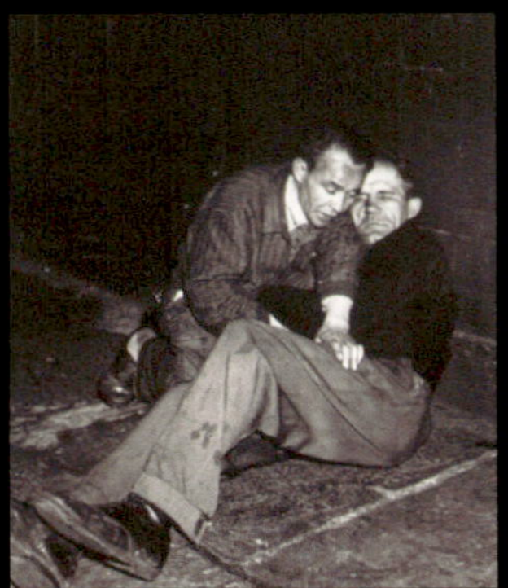

original Bowery user

PROGRAM:

- SLEEP SPACE

NEEDS:

- BED

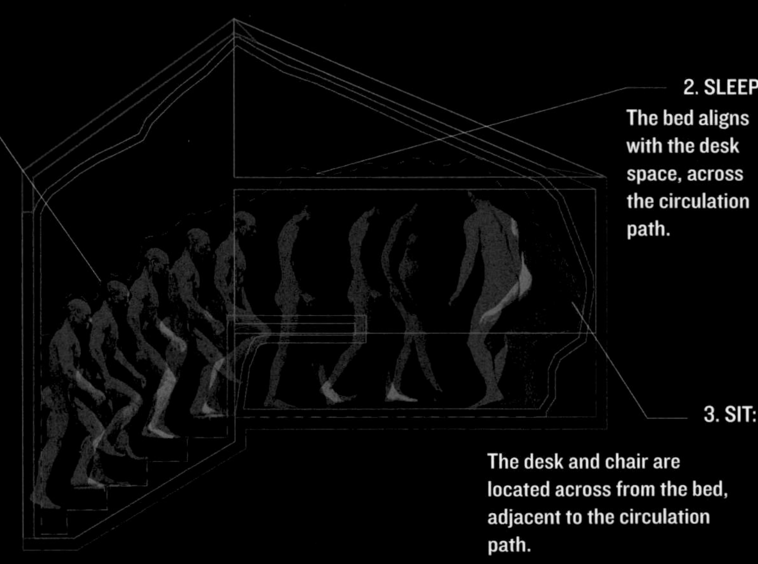
1. ASCEND:
The action performed to ascend to a higher mental state. The stair provides a separation from the ground plane.
2. SLEEP:
The bed aligns with the desk space, across the circulation path.
3. SIT:
The desk and chair are located across from the bed, adjacent to the circulation path.

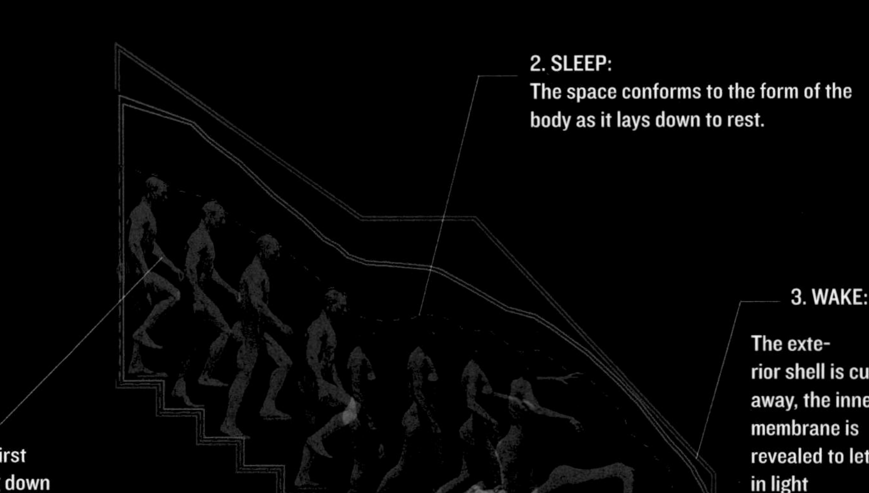
2. SLEEP:
The space conforms to the form of the body as it lays down to rest.
3. WAKE:
The exterior shell is cut away, the inner membrane is revealed to let in light
1. DESCEND:
The descent marks the first step made toward laying down to rest.

UNITS configured

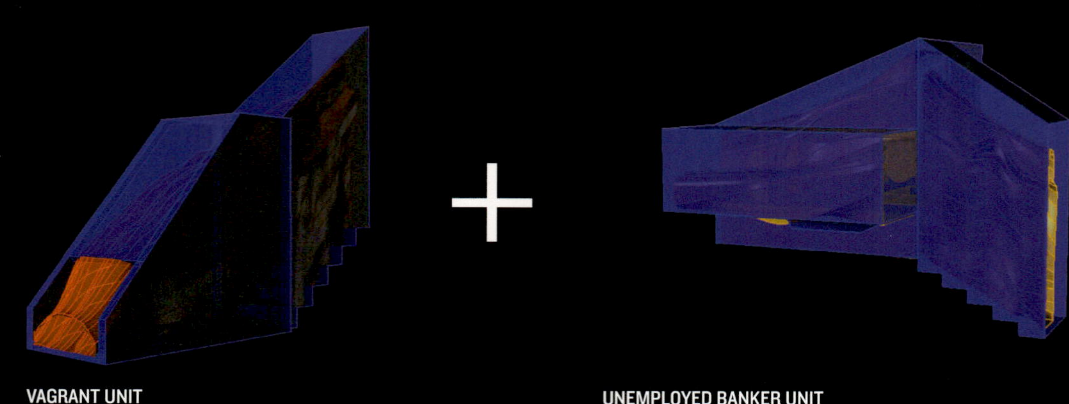

In this design, the original vagrant and the contemporary vagrant are juxtaposed to reflect a reconciliation between the old Bowery and the new. The relationship between these two Bowery users becomes a physical one when the units are fused. Both users enter their respective units at the same level. In this way, an underlying socio-economic equality between these seemingly disparate people becomes apparent through this spatial proximity.

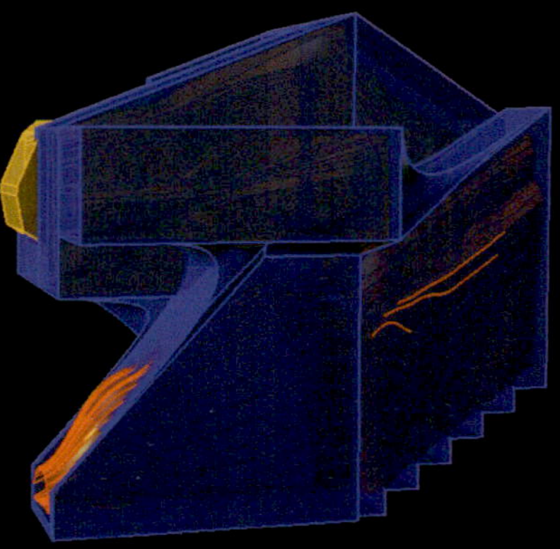

FUSED UNIT

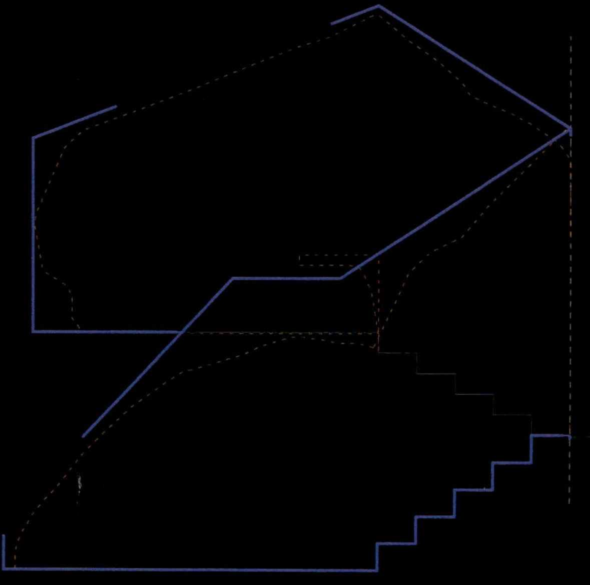

SECTION FUSED UNIT

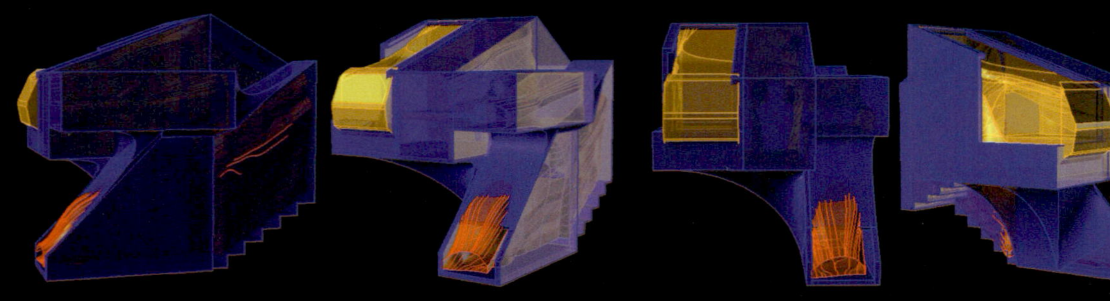

FLOPHOUSE

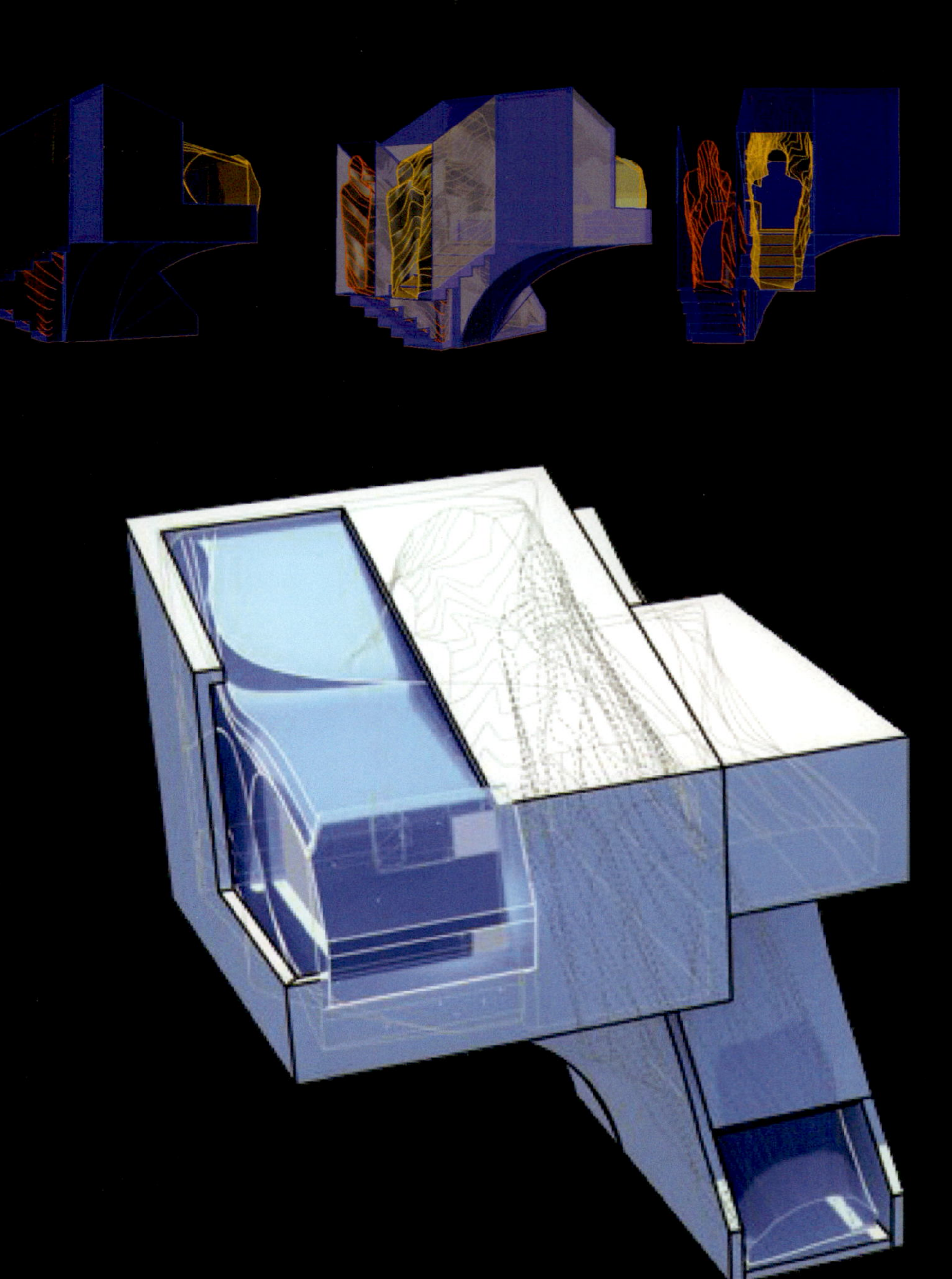

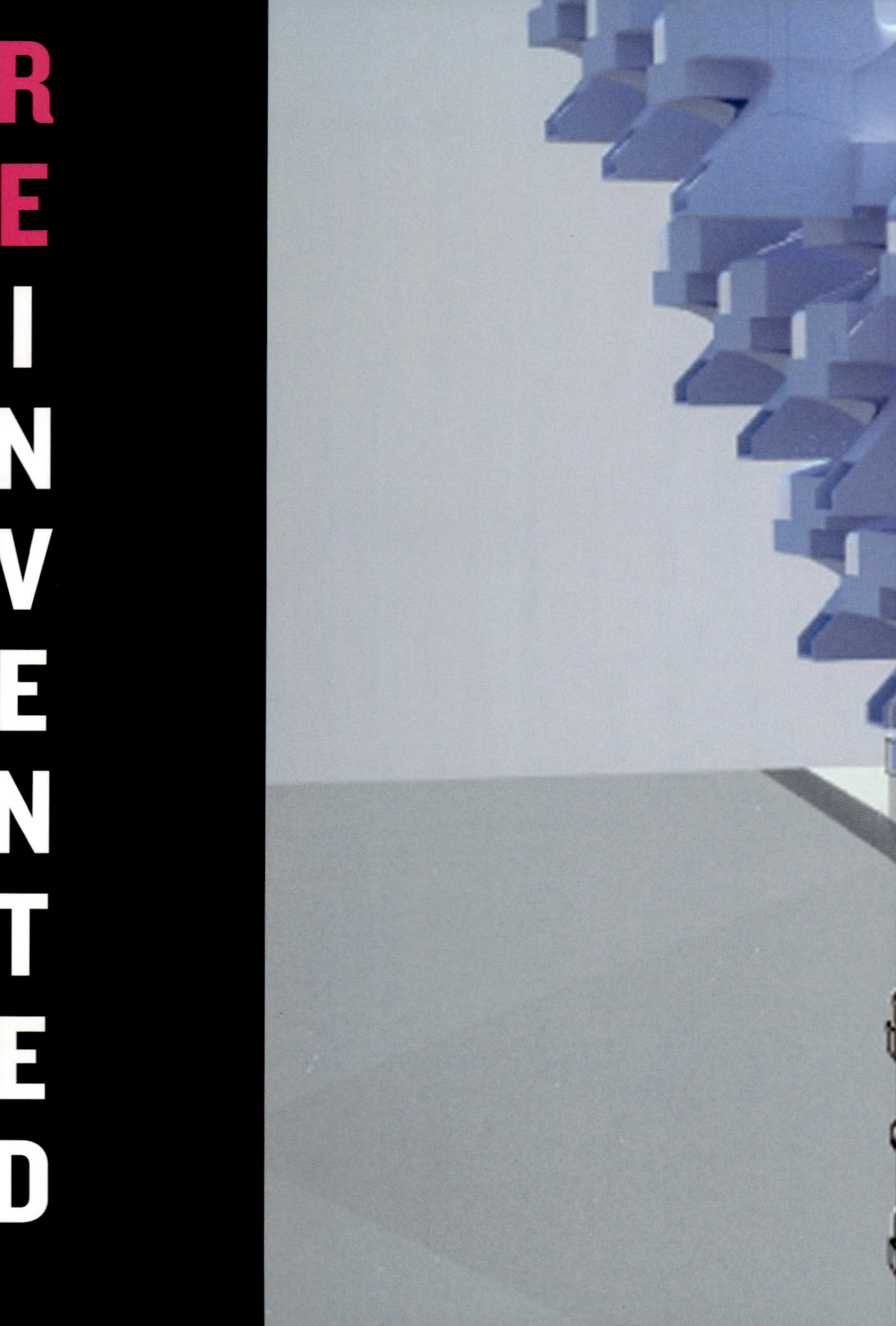
REINVENTED

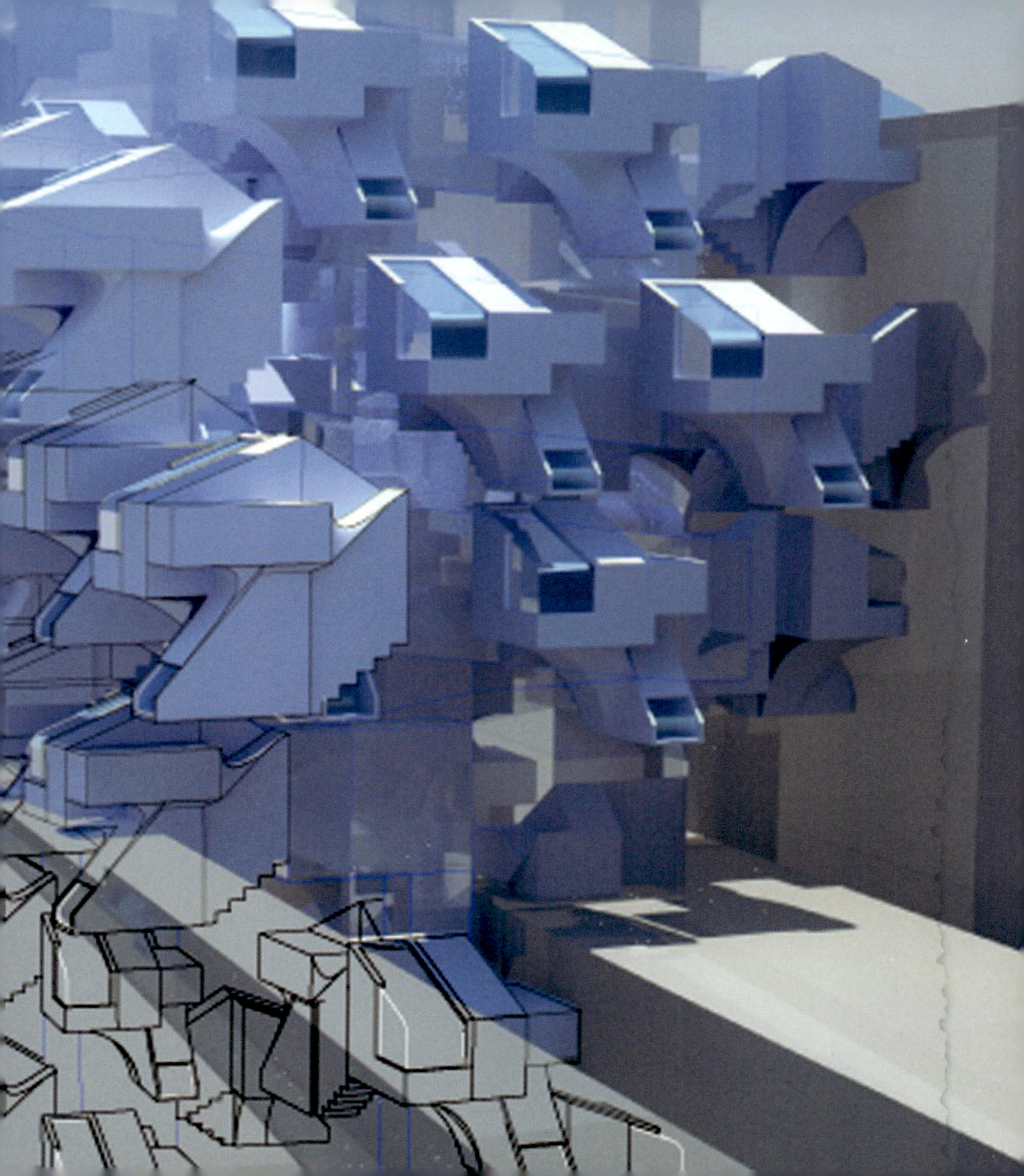

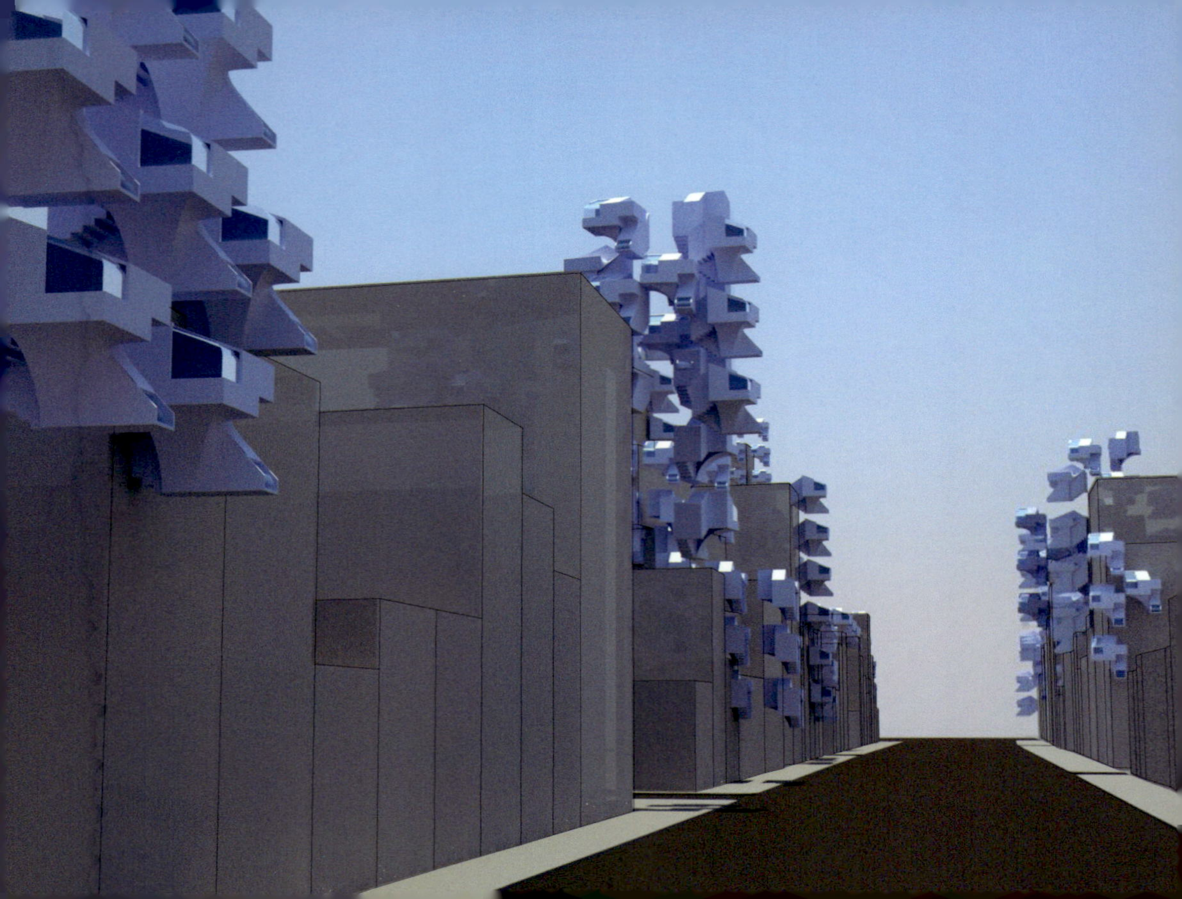

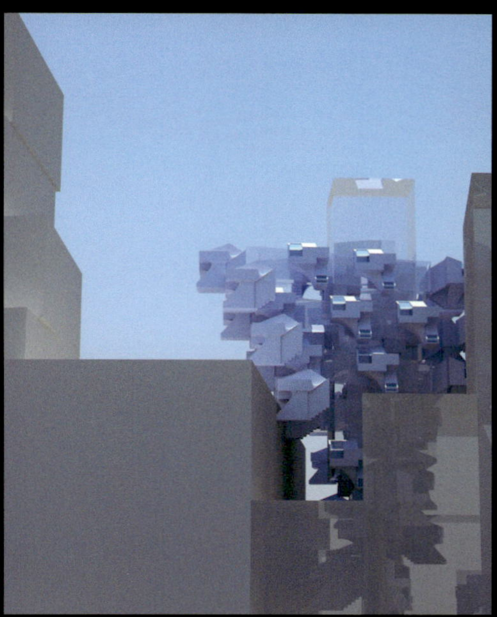

The units agglomerate around a circulation path, which snakes through the building, infecting it like a virus, until it becomes a structure in itself.

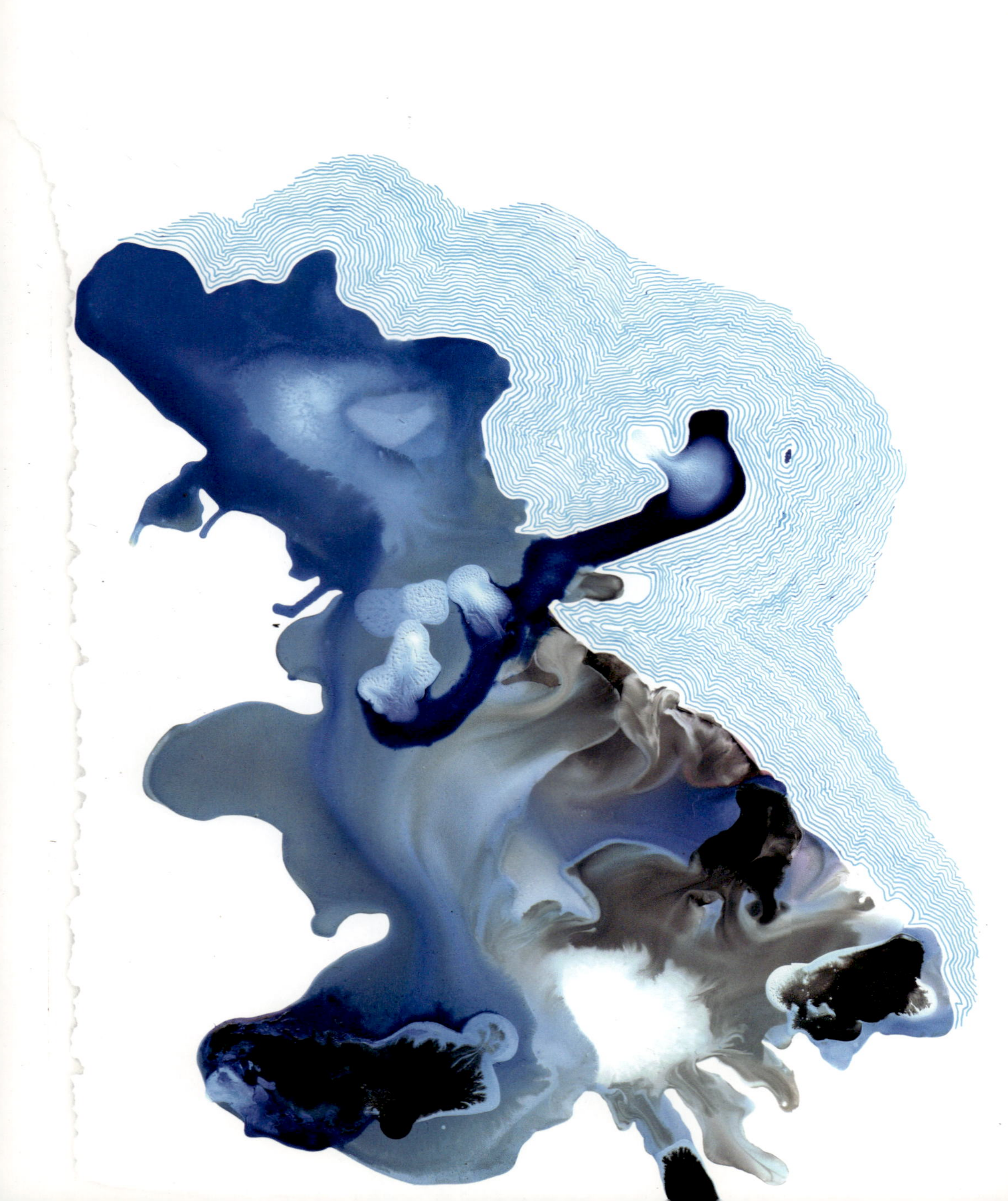

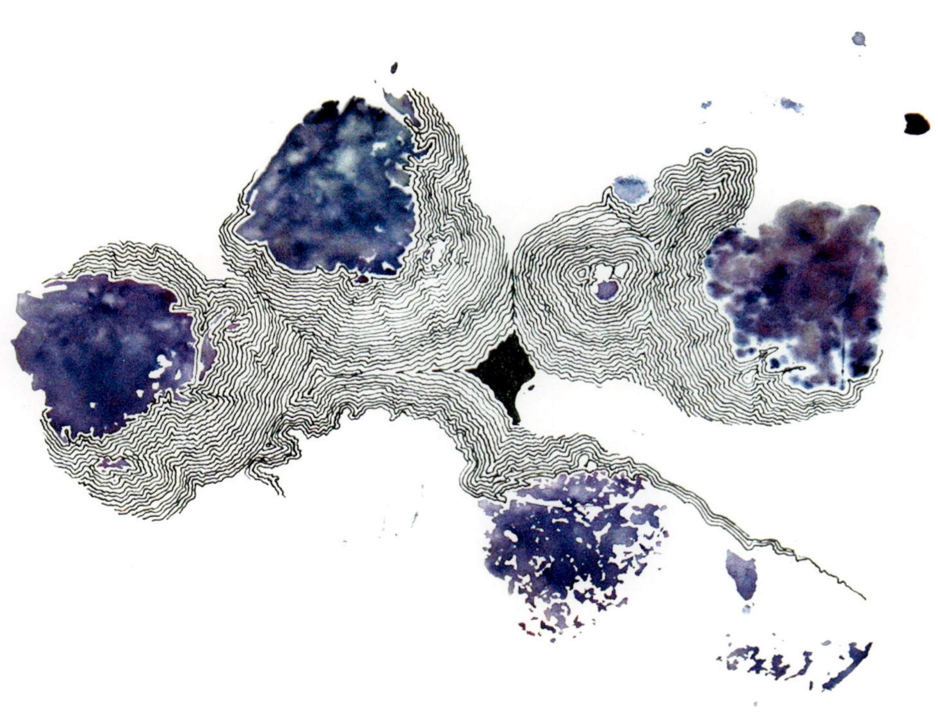

Courtesy of Yasmina Khan

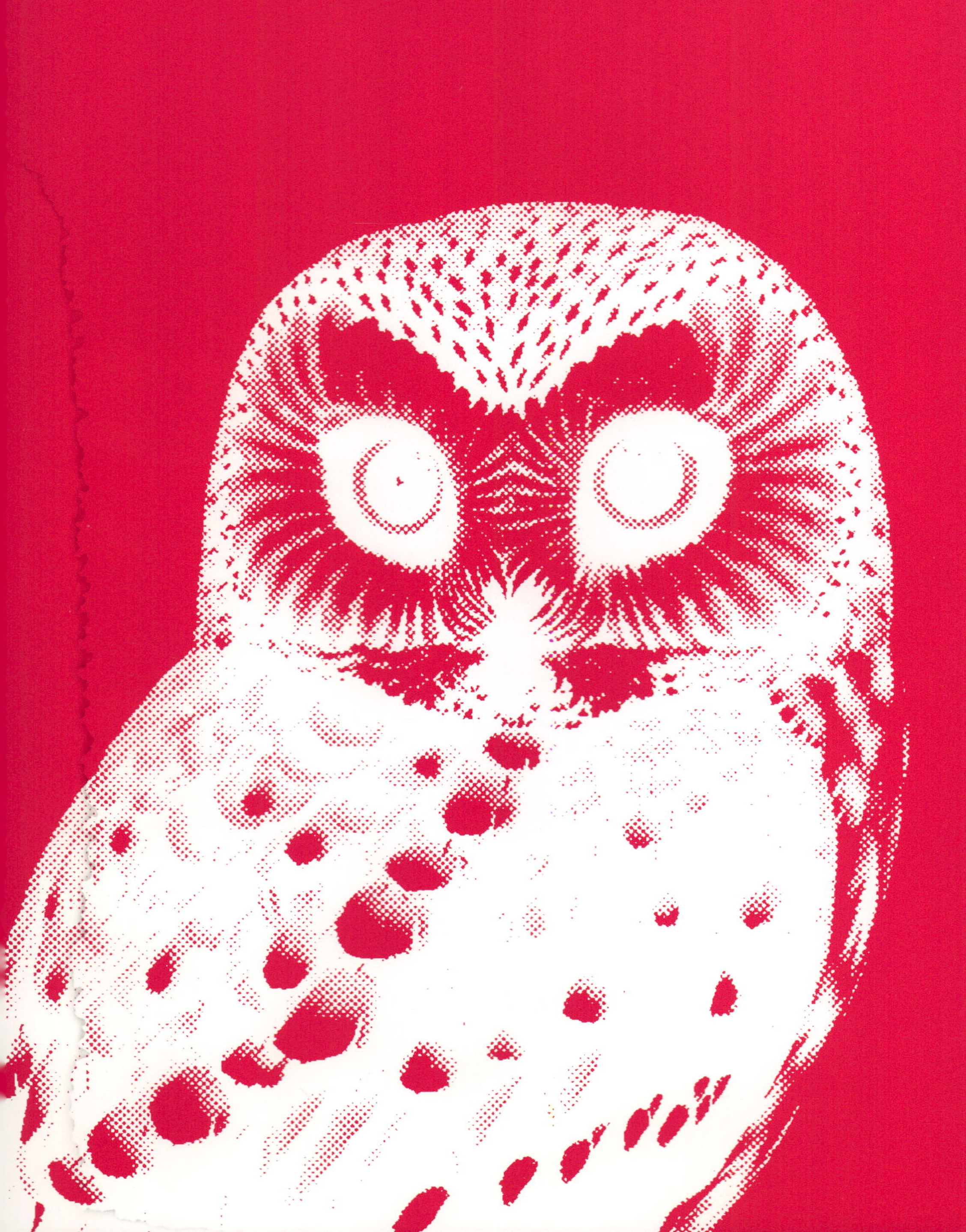

BEN CLAGUE

THE SHOOTING

It had been raining for three days when I heard a man named Steve Wallace had just killed a famous old football coach in Harrisburg, a town in a corner of the state neither my boyfriend Alex nor I had ever visited. *The Daily Iowan,* the university paper I worked for, asked me to extensively cover the story for the State section. This was all over the phone. The editor told me the paper would put me up in a motel room for as long as it took to get the story. He was vague on what he wanted the story to be, told me to poke around and find something big. He told me I could bring Alex. He told me such extensive coverage would look good on my graduate school résumé and then he told me the facts. Wallace, a twenty-five-year-old former reserve player for the football team, had walked into the high school's weight room where the coach was working with some current players, and he had shot the old man dead. But it wasn't just the old coach—everything was dying.

We got our things, Alex and I. There had been a fight but we were trying to gather everything up and piece it back together. We put our clothes in small suitcases and I filled a backpack with my laptop, my notebook, my recorder, some pencils, and my contact cards. We got directions and a mug shot of Wallace from the computer. We drove up to the town from Iowa City in Alex's red compact he had bought from a man in the country who repaired junked cars.

"The gas mileage is great," Alex said as we left town. I had not been in the car yet. He bought it in the foggy weeks between the fight and now. "Something like twenty-eight, twenty-nine. Good for an old car." He had a thin three-day's beard covering the lower half of his long face. It looked like someone had shaken pepper along his jawline.

The highway we drove on had once been a main line from north to south throughout the country, but was now just a skinny secondary route with tar scratches and eroding yellow separating lines. It sliced through fields and on either side of us stubby cornstalks stuck up through the soil. The soil, we were told in grade school, was something of which we should be proud—not every state, after all, was so fertile. Few states fed so much of the world.

It had not rained yet this morning but great gray clouds boiled above us. I explained to Alex that I forgot the CDs. I was very careful about it. There was a level of fear in my voice, I suppose, a restrained level.

"Radio is better for long drives, anyway," he said, and he turned the knobs through the hiss of white noise until he found an AM station. "Talk radio," he said. "That's where the nutjobs are. I bet Wallace called in sometimes."

"It's better to let the crazy people just talk and talk and talk. Otherwise they bottle it up and it becomes too much," I said.

He put my hand on the stick and put his on top. His palm was dry and calloused but it felt nice, the way that coming home to your own trailer can still feel nice, even though there are higher-quality homes across the street.

I had the directions on my lap. Occasionally I looked at them to see that we had not erred but the route was very simple, just a couple of highways from Iowa City to Harrisburg, and so I guess I mostly looked because I like the way roads look on maps, gnarled and humped like an old man's finger.

The morning fog lifted slowly from the fields like a ghost from the grave.

At noon we stopped for lunch about an hour from Harrisburg in a little town called Stewart. All morning we had watched the clouds roll in, stretching to the ceiling of the sky. Now they stood over us and we got out of the car and turned up our heads to look at their bellies, wondering when the clouds would burst and soak us, or if we got back into the car first, when their potent drops would shatter on our windshield into a million tiny beads that would race down the glass to the bottom or be obliterated by the wipers. I could hear the serene beat of the wipers in my head.

We ate at a small roadside shack called Rube's. The front was all glass and a small door that opened in both directions. Inside the lights were off and the lack of sunlight made the inside dim. The stuffing bulged from our booth seats like a white beard and brushed our legs but neither of us minded. We ordered tenderloin sandwiches. This was another thing we were told to be proud of in school—our pork was excellent and rest assured, young lady, you will not be finding a tenderloin sandwich that compares to ours.

The waitress who took our order came back and sat at our booth. She had hips wide enough to birth cattle and a greasy face so flat and large it looked as though someone had smashed it in with a dirty skillet. She smelled like canola oil.

"He admitted to the murder," she said. "Wallace. He's already admitted to doing it. Says he heard voices."

"Nutjob," Alex said. He smiled at me. I didn't mind his yellow teeth. I really didn't. Some people minded them but I found it comforting, to see so constantly someone's physical flaws—there are a lot of people whose ugliness you don't see until you've stripped them naked, but with Alex his worst features were upfront, his yellow teeth and his acne, the great mountainous pimples with whitehead peaks like snowcaps. I was trying to not mind these things. What did they matter?

"I'm going to try and get some quotes," I said. "I'm a journalist for the *Daily Iowan.*" I figured this woman might say something obvious enough to work with. In class they told you things like, get the best or most interesting quote but the truth was nobody wanted to read about a sociologist or therapist talking about the human psyche and all its deep, unidentifiable nooks—not in a newspaper; they wanted to hear big women in roadside shacks say, oh, what a horrible tragedy or, I knew the coach or, my son played for him fifteen years ago and here is my story.

The waitress looked at me and said, "Oh." She stood up. "Looks like rain again," she said. Another customer walked in the door and she crossed the red-paneled floor to seat them.

"Have you heard anything from your dad?" Alex asked me. He took my hand again.

"No," I said. He meant about the factory closing. I hadn't heard much from my dad but I thought about him sitting in his trailer drinking, unsure of what to do next. And then sometimes I thought about if he was even considering what to do next, or if he knew the score and realized that really, there was very little for him. Because what could a guy who'd worked in a factory for thirty years do? Work in another factory? All the other factories were dead or would be in a few months.

I looked at Alex for a long time.

"I was just asking, is all," Alex said.

"I know."

"Just trying to be considerate."

"I know, Alex."

The waitress brought our sandwiches. We swept the fries to one side and poured ketchup from the glass bottle onto our plates and then the sandwiches. We ate for a while in silence and I thought about how good the breadcrumbs were. I looked down at my torso and saw it straining against my white shirt. I thought about how nice it was to be growing a little belly after being told throughout school as well as my personal life that I was too skinny. Now I was beginning to grow. Even if everything else was dying, I was growing.

"If you don't want me to ask anymore, I won't," Alex said. He looked at his plate.

"Alex," I said.

Splotches of rain dashed against the windows. We watched the window grow bleary and the compact transformed from a definable car to a vague landmark, something we would make for after we finished.

The rest of the meal we ate looking at our plates. I tried to form in my mind some questions to ask the townspeople to coax out the right answers. Alex slid me his plate and told me to eat, that I needed the extra calories. I wanted to ask him why he was suddenly qualified to tell me how to eat.

When we paid the check, the waitress told us she heard on the radio that the rain would continue for days. She told us that this year's crop would probably die from too much water. The rivers were beginning to rise, she told us. We said, have a nice day.

The rain looked cinematic. The drops themselves were gigantic and they struck the gravel and exploded or landed on one another and formed small pools we stretched our legs over in order to keep our socks dry. We reached the car and jerked our doors open and threw ourselves in the seats. We slammed the doors shut. We sat there in the car, in the rain, and we listened to the chatter of the water coming apart on top of the roof. Here was where the movie stars usually kissed with a deep passion, but we just sat there.

In the car, I studied the photo of Steve Wallace's face. He had a second chin and the beginnings of a third. Rogue hairs from his left eyebrow crept toward the right. His head was tilted back, and in his nostrils a small streak of snot stretched back into the darkness of his nasal passage. Under blue his eyes slumped purple bags. His long brown hair was tucked behind his ears and he held his number up for the camera. 3698. Prison inmate 3698 in the orange jumpsuit, in for murder.

We passed through towns that were closing their own school districts and merging with other towns to form acronyms. I had done a piece on the dying schools and how communities would cope. I got lots of quotes from people at a loss. Thinking about the story now made me think of my dad.

"Do you think people will freak out when you ask them questions about the guy?" Alex asked me. He didn't turn to me when he spoke but stared ahead through the rain, both hands atop the wheel.

"Why would they?" I asked.

"I mean that it was traumatic for a lot of people," he said.

We passed a sign that said: HARRISBURG 12 MILES.

"Sometimes it's therapeutic to talk about terrible things," I said. "Maybe if Steve Wallace had talked about terrible things he wouldn't have done them."

"He killed someone because he thought he was hearing voices," Alex said. He turned to me briefly. "Hearing voices." He turned back to the road and leaned forward, his chin nearly to the wheel.

"What I wonder about is the coach," I said. "Everybody tells you about his accomplishments, about all the guys he coached who eventually went pro, about what he did for the community. But what was he like to Steve Wallace? Was he abusive? Was he a monster?"

"Sometimes people just kill people. Sometimes there isn't some hidden story that needs busting open."

I didn't say anything back. Instead I listened to the radio. The talk hosts kept jumping back between the rain and the Becker story. It was raining all across the state, they said, and a big front had stalled over us—all of us, I mean, we Iowans. And they said that Steve Wallace should be killed, that we should all clamor for his public death—the "we" being, again, all of us.

We came into Harrisburg. The town was so small you could almost see the fields at the other end and all the homes were squat one stories painted white. Many houses on the highway were boarded up or simply decrepit, gutters full of leaves, porches sagging.

Main Street intersected with the highway and we turned onto it. We passed storefronts with McCain signs in the windows and boarded up storefronts and storefronts into which residents stopped and peered or passed by without notice. There was often a second floor of apartments, and occasionally we saw people walking through their curtainless windows, caught for a brief moment eating soup or scratching their arms or carrying their cats.

Alex pulled the car into an open space on Main Street. I leaned into the back and took from my unzipped backpack the laptop and slid it under my seat, and then I zipped up the backpack and took it with me. We got out, soaked immediately by the rain. We jogged to a storefront with a canopy over the sidewalk and stood there.

We decided we ought to walk from store to store and get some quotes from residents. We moved at two speeds. When we were in the rain, we ran in long strides and then, under the canopies, we jerked to a slow walk, stalling our plunge back out into the rain. While we did this I was thinking about what Alex said, about the people getting upset when I asked them questions. I wasn't worried they would cry, so much as they might shoot me. It was an insane thought and yet there it was, in my brain, blinking like a faulty neon sign, images of guns wielded by men who looked suspiciously like Steve Wallace, foreheads compressed as they caught me in their sights and pulled the trigger. I realized that of course no one would shoot me, that I was being sent up here because this kind of thing happened so rarely. But when a killing gets in your blood stream it has this way of congesting your brain until you just think about people shooting people and all of your actions must be processed through the filter of will someone shoot me for this or not before they can be carried out.

Most of the stores were empty except for the owners. They explained to us that residents did the bulk of their shopping in the morning and that we had just missed the rush. I told them I was a reporter and sometimes they gave me good quotes about the terror they felt, how they had moved to a place like Harrisburg precisely because it seemed immune to this sort of mind-blowing violence. One woman invited us to the funeral and said the whole town would be there. Others said very little. We met one cashier at the grocery store who knew Steve Wallace but he refused to speak to us, called his manager over and said we were hassling him. The residents told us about the Cantilla noodle factory closing. We stood in shops together and watched the rainwater race down the sewers and then, later in the day, watch it gurgle back up and fill the streets. They said they didn't know what would happen to the town after the factory closing. I felt stupid, walking around all afternoon with Alex behind me like a reporter pimp, his arms crossed over his chest. He felt left out, I knew, like I wasn't giving him enough attention, but I found it hard to really care the more I heard about Harrisburg and Steve Wallace. Someday you'll realize just how much this state has to offer, my teachers had told me. There's a whole bunch of things to see.

Walking back to the car we passed the jail where Steve Wallace was being kept. I stood in front of the red brick building and stared.

"He's in there," I said. "I'd love to get an interview with him. Imagine what he has to say."

"'I'm a killer!'" Alex said.

That evening I asked Alex to drive us by the high school so that we could see the scene of the crime.

"There won't be anything to see," he said, looking in his rearview mirror. "They're not going to have the coach's dead body lying on display."

"I know that," I said. "I'm not stupid. I just need to visualize this." The truth was I wanted to see what Steve Wallace saw. All afternoon I had been doing that, looking at the cashiers behind their tan registers and the townspeople on the streets wet with rain as though I was Steve Wallace. I tried to imagine how he deciphered the world, what his codes were. I wondered what I would find if I slashed his head open and shook the contents onto a table. Could I untangle the wires and see, pulsing like a cartoon heart, the node that brought the gun up to eye level? And I was so close to him. It was almost like I could feel him just around the block. I was terrified and thrilled all at once.

The roads were washing out and twice we hydroplaned. I could feel the loss of traction, the car sliding and the belches of the water.

We passed a Super 8 and Alex said, "We'll see the high school tomorrow." He pulled into the drive of the motel and when he had parked, we grabbed our things from the back seat and ran inside. We got a room and when the clerk asked how many beds we looked at each other for what seemed like a full change of seasons and then Alex said just one, please.

Someone who rented the room before us had been a smoker. My head began to spin just a bit and my stomach grew nauseated. The walls were the shade of vivacious yellow that threatened us with insanity. In the middle of the room was the bed, and all around it green carpet with tar smudges and cigarette burns. I peeled back the comforter and threw it on the floor.

Alex was sitting in a chair by the television and he looked at me.

"I read somewhere that there is a lot of semen on comforters," I said. It was true.

He turned on the television and found a national sports station that was showing the day's sports highlights.

I leaned over the small desk to the window and cranked the handle until the glass was all the way open. There was a screen separating the room from the outside but I still felt the rain on my hands. I breathed in the fresh air until the nausea left my body. Outside the gray clouds took on the dim texture of late evening. I crossed the room. Near the door was my backpack and I took from it my cell phone and went into the bathroom and shut and locked the door.

I called my dad.

"Hello, dad," I said when I heard his voice. "How are you?"

"Fine," he said. He yawned. "Just fine."

I listened for the obvious sounds: bottles clanking, loud music, other voices peaking the volumes reserved for the drunk and the irate. There was nothing.

"Okay," I said. "I'm in Harrisburg."

"For the paper?" he asked. "They're still letting you travel?"

"Yes," I said. "This is a big story."

"I just can't believe that happened. There are a lot of things I'm willing to believe but I've been watching the news, waiting for some revelation. There isn't one coming."

"Just wait," I said. "There might be. You never know." I pulled up my shirt and examined my stomach in the bathroom mirror. It was beginning to round nicely. I put my hand under my belly and held it. Into the phone I said, "Hey. How are things there?"

"Nothing yet," he said. "I'll just have to wait and see. I don't know." There was silence on his end and then he said again, "I don't know."

After I hung up, I looked into the mirror. Was I glowing? I could never tell. Other people told me I was, but people often said things they didn't mean.

When I went into the room again, Alex was still watching television. I climbed into the bed and lay down on my back with a pillow under my head. I could see his frail outline in the chair. The scent of rain rolled in through the window sweet and crisp.

He got into bed and we lay there, looking at the ceiling. It had been a long day and we were tired and soon he fell asleep. I got up slowly and went to my backpack and dug out the picture of Steve Wallace and brought it back to bed. I looked through it, as though behind the image was his soul. The residents had told me he had never really been trouble, that sure, maybe, he had been mixed up in the wrong crowd and maybe he had been a little weird, but there had never been any signs that pointed to murder. But then he had broken into a house the night before the shooting, convinced that its owner was controlling him via remote. I thought about all this, tried to see him, a gigantic maniac pawing like a dog at the window, so sure that behind the glass stood a man with a remote injecting voices into his head, telling him to buy a gun, to drive to the school and kill his old coach.

The thoughts began to disturb me so I turned on the television and watched the newscasters warn everyone that our rivers, our great, beautiful rivers, were overflowing. Just north of Harrisburg was the Cedar River, but I wasn't worried. There was some calm about me, like I knew a town with a murder couldn't be a town with a flood, too. The newscasters went on. Get to high ground, they warned. Evacuate if you're near a river, they warned. I fell asleep to their pleas.

It was hard to tell the morning had come. Dawn had not broken so much as the darkness had shrunk away, recessed into a corner where it stood, waiting. Out the window the storm clouds had been permanently etched onto the sky. The rain still came down as though God had wrenched open a faucet and broken off the knob. Alex was snoring.

I had slept little during the night. I kept thinking someone was rattling the knob of the room's door. In the bed, Alex's body next to mine had not seemed like adequate protection—I got the feeling that if someone kicked down the door he would simply roll over and give up or try and prove how flawed the intruder's line of thinking was, how neither of us could understand this man in our room, and how there was no use trying.

Now I sipped coffee and sat at the chair in front of the television, which I had switched off when I woke. The clock showed 7:32 a.m. and I wondered what there was to do in Harrisburg at such a time. I pulled on a gray UI t-shirt and black cotton shorts and slipped into my sandals, and then I walked down the hallway. The carpet matched that of our room, and the hallways were wallpapered the same lunatic yellow. I came to an open doorway and heard a clacking. Steve Wallace was there, ready to kill me. But the sound was only the ice cubes shifting in the icemaker.

At the front desk a girl slept, her fist under her chin. She was little and had glasses and straight blonde hair so white and thin I could see her salmon scalp beneath.

"Hello," I said.

She jumped.

"Sorry," I said. "I didn't know how else to wake you."

She straightened herself and looked at me. "Yes?" she said.

"What can I do right now? Is there anything to do here? I mean anything. Indoors, of course."

The girl shrugged. "There's not really much."

I nodded. "Can I ask you some questions, then? About Steve Wallace?"

"Sure," she said. She looked at her hands, ran the index finger and thumb of her left hand all along the index finger of her right hand, stopping at both knuckles to pinch the skin together so that the wrinkles rolled into one another and formed miniscule valleys. Then she said, "My friend was in the weight room when it happened, you know. She said she saw Steve come through the door and raise the gun at Coach and shoot him in the back three times. But not boom-boom-boom. Like, slowed. Boom. Boom. Boom." The girl brought her two hands together like she was about to pray, the fingers interlocked except the indexes, which ran parallel. She recoiled with each imaginary shot.

"How is the community responding?" It was a dumb question. I saw on the girl's face, the way her eyes withdrew, that I had asked something very obvious. But I didn't know what else to ask.

"We don't know what to do," the girl said in a monotone voice.

"What was he like, Steve Wallace? Did you know him? Did your friends?"

"No, none of us knew him. I didn't really know the Wallace family, either. But they seemed nice, the couple times I saw them."

I thanked her and went back down the hall to the room.

In the room I took the laptop to the small desk by the window and began to type in a Word document. I wanted to get a sketch down. It wasn't the assignment, I knew, but I wanted to imagine Steve Wallace. I thought I might develop a better angle on the story if I knew what he was like. I wrote about how he sat in his house every day after dropping out of community college, in his small room, and he tried to keep it together, he read and wrote and took his medicines, he watched his small metal-caged fan oscillate, he charted stars and planets, he looked in dictionaries for new words, and he tried to force out the sounds of his father and mother in the kitchen. But after a while I knew I was fictionalizing a murderer and projecting a bit of myself onto him, so I stopped.

I called the police office. "Hello," I said. "I'm calling about an interview with Steve Wallace."

"Denied," they said.

I watched Alex sleep. In me there was the impulse that I should kick him in the head or smother him with my ever-growing stomach. There was a bit of Steve Wallace inside of us all, but maybe we had the right combination of brain chemicals to diminish the impulses while Wallace had a mad scientist inside his head pouring mutant concoctions into his veins. And anyway, kicking someone in the head is not the same as shooting an old coach.

I turned on the television and on the news they were showing the rivers rising, pouring out from the banks, water like glaciers moving again across the plains, slowly but totally, swallowing up each inch of our fertile soil. There were videos of sandbagging in Des Moines and Iowa City and all along the Mississippi. No end to the rain in sight, the newscasters said. A dire time for towns across the state, the newscasters said. I was not worried. In school it was made clear to us that Iowans have a sense of community unlike any other group of people. You can leave your doors unlocked at night. Try that in Chicago.

The river was only a few blocks from the motel so I got directions to a bridge where I could stand and look and walked there. On the bridge there were residents in oversized shirts and gray cotton shorts with the white drawstrings hanging out front, old woman with gray curly mullets and thick glasses. I recognized some of them from the day before and I nodded as I came near. But I kept to myself, stood near the far side of the bridge. We were all sopping in the rain.

Nobody could believe it. They kept asking each other, can you believe it? and shaking their heads in response. I put my hands on my hips and watched the water spread from the river. The river looked so incorrect without any banks or designated level. The residents were talking about the roads that might be blocked off. I approached one of the women I had spoken with the day before and said, "I can't believe it."

"I don't know what we did," the woman said, "to deserve this."

"You think it's a God thing?" I asked. I put a hand on the woman's shoulder. We connected in this moment, I felt, like a tortured, confused, deaf, dumb and blind mother and daughter, because we both had some questions for this God and we had nowhere to direct them.

Alex was running up the road. He came to me out of breath. When he regained his breath he said, "We should go before the roads are all washed out."

"I can't leave before the funeral," I said. "I've got to stay here and cover that."

He looked at me. "It's a flood," he said. He seemed irate. "Your editor will understand."

"I've got a commitment," I said, and before that I hadn't really felt one—more like a vague curiosity, maybe simply a morbid one—but now a supreme duty for covering this story was birthed in my heart. "I can't abandon this story."

"I'm not going to be trapped here," Alex said. The residents stared at him and he waved them off. "What are we going to do? I've got work on Monday."

"You go back, then. You've got nothing to do here except follow me around and that doesn't help my interviews."

"What? Come with me. You shouldn't be out in the rain like this. You can't get sick right now."

"I'm staying," I said, much louder than I originally meant but, like my newfound commitment, I allowed for this aggression, took it into my chest.

Alex shook his head and looked downriver. Then he turned back to me and said, "Okay. Be my guest. Stay here in this dinky town, covering your story. I'll be back in a couple of days."

I watched him walk with his hands in his pockets until he turned the corner to the motel. I was glad to see him go, I suppose, but I also felt very alone in that moment, and I put my hand under my belly again not because I needed to but because it felt like the only marked increase of my life left anymore.

I spent the rest of the morning and afternoon in the room. I ordered a pizza and ate the whole thing while watching the news. It rained all day with the same ferocity. I tried to summon again the commitment I had felt on the bridge but I felt no rush of passion, no thrust of obligation.

That evening I put on a pair of slacks and a dress shirt and then I put my notebook, my cards, and my pencils into my backpack and slung it over my shoulder. I left the room and walked down the hallway and out of the motel.

I walked in the rain through Harrisburg, down Main Street. Almost immediately my clothing was wet, and soon the water began to work its way through my shirt and onto my skin until my arms and legs were slick and my shoulder blades became like mountains at the base of a gigantic lake. I could hear the river gushing even as I walked in the opposite direction. There was no one on the streets except for me. I waited for someone to appear in the crosswalk, under the orange bulb of the streetlight, closing up a storefront, leaning out from a house window, sipping whiskey on a porch, but there was no one. Alex's car, I thought, that's what I'll see. But I saw no headlights. I had the world to myself but I didn't feel as though it was mine, I felt as though it was still someone else's world and he or she watched from above as I crossed, like a solitary ant on a tree root in a great park, some miniscule patch of land, clutching to my loneliness as though it were a granule of sugar.

Alex could leave me here in the rain. He expected me to give in, to say, at the last moment, as he unlocked the car's driver side door, Wait, wait! Here I come, my bags clutched in my hand, and off we would go back to Iowa City to finish our degrees and start our lives together, quiet and with considerable space between us, not just the space of a living room but of entire inner gorges. But I would prove him wrong. I would make this story something great. And yet still I felt no flush of dedication, of determination, but only a small kindling in my heart for my dad. If I saw him now, I thought, we could understand each other, come to some sort of great truth about the toughness of the world.

I found myself in front of the police office, where I was supposed to be all along, I knew. I hadn't known it when I left the motel but I knew it now. I put my hand on the brick wall and ran my fingers through the caulking from the bottom of one brick, down the side of the next, and on top of the one below that, as though I were tracing a highway on the map in Alex's car. Here, inside of here, inside a cell, was my future. Hello, Steve, I would say. I would look deep into his blue eyes. I'm here to talk to you, I would say, and I would say it slowly and deeply. I didn't think he would save me—that's not why I wanted to talk to him. I just wanted to make sure I wasn't missing anything. I got the feeling that if I dug deep enough, took out my shovel and excavated enough space, I would find a nugget that would shake everything back into some sort of sense that I could clutch. I took a breath and pushed open the police station door.

There was a long hallway ahead of me and a booth to my right, where a female officer with lips so big you could land a plane on them sat. Separating us was a thick glass window with a half-circle hole near the bottom. Behind the officer was a map of Harrisburg. Even through the glass I could smell cigarette smoke and I had to breathe deep and slow again in order to fight the nausea forcing itself down on my head and stomach.

"Can I help you?" the female officer said.

"Yes," I said. "I'm here to see Steve."

She looked at me from behind the glass with the same look Alex had given me in the car, a long look where her eyeballs kept stretching until they inhabited every inch of her sockets.

"I'm sorry," she said, "but Steve Wallace is taking no visitors."

"I understand that," I said. I nodded to show how much I understood. "But it would mean a lot to me if you could let me see Steve. I'm a reporter."

"Sorry," she said.

I turned to the bench on my left. "I'll just sit here," I said, pointing. "Maybe he'll have a change of heart. Can you at least tell Steve he has a visitor?"

She shrugged.

I sat down on the bench feeling tired. The joints in my knees were wet. The ridges of cartilage under the skin of my ears were wet. The shafts of my femurs were wet. I wanted to strip down naked, to take everything off and throw it on the ground and never put any of it back on again, just stretch out my legs and stare at my big, fat feet, watch them swell.

I woke to a voice on a radio telling residents to evacuate. The voice said that fifty people were sandbagging the river but town officials didn't expect the barricade to hold. This will be the end of Harrisburg, the voice said. Later I heard, half-asleep, the voice announcing the Iowa River had flooded the university and ruined several buildings in which I had taken classes.

A hand shook me.

"Get up," said a male officer standing over me.

"Will Steve see me?"

"No," he said.

"Then I'll stay."

The officer pulled me up by my waist with care. He put his hands on my shoulder. "Miss," he said, "that man is not going to see you. Go home."

"No," I said. I felt so tired, so weak. My legs shook. But I didn't want to go home, wherever he meant—the motel room, the apartment in Iowa City, my dad's trailer, none of that was where I wanted to be. On this bench. In that cell. "I'll stay."

The officer took me by the wrist, his fingers meeting his thumb underneath, to the door. He pushed on the smudged glass and the door swung open. He escorted me outside and said, "You shouldn't be by yourself. Do you have family we can call?"

"Call my father," I said. "My information is in my backpack." When the officer turned around I walked away at a quick pace. My clothes clung to my body like timid children but I strode with as much speed as I could toward the river, through the town square with the dark, shuttered buildings, past the quiet side streets and finally across the glow of the motel vacancy sign. Let them find my dad in my emergency contacts. He couldn't be here for hours.

As I neared the river, I tried to shake Alex's being from me but he hung on me just as my clothes did, his face always right over my shoulder. I could see him shaking his head, thinking, poor little girl, she doesn't know what she's gotten herself into. Stumbling around Harrisburg sniffing for a story like a dog. Well, maybe. Maybe that was not so far from the truth. The bridge was straight ahead, the middle section still above water, and I made for it, pushing Alex from my head with the strength I had left. I wasn't carrying anything anymore, beside myself.

Behind the bridge was the rural night, blacker than my eyes could register, unshaped, like the world ended right across the river, like God hadn't bothered creating anything past that point.

The line of sandbags stood behind the bridge like a crumbling wall, uneven and lumpy. Residents, mostly older men, passed bags from one end to the other, their arms low and their backs bent. There were a few women too, most of them young, handing off sandbags near the front of the line. Behind the sandbags the water sloshed as though it were in a careless child's cup. Limbs appeared in the headlights like fireflies, an arm briefly jutting out, a knee bending and retracting and then sinking back into the dark.

I walked to the front of the line and said, "I'd like to help."

An older man looked at me and said, "Not like that you won't. Time for you to go home."

I pushed my hair behind my ears and said, "I'm fine, really. Very healthy."

A woman came up to me and took me by the shoulders. It was the woman I had spoken with earlier on the bridge. I could feel each of her fingers on my shoulders and they were all fat and gummy. "Come on, let's get you back to the motel."

"No," I said. I threw her hands off me and walked over to the piles of sandbags. I bent my knees and slid my hands under one bag. Its grainy texture chafed against my forearms but I lifted. I nearly fell over but staggered. "Front of the line," I said. "I can handle this one myself."

Then I felt a deep anguish below my stomach, like a bomb had detonated, and besides the explosion I felt the pain of the dead, too. I groaned and refocused myself, and then I took two steps forward.

"Christ, lady," the older man said. "Give me that."

I took another step. The fires inside me were raging. I took another step. My eyes showed bright lights in the corners when I looked ahead. I could hear the water sloshing as I took another step. It slapped against the sandbags. My knees gave and I dropped onto the pavement.

There was a great gathering around me. I could make out the sounds of people I did not know but I felt just then as though I were their dog, hit by a car on the street.

My dad was holding my hand in the white hospital room. His cheeks were very big and red and he had not shaved. His hands were coarse.

"Your hands," I said. The bed I rested on was comfortable.

"Some sort of product at the factory," he said.

"You can sue them for that," I said.

"No," he said, "I can't. They did everything they could. There's nothing to be done."

We gazed to different spots in the room. I looked at the television, where a muted game show was taking a commercial break. My dad's heavy breathing dominated the sterile room.

"You lost it," he said without looking at me.

"I figured," I said. I barely wondered where Alex was. I didn't miss him much at all.

"What next?" my dad said. His belly rested on the bed. He was so big. I was like toothpick shaved from his big family tree trunk.

"What a question," I said. I looked at him until he faced me. "I don't think I want to go back to school for a while. I think I'd like to move in with you for a little bit."

"Sure," he said.

The rain, I saw, had not let up. My dad sat down in the chair by the bed and we didn't speak but instead listened to the sounds of the hospital and watched the muted game show.

TODD COLBY

Guidance Councilor

Weather is just math so you can add it up
and see where you are in the year. A group
of people called real people. The manger is
on fire. Gangly orange light. Memory of heat waves
rising from the sand in summer. Pink and cherry glowing
pale blue by evening, milkier by noon the next
day. What color is remembering? Oh you precious
poets drawn to nothing where nothing is.
The slope of winter just tilted, go rub some
butter on your toast and do something
American. Heart thumping in blue chest,
wake up in memory of panic. The pliers
go mushy in my hand, I can't fix anything.

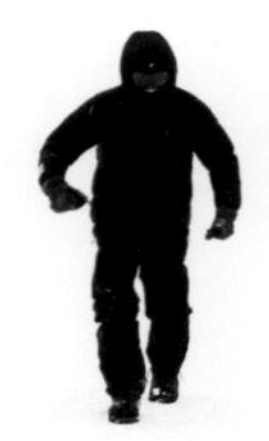

GEERT GIORIS

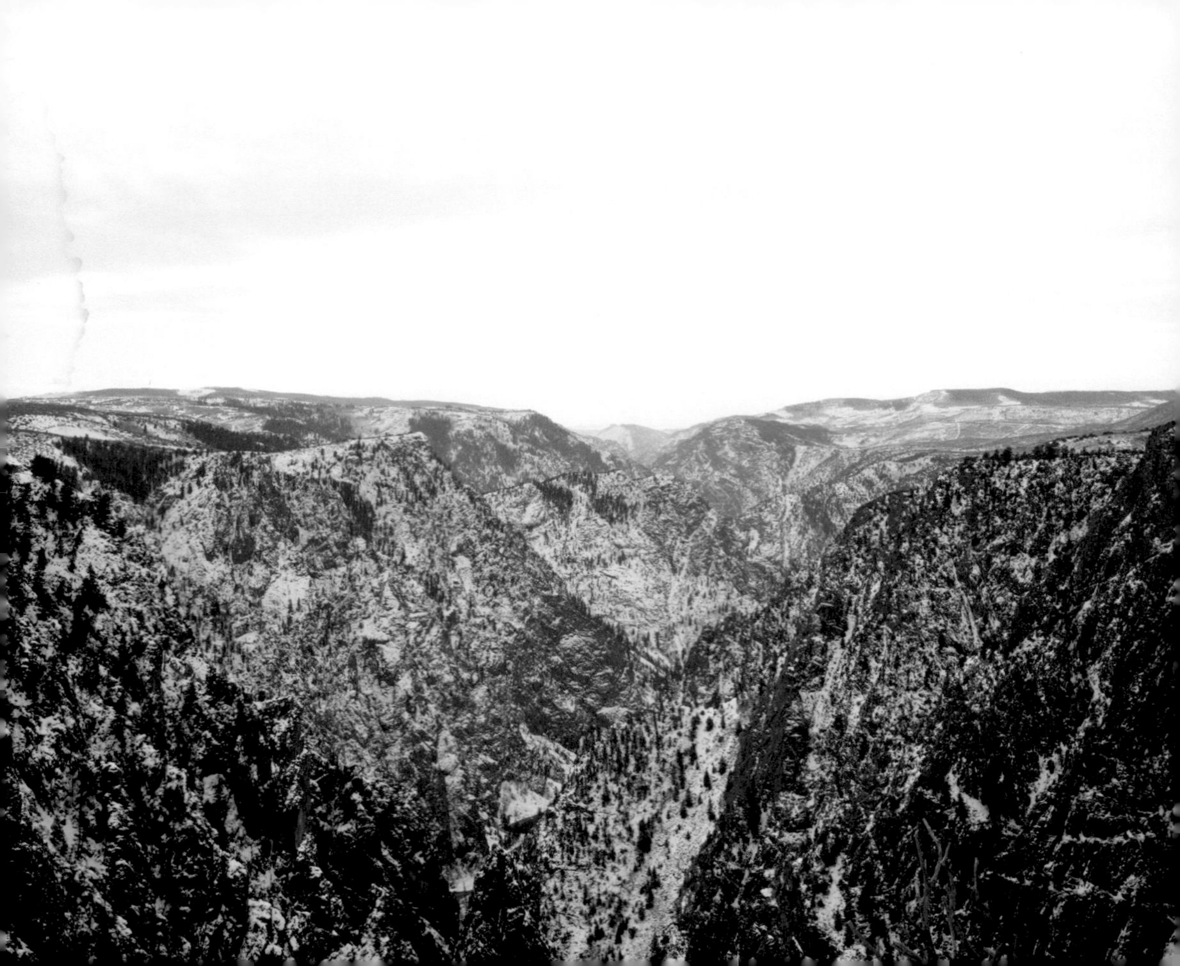

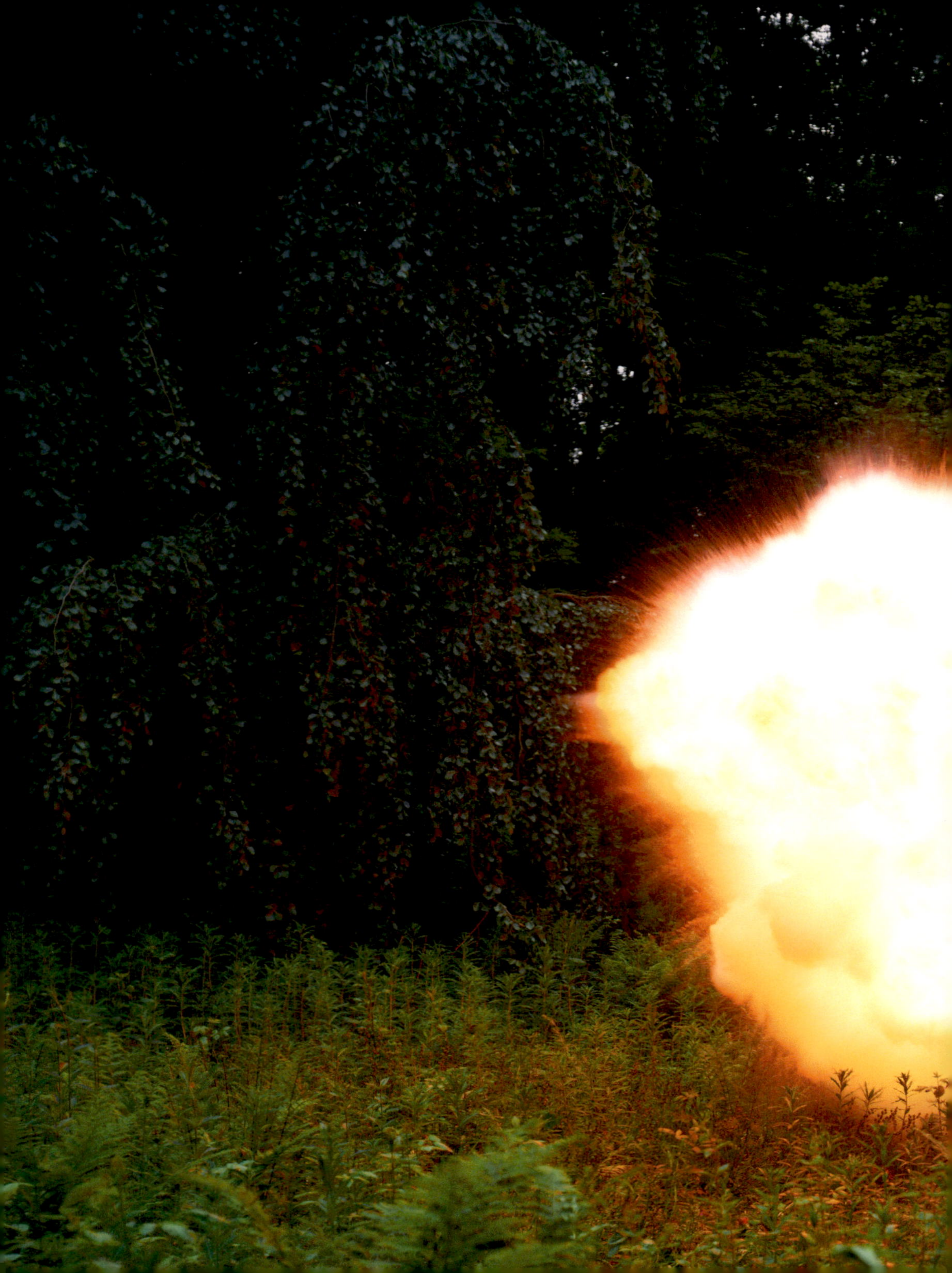

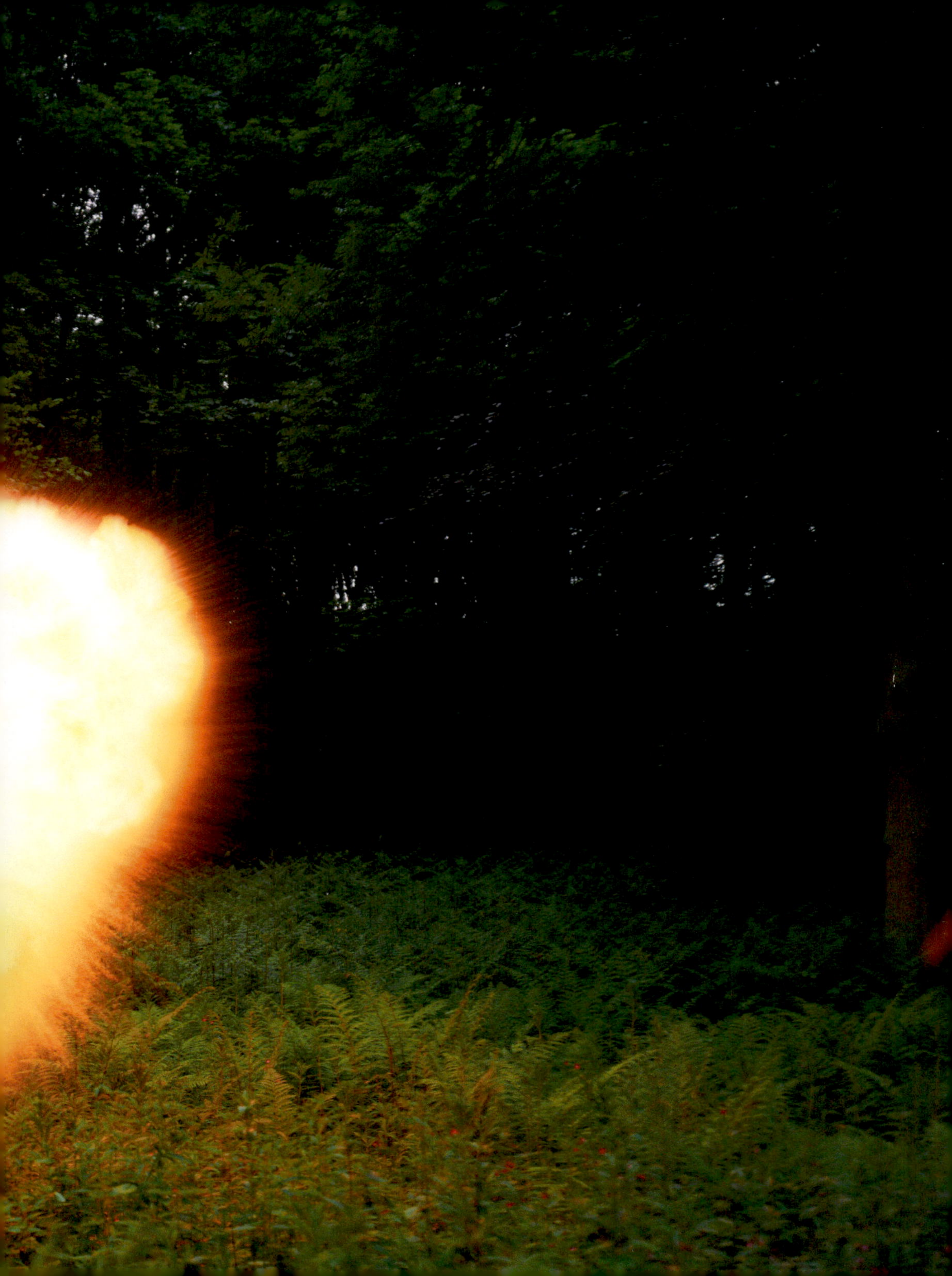

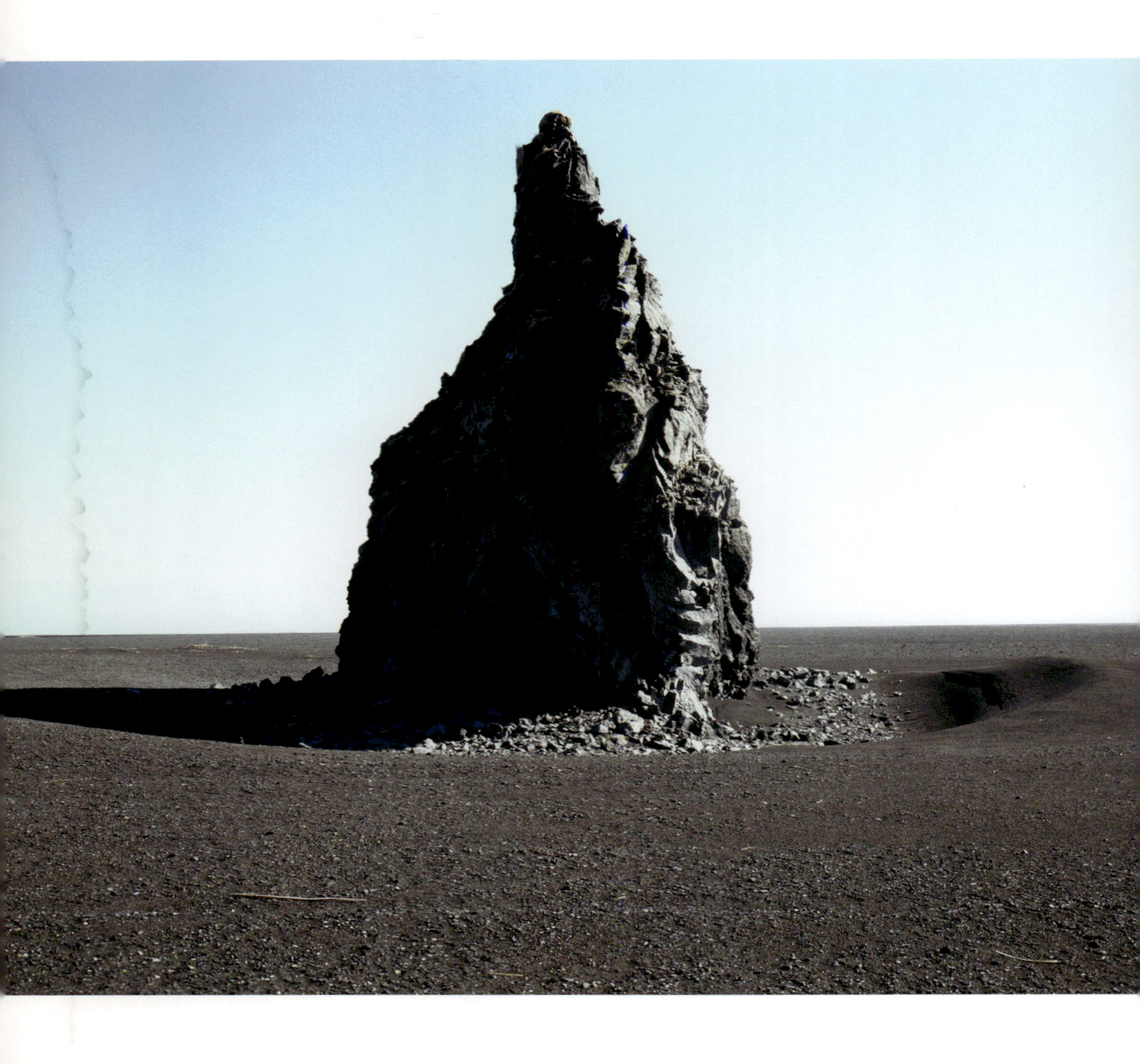

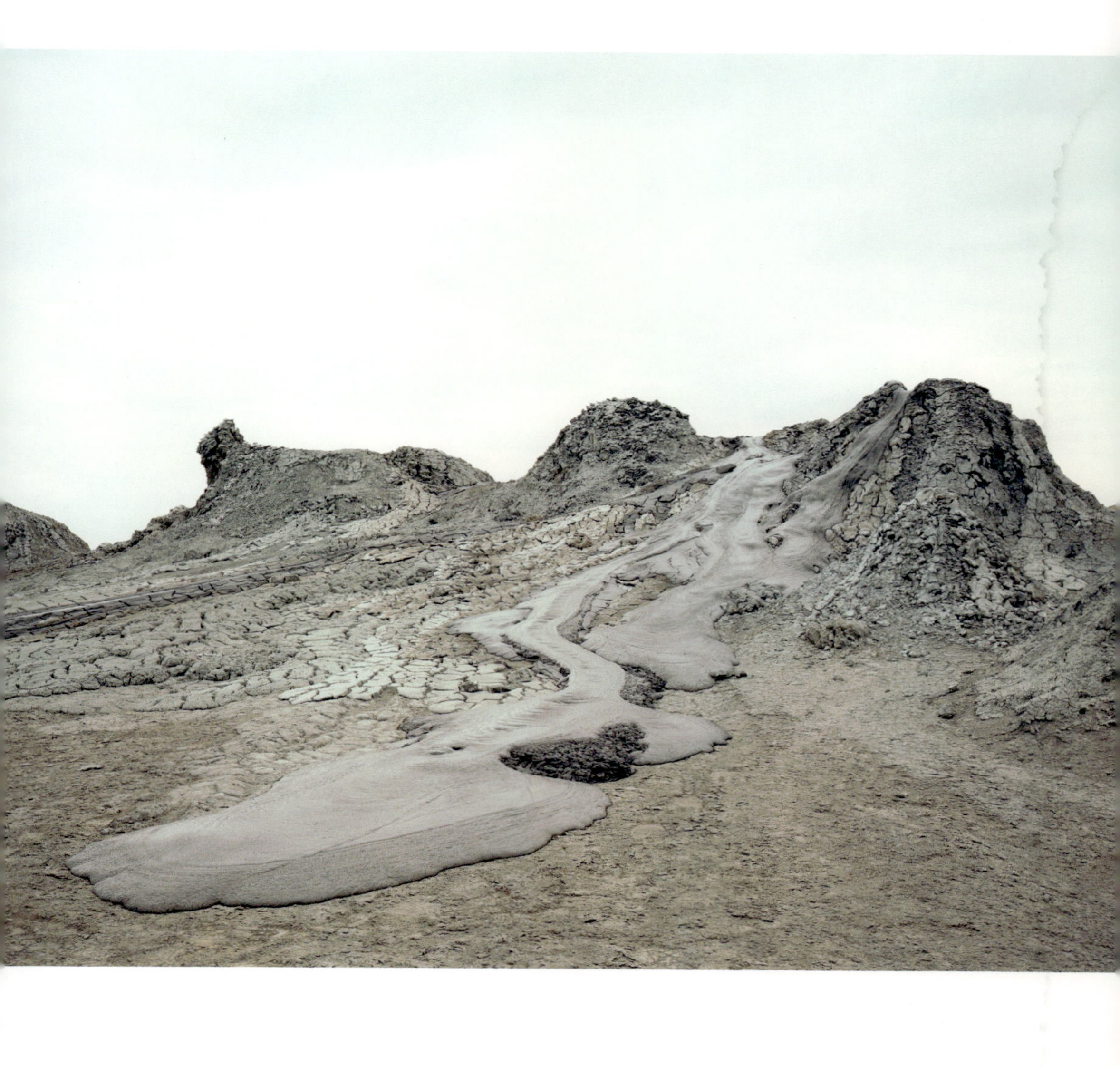

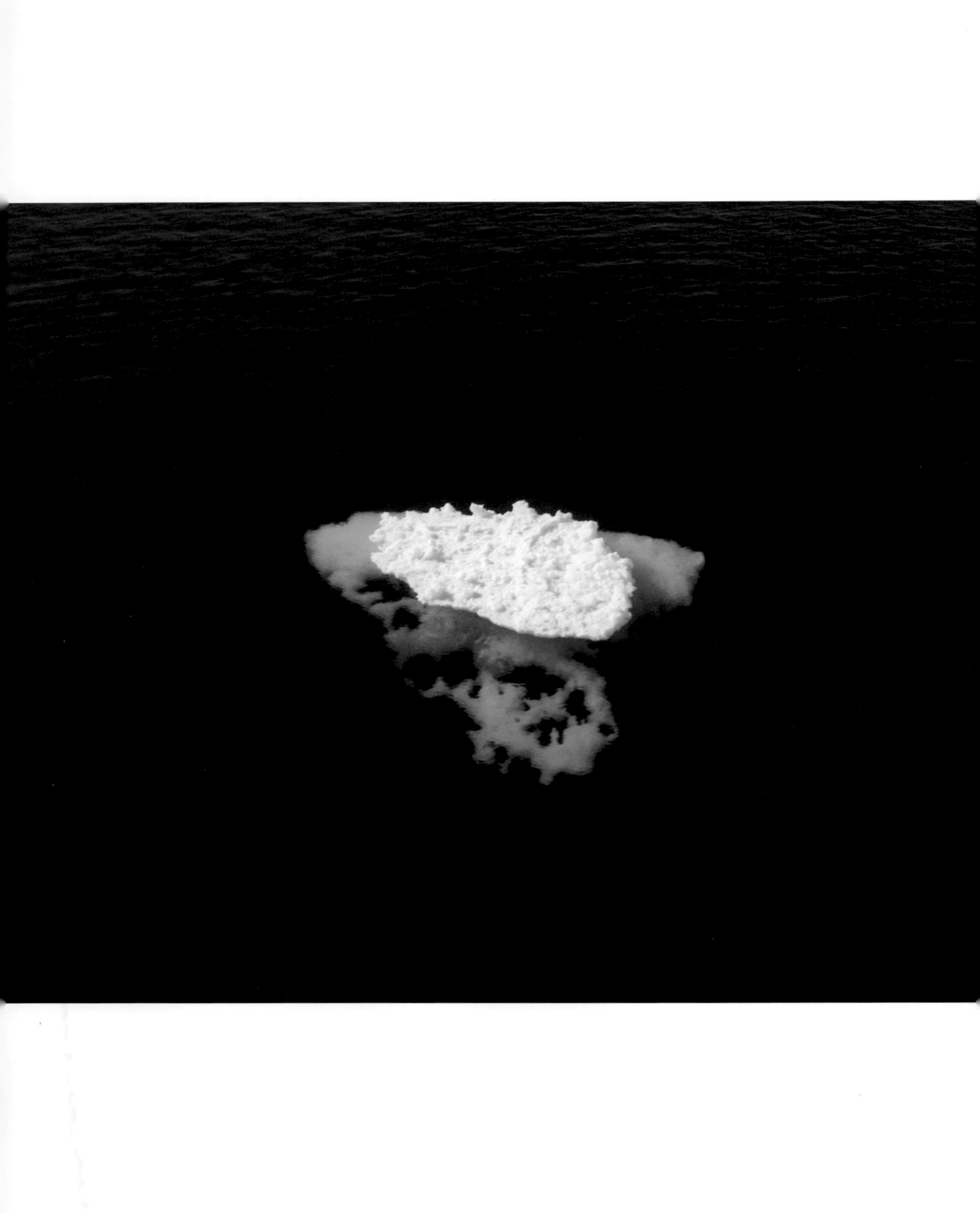

NICHOLAS A. DEBOER

A Hood of Valleys
CXI(111)

as cataracts focused in stream
& heat of a cavernous mouth
the body chronicles

shark teeth gleam rows & rows
down these walls a cage
shadows writhe whistles
fingers grazed the try
extricate my palm

it is must pull the
burn from stakes lift
stones from accusations

shall i lead shadows
of tyranny out into
our community?

bathe us of opposite:
give forth explication
of demons

"power is not of an essence
strives for alienation"
tower simple towers
one shade red
dagger sticks

lunar cobwebs
score a across the cavern

"could there be unity in fragments?"

a small section
bare & hung in effigy
a post-bag
leans and
falls

inside hotbed of decayed organic upstart

in this life i may be
quieted but fight on
the front stays stays

red ore streaks the soil
scrapes flesh down

arrivants carry on (the fields)
people are not
labyrinthine
but embroidery
endowed with

down here fireflies illume
speleothem roots

to falter crumble exhaust
gives pause rest brief:

the spectacle roots
under soft lidded sight

"and what does one do
but crawl travel on static?"

gray at the change at
the meaning of a word

so says night terror
pain reveals in hand
below tongue

a deep love carries
resources over
dark water

down & deep this cage
is sleepy a little pool
to drink to
dip arms

to wake free
a single flickering screen
lure lures
i saturate
multiple images

wet pieces of molded
paper over face

walk past a oculus dome above
vent dim light
spills faint orange
hear water shift

skin foam gauze: a damaged body
cavern's heap

see:

another boat it
is always another boat
to beat against the
surf!

i say

i melt
in
air

nude light at underside
hold close

situationist stone

passage sheaves
wander
choke tears that fit with dead love:

widow/ eir wait mourn
a sight stretches wind

ey who heaves this ship
always this
ship

onto its long course

i gather
a hood
dark fur
escape is just an out

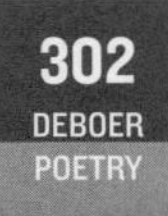

PETER KAMINSKY

THE ARISTOCRAT

My grandpa Jan grew up in the town of Narev, Poland. At that time, as it often was during its long war-torn history, that region was part of the Russian Empire. Narev, which Simon Schama wrote about in the beginning of Landscape and Memory, adjoined the Bialowiez forest, which Grandpa Jan never failed to mention was the largest stand of virgin forest in Europe. Subsequent research for my book Pig Perfect: Encounters With Remarkable Swine *indicated that the term virgin," when applied to European forests, is often an exaggeration. In ancient times, when mammoths, bison, and other large animals roamed the continent in huge herds, the Western European forest was as much grassland as it was forest. That's what happens when you have a lot of big, plant-eating creatures roaming the land. When people enter the picture and get rid of the large creatures, or fence them in, you get deep dark forests.*

Questions of the virginity of the forest aside, Grandpa, once a revolutionary, and always a poet, never tired of telling a tale of royal malfeasance that has passed into my family's store of ancestral lore.

"I was nine or ten," Grandpa said (so it must have been 1904 or 1905). "The Czar kept Bialowiez as a royal hunting preserve and retreat. One summer the Czarina was coming with Rasputin and her young son, who was a hemophiliac. The Czar sent his brother, the Grand Duke Michael to make sure everything was in order. I will never forget it: the whole village came out to greet the Czar's brother. The mayor was there wearing a wide sash. All the little girls were dressed up in traditional clothes with flowers in their hair. The town band was there and I was a member of the church choir.

"So we all waited at the train station. The Grand Duke's train pulled up. It was white and gold, with a big Romanov eagle above the cowcatcher. It was quite a sight, like a piece of jewelry weighing a hundred tons, with steam coming out of it.

"As the train came to a halt, the Grand Duke Michael, bewhiskered and bemedalled, climbed down to the platform." At this point Grandpa would imitate an overfed burgher, red-facedly trying to look graceful while he struggled to move his considerable bulk, a task made more difficult by high boots, a starched collar and a saber. I imagined a mental picture of Oliver Hardy at his klutziest.

"The little girls came forward with the mayor to present flowers. The band played. The choir started to sing along, but the Grand Duke walked right past us and continued down the platform about twenty steps. Then he unbuttoned his tunic, undid his pants buttons, and proceeded to urinate right there! To him, having a piss in front of all of us was no more indecorous than going in front of some farm animals. That's how the aristocracy thought of the rest of us. We weren't people!

"Then he buttoned up his fly, came over, took the flowers, kissed the girls, shook the mayor's hand, and off he went in his coach and four."

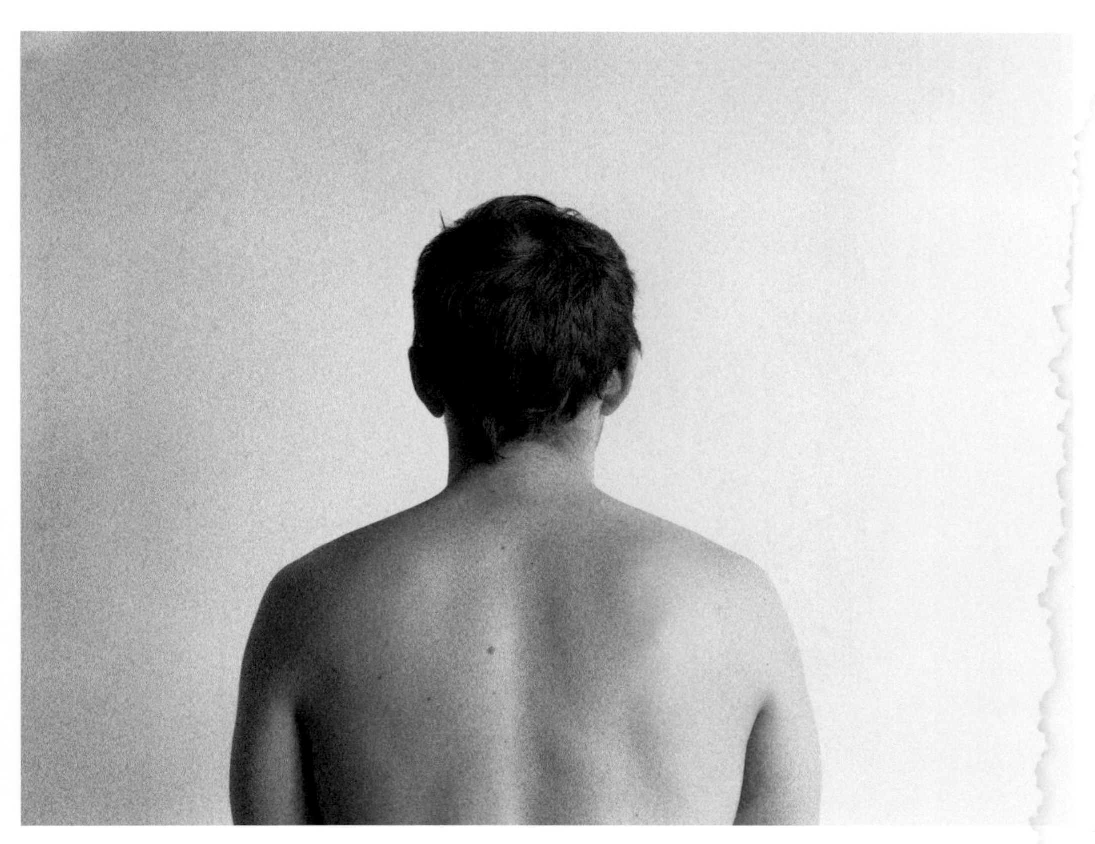

PACIFICO SILANO

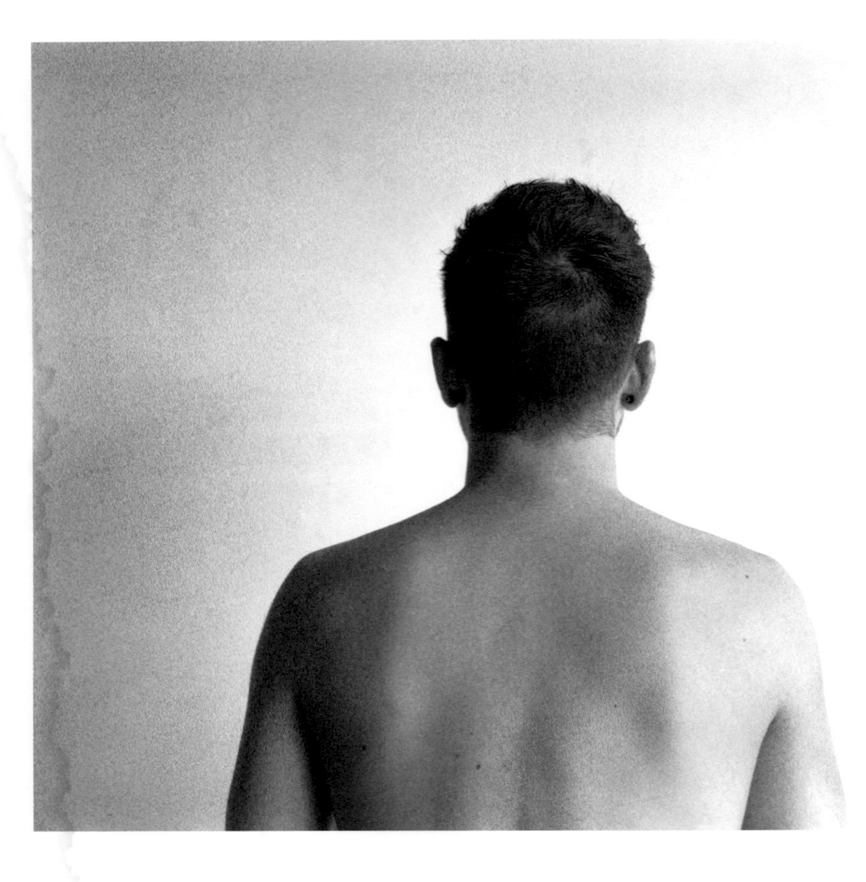

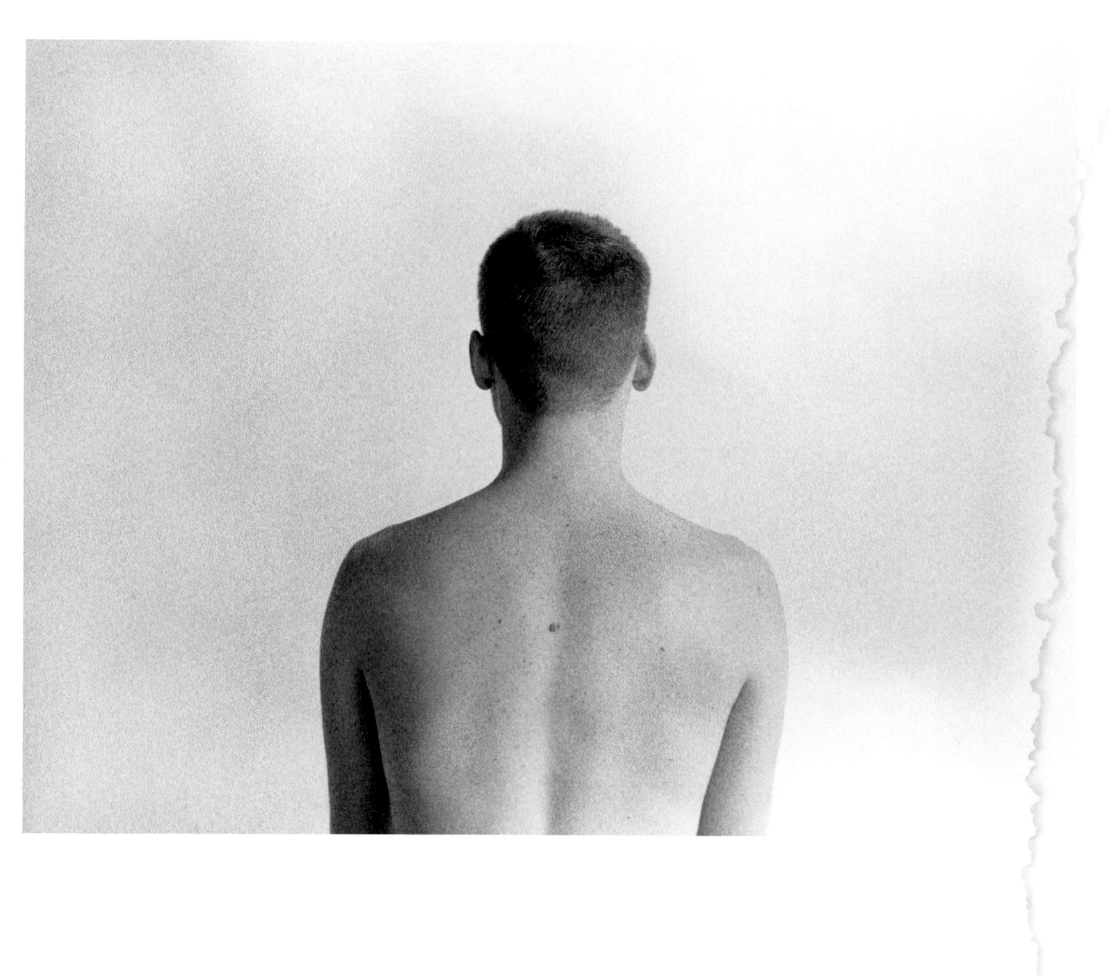

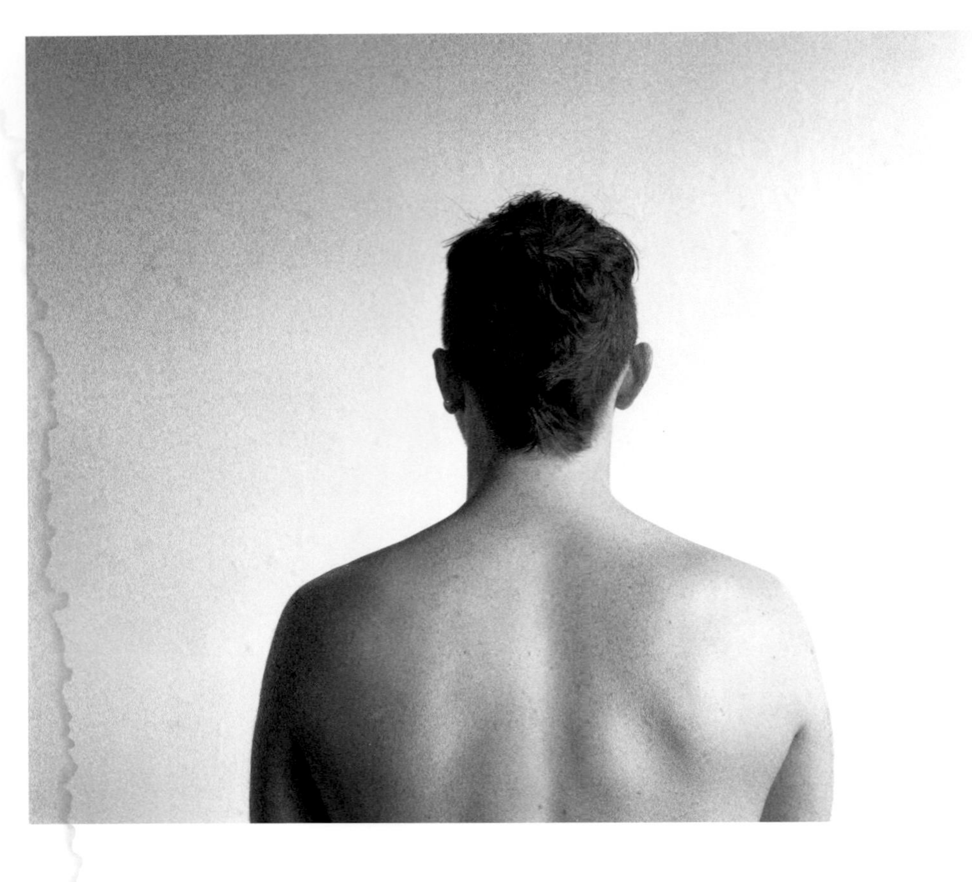

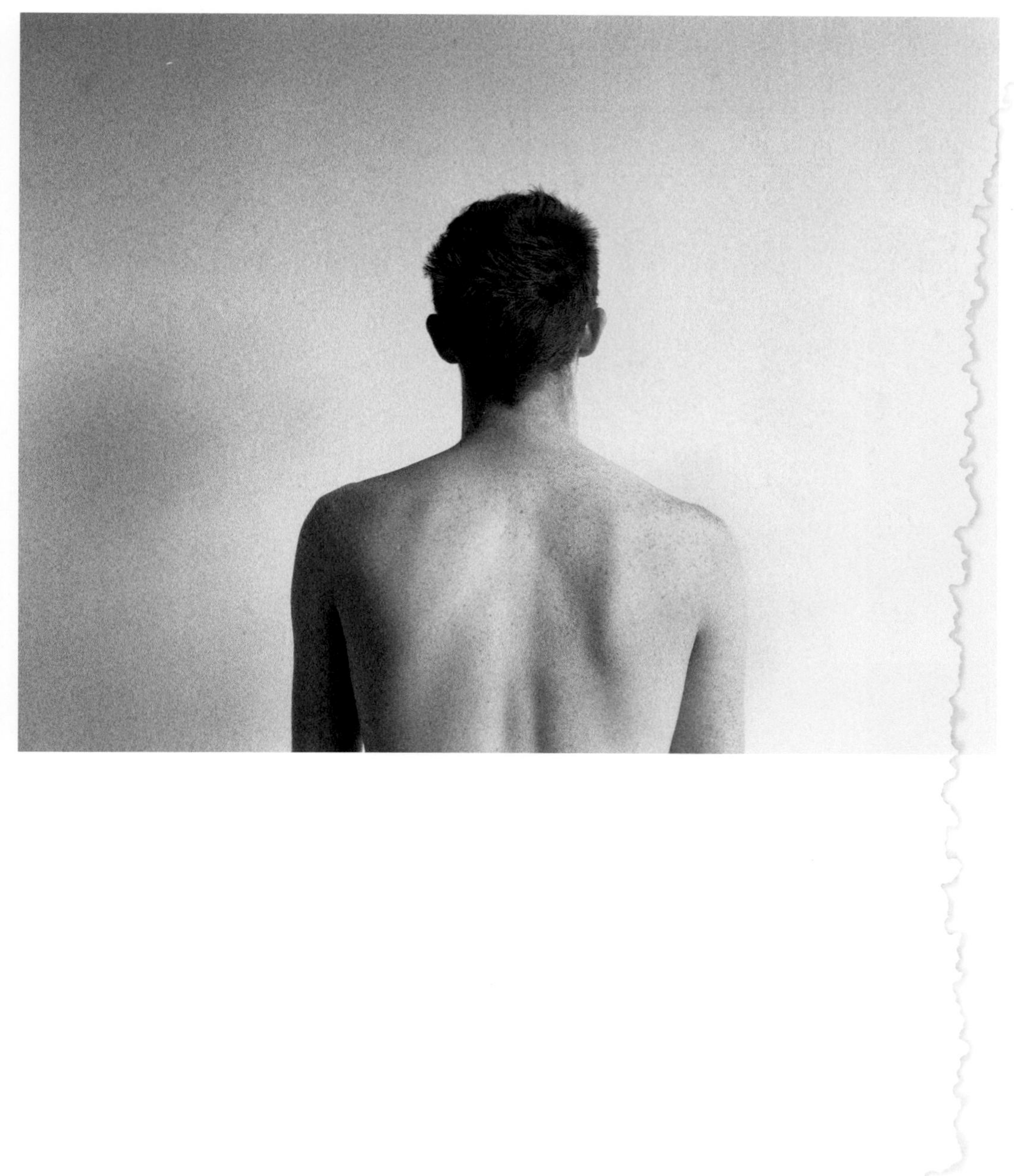

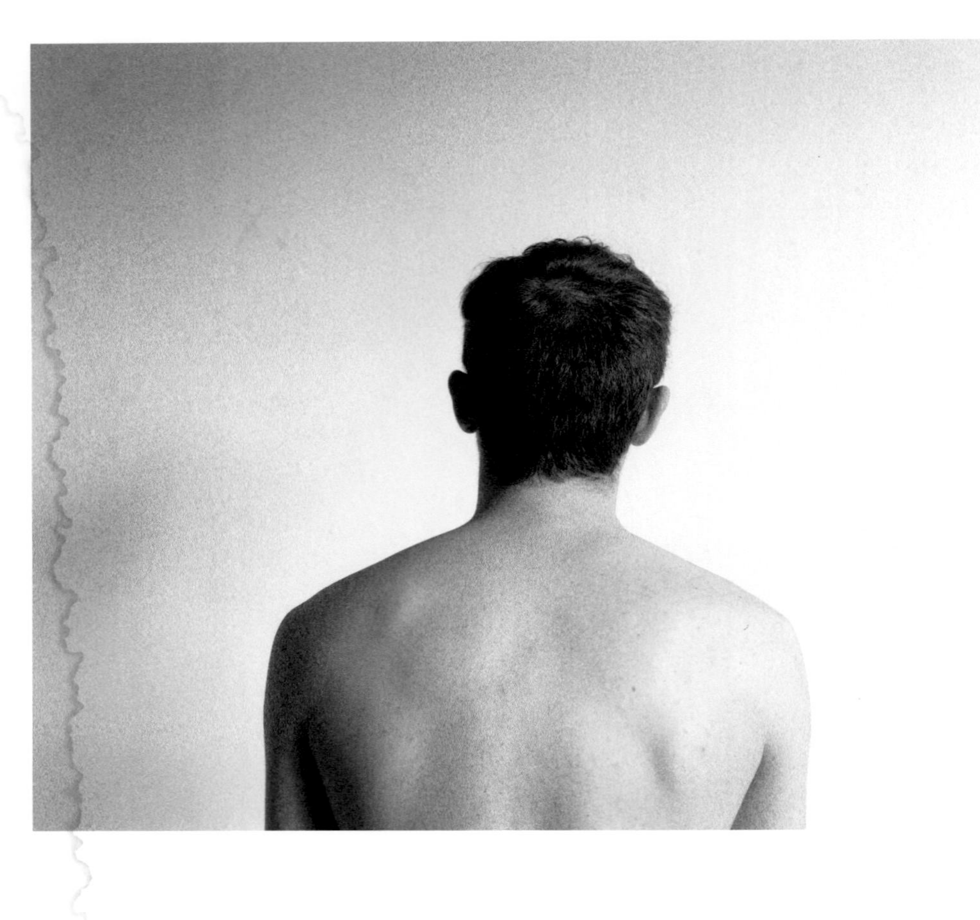

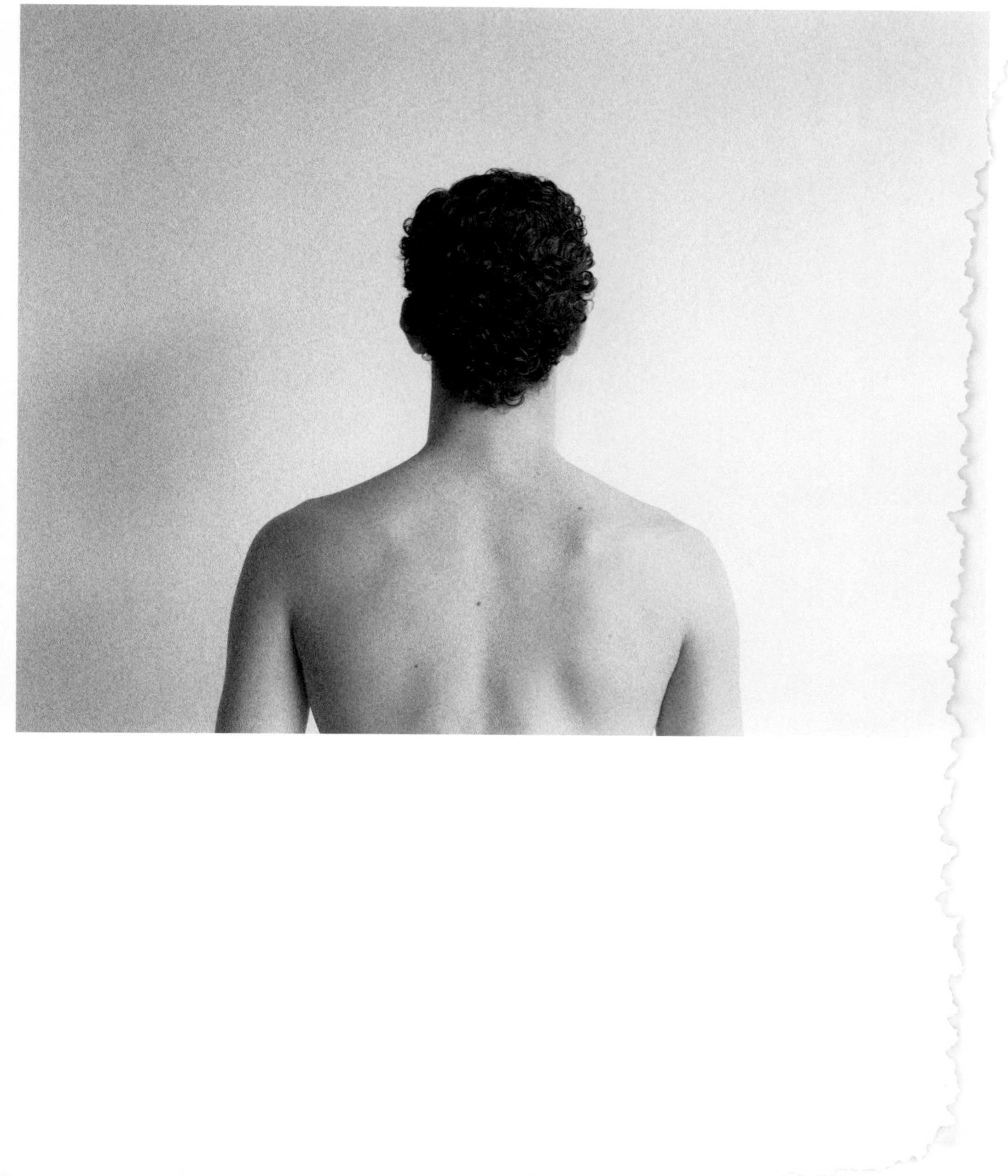

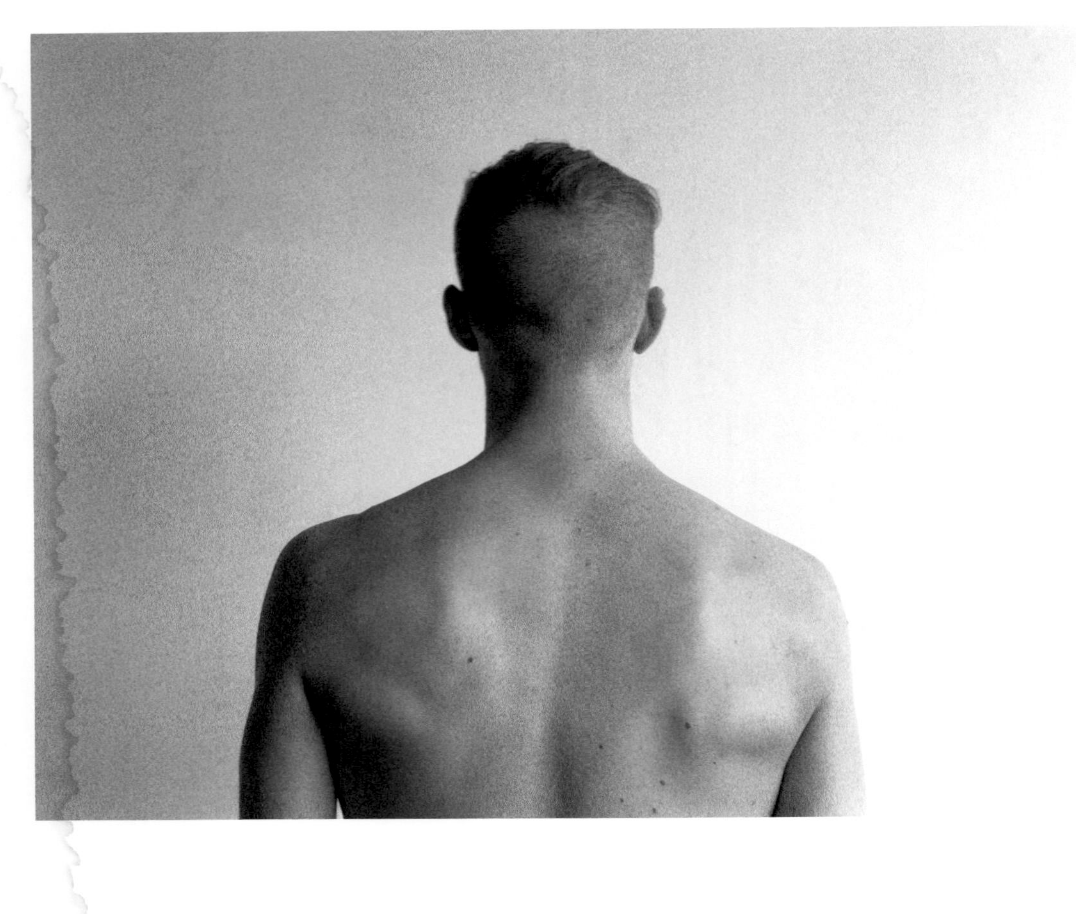

NICK SMITH

KALI DANCED IN THE NO MO ZONE

If you have only one *chapatti* a day, you will not have a fluffy stomach. You see, the travel thing is really not a walk in the park like it is in Europe. That place, with its stone-faced Beefeaters, charming waiters, and garrulous gondoliers, might as well be some quaint Disneyland. But here it's not easy, especially if you're a babe in the woods. First, you have to go to the Tourists Only Railway Ticket Office. It's in the Writers' Building in the old part of Calcutta. They haven't done a stick of repairs there since maybe about 1848. Large falcons survey the city from its ramshackle pinnacles, now and then swooping down on hapless crows and sparrows. Once inside, you see the bureaucrats reading their newspapers and taking their time. Like the *alaap* section of an Indian *raga,* they're in no big hurry to get through this tune. Things will happen when they want them to happen. You will soon discover that the word for "tip" and the word for "bribe" are one and the same. At that point, the rats start coming out of the holes in the walls. They strut around like they own the place and they kinda sorta do. You half expect them to say, "Hey buddy, how're ya doing?" in a low raspy voice. But they don't, so you sign the required forms, the bureaucrats slump to attention, and suddenly there are lots of the critters scampering around. Your wife begins to get pissed because the tail of one of them has slithered across her bare foot. Well, you get the drift. So, having gotten your tickets, you use the city as your home base and set off for side trips around the country. You zigzag across the land.

The trip back to Calcutta started uneventfully except for the occasional passed-out peasant lying facedown in the middle of the steep winding road.

We were descending from the foothills of the Himalayas. The driver would come around a sharp turn and there the peasant was—dead drunk on the worn median strip.

"Shouldn't we stop and help him out?" I inquired. The driver smiled and hunched over his wheel, deep in concentration. I pondered the bald tires I'd seen earlier and figured, what the hell, this guy looked like a great driver. After all, he was still alive.

Mrs. Dhutt, a plump Brahmin matron from West Bengal, burst out laughing, slapping her pink-saried thigh.

"What? You must be joking. No, no, no. It's just one of those country people. He's tied one on. Too much toddy. He's lucky not to go blind. Let him sleep it off. That's if he's really drunk, but he probably isn't."

"What do you mean by that?" I replied.

"Most likely, he's stone-cold sober and if we get out to help, his friends will come out of the woods and rob us."

I was incredulous. Sachiko was incredulous too, blurting out a loud *"Mo."* It's Japanese for "For shame"—short in her native tongue for *"Mo-eeh-yo."*

"Stop it, Sachiko." I ordered. "Don't you know this is a no mo zone?"

She burst into tears.

Manipur was definitely the dangerous place we'd expected. Everywhere there were all sorts of security personnel, roadblocks, and checkpoint Charlies. Understand that the place was trying to secede and had been trying for a long time. The authorities had put a curfew in place for six o'clock because the week before, some kid waiting for a bus had been shot by the trigger-happy soldiers. Tall opium poppies adorned the hotel's front lawn.

"It's a problem here!" exclaimed the lady at the check-in desk as she gestured to the addictive plants.

This particular establishment had been a big deal at one time, but since you needed to get special permission to even get into Manipur these days, it had kind of gone to seed. Our hosts were constantly arguing over which of them would have the honor of squiring us around their fair city.

The strangest part of this side trip was when our Hindu host Dr. Singh took us to a "VIP" party in the old section of Imphal. Suddenly, it became quite clear that Sachiko and I were the guests of honor. There were so few Westerners who ever managed to gain entry that when they did, it was an excuse to throw a party for their benefit. And what a party it was. The men were dressed in tuxedos and their wives wore what looked like 1950s prom dresses. They were indeed the VIPs that Dr. Singh had promised. The gang was all present and accounted for; these doctors, lawyers, politicians, police captains, and even a general or two, were the people who pulled the strings in this town. One of the generals drunkenly informed me that no Manipuri party would be complete without a round of songs. I glanced anxiously at Sachiko. She looked nervous. She was out of her realm. That was not good.

"Ev'y one mustht thing a thong of hith choosing," announced the general. "You thee Joe. We haf Jack Daniels here too."

I watched as each of the elegantly dressed inebriated couples got up and performed beautiful songs I would probably hear once, and only once, in my entire life. Sometimes the revelers even looked a bit like Fred and Ginger as they cavorted around the room. The burly Chief of Police and I each took turns accompanying the show. We traded off playing *tabla,* a folk drum used in a variety of Indian music. Soon it was my turn to sing. I chose to sing The Beatles' "Within You, Without You" and got quite a reception. They had never heard it before.

Then it was the Police Chief's turn to play *tabla.* He glanced at his hands, held them up for all to see and exclaimed, "These hands beat prisoners all livelong day. Now they need another place to come out again to play."

I looked again for Sachiko in the drunken crowd. She looked alone and crestfallen in the corner of the room. Someone was trying to feel her up. I gently removed the groping hand and reached out to her, but she pushed me away.

"It's okay, Sachiko. We don't want to get in trouble here. Sometimes I even get felt up."

Fast forward to a week later: we were back in Calcutta taking *sitar* music lessons from one of the great pundits. I was playing *tabla* again, this time for the great pundit's class. I loved playing the drum and looking up to see the entire class playing the same sitar melodies over and over until they got the hang of it. James, an American from the Midwest, was one of the students. He was by far the best pupil, and the pundit was very happy with him. Often, the pundit would hold James up as a shining example of the ideal *sitar* player, comparing him to his son who was, quite frankly, a bit of a disappointment for Panditji. You see, pundits are always looking for reliable students to whom they can pass on a lifetime's worth of musical treasures, and Panditji's son was more interested in computer hacking and cricket matches. James milked it up, and he also hit it off really well with Sachiko. Sometimes, back at the apartment in Lake Gardens, she would even say, "Joe, why can't you be more like James?" James, James, I thought. I'd only met him a few times and didn't get much of an impression except that he seemed like the type who wrote the most beautiful songs that no one would ever hear. I recalled going over to James' house. The man's cat had made more of an impression on me. Then there were a few times when I'd come back to the apartment and fall asleep under the fan, and Sachiko would come back two hours later from an errand in the city. She would definitely be in a better mood.

I stepped out into the heat of the day. Varanasi was like that, a labyrinth of ancient narrow streets where the stray dogs and the monkeys were in a state of perpetual war, and goggle-eyed young Turks chewed *pan,* shoving their way through the crowds, all the while revving the engines of their shining motor scooters. I was alone this time, and Sachiko was back in the hotel trying to get a hold of herself. I wished he could've slapped her silly, but naah, I wasn't the type. That sort of thing was a note that just wasn't in this *raga.* But I was slowly discovering that that was really what she wanted. True, unpleasant things had happened. The train had been hijacked, which was about par for the course, and we'd been held hostage from about eleven at night until seven in the morning. We'd been forced to listen to political speeches in Hindi the whole time, and I'd asked an old man what the hijackers were talking about and the guy sorta shrugged his shoulders. Eventually, the local warlord, satisfied that had made his show of strength, let the train proceed on its way. He was so darned gentlemanly about it that he even bowed to my wife. Sachiko, however, was unimpressed. "It's all your fault! It's all your fault!" she yelled. Things were starting to take a turn for the worse.

I decided to go to the burning *ghats.* I was having a cup of tea from an indoor stall near the great sacred river when a loud crashing sound had interrupted my daydreams. I didn't give it much thought until the crash happened again, reverberating every ten seconds or so, through the walls of the tiny restaurant. I rushed outside to see an enormous dead cow being pushed down the steps of the burning *ghat.* A French tourist off to the side informed me that the farmers were pushing the carcass towards the river. The crashing continued until at last the straining farmers managed to get the beast into the water and the tourist and I watched it get carried away in the slow current, its stiffened legs peeking out from the ripples. I took a deep breath and invited the tourist to join me for tea. The tourist introduced himself as one Claude Ferrier from Paris. Soon Claude was ranting to me about how India wasn't living up to his expectations. Claude seemed like the type of person who never let a very skimpy command of a language other than his own ever get in the way of having a deep discussion. He would make his point like some sort of bulldozer, which I found to be very endearing. In fact, I found myself egging him on, urging him to describe indiscretions that I would never dream of doing myself. In my mind's eye, I kept saying, "Do it! Do it!" "No," I thought, but didn't say, "it's better to let other people do your acting out for you." Claude's favorite words were "arriving "and" transforming." Everything about India could be assessed with those two words. Basically, Claude was bummin' and bummin' bad. Apparently, he had expected some sort of old Vedic culture and what he got instead was this dog-eat-dog, smash-and-grab, hocus pocus shuck and jive, or something akin to crashing cows.

I reassured him: "No pain no gain. Take me, for example. I'm going through lots of pain right now. My wife is acting like a spoiled child. This country brings out the best and the worst."

Claude nodded and looked into the bottom of his tea cup. He was unpleasantly surprised to see several strands of matted human hair. He was deeply alarmed. I reminded the tourist that this was Varanasi, city of death, city of grossness—the place where dyed-in-the-wool Hindus go to die—the place that will never host the next Olympics. The tourist smiled nervously.

"It's okay," I said. "This water has been boiled to the right temperature. You won't get sick.

"You tourists," I continued. "You're so worried about getting sick. Don't you know you'll get sick? You must get sick. It's only a matter of time. One of the tourists that Sachiko and I met is this guy named James. He's a rich kid from Ohio who's determined not to get sick. Tells me that the only way to accomplish this is to eat strictly at expensive tourist traps like the Taj Bengal. I, on the other hand, continue to dine and tempt fate at all the funky *chapatti* and *masala dosa* stands in Dalhousie Square. I tell this guy I'm building up my immune system and then I flex a bicep. So, James decides to take a two-week side trip to Bangkok, the capital of sin on this planet. After that, James is back in Calcutta regaling me with stories about his adventures in an endless succession of cat houses in Sin City. And this was the guy who was so worried about getting sick?"

Claude nodded and laughed.

"Joe, *mon ami.* You are arriving and transforming."

"Claude, my friend, I think she's having an affair with him."

"Mon dieu! Say it isn't so. How do you know?"

"I just know it. To tell you the truth, I'm at my wit's end. She's the one who teased for this trip, and she's got the sourest attitude you could ever imagine. Talk about arriving and transforming. Except for a few things, she hates it here. I think she can't wait to get back. Me, on the other hand—I could just as easily stay here for the rest of my life. I rather like all the chaos. Everything from purchasing bottled water to a recording device is a protracted negotiation. Just the other day, I said to a storekeeper, 'I'm leaving the store with the merchandise now. There are fifty rupees on the counter. If there's a problem, please stop me before I get to the door.' Well, I just kept walking, and he didn't come after me."

"If she's really having an affair with him, why don't you take the wind out of his sails? Why don't you trade her for something?"

"You can't be serious!"

Now Claude was the one who was doing the egging on. I felt an uneasy sense of camaraderie, a feeling that we could be partners in crime.

"Joe, trade her and trade her soon. It'll only get worse."

I'd always liked people who would volunteer for someone else.

I left the teahouse and started back to the hotel. The sun beat down relentlessly. It was the hammer and the street was the anvil. A small procession was coming, no doubt heading for the burning *ghats.* There was a young woman laid out on a hand-pulled rickshaw. She was surrounded by relatives who were sprinkling rose petals on her motionless form clad in a white winding sheet. Already her serene face was changing color. Now there was a lady on her last rickshaw ride, going to the same place as the crashing cow, but with a stop at the *ghat* first! I suddenly felt an impossible sadness, a sadness without end. I desperately wished I could rescue her—tap her on the shoulder, so she would wake up and go down to the bazaar to buy herself a pretty new *sari* and some bangles.

You see, in Calcutta it's like this: when you rent a house, the servants come with it. Mrs. Bhattacharyya, who would be our landlady for all those times when we weren't on the road, had explained this to us, but it really didn't sink in until the kids of the servants would show up at the window sill in the morning. Sachiko was quite taken by the two-year-old named Kuti. What a charmer! He was always doing some cute little dance or asking me to take him by his tiny hands and give him a twirl. He would get dizzy from that and fall in a heap on the floor only to get up again and say, "Joe, *abai, abai* (again, again)." He loved to be twirled.

Sachiko was so in love with the little tyke that she wanted to kidnap him. Sometimes, usually when the heat of Calcutta got too oppressive, she would sleep out in the outer room where there was a bigger fan. When I awoke in the morning, I'd go to that room and there would be Sachiko and Kuti curled up together, still deep in sleep. In those moments, I wanted to rescue someone again. She would wake up and say, "C'mon, Joe. Let's take him back to New York with us."

"Don't you think his parents might object to that?" I asked.

"Joe, I'm joking of course."

But I knew that she wasn't. I could imagine what it would be like if we took Kuti back to New York. In no time at all, he'd be wearing backwards baseball caps and surfing the web. Maybe, as an alternative, I should just stay there in Calcutta, and Sachiko and James could go back to Ohio or wherever. I began to ponder Claude's proposal, the one about trading her for something. Oh, how I wished I could wake her up. It was the same feeling I'd had about the dead lady on the rickshaw. But that one was gone. Nothing could bring her back. Lesson to be learned: she must be worthy of rescue. Yeah, something in Sachiko was dead. Something irrevocable, something irretrievable. Ha! That was weird because in light of this new revelation, she had managed to redeem, in my eyes, some small measure of desirability. Yeah, but she was really gone. Gone forever. That was the allure. And like the rickshaw lady, being gone didn't necessarily mean that she would be out of mind. Rickshaw Girl, like the crashing cow, may have become a part of the great sacred river, but she would always have a certain power over me. No doubt Rickshaw Girl was acutely aware of this as, yawning seductively in some nebulous afterlife, she found herself laughing coquettishly at me. "Hey guy, put that in your pipe and smoke it!" she giggled. But perhaps I should exchange this feeling for something new? Claude was right. An exchange must take place. *Quid pro quo.* It was as it should be.

But another development was happening. I was acquiring a fondness for *tabla,* that musical instrument I'd been playing at Panditji's *sitar* class. I loved the voluptuousness of it, how you could bend notes on the larger of the two drums. And once you knew the rules, you could solo on it. Musically, it was like an enormous labyrinth in which you could wander around at will, checking out what each side room had to offer. And what surprises they were!

This was quite different from the usual rock and roll stuff that I was used to. Also, unlike that world, there was surprisingly little arguing. The beats all had names, and if someone didn't like them, well tough. Here they were never trying to force a drum to be something else—as if it should be ashamed of itself for making such a glorious racket.

At first Sachiko and I liked the idea that the servants came with the bed and breakfast/ paying guest accommodations. It was an unexpected perk, but we soon discovered that it had one disadvantage: we had to be back by 11:00 p.m., or Mrs. Bhattacharyya would be very upset about our waking up the household. Twice we were admonished of this rule, and we both made a concerted effort to be back on time. This worked out well for a time.

However, the problem all came to head when my *tabla* teacher, Kishan, invited us to one of his concerts at a Hindu temple about an hour's drive outside of Calcutta. We went in Kishan's car and got a bit of a late start, being that there was traffic on the Hoogly Bridge. There was always a traffic jam on the Hoogly Bridge. Kishan informed us that there would be a very fine girl *tabla* player named Vidya playing before him, and perhaps if we hurried, we might even get to see part of her performance.

"Take my word, Joe," said Kishan. "She's one of the best. She can really make the mountains move with her playing."

But soon it became clear that we were probably not going to catch the beginning of Vidya's set. We were almost at our destination when the weather became an added factor. Suddenly, the rain came out of the sky in torrents, and the thunderclaps started in. Sachiko and I looked out over a ridge to the right and could see power lines snapping, lighting up the night sky like writhing incandescent snakes. The wind became ferocious, buffeting the car back and forth. I was genuinely afraid.

Sachiko looked anxious. She whispered in my ear, "Why did we have to come? Now we probably won't be able to get back in time, and Mrs. Bhattacharya will be very angry. "

Kishan reassured us, "It's only a little squall coming in from the Bay of Bengal. Not to worry. The goddess Kali is doing her thing. But it looks as though we may miss Vidya's part of the concert. However, I'll put on a good show. So, you have that to look forward to."

The storm subsided as quickly as it began, and we pulled into the parking lot of the Hindu temple. But when we got to the site of the small outdoor stage, we found the place in a shambles. The stage had been trashed, and the rest of the show had been cancelled. The promoter, who was a close friend of Kishan, was in tears. He had been planning this concert for months and now it had been destroyed by the weather. It seemed that as Vidya had reached the high point of her *tabla* performance, someone in the audience had spotted a mini-tornado, so everyone had to leave and run for cover. When they got back after the storm had abated, it was clear that the show could not go on.

"It's okay, my friend." Kishan was consoling the promoter. "We'll reschedule. All is not in vain." Kishan turned to Vidya who was dressed in a red *sari* with pink highlights. Despite the disappointment of the storm, she was beaming. "And they tell me you played quite a program. Yes, you almost made the mountains move, but you certainly made the stage move. Hey Joe, I think you should study with her too. She would make a great teacher, in addition to me of course."

I was thunderstruck. Vidya was a spitting image of Rickshaw Girl. I thought I was looking at a ghost. That sweet little Kali, Miss Goddess of Who-Knows-What?, had come back to me. And she had a look on her face as if to say she knew something I didn't.

We all adjourned to the promoter's nearby house and discussed when to reschedule. The talks went deep into the evening. Sachiko got more and more angry. Finally, we piled back into Kishan's car and he drove us back to Calcutta .

"I'll drop you in Jadavpur and you can get a hand-pulled rickshaw from there," he explained.

Sure enough, as he pulled into Jadavpur, I could see the long line of rickshaw drivers fast asleep on their rigs. Sachiko and I said goodbye to Kishan and got out of the car. We got into the first rickshaw in the queue and I gave the man directions in Bengali. Immediately, I had to endure a constant barrage of verbal assault from Sachiko.

"*Mo* Joe, what's the matter with you? You bastard! You knew this concert would go late. Now Mrs. Bhattacharyya will be so angry 'cause we'll wake up all the servants."

"Baby, how did I know it would go over? I'm doing the best I can. Besides, I thought I told you this is a no mo zone."

Her tirade went on and on until she topped it off with a round of vicious slugs to my back and shoulders. I just braced myself and turned away. I didn't do anything to protect myself. As the assault grew worse, the rickshaw driver suddenly laughed. He burst out first in a stifled guffaw which heightened in intensity causing the rickshaw to wobble. This only made Sachiko angrier, and she started yelling at him.

I blurted out, "It's okay, my good fellow! Your driving is impeccable. A very good *baksheesh* is in store for you! Carry on, my man!"

Yes, my life was clearer now. Tomorrow I would have to make the trade that Claude had spoken of. Perhaps I could get James' cat. In the meantime, I would have to give this driver say 300 rupees and take him out for a toddy.

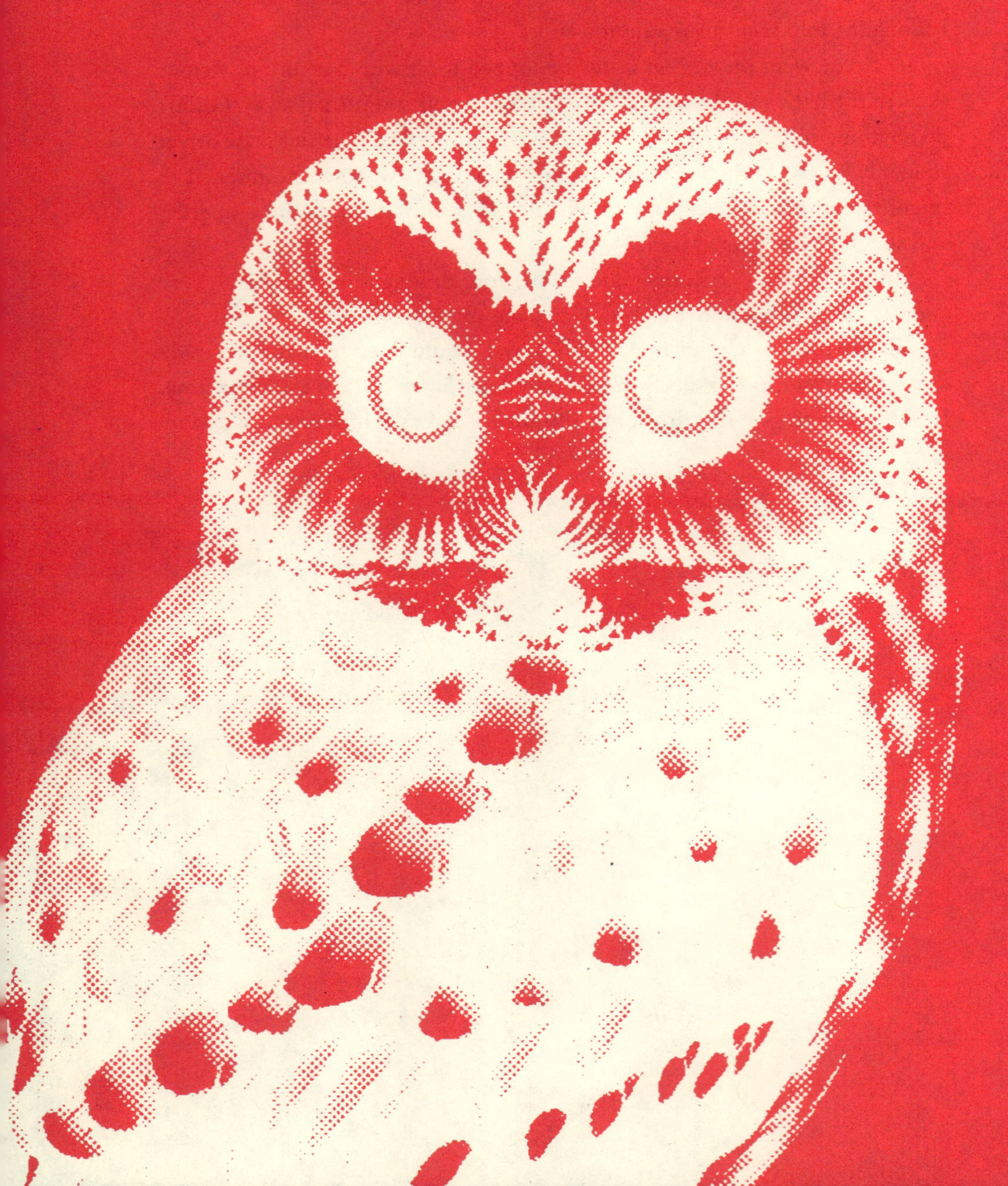

NOAH WARREN

diatomaceous earth

Charles repairs his garden. The corn stalks
he rights and ties with hemp string,
while in the groove of earth
between them he plants pole beans.
He sifts the soil for stones
and checks roots for cutworms,
his hands steady, then shaking.

In the story about his past that we told him
when he came home,
his body was a narrow empty space:
no one's purview.
We meant this as a salve.

When he stands the light
that the trees let pass fills his face;
when he crouches it bars him.
He sinks down to sit in the dirt,
pinching a potato beetle
in the leaf it eats.

I have no idea
how long I have been
looking out from the hollow
that a window carves in the room.

the tines

My father threw his weight into the shaft
and sunk a pitchfork in the moist mound
of old straw—the smell of rot—my body
was so small, the muscles were mere
ideas, tender and beautiful, and I thought the tines
of the tool were beautiful too—standing in that dim barn
that the weather roamed through I was pierced
over and over by a reverence for the edges
men wielded, razors, shears, for the straight lines
spoken between them, so easily, an ache,
because whenever I opened my mouth to talk,
even something trivial, I'm tired,
I'd like to go home, the world stormed in—
stammering beneath gray eyes, my face broke
and I cried—every muscle of my father's back gathered
and tensed, he lifted, an enormous load,
but at that moment I could only watch the tines,
long and cold, as they caught the light
and gleamed, as my father staggered
toward the white noon and the wheelbarrow
waiting in it.

we visit the clinic

It was you, wasn't it
you who spoke to me about the summer morning, the curtains
above tropez, and those times when the wind
buries itself in them,
and they rustle in return
for an instant...when the sun lights
on them and you, deep in the breakfast parlor
of the grand hotel, and throws ovals
through the broken crystal
and across the floor, and you find
then in your reflection such a sadness,
your smile twisted, your great blue eyes
taken out of context and unable to bear
the sudden slight, or the crape
of the hangings or the green of a sea
from which the swells crest sharply
and lick with longing at the narrow cliffs.

calyx

when the sun emerged it lifted the water
from the floor of the tub, a passage
that took weeks—it was so cold
in alberta, mornings opened stiffly
then shriveled, and the wooden house
loved to sigh—and yet
the tub filled itself with verdure
through march, or verdure entered it,
pushing its way in, certainly the small things—
algae, mold—but equally in time the less
explicable life, sphagnum moss, liverworts,
a water lily—
and wind continued to pour south
from the blank pole, scraping the plains
like a steel brush, and the house remained empty
no matter how I raged, and the water
was water—how I dreaded
the sun—

movie scene

Brother Martin slumbered through the Central Valley.
A red tongue slipped out of his open teeth.

He dreamed he was sparrow, or that his faith
was a sparrow. Then he dreamed a marble city.

I want to ask you a question, he said to the driver
in the middle of a strawberry field, Is that okay.

What happens to birds in the winter,
he asked, then, a little later, Where are you taking me?

REGARDING THE CONTRIBUTORS

CHRISTOPHE AGOU'S work is held in the collections of the Museum of Fine Arts, Houston; Neuberger Museum of Art, Purchase; Smithsonian American Art Museum, Washington, D.C.; and many more.

MEG ATKINSON'S work has appeared at the Paramount Gallery, the Fine Arts Museum of Long Island, Pierogi, P.S. 122, Rotunda Gallery, Franklin Furnace, Graphic Eye Gallery, the Alternative Museum and many other venues. She lives in Brooklyn.

NICK BERTOZZI is the creator of *Pecan Sandy* and *Persimmon Cup*, author of *Lewis & Clark* (First Second), and *The Salon* (St Martin's Press), a graphic novel about Picasso and magical absinthe. He collaborated with Jason Lutes on the cartoon-biography *Houdini: The Handcuff King* (Hyperion). He has been teaching cartooning at NYC's School of Visual Arts and lives in New York City with his wife and daughters.

ARTHUR BRADFORD is the author of *Dogwalker* (Knopf 2001), and has a children's book coming out fall 2011 with McSweeney's. He is also the creator and director of the documentary series *How's Your News?* He lives in Portland, Oregon and in the summertime directs Camp Jabberwocky, a residential camp for people with disabilities.

TODD COLBY has published four books of poetry with Soft Skull Press. He posts new writing and art on gleefarm.blogspot.com.

DARRYL CUNNINGHAM is the author of the graphic novel *Psychiatric Tales*, out from Blank Slate in the UK and Bloomsbury in the US. His book *Uncle Bob Adventures* will be out from Blank Slate in the summer of 2011. His comic strip *The Streets Of San Diablo* was serialized on the ACT-I-VATE website. He lives in Yorkshire, England. Visit darryl-cunningham.blogspot.com.

NICHOLAS DEBOER has been published in *Fact-Simile, Bombay Gin, Eccolinguistics,* and *Apparent Mag.*

SIMON DINNERSTEIN graduated from CCNY with a BA in history, studied painting and drawing at the Brooklyn Museum Art School, and has had twenty-two solo exhibitions. Among his numerous awards are a Fulbright Fellowship to Germany, the Rome Prize for living and working in Italy at the American Academy in Rome, a Louis Confort Tiffany Grant, the Ingram Merrill Award for Painting, and a New York State Foundation for the Arts Grant. In 1999-2000, a retrospective of his work toured the country, sponsored in part by a grant from the Robert Lehman Foundation. Two monographs, *The Art of Simon Dinnerstein* (University of Arkansas Press, 1990) and *Simon Dinnerstein: Paintings and Drawings* (Hudson Hills Press, 2000) have been published on his work. A member of the National Academy of Design, Dinnerstein has been represented in past years by Staempfli Gallery and ACA Galleries in New York. He resides in Brooklyn. Visit www.simondinnerstein.com.

JEN FERGUSON is an artist working in DUMBO Brooklyn, New York. Her art is featured in the Blue Ribbon Restaurants where she created the menu art and décor since its inception, and is published in *Art of the Brooklyn Bridge: A Visual History* (Routledge, 2008). Her most recent projects include collaborations with writer Tim Hall on *Uplift The Positivicals* and *Monster Mash-Ups*, and she made her Marvel Comics debut in *Cyclops #1*. She's created art for Brooklyn Oenology, and Railbirds, a drawing project inspired by the Aqueduct Racetrack. Jen's art is also featured on the HBO show *Bored To Death*. Visit www.artinchaos.com.

MICHEL FIFFE is the creator and publisher of the comic *ZEGAS* and is also the editor for the forthcoming Image Comics anthology *Twisted Savage Dragon Funnies*. Drop him a line at his art blog: michelfiffe.com.

SUZANNA FINLEY has traveled and lived widely in South Asia teaching, volunteering, and photographing with non-profit organizations. Major themes in Finley's work include globalization, post-colonial identity, and cultural survival. Her work has been exhibited in New York and Seattle, and she has been published in a number of magazines and web publications including *Yes! Magazine* and *Real Change News*. Finley is currently working as a freelance photographer in New York City.

SIMON FRASER is a widely traveled Scots comic artist best known for his work in the British sci-fi weekly *2000AD* where he has drawn Judge Dredd and co-created Nikolai Dante. He helps run the New York-based webcomics collective ACT-I-VATE and the DRAWBRIDGE sketchblog. His creator-owned hard sci-fi webcomic *Lilly Mackenzie & the Mines of Charybdis* debuted on ACT-I-VATE and has since been published in the *Judge Dredd Megazine*. Simon is currently working on the sequel *Lilly Mackenzie & The Treasure of Paros*. He currently lives in Brooklyn.

BENJAMIN GANTCHER'S poems have appeared in several publications, including *Tin House*, the *Brooklyn Rail, Quarterly West, Slate*, and *Drunken Boat*. His first book, *If a Lettuce*, was a finalist in the 2007 National Poetry Series and Bright Hill Press contests. He has been nominated for a Pushcart Prize, attended Ucross and Art/Omi's Ledig House, and been both a poetry editor of the online journal *failbetter* and a correspondent for the *Hyde Park Review of Books*. He lives and teaches in New York City.

RACHEL B. GLASER is the author of the story collection *Pee On Water* (Publishing Genius Press) and the poetry chapbook *Heroes Are So Long* (Minutes Books). Her work has appeared in the *New York Tyrant*, *American Short Fiction*, and *McSweeney's*. Glaser lives in Northampton, MA. For more information, check out rachelbglaser.blogspot.com.

GEERT GOIRIS is a photographer concentrating on the notion of the "first encounter." His analogue photographs investigate traumatic realism, wilderness as metaphor, and cabin fever. Goiris teaches practice based research at Hogeschool Sint-Lukas Brussels and has exhibited and published extensively. www.geertgoiris.info

ANDREW GORIN is the Poetry Editor at the *Faster Times* and an MFA candidate at Brooklyn College. His writing has appeared or is forthcoming in *Stonecutter*, *SUPERMACHINE*, *Ostranenie*, the *Huffington Post*, and elsewhere. He has worked for Ugly Duckling Presse, Tibor de Nagy Gallery, and David Zwirner Gallery.

JAMES GUIDA is the author of *Marbles*, a book of aphorisms published by Turtle Point Press. He grew up in Australia and currently lives in New York.

DEAN HASPIEL is an Emmy Award winning artist who created the Eisner Award nominated *Billy Dogma*. Dean has drawn many great superhero and semi-autobiographical comic books for major publishers, including graphic novel collaborations with Harvey Pekar, Jonathan Ames, and Inverna Lockpez. He illustrates for HBO's *Bored To Death*.

LILLIAN HEEHS studied creative writing first at Eugene Lang College at the New School University in New York City before transferring to Naropa University, where she went on to major in Creative Writing and Somatic Psychology. She has published short stories as well as a number of poems in Flaneur Foundry Press, *Beehive Magazine*, *Monkey Puzzle Magazine,* and *Wicked Alice Poetry Journal*, among others. She lives in Brooklyn.

H. L. HIX has published poetry, essays, and other works in *McSweeney's*, *Georgia Review*, *Harvard Review*, *Boston Review*, *Poetry*, and other journals. He holds an NEA Fellowship, the Grolier Prize, the T. S. Eliot Prize, and the Peregrine Smith Award, and has been translated into several languages. He lives in Laramie, Wyoming. Visit www.hlhix.com.

PETER KAMINSKY is the author of *The Moon Pulled Up An Acre of Bass* and *Pig Perfect: Encounters With Remarkable Swine.* Forthcoming from Knopf, *Boys Have Stomachs And Men Have Bellies.* Kaminsky is a creator, executive producer and head writer of The Kennedy Center Mark Twain Prize for American Humor and The Library of Congress Gershwin Prize for Popular Song. He lives in Brooklyn, New York.

YASMINA KHAN received a $10,000 award from the Thornton Tomasetti Foundation for her plan to implement Green Homes for Urban Development. She has pursued work in sustainable design, museum education, and exhibition design. She will soon attend Columbia University's Graduate School for Architecture, Planning and Preservation.

JHUMPA LAHIRI is the recipient of a Guggenheim Fellowship. Her debut collection of stories, *Interpreter of Maladies*, was awarded the Pulitzer Prize, the PEN/Hemingway Award and The New Yorker Debut of the Year. Her novel *The Namesake* was a New York Times Notable Book, and a Los Angeles Times Book Prize finalist. She lives in Brooklyn, New York.

JOCELYN LEE received a BA in philosophy and visual arts from Yale University and an MFA in photography from Hunter College. In 2001 she won a Guggenheim Fellowship. She has been exhibited nationally, most recently in a group show titled *Feature Photography* at The National Portrait Gallery, of the Smithsonian Institute, in Washington, D.C. in 2008; and in solo shows at Pace MacGill Gallery in New York in 2007 and 2010. Her work has appeared in many national publications and she is represented by Pace MacGill Gallery in New York and The Institute for Artists Management. The new monograph *Nowhere but here* (Steidl 2011) represents nearly 15 years of her work. A selection of her portraits entitled *Women are Beautiful* will be published later this year by Fisher Press. She teaches at Princeton University.

ANDREW MOORE'S photographs are held in the collections of the Metropolitan Museum of Art, the Whitney Museum of American Art, the Yale University Art Gallery, Museum of Fine Arts Houston, the George Eastman House, and the Library of Congress. Moore presently teaches a graduate seminar in the MFA Photography Video and Related Media program at the School of Visual Arts in New York City.

JOSH NEUFELD is the writer/artist of the New York Times bestseller *A.D.: New Orleans After the Deluge*. His latest project is *The Influencing Machine*, a collaboration with *NPR*'s Brooke Gladstone. Neufeld is a founding member of the comics collective ACT-I-VATE. He lives in Brooklyn.

ERNESTO QUIÑONEZ'S debut novel, *Bodega Dreams* (Vintage Contemporary Originals) was chosen as a *Los Angeles Times* and *New York Times* Notable books of the year. He's also the author of *Chango's Fire*. Bodega Dreams has become a landmark in contemporary literature and is now required reading in many high schools and colleges around the country. He currently teaches at Cornell University's MFA program in creative writing.

EMILY RABOTEAU is the author of *The Professor's Daughter* (Henry Holt 2005) and her writing has appeared in *Narrative Magazine*, *Nerve*, and *The Best American Short Stories 2003*. She has received the Pushcart Prize, a Nelson Algren Award, a New York Foundation for the Arts Fellowship, and a Literature Fellowship from the National Endowment for the Arts. She teaches English at City College of New York.

NATHANIEL RICH is the author of *The Mayor's Tongue (*Riverhead 2008). His second novel is forthcoming from Farrar, Straus & Giroux.

DIANA SCHERER has studied fine art and photography at the Gerrit Rietveld Academy in Amsterdam. Her work has appeared in solo and group exhibitions in Paris, Hyeres, Amsterdam, Berlin and Seoul. She has received a Gregers Nielsen Award. Her work has been published in *capricious*, *piknik mgazine,* and *liberation*, among others. Visit: www.dianascherer.nl.

MICHAEL SIGNORELLI is an editor at HarperCollins Publishers. His work has appeared online at *McSweeney's Internet Tendency*, *Mr. Beller's Neighborhood*, *Saltgrass*, and *Stone Canoe*, among other places. He lives in New York City.

PACIFICO SILANO is currently an MFA candidate in the Photo, Video and Related Media program at School of Visual Arts. His most recent work explores issues of identity, virility, and the politics of sexuality. He lives and works in Brooklyn, New York.

JAMES SMITH is the Brooklyn-based writer and artist of the web sensation *Gang of Fools*. He supplies graphics and FX for the occasional music video. Find him online at jamesmith.com and activatecomix.com.

NICK SMITH is currently at work on his first novel entitled *Joe the Neanderthal*. He lives in Brooklyn, New York.

EMMA STRAUB is the author of the short story collection *Other People We Married* and the forthcoming novel *Laura Lamont's Life in Pictures* from Riverhead books. More information can be found at www.emmastraub.net.

JG THIRLWELL is a composer/producer/performer based in Brooklyn, who also works under many pseudonyms including Foetus, Steroid Maximus, Manorexia, Baby Zizanie, Hydroze Plus, Clint Ruin and Wiseblood. Thirlwell has been featured as producer or remixer on a variety of recordings, including releases for artists like Nine Inch Nails, Jon Spencer Blues Explosion, Lydia Lunch, White Zombie, and Swans. JG has completed commissions for Kronos Quartet, Bang On A Can and LEMUR and is also a member of the "freq_out" sound-art collective. Visit www.foetus.org.

YVONNE TODD photographs people and objects with a decrepit large format camera. Her cast of humans, a "rainbow of affliction," is informed by mass-market fiction, religious cults, glamour, and advertising. Her product shots utilize an array of meaningless merchandise. Todd exhibits work in New Zealand, Australia, and beyond. She Live in Auckland. www.ervon.com

NOAH WARREN will soon be studying the poetics of revolution in Cuba and Venezuela. His writing has previously appeared in the *Yale Literary Magazine*.